1999

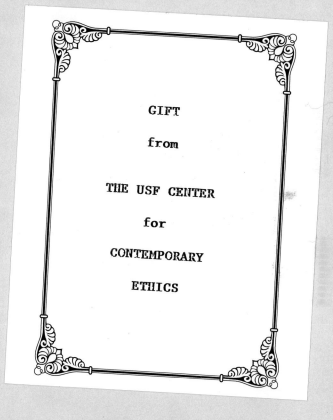

CODES OF CONDUCT

CODES OF CONDUCT
Behavioral Research into Business Ethics

DAVID M. MESSICK AND ANN E. TENBRUNSEL
EDITORS

Russell Sage Foundation / New York

The Russell Sage Foundation

Library of Congress Cataloging-in-Publication Data

Codes of conduct : behavioral research into business ethics/
    David M. Messick and Ann E. Tenbrunsel, editors.
        p. cm.
    Includes bibliographical references and index.
    ISBN 0-87154-594-2 (cloth : alk. paper)
    1. Business ethics—Congresses.   2. Corporate culture—Congresses.   I. Messick,
David M.   II. Tenbrunsel, Ann E.
    HF5387.C6 1996
    174'.4–dc20
                                                                                        96-33374
                                                                                        CIP

Text design by Rozlyn Coleman.

RUSSELL SAGE FOUNDATION
112 East 64th Street, New York, New York 10021
10 9 8 7 6 5 4 3 2

Contents

Contributors

David M. Messick	Kellogg School, Northwestern University
Ann E. Tenbrunsel	College of Business Administration, University of Notre Dame

Jonathan Baron	University of Pennsylvania
Max H. Bazerman	Kellogg School, Northwestern University
Maura A. Belliveau	Fuqua School, Duke University
Francisco J. Benzoni	Divinity School, University of Chicago
Robert J. Bies	School of Business, Georgetown University
Marilynn B. Brewer	Ohio State University
Robert B. Cialdini	Arizona State University
John M. Darley	Princeton University
Robyn M. Dawes	Carnegie Mellon University
Thomas Donaldson	School of Business, Georgetown University
Baruch Fischhoff	Carnegie Mellon University
Susan T. Fiske	University of Massachusetts at Amherst
Robert H. Frank	Johnson School, Cornell University
Stephanie A. Goodwin	University of Massachusetts at Amherst
Russell Hardin	New York University
Helmut Jungermann	Institut für Psychologie, Tehnische Universitaet Berlin
Joshua Klayman	Graduate School of Business, University of Chicago
Roderick M. Kramer	Graduate School of Business, Stanford University
George Loewenstein	Carnegie Mellon University
Robert Mauro	University of Oregon at Eugene
Ann L. McGill	Kellogg School, Northwestern University
Myron Rothbart	University of Oregon at Eugene
Tom R. Tyler	University of California at Berkeley
Kimberly A. Wade-Benzoni	Kellogg School, Northwestern University
Willem A. Wagenaar	Leiden University
Patricia H. Werhane	Darden School, University of Virginia

Preface

The papers in this book were presented at a conference on Behavioral Research and Business Ethics that was held at Northwestern University in the summer of 1994. The conference was the first major project sponsored by the Center for the Study of Ethical Issues in Business of the J. L. Kellogg Graduate School of Management. The purpose of the center is to conduct, promote, and support psychological and behavioral research on ethical issues that arise in business settings. The conference and the publications resulting therefrom—this book and a special issue of the journal *Social Justice Research*—constitute the center's first answer to the question of how psychological and behavioral research can be woven into the study of business ethics.

The conference was supported by generous grants from the James S. Kemper Foundation and the Russell Sage Foundation. We are deeply grateful for this support. We are also grateful to the many people, including the participants, who helped manage the mundane details to make the conference a success.

David M. Messick
Ann E. Tenbrunsel

Introduction

Behavioral Research into Business Ethics

David M. Messick and Ann E. Tenbrunsel

Who is at fault when a worker on an oil platform falls to his death? Is it possible for well-intentioned organizations to socialize their employees unwittingly into committing illegal and immoral acts? How would such a process work? Does racial discrimination require intentional acts of suppression of racial minorities? What are the ethical obligations of persons, such as experts or consultants, who claim knowledge or skill that is beyond that of the average person? These are a few of the complex issues that are the concerns of the field of business ethics.

Business ethics, the study of the moral and ethical dimensions of business, is a branch of moral philosophy. It is an area of applied philosophy and, as such, must bridge the gap between the foundational principles of moral belief and conduct, on the one hand, and the reality of the business world, on the other. William Kahn (1990) describes this distinction as the difference between *normative* and *contextual* issues. Normative ethics is the study of what is good and morally correct and the arguments that support such judgments. The contextual or descriptive component involves the empirical study of the environments in which real people work, the cultures of the organizations and institutions that transact business, what people believe is right and wrong, and what they actually do. It is in this latter domain that business ethics overlaps the scientific study of human behavior.

Most scholars with a concern for business ethics recognize the importance of good empirical research. Many questions that are relevant to the moral conduct of business can be answered only through such careful research. Do different policies differ measurably in their effectiveness against employee theft? Do corporate codes of ethics have an impact on the behavior of managers? Are employees more willing to accept surveillance and monitoring if they are consulted on the forms that it will take than if they are not? Is there objective evidence of discrimination against women and minorities in the workplace? Do managers feel that ethical behavior in the workplace is improving or deteriorating? These and scores of ethics-related questions like them can be answered only through empirical research.

The hypothesis underlying this book goes beyond the mere assertion that empirical research is a necessary component of a comprehensive study of business ethics. The hypothesis is more specifically that the theories, findings, and methods of the behavioral sciences will provide new insights, data, and principles that can be blended with the concepts of philosophy to create a multidisciplinary field of business ethics in which questions of "ought" can be considered alongside questions of "how." We can agree that it is morally objectionable to use a person's race or gender against that person in business (or other) contexts; understanding how discrimination works in specific contexts—for instance, in mortgage lending—is an empirical issue of some complexity that requires scientific scrutiny (Messick 1994).

This book is based on the conviction that there are many domains of research in psychology and behavioral economics that are relevant to business ethics. Since the evidence for this claim is spelled out in the chapters that follow, we will not argue it at length here. We will rather mention some of the general themes that are shared by these areas of scholarship.

Many of the research areas of social psychology began as efforts to comprehend the dark side of the human experience. Implicit in these early efforts was the assumption that comprehension could lead to improvement. For instance, some of the earliest social psychological research dealt with causes and consequences of aggression. The important frustration-aggression hypothesis proposed by John Dollard and his colleagues (1939) not only offered an alternative to the prevailing Freudian theories of aggression but specifically addressed social problems of racial and religious prejudice and intergroup hostility. In addition to marshaling the evidence in favor of the hypothesis that aggression is *always* caused by frustration, Dollard's team examined the implications of that position for the reduction of aggression.

Frustration-aggression theory was the intellectual precursor of realistic group conflict theory (Sherif and Sherif 1953), which proposes that intergroup violence and hostility stem from real or perceived differences between the interests of the groups. This theory also was more than just a way to explain the willingness of strangers to kill or harm other strangers simply because they were members of different groups. Always associated with this idea was a corollary theory of how intergroup hostility could be reduced.

An important element of group conflict theory concerned the formation of attitudes to in-group and out-group members. The study of attitudes has been viewed as the core of social psychology, and research that grew from Sherif and Sherif's theory has focused on how attitudes are formed, how they are organized, and, importantly, how they can be changed, a focus that reflects the underlying aspiration to improve the human condition through a better understanding of psychological processes. It is in the conviction that psychology and behavioral discoveries can be used for the betterment of humankind that the goals of behavioral researchers and those of business ethicists, who must believe in the improvability of the business environment, coincide.

There are four broad themes that pervade the chapters in this book. Each of them embodies a research literature in psychology and behavioral economics that has a long and rich history. In most cases the relevance of the themes to business ethics is obvious. Where the relevance may be obscure, it will be illuminated.

The first of the themes has to do with power, influence, and authority. Social psychologists became interested in this cluster of issues following the Second World War, when scholars were puzzled by the apparent ease with which citizens of one of the world's most civilized nations, Germany, acted brutally toward citizens of other nations and to many of their own citizens as well. The pioneering research of Stanley Milgram (1965) on obedience to authority was shocking in its implications that most people may be more easily induced to harm others than we would like to acknowledge. Much of the evil that was done by the fascist state was done "institutionally"—that is, within the context of organizations in which people, influenced by the prevailing organizational cultures, followed or gave orders, doing what they thought others wanted and expected of them. This broad theme also includes issues of conformity, social influence and persuasion, and group control of individuals.

A second theme concerns prejudice, discrimination, bigotry, and stereotyping. The Second World War not only kindled interest in the dynamics of authority (and authoritarian people) but also brought the issues of anti-Semitism and racial prejudice to center stage. Social psychologists had long been interested in these topics, almost from the beginning of their disciplines, but the cataclysm of the war made the destructive potential of such beliefs blatant. The decades of research conducted since Gordon Allport (1954b) wrote about the nature of prejudice have produced valuable insights, theories, and methods of immediate applicability in modern business environments. Nonetheless, the reliance on racial or gender stereotypes in decision making, although unethical and often illegal, has certainly not disappeared.

Cognitive psychologists have had a longstanding concern with the nature of human decision processes, especially with the extent to which real human decision makers fit an ideal of rationality. The third theme of this book involves the ways in which humans fall short of our ideal models of decision making and the ethical consequences of these deficiencies. The discovery that people are not perfectly rational decision makers is not a terribly useful fact unless one can specify with some precision the processes that lead to deviations from the ideal. This type of knowledge can then be woven into policies and procedures that help organizations and their employees achieve their business goals while abiding by their ethical values (Messick and Bazerman 1996).

The final theme of the book is the management of risk. Clearly, risk is a central aspect of decision making, but ethical considerations are inherent in the management of harm and potential harm. The ways in which people cope with risky situations, the ways in which they explain and describe misfortunes, and the policies that are intended to minimize risk and maximize safety are crucial ethical concerns. These issues have been examined in some detail by cognitive psychologists, but only relatively recently has attention been directed to their ethical aspects.

It is important to note that there is one area of research that is not well represented in this book, and that is the topic of justice. The reason is that research on justice is already well established in business. Many of the leading researchers in this area teach and conduct their research in business schools, and psychological concepts of justice have already been integrated into contemporary thinking about business ethics. We therefore made a conscious decision to concentrate on areas of behavioral research that have had less penetration into modern business ethics.

This book is organized into two general sections, one dealing with organizational and social psychological issues and the other dealing with risk, reasoning, and decision making. Many of the chapters would have been equally comfortable in either section, so our classification is somewhat arbitrary. Roughly speaking, the first section includes papers dealing with the first two of the themes just discussed, and the second section contains papers dealing with the second two. There is much overlap, however, which we see as a virtue rather than a flaw. Just as real problems usually involve many psychological issues and processes, behavioral principles may find applications in many different organizational domains. Managing diversity, for instance, involves risk as well as stereotypes, and problems of safety often involve occupational stereotypes as well as issues of risk management.

Within each of these sections, the chapters also vary in the extent to which the phenomena they highlight are individual or organizational. For example, while John Darley outlines ways in which organizational processes induce people to violate their personal ethical values, George Loewenstein examines the ways in which cognitive biases permit people to behave in unethical ways. The focus in the former chapter is on the role of the organization as a source of trouble, while the theme of the latter is the mischief that can be caused by rather simple cognitive processes. While this distinction is a useful one, it should be thought of as a continuum rather than as a dichotomy. Behavior in business, as anywhere, is the product of the interaction between environmental (organizational) factors and internal (cognitive) processes.

Part 1 begins with John Darley's chapter on the organizational pressures that induce employees to behave in unethical and destructive ways. Darley notes that most evil is not done by individuals acting singly but by people in organizations with rules, structures, and plans. Darley probes what it is in the nature of organizations that empowers them to evoke evil behavior from ordinary people. In some ways his analysis is a social psychological parallel to Hannah Arendt's famous position on the "banality of evil" (1963). In covering the trial of Adolph Eichmann in Jerusalem, Arendt described the man who was responsible for the extermination of millions of Jews as an ordinary, rather dull bureaucrat who did his job in pursuing an undistinguished career. She did not see the deranged and evil killer that the prosecution was trying to portray; it was a relatively inept organization man who had created evil. While modern corporations are a far cry from the Nazi party, all organizations, according to Darley, have the potential to socialize their members into doing evil, and this potential must be understood to be effectively controlled.

Chapter 2, by Robert Cialdini, examines the consequences to the organization that permits wrongdoing and dishonesty. The short-term gains that the firm may reap from wrongdoing will be erased by long-term costs. For example, an organization that tolerates or rewards dishonesty will tend to attract employees whose values are compatible with dishonesty, and these employees may prove to be more costly to the firm than employees who value honesty more highly. The dishonest employees may require costly surveillance, which itself may send the message to the employees that they are not trusted and in turn may reinforce their tendencies to behave dishonestly. Decisions can have snowballing consequences, and firms that ignore the remote consequences of their policies may find themselves struggling in the long term.

In chapter 3, Roderick Kramer and David Messick address some of the issues raised in the first two chapters from the employee's perspective. They propose that managers may behave like intuitive lawyers, whose motives are to promote and defend their own interests, possibly at a cost to the organization. When decisions are complex and multifaceted, as are many of the types of social dilemmas faced in business, people can find justifications for behaving in ways that are beneficial personally but not organizationally. Complex organizational dilemmas become grist for the intuitive lawyer's mill, providing the means to reframe the issues, outcomes, and choices so as to profit the decision maker but not the firm.

How realistic, then, is the goal of ethicality? Despite Cialdini's claim that dishonesty is, in the long run, more costly than honesty, it may be that firms cannot afford the short-term costs of honesty and responsibility. In chapter 4, Robert Frank argues that distinct benefits accrue to firms that occupy the moral high ground, even if doing so entails costs. One of the benefits is that socially responsible firms may be able to hire talented employees with high ethical values at lower salaries than less ethical firms. The data that Frank presents to support this argument provide additional evidence in favor of Cialdini's position. Not only do dishonest firms tend to attract dishonest employees, but they have to pay a premium to hire them. Frank makes it clear that while doing ethical business may increase costs in some areas, it may also reduce them in others.

In chapter 5, Robert Bies discusses one subtle aspect of the perceived ethicality of organizations, namely the extent to which they adopt procedures that intrude on the privacy of the employees. Firms need to maintain information about employees to make decisions about job assignments, promotions, and bonuses and, in some cases, to forestall serious problems with issues like drug or alcohol abuse or tendencies to prey sexually on other employees. How this information is gathered and maintained is a concern of growing importance, not only because the information may be personal in nature but also because employees may retaliate if they feel that their privacy is being improperly invaded by their employer. Bies reviews some of the ethical issues involved with privacy in organizations as well as some of the psychological research that has been conducted on perceptions of privacy rights.

Chapter 6 by Stephanie Goodwin and Susan Fiske deals with social information processing, one of the central problem areas in social psychology. The authors describe a model that posits a continuum between reacting to people in terms of generic categories like gender or race and reacting to them in terms of their individual qualities. This model proposes that people think more carefully and personally when they are motivated to do so and when they have the necessary capacity to concentrate on the task. The authors also address the question of what happens when we simply lack sufficient information to make a judgment about another. We have judgment standards that prevent us from making judgments or that influence the judgments we are willing to make. As the diversity of the work force increases and legal and social norms proscribe race-, ethnicity-, or gender-based decision making, an understanding of factors that influence such tendencies is essential.

The theme is carried further in chapter 7 by Myron Rothbart and Robert Mauro, who point out that making judgments about people on the basis of categories is a way of simplifying the social world and making it navigable. The simplification comes at a cost, however, often in the form of errors in judgments about people, especially when the categories involve race, ethnicity, or gender. The dilemma these authors wrestle with is that sometimes it may be useful (valid) to use racial categories to make predictions about future actions, but at the same time it may be unethical to do so. The accuracy with which we can predict future outcomes is extremely important here, and the question arises of how the technical and ethical issues are fused into effective policies. Some of the issues raised are echoed in Robyn Dawes's chapter in the second section of the book, where Dawes addresses the value of experts in predicting people's future behavior.

The use of categorical information in making judgments about people often involves discrimination against members of certain groups. One traditional view of this process is that members of these groups, frequently defined by race, ethnicity, or gender, are unqualified for responsibility and hence do not merit important jobs or other rewards offered to responsible people in our society. In chapter 8, Marilynn Brewer describes research that suggests that the process of discrimination may work in a somewhat different manner, through a process of in-group favoritism. Drawing on social psychological research, she argues that discrimination may involve not so much depriving qualified out-group members of their just desserts as affording rewards unjustly to in-group members. In many cases these processes would create identical discriminatory outcomes, but the psychological processes underlying the discrimination are very different. The latter process does not need to involve hostility toward out-groups, only an inappropriate helpfulness to in-groups. Heightened sensitivity to out-group members may not eliminate discrimination of this latter type.

As the demographic complexion of the work force changes, there is an increasing need to manage not only racial and gender diversity but also diversity of values. Chapter 9 by Tom Tyler and Maura Belliveau addresses the question of whether procedures can be adopted to reduce or avoid the potential conflicts that diversity may entail. They argue that the perception of fairness in the workplace, as in government, creates a climate in which people with different interests can accept even disappointing outcomes. The existence of fair procedures may permit preferential hiring or promotion policies to succeed in organizations that have traditionally been white male bastions. There is also a relationship between the value that people place on procedural fairness, as opposed to outcome favorability, and their identification with superordinate groups. For people who identify more with America than with their ethnic group, procedural issues were more important than instrumental issues (winning or losing), whereas the relationship was reversed for persons who identify more with their ethnic group. Application of some of the principles described in this chapter may lead to fewer diversity-based conflicts in organizations.

The second half of the book includes chapters that focus on the themes of risk, reasoning, and decision making. The early chapters explore the reasoning and decision making processes of individuals faced with making ethical decisions, while the later ones concentrate on the organizational implications of risk management and uncertainty. The first five chapters in this section focus on individual reasoning about ethical dilemmas and the systematic flaws that can occur in this reasoning process. Jonathan Baron, in chapter 10, starts the section off by analyzing the relationship between utilitarianism, maximizing social welfare, and the omission/commission distinction. Baron suggests that one of the reasons we often see deviations from the utilitarian philosophy is that individuals make a cognitive distinction between omissions and commissions, a distinction that is not made in the utilitarian philosophy. Baron further asserts that these "nonutilitarian intuitions" have some important implications, including a tendency to oppose government policies that people believe to be beneficial and a willingness to accept more harm produced by omission than less harm produced through commission.

In chapter 17, George Loewenstein suggests that ethical dilemmas can be characterized by a trade-off between self-interest and the well-being of others and that the decisions made by individuals are often skewed in the direction of the self. Loewenstein identifies several reasons for an overemphasis on the self, including the weak force of altruism, the unidentifiability (or "statistical nature") of the victims of unethical behavior, inappropriate time discounting, and the powerful human ability to rationalize or justify actions. He uses the auditing profession to illustrate the operation of these factors.

Ann McGill, in chapter 12, draws on the causal reasoning literature to examine how individuals form causal explanations and how these explanations may be related to judgments of blame and responsibility. McGill asserts that individuals explain an event by comparing the event with a causal background. Different explanations can be made for the same event, however, because the causal background selected is not constant but rather is dependent on management perspective, culture, and the perceived mutability of events. McGill concludes with a proposal for a normative theory of the selection of causal backgrounds.

In chapter 13, Joshua Klayman concentrates on the cognitive processes that result in resistance to change, in particular examining the ways in which these processes may be particularly characteristic of ethical situations. He pinpoints four cognitive processes that tend to favor the status quo: the tendency to conduct positive tests of our hypotheses, the belief that we are unique, the biased interpretation of data, and an underemphasis on alternatives. Klayman suggests that certain characteristics of ethical dilemmas make them particularly resistant to solution. His analysis is similar in many respects to that offered by Kramer and Messick in chapter 3.

Chapter 14 focuses on a particular niche of ethical decision making: the environment. Max Bazerman, Kim Wade-Benzoni, and Francisco Benzoni identify a gap between the general attitude that people want to preserve the environment and particular behaviors that result in harm to the environment. They offer four reasons for this attitude/behavior gap, including inappropriate time discounting (also mentioned by Loewenstein), self-serving biases, preference reversals and lability, and problem censoring.

The remaining four chapters focus on the management and communication of risk. In chapter 15, Baruch Fischhoff examines reasons why there are disagreements between the public and the experts about risks. He suggests that such disagreements are not due to a conflict between actual and perceived risks but rather result from terminology differences, the different problems that the two groups are trying to solve, disputes over form versus substance, disagreements about what is feasible, and different interpretations of the facts. Fischhoff concludes by suggesting some implications of these differences, including when to involve the public in policy decisions and how to determine whether public or expert opinions are appropriate to a given situation.

As suggested by Fischhoff, one way that we have historically managed risk and uncertainty has been to rely on the advice of experts. In chapter 16, Robyn Dawes calls into question the usefulness of such experts. Dawes proposes that experts should provide "incremental validity" (an improvement in the quality of the predictions that would be achieved without the expert) and that the concept of incremental validity should include both positive features (for example, knowledge and assistance) and negative features (such as dependence on the expert). Dawes raises the ethical question of individuals who label themselves as experts and suggests that it is up to experts to prove that they can provide incremental validity.

Helmut Jungermann, in chapter 17, examines risk communication in situations where all communication options violate at least one ethical standard. Jungermann suggests that there are two dilemmas involved in risk communication: whether and how to present the information and what information to present. Jungermann highlights his points by drawing on real-world examples and closes by discussing the theoretical and practical implications of risk communication dilemmas.

Willem Wagenaar's chapter 18 closes the discussion on risk by suggesting that our tendency to look at safety issues at the site of the accident is often misguided. Wagenaar proposes a General Accident Causation Model that focuses on upper-level management decisions as a primary cause of accidents. Using this model, he proposes that the ethical problem of safety is found at the higher end of the organization, particularly in decisions that involve the trade-off between safety and money, separate budgets, short time horizons, and correction systems that unfairly blame employees for systemic safety problems. Wagenaar concludes that organizations do not have an ethical obligation to spend unlimited money on safety but are ethically responsible for removing structural deficits that result in unsafe conditions.

One of the distinctive features of this book is the commentaries written by three distinguished philosophers. It is rare that philosophers comment on papers written by psychologists and economists, but it is appropriate and important that they do so in this case. After all, business ethics is an area of applied philosophy. The behavioral scientists who wrote chapters for this book were invited to use their own moral common sense to place their research in an ethical context, but philosophers can place the work in a broader philosophical context with which most behavioral researchers are unfamiliar. Thus, Thomas Donaldson discusses the relevance of the first set of papers to stakeholder theory and to social contract theory, two ethical frameworks that enjoy popularity among business ethicists. Patricia Werhane relates the papers on risk management and decision making to philosophical writing about moral imagination, and she explores the possibility of linking cognitive psychology to moral concepts and ethical growth. In the final chapter, Russell Hardin ruminates about the connections between the findings and principles presented by the behavioral researchers and fundamental issues and questions in ethical theory.

These three chapters hold out the promise for an exciting area of research and scholarship in business ethics, an area that blends the empirical research tools of behavioral scientists with the conceptual discipline of moral philosophers and applies the resulting ideas to business and management contexts. This book will be a success if it helps this area grow.

Part I

SOCIAL AND ORGANIZATIONAL PROCESSES

Chapter 1

How Organizations Socialize Individuals into Evildoing

John M. Darley

W hen members of our culture think of acts of doing harm, we tend to think of an individual harm-doer who lies behind these acts, an evil individual who seeks out others and acts on them in evil ways. Perhaps our canonical image is that of a serial murderer, who moves among us, hidden behind the mask of normality, destroying the innocent. Contrary to cultural stereotypes, however, most harmful actions are not committed by palpably evil actors carrying out solitary actions. Instead, the typical evil action is inflicted on victims by individuals acting within an organizational context. Indeed, it may be difficult to identify the individual who perpetrates the evil; the harm may seem to be an organizational product that bears no clear stamp of any individual actor. Further, if we look within the organization and identify the individual who seems most closely connected with the harm—for instance, the foreman who orders the workers down the dangerous mine shaft or the corporate executive who orders the marketing of an unsafe drug—we do not find an individual whom we recognize as evil but someone who looks rather like us. We encounter again what Hannah Arendt (1963) found so striking about the Nazi mass murderer Adolph Eichmann, the banality and ordinariness of an individual whom we expected to be demonic. But that person has been changed; through participation in the organization, the individual has undergone a conversion process and become an autonomous participant in harmful actions.

This generalization, while hard to accept, is the major message arising from a recent set of books (Kelman and Hamilton 1989; Lifton 1986; Milgram 1974; Staub 1989) about organizations of social control that have committed horrible acts of genocide, and its validity is strengthened by the independent convergence of these books on this conclusion. To summarize their findings (see Darley 1992 for a fuller discussion), many evil actions are not the volitional products of individual evildoers but rather essentially organizational products that result when complex social forces interact to cause individuals to commit multiple acts of terrible harm. In that process, the individuals committing the harm are themselves changed. They become evil, although they still do not show the demonic properties that are suggested by our conventional views of evil.

The realization that the specific social forces that alter individuals are produced in organizations raises several questions. What sorts of organizations enlist their members in doing harm? How do the organizational forces work to produce harmful actions? How does the sustained application of those forces alter the character of those individuals caught up in the harmful activities?

WHAT ORGANIZATIONS DO HARM?

What organizations are prone to inflict harm on innocent victims? One possible answer is that it is primarily organizations of social control that do so. "Organizations of social control" are those organizations that society authorizes to control the behavior of members of the society or outsiders. Police forces, prison guards, and military forces are the standard examples. More specifically, these organizations are sometimes captured by leaders who have evil purposes and make the command-driven machinery of the organization achieve those purposes. There is considerable validity to this observation. Certainly Hitler was evil. Certainly, too, the commanders of the Argentine forces who ordered the torture and killing of large segments of Argentinean society completely intended the killings they caused and are evil. But harmful actions are not limited to organizations controlled by evil leaders. Perhaps the most disturbing element of the case I am constructing is that organizations can lurch toward evil in ways not intended by any of the participants in the organization.

As we now know, there were many instances in which the American army massacred civilians during the Vietnam War. I believe that the army leadership structure did not intend these killings. We therefore face the fact that organizations can somehow be subverted or otherwise altered to turn persons within those organizations into evildoers, even when the apex of the organization does not direct the evildoing. We do not have too much trouble understanding how this happens in an organization set up for the purposes of social control. Such an organization is already in the business of harming, perhaps killing, the enemy. What happens is that the definition of who constitutes the enemy widens, and the controls that are put on the occasions for killing them become "inoperative." This propensity of organizations of social control to lurch into morally unacceptable actions is quite well understood.

The analysis constructed so far can be read in the following way. There is a particular subclass of organizations, roughly those concerned with social control, that have the unique capacity to turn those within the organization into evildoers. We have a reasonably clear notion of what those organizations are. Our task, therefore, is to be particularly vigilant in monitoring those organizations so that they do not consciously stray or unconsciously slip into creating evil actions, and in the process evildoers. Success in this task, admittedly not easy to achieve, will protect us from this problem.

This analysis seems to me to be seriously inadequate. The truth is bleaker. While organizations of social control are particularly vulnerable to this process, the implicit contention that other kinds of organizations are not subject to similar problems is demonstrably false. We do not eliminate organizational harm-doing by eliminating it in organizations of social control. Schools and universities, manufacturing firms, research organizations, and government organizations are not conventionally regarded as organizations of social control, yet their potential for the incubation of harm is high, and in many cases that we can cite that potential has become actual. What I suggest is that the division of organizations into those that are engaged in social control and related activities versus those engaged in, for instance, production is less useful for identifying organizations that may engage in doing harm than we might think. Given the focus of this volume on business ethics, I will concentrate on the genesis of harm within firms but will also cite related examples from bureaucracies.

In recent years, a number of books have appeared whose authors are concerned with what they call "corporate crime." For many years "white-collar crime" has been the subject of study, but that category was found to blur the distinctions among what proved to be several quite different kinds of crime. White-collar crime was initially analyzed as crimes committed by workers or executives against their firms. Gradually, a second class of crime has come to be noticed. Corporate crime is crime perpetrated by an organization against either the general public, that segment of the public that uses the organization's products, or the organization's own workers. A generally accepted definition of corporate crime, proposed by Marshall Clinard, is "a form of collective rule breaking in order to achieve the organizational goals." Clinard, a seminal figure in the field, encases a critical realization in this definition, the recognition that some crimes are committed because they fulfill an organization's goals.[1]

Examples of all kinds of organizational crimes are easy to find. Recall the design of the Ford Pinto, sold for years by a company in which many executives were aware that it had a gas tank likely to rupture in low-speed rear-end crashes and incinerate its passengers (Dowie 1987). Consider the Robins Corporation, marketing a contraceptive product that it knew caused disastrous medical consequences to many who used it (Mintz 1985; Perry and Dawson 1985). Recall Watergate or the Iran-Contra affair. Consider the silence of Morton Thiokol executives who were aware of the dangers to the space shuttle O-rings at low launch temperatures (Kramer 1992). Consider any number of defense contractors who have delivered military weapons systems to the Defense Department with faked safety and effectiveness tests and substandard internal electronic components (Vandivier 1987). Recall the suppression of the growing evidence about numerous design flaws in the nuclear reactors used to generate electricity in this country (Faulkner 1987).

There are also numerous examples of organizations that harm their workers. Think about executives who continued to have shipyard workers work with asbestos long after its carcinogenic properties were known to the officials, or government bureaucrats who kept uranium miners at work long after the dangers of that occupation were known to the bureaucrats. Think of miners with black lung disease or cotton mill workers with brown lung disease.

Nor do we lack examples of organizations' inflicting harm on large segments of the general public. Our government's atomic bomb tests in Nevada rained radioactivity on all citizens downwind of the test sites. Matt Tallmer (1987) details the incredible chemical dumping practices of the Hooker Chemical Corporation, the perpetrator of the Love Canal disaster, which have left a trail of illegal poisonous chemical waste in ground water sources from Long Island to California. The Allied Chemical Company, manufacturers of Kepone, a substance known to be toxic, set up a dummy corporation as an "independent contractor" to continue the manufacture of it; the dust from the plant obscured the sight of the plant from those members of the public unlucky enough to be nearby. Eventually, one hundred miles of fisheries on the James River had to be closed because of concentrations of Kepone in the fish. Interestingly, another organization—the city of Hopewell, in which the plant was located—was so obviously complicit in hiding the damages caused by the chemical that it received fines as well.

What this list demonstrates is that many corporations have inflicted serious harm on either the general public, consumers of the products that they manufacture, or the workers engaged in the manufacture of those products. I will return later in the chapter to the question of whether these organizations are in some identifiable way "rogue organizations" or whether these patterns of doing harm are somehow latent in all organizations. First, however, it is important to examine the mechanisms by which organizations—conglomerates of individuals—come to inflict harm on the public, consumers, and workers.

HOW INDIVIDUALS ARE DRAWN INTO DOING HARM

Analyzing evildoing in organizations and the ways in which organizations cause individuals to do evil requires a number of constructs that can be drawn from various fields of social science. Within organizations, processes leading to both the *diffusion of information* and the *diffusion and fragmentation of responsibility* are common. Barry Staw's (Staw and Ross 1987) notion of *sunk costs* is also necessary; organizations get committed to courses of action, and the individuals who generated those courses of action are reluctant or unwilling to change them, even when others would see the need for change. Many decisions prove to have *implicit ethical components* that are hidden at the moment of decision, arising only later, after decisions are made. Finally, there are *concrete decision options* that face various individuals in the organization, as it continues the course of doing harm even after some of the ethical issues become clear. These decision options generally are presented within the context of a hierarchically structured organization, business or governmental, *on which people are dependent for their livelihoods.* Following orders, within some ill-defined sphere of activities, is legitimated, and failure to follow orders may put one's livelihood at risk.

Diffusion and Fragmentation of Information and Responsibility

The processes of diffusion and fragmentation of information and diffusion and fragmentation of responsibility often go together, but they can be separated analytically. When it is discovered that a product that has been designed, manufactured, advertised, and sold is harmful to its consumers, there is often a long period during which the evidence of harm accumulates. This knowledge that the product is potentially or actually harmful may come into various divisions of the organization but remain in an unassembled state, because those divisions are not in perfect communication with each other on issues of harm. The organization has all the information needed to draw the inference of harm, but because the information is not pulled together and put in front of a competent individual, the organization can be said not to know that the product is harmful.[2] And, of course, responsibility requires knowledge. If I do not know that harm is risked, then I am not responsible for preventing that harm.

The Dalkon Shield case (Mintz 1985; Perry and Dawson 1985) provides a clear illustration of the compartmentalization of information within a corporation. The Dalkon Shield was an intrauterine contraceptive device, manufactured and aggressively sold by the Robins Company, that proved to be potentially dangerous to women who used it. One of the product's many dangers was a "string" attached to it, actually a bundle of plastic fibers enclosed by a sheath, that was designed to facilitate removal. If the sheath was perforated, the string drew bacteria into the uterus, causing sometimes life-threatening infections.

Because of successful sales efforts, more shields needed to be manufactured, and the company assigned production to a subsidiary plant, the Chap-Stick plant. The quality control supervisor of that plant, on his own initiative, "examined under a microscope samples of Shields ready to be shipped from the ChapStick plant. He found tiny holes through which body fluids from the vagina could escape into the sterile uterus if wicked up the string" (Perry and Dawson 1985, 81). This information apparently did not get to the relevant medical personnel, however, so that when reports of infections from Shield users began to come in from doctors who had implanted the Shield, the medical personnel initially did not connect these infections with the infection-transmission path documented by the person in the manufacturing arm of the subsidiary. Different elements of relevant information, coming in via different organizational components that are not tightly connected to each other in communication networks, often do not reach the relevant decision makers. Those who make decisions are often walled off from information that is vital to good decision making.

Another example of this failure of communication occurred in the months prior to the space shuttle Challenger disaster. NASA test engineers at the Marshall Space Flight Center wrote a series of memos expressing concerns about potential failures in the pressure seal system, but the project manager did not pass these memos on to the Morton Thiokol engineers (Kramer 1992).

It may seem somewhat naive to cite these examples as cases of an organization's simply "not knowing" of harm their product causes, and with good reason. If a product is producing a profit for the corporation, then one can see a great advantage in the corporation's "not knowing" that the product is dangerous when it in fact knows it full well. Later in the chapter several cases will be considered in which individuals moved to preserve what we might call "strategic ignorance," both for themselves and for the corporation, and the corporate structure was organized to facilitate that claim.[3]

Diffusion of responsibility is another source of organizational harm-doing. Who has responsibility for actions that are seen to cause harm? And what kinds of responsibilities can be said to exist? It has been said that success has a million parents, but failure is an orphan. Assume that an organization has produced and marketed a drug that is later found to have terrible side effects—thalidomide or DES, for instance. One unit can develop a drug and assume that it will be tested for side effects. Another unit can arrange for it to be marketed, assuming that those safety checks have been completed. Those who have actually carried out the tests of the drug may be aware that their tests were incapable of determining side effects with any sort of precision. (In the case of DES, for instance, a drug given to pregnant women to reduce nausea during pregnancy, it was only many years later that the drug was discovered to produce long-term negative effects, including increased likelihood of cancer, among young women who had been in utero when their mothers were taking the drug.) No individual intentionally brought about these side effects. More to the point, it is difficult to identify exactly who within the organization was responsible for allowing the mistake to happen. This fact seems to become recognized in those few cases in which members of organizations are put on trial for the consequences of their actions; rarely are any specific individuals found criminally liable.

Responsibility not only diffuses but also fragments. Within a hierarchical organization, an individual's responsibility is defined by the duties that accrue to that person's position within the organization. If, for example, my role is to receive reports of drug trials being carried out at remote sites in one region, my responsibility may be to summarize and integrate those results and pass them to somebody else, to be merged with reports from other regions. I may know enough to know that one or two reports from my region could point toward worrying side effects, but I do not know if the reports from other regions confirm them. "I have done my duty" if I just flag my worries as I pass the reports along.

One more fact about information flow and individual responsibility is worth noticing. Information about product dangers, as opposed to information about product sales, markets, and profits, is generally "abnormal" information, and the mechanisms for its analysis are not well developed. One can anticipate that it will be collected in less-organized ways, and responsibilities for its analysis will be assigned in less well considered ways.[4]

In organizations, persons are sometimes assigned formal responsibilities for safety monitoring, but are more informally instructed to disregard those responsibilities, or simply learn to disregard them under time demands to complete other activities more directly connected with production. Following a methane explosion that killed twenty-five miners, it was discovered that, although it was formally part of the foreman's responsibilities to test the methane concentration in the shaft, he had long since been socialized not to make the tests and to fake the record entries about them (Caudill 1987).

In the pressure of the moment, definitions of responsibility are often renegotiated downward to accommodate those pressures. During the fateful conference between Morton Thiokol (MTI) engineers and officials and NASA officials, MTI initially recommended that the shuttle Challenger not be launched because of the possible effects of the cold launch temperatures on the O-ring seals. NASA officials would not launch with this recommendation on record but pressured MTI to reverse its recommendations. The MTI management people caucused. One MTI official said that "a management decision was required" (Kramer 1992, 232). One of the MTI engineers was told "to take off his engineering hat and put on his manager's hat" (p. 232), apparently in an attempt to recast the engineers' definitions of their responsibility to the MTI managers; they were to elevate themselves above their own engineering knowledge and function as compromising decision makers.

The reframing also gave the MTI engineers only a reporting responsibility. The two MTI engineers fought their way back into the discussion, arguing not to launch, but were overridden; the MTI executives decided the "data were, indeed, inconclusive, and that they would now recommend that the launch proceed" (Kramer 1992, 232–33). Roger Boisjoly, one of the engineers, summarized the way that the decision was finally framed by the meeting: "This was a meeting where the determination was to launch, and it was up to us to prove beyond a shadow of a doubt that it was not safe to do so. This is the total reverse to what the usual is . . . in a pre-flight review" (quoted in

Kramer, p. 233). Thus the task of the engineers was to prove the launch would fail, and it was the responsibility of the MTI executives to allow launch unless that proof was conclusive.

This last move illustrates a critically important maneuver in the reframing of responsibility. In our culture we have a decision rule that might be called "innocent until proven guilty." The chance for some motivated creativity in the application of this rule arises in identifying which of the decision options counts as "innocent" and which as "guilty." In real-life decision cases, people skilled at framing can claim that the burden of proof falls on those arguing for a decision other than the one proposed. In this instance, "launch" was more or less forcibly equated with "innocent," the option to be chosen unless it could be proven wrong beyond all possible doubt. The standard framing of the launch decision was not to launch unless the engineers were convinced that the launch was safe, but the NASA officials reversed this framing. The launch was going to happen unless the engineers could prove that it would fail. They couldn't prove that it would fail, so they launched, and the launch failed. One is reminded of the Clarence Thomas–Anita Hill hearings, in which the issue was cast as requiring a vote for Thomas's appointment to the Supreme Court unless Hill's allegations could be proved true. Conservatives on the panel framed the hearing task as a court case; either Thomas could be proved guilty or he was "innocent" and therefore, by an odd twist of reasoning, entitled to a position on the Supreme Court.

The assignment of the burden of proof is a very powerful manipulation of decision rules, and one that is more malleable than is widely recognized. Kramer and Messick (chapter 3) suggest that everyone is able to adopt the perspective of the "intuitive lawyer," trained to muster sincerely all the arguments for one point of view.

Take this a step further. Sometimes the burden of proof is a genuine burden in both time and costs. If one organization produces a product, it accrues the profits from that product. If we require that a second organization prove that the product is unsafe, where does that second organization acquire the resources to carry out the relevant tests? Do government agencies assume that burden? If so, profits remain with the producer, while certain of the costs that might be associated with the product fall on the public. Further, general reductions in government resources may remove the resources necessary to conduct those tests.

To summarize, the information that a product or an act is potentially harmful may exist within the organization in an unassembled form, so that the decision makers are unaware of the potential harm. Those who report to the decision makers may be very aware of the possibilities of harm, but feel that they have fulfilled their responsibilities by providing information to the decision makers from which the possibilities of harm might be inferred by careful analysis. Further, the framing of the decision is important. To halt ongoing processes because of potential future harms requires an action, a decision, while allowing the continuation of normal processes requires no action. Thus, the decision to intervene is often framed as requiring clear and overwhelming evidence before it is taken, while the original construction, that processes should not go forward, or products should not be produced, unless their safety is assured, is lost.

It is important to see how these processes, each of which can work independently to produce harm, can also work together to magnify the possibilities of harm. If evidence of potential harm is unassembled and fragmented, and if those who feel that it might occur are not responsible for making that point, then the evidence of potential harm will rarely rise to a level of conclusiveness to convince those caught up in the pressures to continue with normal activities to suspend those activities because of the possibility of dimly perceived, poorly documented, harms.

One further point needs to be made. Because these processes so naturally occur within any organization, it is possible to set up conditions that promote their occurrence and create an organization "optimized" for the denial of the harms that are done. We will consider examples of this later.

Commitment to Courses of Action

Staw, in an interesting series of studies (see Staw and Ross 1987 for a review), has demonstrated the utility of the notion of "sunk costs," those commitments to a course of action that are generated by some initial decision, often a decision to invest financial or other resources in a course of action. He shows that once these costs are incurred, those individuals incurring them are reluctant to withdraw from that course of action, even when the evidence suggests that withdrawal would be wise. Sometimes organizations get committed to courses of action in ways that are ill-considered, premature, or impulsive. It is hard enough for an individual to reverse a personal decision, even when no one else knows of that decision. In organizational settings, decisions are far harder to reverse. The commitment of the individual is strengthened as he or she advocates a course of action to others in the organization, because that person's reputation within the company is on the line. Then, when the recommendation is accepted, the face of the organization or a sub-unit of the organization is also put on the line. Still later, the commitment to the course of action is further hardened when costly implementation procedures are put in motion. However the commitment is made, once it is made the organization either is reluctant to or cannot retreat from the decision it has made, even if the decision is going to put a harmful product in the marketplace.

Examples of this process are abundant and quite revealing. Consider the Goodrich case. Briefly, the B. F. Goodrich Corporation won a contract to produce aircraft brakes for the LTV Corporation. It was extremely important to Goodrich to succeed at this subcontract, because as a result of a previous subcontract with LTV, the company had been dropped from LTV's list of suppliers for many years. For the new contract, Goodrich had based its proposal on the assumption that it could achieve sufficient braking power with a four-disc brake assembly. Disastrously for the company, however, this assumption proved to be based on erroneous calculations. When the assemblies for the four-disc system had already been ordered and many had been delivered, a subordinate engineer was put in charge of completion of the project, which was conceptualized as choosing the right materials to line the discs. After a series of lining tests, all failures, he began to suspect the original calculations; he reran them and came up with evidence that a five-disc system was going to be needed. He had the equations, but if Goodrich accepted them, three consequences would follow: (1) the company would lose money on the assemblies they had ordered, because they could not be converted to a five-disc configuration—a literal case of "sunk costs"; (2) Goodrich would be hopelessly behind on the delivery date, because new assemblies would have to be ordered; and (3) the company would lose corporate face with LTV, because a major factor in awarding Goodrich the contract was that their brake system was to be light in weight. (Weight was an important consideration in airline economy, and a five-disc system would be noticeably heavier.)

How this situation unfolded is a fascinating story and one that I will return to, but the company's immediate decision is of interest to us now; it was to code the problem as one of finding the "right lining material." The subordinate reported the faultiness of the calculations to the engineer who originally made them, who was known as a person who exploded when his decisions were questioned. This engineer rather obviously regarded that his own face was on line in this decision. Not surprisingly, he denied the validity of the recalculations and the subordinate was sent back to carry out what proved to be a futile search for better disc-lining material.

Abstract Harm and Tangible Gains

In many organizational settings in which an action is taken that will ultimately result in harm to others, there is initially no overt target of the actions committed, no salient other human who is seen to be a victim of the action. The person who decides to let the assembly line use substandard cord in the fabrication of radial tires is not thinking of the accidents that the decision could cause but simply keeping the assembly line moving. "Product safety" at this point is an abstract concern standing in the way of the all-important goal of production. If one examines the steps from product design to the eventual emergence of that product from the assembly line into the marketing organization, there are remarkably few times that the question of the effects of the product on the consumer is raised. Instead, competing issues involving product conceptualization, profits, and fulfillment of production standards are generated and dominate the analysis.

The Ford Pinto case seems to illustrate this process. The Pinto's gas tank was located in a position that made it vulnerable to rupture in even a very low-speed rear-end collision. First, why did this design flaw happen? Because Ford wanted a competitor to the Volkswagen Beetle, production schedules were speeded up. "In order to accomplish this goal, the tooling process was carried out simultaneously with the design, engineering, and quality assurance stages. . . . Ford engineers discovered, prior to production but after tooling was well under way, that rear-end collisions in crash tests would easily rupture the Pinto's fuel system" (Clinard and Yeager 1980, 260).

Still, remedies existed. A relatively cheap retrofit would have rendered the car at least somewhat less dangerous, but it was not done.[5] Why not? Probably because the framing of the task of those building the Pinto was to produce a car rapidly that would meet the "two thousand, two thousand rule." The manager in charge of the entire project had articulated the criteria that the car needed to come in under two thousand pounds body weight and should sell for around two thousand dollars to the consumer. When an engineering or design decision was referred to him, he constantly referenced those two standards in deciding the issue. One gets the feeling that subordinates quickly learned not to refer decisions to him but to decide them in terms of the clear framework of reference he had provided. The process is perhaps easy to envision if one knows that the person in charge of the project was none other than Lee Iacocca, whose forcefulness we have all had a chance to see on our televisions.

To summarize, a number of frameworks generated by requirements of the manufacturing process and the need to have that process run on time, efficiently, and at low cost dominate the analysis of those who are building and even designing a product. The end user of the product is not represented or is represented only in the limited role of "consumer." Since a good many of the forces that cause people to avoid doing harm to others rely on the salient presence of specific or specifically imagined victims, if such victims are not present then restraining forces are considerably weakened. "These opposing forces rest ultimately on the actor's awareness that he or she is connected to a victim," as Herbert Kelman and Lee Hamilton remark in their percipient way (1989, p. 313). Individuals within the organization can lose sight of the fact that people may be harmed in the course of fulfilling the other goals of the corporation or bureaucracy.

All the factors that I cite can be combined in powerful ways. When members of an organization do see potential dangers to workers or customers that might result if certain decisions taken by the organization are put into effect, then those who advocate different decisions are often given the heavy burden of proof discussed earlier.

Employee Self-interest and Job Survival

In most organizations, it is legitimate to give orders, and the cost of disobeying those orders may be loss of one's livelihood. If, therefore, the organization orders—or is seen as ordering—certain actions in furtherance of the production of dangerous products, those involved face some extremely difficult decisions. The Dalkon Shield case provides us with a specific example (Perry and Dawson 1985). At the time that production was begun in the ChapStick plant, the product had previously been manufactured at other plants and widely marketed, and the company was already aware of several safety concerns about the Shield and deep in the process of denial and fabrication. Crowder, the quality control supervisor of the Chap-Stick plant, reported his concerns about wicking to his superior, Ross, and did not get a satisfactory response. He then did a series of experiments proving that the string would wick water—and thus, by inference, bacteria—up into the bodies of women users and reported the results of these experiments to his superiors.

> Ross was anything but pleased. He angrily reminded Crowder that the string was not Crowder's responsibility and that he should leave it alone. Crowder told Ross that he could not, in good conscience, keep quiet about something that he felt could cause infection in the women who wore the Shield.
> "Your conscience doesn't pay your salary," Crowder says Ross replied. Ross also told Crowder that he was being insubordinate for pursuing this matter; if he valued his job he would do as he was told and forget about the string."

Note the psychology of the presentation of the issue to Crowder; although done with a certain crudeness, it was not atypical. First, he was giving Crowder an order. Second, he was offering Crowder a framing of the whole matter as "not his responsibility" along with a threat of job loss to induce him to accept that framing. We will see this threat and framing maneuver in play again, although done with more sophistication; it is quite commonly used in organizations.

Not many respond to it as Crowder did, however. He continued to protest, carried his protests higher up, had them rebuffed, and was finally "let go" in a corporate reorganization some years later. He is a genuine hero, and his heroism cost him his job. Those looking at what happens to whistle-blowers—individuals who report their concerns to outside groups—report similar fates.

Notice I said that if the superiors in the corporation are *seen as* ordering the continuation of a certain course of action, subordinates may feel compelled to fall in with that course of action. In a corporation, to wait to do something until one is ordered to do so can be thought of as a failure of initiative, or worse, a desire to put the superior on the spot. Many subordinates, in those circumstances, can be expected to intuit what orders they would be given and "follow them in advance." One suspects that this is what happened in the Pinto case; the subordinates intuited Iacocca's response to the possibility of fuel tank disasters and rolled straight ahead. An obvious point follows: This process gives the superiors the chance to deny ultimate responsibility for the product or harm while continuing to exert pressure for the harm to continue. Management by objectives, if those objectives largely involve making profits, has a good deal to answer for.

Many organizations have in place some form of corporate code, which generally includes both ethical strictures and references to "fair play" and a "superior product for customers." They also have in place incentive and bonus schemes, competition between various sales forces, promotions based on winning those competitions, and so on. Corporate workers are going to pay particular attention to what happens when those two aspects of corporate culture clash.

Several years ago, the Xerox Corporation, apparently pleased with its new articulation of its corporate code, gave permission for a reporter to observe one of its sales groups in action, no doubt expecting a glowing report on its system. Instead, the reporter (Dorsey 1994) demonstrated how the intense pressures for profits caused the sales force to push their customers to buy machines of far greater capabilities than the customers needed—or often could pay for. They succeeded, it seems, by telling customers about the Xerox Company code, convincing them that the existence of the code somehow ensured that their recommendations of oversized and expensive machines were in the customers' best interest. Corporations that put in place a corporate ethics code and do not consider its relationship to existing corporate practices and bonus and promotion systems seem to me to be engaging in window dressing of a particularly cynical sort. Specifically, unless decisions are made that elevate the ethics code over the profit and promotion system, such codes are empty. And in the end, the corporate structure that promulgated the code loses creditability, and its further pronouncements, in the unlikely event they are sincerely intended, will be ignored.

THE TIME COURSE OF DECISION MAKING: HINDSIGHT AND COVER-UPS

Let us assume that, suddenly and dramatically, it is discovered that the actions of a corporation have already harmed large classes of others. It is now realized that given certain actions of the organization, harmful outcomes are inevitable. Pintos are actually rear-ended, gas tanks actually catch on fire, and actual passengers are horribly killed. Memos exist within the corporation in which design engineers warn about exactly these possibilities. To an outsider observing the situation, it seems apparent that those in the organization must have been aware of the risks of harm, and thus somewhere there must be evil individuals who have knowingly brought about that harm.[6] And sometimes this is true. There are such evil people. One thinks of the bosses of the Film Recovery System Corporation, which recovered precious metals using processes that involved highly dangerous chemicals, taking almost no safety precautions to shield the workers from the effects of these chemicals, and hiring illegal immigrants who spoke little English so they would not understand what was happening or be able to reveal it to others (Frank 1987).

Let us consider a more charitable scenario, that the negative outcomes simply could not have been anticipated; an unexpected side effect of a drug might be an example. Or, more likely, let us say that some evidence existed calling attention to the negative outcomes but that this evidence was not given sufficient attention within the organization. The Pinto case is a perfect example. The people within the organization were focusing on other organizational goals and, because they were "negligent, hurried, sloppy, or overworked" (Kelman and Hamilton 1989, 312), missed the meanings of the danger signals. They were also subject to the interpersonal processes we have considered involving breakdowns of communications and diffusion of responsibility.

However it comes about, harmful actions have been committed, and now the individuals who had some responsibility for those actions have become aware of those consequences. There are several psychological points to be made here. First, the decisions that now face organizational decision makers are not clean ones: they do not offer perfectly positive outcomes and typically involve choosing the least bad option. All too often, the organization does not have the choice of not embarking on a course of action that will cause harm; it has already done so, and some people actually have been harmed. Thus some guilt and liability have already been incurred. The decision makers may have been implicated in decisions that will now be seen as, at best, ill-considered; even if they are not, others to whom they owe loyalties may be implicated.

The role of the well-known hindsight bias here is likely to be destructive. In the classic demonstration of hindsight, an observer to a series of events consistently finds the actual outcome of the events as having been more probable than it was in fact (Fischhoff 1975). It is as if the observer is saying, "Well, of course that was going to happen. I could see it from the beginning." To those responsible for corporate disasters, as to the outside observers, it must seem that the disastrous outcomes were foreseeable once evidence for the disasters has accumulated. Some rather bizarre dynamics ensue. If the organizational decision makers admit, to themselves and others, that harmful outcomes are actually occurring in the present, then because it will seem to them that these outcomes were foreseeable, they will feel culpable for "knowingly" allowing them to happen. And they will certainly feel that others will think the negative consequences were foreseeable and condemn them for allowing them to occur. This dynamic creates a strong pressure for the decision makers to deny that the harmful outcomes are genuine, or genuinely caused by the product in question.

This denial by the higher-ups in the organization may cause subordinates, who are more concretely faced with the evidence of harms, to interpret that denial as a tacit instruction to lie about the existence of those harms or minimize the role of the organizational action in producing them. As the reader will recognize, this begins the process of "the cover-up," a frequent occurrence in organizational harm-doing, and one whose dynamics we may be able to illuminate here.

Certainly organizational case studies give us an enormous number of examples of corporations attempting to cover up harm-doing. Three things strike me about cover-ups. First, they are highly unlikely to succeed. The evidence has become so clear about the harmfulness of the product, and so many people within the organization know about it, that it will surely leak out. Second, cover-ups themselves frequently provide conclusive evidence of the wrongfulness of the actions taken in the first place. So for a company to engage in cover-ups—cover-ups that are also likely to get detected—is a further and more foolish error. Third, because these first two points are true, we can infer that when individuals engage in cover-ups, there is a great deal of pressure on them to do so. Standardly, this pressure is thought to come from fear of negative publicity, possibly leading to job loss or civil or criminal penalties. But we can see how it could also stem from an initial shocked denial on the part of the organizational decision makers, that they were the sort of persons who would bring about disastrous harm to others—a denial aimed at maintaining their own image of self, although quickly coupled with concerns for the more standard consequences as well.[7]

To my mind, this is a critical point in the destruction of the ethical character of those decision makers. The cover-up is now engaged in consciously and deliberately. Covering up past evidence is also likely to lead to maintaining the current practices that have brought about the harms, at least for as long as the cover-up is successful. It is at this point that I think that this organizational actor becomes evil, becomes an independent perpetrator of further negative acts that are now knowingly done. When, for example, individuals in corporations discovered that the asbestos used by its workers was leading to a high rate of cases of lung cancer, they sometimes chose to conceal that fact, perhaps because they were concerned with all the factors we have discussed and the liabilities they would incur if they revealed that information. But they also continued having the workers work in what they now knew were dangerous settings. They now were doing intentionally what they had previously done unknowingly.

As cover-ups continue, other processes of concealment are likely to be necessary, even ones that were perhaps not contemplated by the organizational actor at the moment of choice between acknowledging and denying the harms done. The evidence of previous harms had better disappear. Those in the organization who might discover the previous harms had better be hindered or muzzled. Meetings have to be held to rehearse the next set of lies to be told. All the participants have to get their stories straight. A number of repugnant moral actions are found to be required following the initial decision to conceal the initial harm.

What has been described here, I claim, is a very important way in which an individual can be caught up in a harmful process and altered by it. Whatever else might be said about the Nazi doctor who stood on the selection ramp, designating those who would live and those who would die, he knew that was what he was doing. But often an individual within an organization carries out what seem to be routine actions but later turn out to have negative consequences that in retrospect seem to have been foreseeable. Whether that person denies the negativity of the consequences, denies the responsibility for those consequences, or conceals those consequences and becomes meshed in a widening circle of actions necessary to continue the concealment, he or she has become an independent and autonomous perpetuator of the harms done. That person has become evil. What is important to see here is that the process is an after-the-fact one, in which the person faces not the prospective choice to do harm but the retrospective choice to acknowledge that his or her actions have already done harm. The more it becomes clear that those harms should have been foreseen, the more guilt, shame, and blame are acquired in the acknowledgment of past harms. But often failing to acknowledge past harms means continuing to commit those harms in the present.

The Goodrich Case: Cascading Processes

This account of the processes by which corporations lurch into corruption and follow it with cover-up has not revealed the rapid and dynamic application of all the processes in tandem. It therefore does not convey the full force of the pressure that is experienced by any individual who seeks to stop the march toward disaster. A further description of the Goodrich case will illustrate the cascading nature of the processes. There are three reasons for examining this case in some detail. The first is that, quite unusually, we have a firsthand narrative account of it from one of the participants, who was willing to be candid about his own actions. Firsthand accounts are rare, unfortunately, for they are highly illuminating.[8] Second, the case is remarkable in the certainty with which the cover-up was doomed to failure. The Goodrich Corporation delivered a brake assembly guaranteed to be discovered a failure by the LTV group when they did their first flight tests of the plane. This fact allows us to rule out the possibility of corporate gain as a motivator of the incident and to see what we might call "the internal momentum" of the dynamics of corruption. Third, the case is one that is familiar to many who teach business ethics, and a social psychological perspective on the case might be useful.

The story is told by Kermit Vandivier, who worked in the testing division of the Troy, Ohio, plant of the B. F. Goodrich Corporation (Vandivier 1987). Since the contract was to supply brake assemblies for a military plane, the brake system would finally have to undergo an intensive set of tests called qualification tests, and the specifications for conducting and reporting the results of those tests were rigidly specified.

Recall that Goodrich really wanted to get back into subcontracting for LTV. According to Vandivier, "The brake was designed by one of Goodrich's most capable engineers, John Warren. . . . The happy-go-lucky manner he usually maintained belied a temper which exploded whenever anyone ventured to offer any criticism of his work, no matter how small. . . . As his co-workers learned the consequences of criticizing him, they did so less and less readily, and when he submitted his preliminary design for the A7D brake, it was accepted without question" (p. 146). Goodrich bid for the contract on the basis of that design, which called for a relatively small brake, using only four discs of stopping surface. Here was where the core mistake was made; apparently nobody checked Warren's calculations.[9]

When the contract was won, a subordinate engineer named Lawson was assigned to work out the final plans for production. The task was largely to figure out the best materials for the disc linings. He rigged a simulation of the brake system, lined it, and found that it produced braking temperatures that exceeded the normal maximum temperatures by 50 percent. The linings crumbled and failed. After repeated tests, all with the same result, Lawson redid Warren's calculations and discovered that "the brake was too small. There simply was not enough surface area on the disc to stop the aircraft without generating the excessive heat that caused the linings to fail. . . . The answer to the problem was obvious but far from simple—the four-disc brake would have to be scrapped" (Vandivier 1987, 148).

But various kinds of commitment processes were already in play. Replacing all the four-disc brake subassemblies would be costly in both money and time and might jeopardize the promised delivery date. Perhaps the major commitment was Warren's: Despite the evidence of the abortive tests and Lawson's careful computations, Warren rejected the idea that the four-disc brake was inadequate. As Vandivier has noted, "It would have been difficult for Warren to admit not only that he had made a serious error in his calculations and original design but that his mistakes had been caught by a green kid, barely out of college" (pp. 148–9)—another kind of sunk costs. Warren's professional status had been committed to the proposition that the four-disc system would work.

Other members of the organization had also made commitments. The projects manager in the Goodrich organization had already reported to LTV that the preliminary tests on the four-disc brake had been successful. In this fashion, the face of the production unit was committed. One wonders how many similar disastrous commitments have been hardened when someone automatically answered "no problem" in ignorance of the facts.

Lawson, convinced of the validity of his calculations, and rejecting the implicit framing of his responsibilities as continuing to test lining materials, courageously took his case the next step up the hierarchy. Unfortunately, the next step up was to the previously mentioned projects manager, a man named Sink who did not have an engineering degree but had risen through the organization for somewhat unclear reasons. Sink listened and examined the calculations. "Despite the fact that he was not a qualified engineer, it must certainly have been obvious to Sink that Lawson's calculations were correct and that a four-disc brake would never have worked on the A7D. . . . But other things of equal importance were also obvious. . . . [If he conceded] that Warren's calculations were incorrect . . . he would also have to admit that he had erred in trusting Warren's judgments. It also meant that, as project manager, it would be he who would have to explain the whole messy situation to the Goodrich hierarchy . . . and he had assured LTV . . . that about all there was left to do on the brake was to pack it in a crate and ship it out the door" (Vandivier 1987, 149).

Look at the decision that faced Sink. Assume that he might have figured that there was one chance in a hundred that some miraculous material for brake linings might appear and bail him out. Probably the corporation would not have wanted to risk the possibility of the 99 percent chance of failure, but Sink might. If he now decided against a four-disc assembly, all the consequences just mentioned would be triggered immediately. His job might be at risk. George Loewenstein has pointed out in chapter 11 that individuals heavily discount future consequences and underestimate consequences for others. This point is very relevant here; Sink faced immediate, certain, and negative consequences for himself if he decided against the four-brake assembly and uncertain consequences at some distant time if he decided not to scrap it. There was also the possibility that the responsibility for the whole situation could be diffused among the various players as time passed; indeed, as we will see, Sink took steps to see that it was.[10]

So, not so astoundingly, he sent Lawson back to try more linings. Lawson did, and they failed. Flight test dates came closer. Lab technicians and others in the plant became aware of the situation. "It was no longer possible for anyone to ignore the glaring truth that the brake was a dismal failure" (Vandivier 1987, 150). To their dismay, they saw the Goodrich organization marching toward delivering a brake that would inevitably fail when it was flight tested, causing acute danger for the test pilots.

In passing, Vandivier mentions that an LTV engineering team visited the Goodrich plant for a few days. Although their purpose was to see the brake in action, the Goodrich engineers managed to cover up the facts. I suspect that this cover-up action, which would have required the participation of a number of the Goodrich personnel, played a major causal role in committing them to what followed. Almost instinctively, one conceals evidence of disasters from outsiders, out of loyalty to one's co-workers, but then, retrospectively, one may see that doing so has placed one in a compromised position. When the Goodrich workers faced later decisions to participate in the fraud, they found themselves already committed or co-opted. A decision that had been made rapidly and on the basis of loyalty considerations had hidden ethical components that would become visible only later.

The brake now entered the qualification test phase. This was serious business. The qualification reports would be used as documentary proof that the brake had met all the requirements and was safe for flight testing. Reports of qualifications tests, signed by the testers, were to be sent to LTV and the government. Vandivier now personally entered the scene, as a part of the test lab team. His report of conversations among various Goodrich personnel (Vandivier 1987) provides a rare opportunity to follow the events as they unfolded. "I noticed that many irregularities in testing methods had been noted on the test logs." One blatant one involved a deliberate miscalibration of the brake pressure–recording instrument. "I showed the test logs to the test lab supervisor, Ralph Gretzinger, who said that he had learned from the technician who had miscalibrated the instrument that he had been asked to do so by Lawson." So now Lawson, who had up to then been quite courageous, had begun to participate in the deception. "Lawson . . . readily admitted asking for the miscalibration, saying he had been told to do so by Sink." When the hierarchy strikes, people begin to fear for their livelihoods.

Vandivier and Lawson talked, and Lawson was candid about the whole situation, "saying, 'I just can't believe this is really happening.' " He then made a prescient remark to Vandivier, showing that he already knew how things would unfold. " 'You wait,' he warned. 'You're going to get in the act too. . . . Regardless of what the brake does on test, it's going to be qualified.' . . . He said he had been told in those exact words by Sink and Van Horn."

A new player now emerged; Van Horn was Sink's boss, manager of the design engineering section. Higher-ups were now engaged in the deception. Vandivier reported this rather alarming comment to Gretzinger, who declared that " 'No false data or false reports are going to come out of this lab.' " Further pressures were put on the test labs to write a false qualification report, and Gretzinger angrily took the matter to his boss, Russell Line.[11] He came back shaken. " 'You know,' he went on uncertainly, looking down at his desk, 'I've been an engineer for a long time, and I've always believed that ethics and integrity were every bit as important as theorems and formulas, and never once has anything happened to change my beliefs. Now this. . . . Hell, I've got two sons to put through school, and I just. . . . ' His voice trailed off." Subject to hierarchical pressures, he had compromised, agreeing to have the test lab do the graphics section of the report but not to do the narrative section or to have the test lab sign the overall report. He had redefined his responsibility: " 'We're just drawing some curves. What happens to them after they leave here, well, we're not responsible.' "

Vandivier, showing considerable courage, confronted Line and was told that it was none of Line's business and none of Vandivier's business. Vandivier asked how he would feel if a test pilot were injured or killed during test flights.[12] Line answered with the sentence that gave Vandivier the title for his report: " 'I just told you I have no control over this thing. Why should my conscience bother me?' " Responsibilities fragment and disappear because people are motivated to make them do so.

Vandivier, thinking on his seven children and the house he had just bought, agreed to draft the report. He and Lawson drafted for a month, "normalizing" test results by filling in acceptable numbers for ones that would reveal the brakes had failed. Remarkably, they had several tortured conversations about their own guilt and even about the Nuremberg trials. When the graphics section of the draft was finished, Gretzinger took it to the chief plant engineer (essentially the highest-level executive in the Troy plant), whose engineers were to complete the report, only to find that he had been double-crossed. The chief engineer said that his people were "too busy" and said that the testing group would have to complete it. It is my opinion that he was well aware of the fraud in progress and was preserving his ability to deny involvement. This aspect of cover-ups is a very important part of the process. Higher-ups have a good deal of room to maneuver to keep cover-ups on track without leaving evidence of their complicity. Thus they can participate in evil without leaving a trail and can generally escape the sanctions that, at least occasionally, are visited on some middle-level personnel.

Gretzinger, whom I continue to admire, told the chief engineer he would not write the report and told his superior, Line, about the matter, expecting to be backed up. Line ordered him to write it.

Vandivier's response was interesting. "As far as I was concerned, we were all up to our necks in the thing anyway, and writing the narrative portion of the report couldn't make me any more guilty than I already felt myself to be." This was a complex response. Clearly he felt that his earlier actions, which I have found generally admirable, were sufficiently complicit in the fraud that he was already flawed in his own eyes. I suspect that there were other options that might have been available to Gretzinger and Vandivier, but they felt so implicated and were so burned out and compromised by this time that they did not explore those options.

Vandivier finished the report, which I suppose was generally faked to indicate that the brake complied with specifications, but ended it with the following sentence: "The . . . brake assembly does not meet the intent or the requirements of the application specification documents and therefore is not qualified." He felt that this gesture was meaningless, because the sentence would be changed by somebody else, but I don't find it meaningless. Vandivier, Lawson, and, interestingly, Warren, who got the group into the problem in the first place, all refused to sign the report. Sink forwarded it without a signature.

There is one more comment to make on this rather sorry story. Those who write about ethics often do so illuminated by the bright light of hindsight. What we expect to see, and therefore often create, is the one clear moment when an unethical decision was made by an actively unethical individual. We then expect to condemn the person who made the decision. But rarely can we find that moment. In analyzing the choices made by the various individuals in these incidents, we find that their alternatives are generally confused and ethically unclear. They are also incremental; as Joshua Klayman points out in chapter 13, people move toward these disasters in small steps, and the later steps seem no different from the earlier ones. When one faces the realization that something ethically untoward is going on, one seems somehow committed to allowing and assisting in its continuance, because of the commitments generated by the previous actions.

To return to the Goodrich case, the qualifying report was accepted, brakes were delivered, and LTV went to flight testing. There were several near crashes during landing—caused by problems with the brakes. The inevitable had occurred; the deception had failed, as it had to fail. Goodrich went into cover-up mode, but others did not. Vandivier and then Lawson went to an attorney and told what happened. They were sent by the attorney to the FBI, which started an undercover inquiry. (Because federal contracts were involved, faking a qualification report was a criminal offense.) Perhaps triggered by this, or its own suspicions, LTV requested the testing raw data, and Sink called a meeting, saying that they were going to level with LTV. Lawson and Vandivier asked whether they were going to admit lying. Vandivier reports that Sink said, "We're not really lying. All we were doing was interpreting the figures the way they should be. We were just exercising engineering license." Not long after the meeting, Vandivier and Lawson resigned from Goodrich, and Vandivier detailed the fraud in his resignation letter. Sunderland, the plant manager, called him in and asked him how he dared accuse the company of fraud, accepted the resignation, and asked Vandivier to leave immediately because of his disloyalty. Later Lawson and Vandivier testified at a congressional hearing about the event. Sink and a lawyer who was a corporate vice-president testified for Goodrich, saying that no fraud had happened and that changes in data on qualifying reports were normal procedure. No sanctions were applied to Goodrich; those mentioned here continued to work for Goodrich, and Vandivier knows of no corporate sanctions applied to them. Line and Sink apparently were promoted. Vandivier became a newspaper reporter.

This conclusion to the story is fairly typical. Whistle-blowers get fired or harassed; recall what happened to the engineers who argued that the Challenger O-rings were unsafe. In another case, an engineer who worked for the Nuclear Services Corporation presented a report to a congressional committee, detailing engineering deficiencies in nuclear power systems then on the market (see Faulkner 1987). He was fired some weeks later; the accident at Three Mile Island followed five years later.

What happens to the executives who commit the harm-doing actions in the first place and then engage in the cover-up? Since the organizations are generally involved in denying the existence of the harm or of the cover-up, they are in an awkward position. If they punish the executives, they will be admitting to their corporate misrepresentations. Also, the wiser executives, as a price for participation in the cover-up, may extract guarantees of no retaliation. Still, one would not be surprised if their careers were quietly dead-ended. Iacocca's career, one notices, was not dead-ended.

Let us summarize the processes that are revealed in the Goodrich case. Poor calculations, made under time pressure, caused the corporation to commit to manufacture a product that was soon discovered to be bound to fail, and fail dangerously. Costs were incurred that would be sunk costs if that realization of failure were allowed. The costs were not only literal costs spent on subassemblies but—perhaps more powerfully—costs of loss of individual and corporate face. In this hierarchical organization, the possibilities of lost jobs must have been apparent. With these considerations in place, all the concrete decisions taken were tilted in the direction of continuation of the flawed course of action. Loyalties to the immediate group were mobilized. The possible harm caused by possible product failure was probabilistic and remote, and only unknown others were at risk. Under hierarchical pressures, individual responsibilities were redefined and narrowed, so that each person would continue to participate in the flawed course of action. Superiors simultaneously arranged "not to know" of the flaw and reinforced the hierarchical pressures to continue to fragment the responsibility of the individuals. These intertwined processes inevitably led to the production of a product that would certainly fail. Looking ahead to that failure, many within the organization acted to create a case that they themselves were not implicated in that failure, making the failure more likely and eventually certain.

Phenomenology and Responsibility

The analysis of the Goodrich case presented here is what can be called a phenomenological analysis. There is a danger in this sort of analysis. Typically it can lead to a perception that since we can understand the decisions taken by all participants, sympathize with their plight, and even realize that we might not have acted so differently, no ethical transgressions have been committed; to understand is to forgive. This perception must be rejected. To do so, it is useful to draw on another conceptual system, one that will allow us to assess both blame for individuals and the complex question of blame for the corporation.

For the purposes of discussion, let us assume that an LTV test pilot was killed in a test flight because of brake failure. One could hunt for a murderer or a manslaughterer among the Goodrich employees, but the specific state-of-mind requirements for such felonies are not met. That path seems not the one to take. There is also a set of government requirements about the qualification reports, and penalties might be associated with falsifying those; I assume that this was what Sink thought he was avoiding when he had the report sent in with no signature. Again, this approach seems to me to take us down a potentially morally confused path. What has happened seems to me to be more persuasively analyzed in terms of a responsibility analysis used in military settings. Existing as it does in a world in which its agents can easily harm others, the military has thought through various of the issues in this case. The concepts that we might extract from military justice center around duty and dereliction of duty and around command responsibility and the failure of command responsibility. The duties and responsibilities in the Goodrich case are to the organization, which is where the failures seem to lie. Most of the managers, specifically Sink, Van Horn, and Line, were derelict in their duty; further, they attempted to cover up the matter, in the process revealing that they knew that they had been derelict. Discharge from the organization seems an appropriate penalty. Vandivier, Gretzinger, and Lawton took irresponsible actions at various times and therefore perhaps were derelict in their duties, but they acted responsibly at other times, even making vigorous attempts to stop the deceit. The wise organization might retain them, with the admonishment "never again."

Notice now the facts that can only be inferred by the absence of certain happenings. No reference is made to any corporate code of ethics; more importantly, no reference is made to any mechanism for reporting incidents or actions that a worker thinks are wrong. As I understand modern liability thinking, the corporation that has mechanisms in place outside the standard lines of authority for the reporting and disposition of such incidents has at least some defense against the claim of corporate negligence. Goodrich seems to have had none. Thus there is a very clear sense in which the corporation is responsible for the failure, and penalties directed against the corporation are appropriate.

This lack of mechanisms points back to the individual level, to another set of individuals who failed ethically because they failed to supply such mechanisms. The plant manager, Sunderland, clearly had failed to create such mechanisms. Further, he obviously tolerated a perception of authority relationships within the plant that were unhealthy, in that they emphasized blind obedience to orders. Moreover, since most of the workers in the plant knew what was happening, Sunderland either knew it "unofficially" or didn't know it. Therefore he is derelict in his duties in several ways, and he failed to fulfill certain affirmative duties that he assumed when he took on his job. He should be fired. Finally, the corporate headquarters staff, which appeared in the story only to testify that faking reports was "engineering license," obviously failed in its command responsibilities.

I mention these judgments not because I am convinced that I have them right, but to make two points. First, it is often suggested that doing a phenomenological analysis that takes the point of view of one or more participants inevitably removes any sense of moral condemnation for the participants' actions. I hope that I have dispelled that notion in this instance; it seems to me that we can quite clearly make judgments about several failures to take moral responsibility by various of the participants. The second point is a related one; the appropriate analysis is one that recognizes that the individuals being judged are situated within an organization, and uses an analysis that emphasizes the duties of individuals in organizational settings.

Characteristics of Organizations That Do Harm

Enough cases of corporate wrongdoing have been cited here to make it clear that many corporations often engage in harmful actions toward their workers, the consumers of their products and services, or the general public. Let us define an "intentionally unethical" corporation as one that knowingly or recklessly does harm to others in the service of making profits. Intentionally unethical companies do harm because the corporate controllers are willing to do so. Their corporate ideologies make it appropriate to harm others, and the structural conditions within the organization facilitate the doing of harm. Workers, fearful of losing their jobs, participate in the harm-doing, or taking a narrow definition of their responsibilities, do not seek to end it.

A number of forces can lead to the depersonalization of those that the corporation harms and provide rationalizations for the harms inflicted on them. Union-management relations, often zero sum in nature, can lead the managers to regard the workers as stupid and careless, and this can lead to blaming the workers for work accidents that are actually the product of unsafe machinery and work practices. If I as a tobacco company executive can deny that nicotine is addictive, then it is possible for me to see those who buy cigarettes as simply exercising their right of free consumer choice. If I am selling bogus health policies to the elderly, it helps my activities if I conceive of the elderly as living too well on unearned incomes. Many rationalizations exist for making others the targets of our own harm-doing activities.

The thought that most corporate wrongdoing is done by intentionally unethical corporations is oddly reassuring. It would be possible to recognize such corporations by the internal structures they have set up to facilitate harm-doing, and by the rationalizations they have developed for the depersonalization of those to whom they do harm. Unfortunately, we cannot conclude that all or even most corporate wrongdoing is done by intentionally unethical companies. There are cases like the Film Recovery Systems Corporation that fit the bill, but there are cases of great organizational harm-doing that are done by corporations that are not intentionally unethical.

All corporations, because of their emphasis on corporate profitability, and because of the complex interactional forces that I have documented, have the potential to drift into harm-doing, with the corrupting forces I have described leading to a continuation of those actions rather than a halting of them.

CORPORATE SOCIALIZATION AND THE REPRODUCTION OF CORRUPTION

Like other innovations, innovations of corrupt practices spread. The question of how corrupt organizations reproduce themselves and grow in size is quite easy to answer. Organizations such as the ones involved in the Nazi death camps have not one but two outputs. They produce death, and they produce individuals who become autonomously capable of and committed to producing other deaths. The evil individuals they produce become available for the reproduction of the evil organization. Concretely, SS officers and soldiers who first murdered civilians on the eastern front could be used to staff the concentration camps and initiate and socialize other individuals into the new organizations. Older soldiers in the U.S. Army in Vietnam made clear to the new inductees how the war was really to be fought. On the trading floor of Salomon Brothers, cohorts of new recruits were reliably socialized into patterns of betrayal of customers' interests.

Let us examine how corporations come to the perception of their customers as fools to whom no moral obligations are owed. Michael Lewis (1989) provides a richly detailed description of how those joining the stock brokerage firm of Salomon Brothers were socialized into regarding their customers as sheep to be fleeced. A good many customers' lives were destroyed in the process, as his book reveals. In one incident described by Lewis, he sold a customer a bond that somebody within his brokerage house advised him was a good bond to sell. The bond fell, taking the customer down with it, and Lewis learned that it was indeed "a good bond to *sell*"; the brokerage house held a large inventory on it and had inside information that it was going to fall. The firm therefore moved the bonds out of inventory onto customers, letting the customers take the ensuing loss, to the delight of the brokerage house. Lewis left the firm, but the socialization process that he has described corrupted many others. Of course, it was intended to. As Lewis's book makes clear, the firm's managers were willing participants in the corruption and made calculated efforts to corrupt the lower-level staff. For example, higher commissions were paid for moving poor-quality bonds off on unwary customers, a fact of which the customers were kept unaware. One is reminded of the case of the now-defunct Lincoln Savings and Loan Company, which sold a good many non-government-insured investments to elderly customers, while allowing the customers to believe that they were insured. Many lost their life savings.

The corporate case of Salomon Brothers also illustrates how unethical practices diffuse through an industry. The salespeople who successfully foisted bonds off on customers made a good deal of money for the corporation, with two consequences. First, the status hierarchy within the organization was reordered. Those individuals were rewarded with large bonuses, a signal that the corporation approved their trading practices, and others in the corporation vied for assignment to their departments. Since entry to the departments in which these practices went on was prestigious and likely to be highly profitable, newcomers were easily socialized into these ways. Newcomers went along with the attitudes professed and the practices employed or faced the threat of rejection and expulsion. The financial and psychological incentives for corruption were high.

A second consequence involved the spread of corruption to competing firms. Inevitably, word of Salomon's success got around in the small world of Wall Street. Many of the firm's major sales people were raided by other trading firms, who offered them astronomical salaries and bonuses in order to break into the areas that the Salomon staff had pioneered. That the migrants from Salomon Brothers took with them to their new firms the innovative financial instruments that they had invented was explicitly expected; that they also took with them their attitudes of scorn for the customer seems highly likely. In this way a single evil organization can produce a surplus of individuals who go on to replicate the organization in other settings. Given that those who have been "processed" by the evil organization have been brought to a point where they use their intelligence in the service of their evil actions, the replicated organizations can be counted on to transcend whatever local obstacles stand in the way of reproducing the results of the original organization.

The realization that evildoing organizations have the capacity for self-replication provides part of the explanation for one of the facts that so bewilder us about corporate corruption: why so many individuals are willing to participate in a corporation's immoral activities. One answer is that individuals in organizations are "trained" (an unfortunate use of this word) at different times, and those trained earlier train others, providing a multiplicative effect on the pool of available evildoers. They also carry their corruption to other firms. All this follows from what we know about normative socialization of individuals within organizations. It is the task of the individual, when entering an organization, to catch on to the real operating practices and rules of the organization, and this is a skill that most people acquire.

CAN ORGANIZATIONAL CORRUPTION BE CONTROLLED?

Given this analysis of corporate wrongdoing, what can be said about preventing it? Recall that I have distinguished two ways that a corporation can lapse into corruption. One is intentional; the organizational superiors plan for the organization to function corruptly, in a way that harms sets of people, either workers within the organization or consumers of its products and services. The Film Recovery Systems Corporation case is one example; the corporation deliberately set up practices that harmed almost all its workers and finally killed one. The Salomon Brothers case is another example; the corporate bosses knew of the bond-dumping practices and rather obviously condoned them, celebrating and rewarding the practitioners. (For further evidence, read Lewis's [1989] description of the training program that the organization conducted.) The first question that arises is whether the conduct at issue was criminal in nature and prosecutable under criminal statutes. In the case of the Film Recovery Systems Corporation, the state was able to prosecute the executives successfully for murder, and the corporation was convicted of manslaughter. While one no doubt applauds this verdict, there are legal complexities (N. Frank 1987). Generally, to commit murder requires not only knowledge of the risk of death caused by one's actions but actual intent to kill. The behavior of the defendants who exposed the workers to the risk of harm and death fits the first criterion but not the second.

How efficacious, then, are criminal prosecutions in preventing the sorts of incidents we are describing? The answer seems to be, not very. The prosecution of Film Recovery Systems, which took place in 1985, "was the first recorded case of an employer being charged with murder for the work related death of an employee" (N. Frank 1987, 104). Nor has there been a wave of such cases since. The corporation, incidentally, was fined the enormous sum of ten thousand dollars. As the more radical commentators have discussed in some anger, corporations do not go to jail.[13]

In most cases the harms corporations inflict on their workers come under occupational health and safety codes rather than criminal codes, and those they inflict on consumers are not subject to criminal sanctions but only to the somewhat chancy application of tort acts of recovery. What of the occupational health and safely codes? Under Reagan administration guidelines, an OSHA inspector who visited the Film Recovery Systems plant was not allowed to conduct an on-site inspection (N. Frank 1987). And what would the fines have been if he had? One speculates that members of Congress who depend on corporate campaign contributions would have intervened to moderate the damages.

What of tort actions? Bringing such actions is not easy for individuals; more frequently such suits are class actions. Deceit, denial, and delay are frequent tactics of the defendants, who, having their own lawyers on retainer, are willing to expend enormous sums defending individual cases. Nonetheless, these actions for corporate negligence or product liability are probably the most relevant control on the cases we are discussing.

In many cases, typified by the Salomon Brothers case, the activities in question, although of doubtful ethical standing, are not illegal. Trading in stocks and bonds is largely governed by what are called voluntary associational practices, given some force by government backing, with the occasional patchwork intrusion of governmental standards, such as the criminalization of insider trading, "stock parking," and a few other offenses that allow for the occasional criminal prosecution of a few deviant offenders. Currently there is some talk of requiring stockbrokers to reveal the differential commissions they are paid on the different products they tout to consumers.[14] It remains to be seen what comes of this talk.

It seems to me one chance of effectively controlling rogue organizations lies in the admittedly somewhat disorganized consumer boycotts that sometimes occur when a corporation is caught producing some particularly horrendous consumer product or inflicting particularly horrendous harm on its workers.

Finally, in a time of employment downsizing, unsafe working conditions do not seem to hamper corporations' ability to hire workers for hazardous jobs. Too many sad stories reach us about workers protesting the application of health and safety standards that would protect them, since the corporation manages to convince them that would mean "closing the mine."

Thus criminal sanctions do not have much coercive force in hindering organizations that set out on courses of action that they know will harm consumers or workers. But what about other organizations, those in which the hierarchy genuinely seeks to prevent these occurrences? What can be done to prevent their lurching into harm-doing and cover-up in the ways illustrated by several of the cases in this chapter? Unfortunately, there are no easy answers. Obviously, any corporation needs to have a reasonably explicit code of acceptable behavior in place that is of sufficient specificity to make clear what actions are ruled out. However, although the corporations have genuinely meant the codes to guide behavior, they have left in place other systems, such as sales bonus plans, that generate forces to behave in ways that run counter to the official code. These other forces are likely to first generate behaviors that cut corners rather than directly contradict the code. If detection mechanisms are not in place to discover and halt these actions, the inadvertent but clear message to the work force is that the code is to be subordinated to the other imperatives, and soon the code is more blatantly violated. Further, we have seen how the forces of subunits of the organization are often mobilized to conceal harm-doing and how powerful pressure is placed on the players in the subunit to participate in this concealment.

It seems to me to be essential that the corporation recognize that these inadvertently corrupting actions can occur, and can leave behind a continuing tradition of harm-doing. Recognizing this, it is the responsibility of the corporation to put in place a system for detecting and eliminating the effects of this corruption of the system. What might this sort of system look like? I suppose that the wise company would have some sort of mechanism by means of which an employee who saw such actions beginning could report them, perhaps anonymously and out of channels. There would then be a mechanism in place to investigate the allegations and, more to the point, to make clear to the subunit that denial and deception were not the way to proceed. The investigation group would need to be relatively independent of the standard lines of authority and perhaps report to an independent committee of outside directors. Its task, though, would be less to provide reports on disasters after they occurred than to set forces in motion that would keep them from developing after someone has seen them begin. Would this work, or have I just created a mechanism that would bring out further motives to deny and cover up on the part of the units investigated? And what would happen if the investigating unit uncovered actions, such as suppressing reports of drug side effects or faking qualification test runs, that were violations of the law? The investigators would, I suppose, be bound to report them, somewhat limiting the relationship of trust that they should have with the corporate units they were investigating.

CONCLUSIONS

The discipline of psychology has well-developed concepts concerning the origins of antisocial acts in the personality structures of those who commit those acts. But that individual-level psychology is largely irrelevant to the occurrence of a much more common source of evil actions, the sorts of evil actions that are produced by what I will call "organizational pathology." There is now a need to create a social science describing how human institutions can purposely move or accidentally lurch toward causing these actions, somehow neutralizing or suspending or overriding or replacing the moral scruples of their members. The psychology that contributes to this science will inevitably be a social and organizational one, rather than one centered on the individual acting alone, although it will draw on the conceptualizations of an individual-level psychology, particularly to explain how the individual participates in being trained in the social movement and continues to access individual-level skills in the service of the pathological group projects.

I have attempted to point out some implications for those managing corporations. First, I have suggested that while it is true that some organizations are essentially created in corruption, all are vulnerable to being corrupted by a set of dynamics that follow from the discovery that some product or process to which the organization is committed has the potential to do harm. For corporations concerned to avoid that sort of corruption, I have suggested a perspective of "command responsibility" and an emphasis on the various duties of individuals, including the duty not to overlook harm, and the duty to carry out positional responsibilities. Whether the perspective is correct is unclear to me; I suggest it to provoke responses, because I consider the problem that it addresses a major and critical one.

ENDNOTES

1. Braithwaite (1985) suggests that the term "organizational crime" is a more useful one, because it recognizes the similarity between the ways in which public organizations and corporations can offend.

2. Note the complexities of speaking of an organization's "knowing." Knowing is a concept we apply to individuals, and its meaning loses precision when we extend it to organizations. When we are engaging in moral analysis, which is centrally an analysis of individual cognition, our thoughts become confused when we try to examine "the morality of organizations." While this idea cannot be fully developed here, two comments are in order. First, we are frequently forced to analyze the organization as individual by the "legal fiction" of the organization as individual. Second, the moral confusion engendered when we attempt to analyze an organization by the moral standards we use for individuals frequently works to the advantage of the organization that is doing harm.

3. One of the arguments for an aggressive product liability recovery system, pursued by contingency-compensated lawyers, is that it lessens the utility of strategic ignorance for the corporation. If the corporation is going to be hit with large punitive damage awards, then the sooner it can discover that it is incurring this liability the sooner it can cease to incur it.

4. This would not be true of corporations making products in which the possibility of danger is generally known to be present. Makers of prescription drugs are the paradigmatic example. They should have in place routine systems to collect, process, and analyze information about product safety—side effects, in their terms. From an unsystematic scanning of newspaper reports on the topic, I am not greatly impressed by their efficiency.

5. The retrofit is generally described as cheap by those who write about this case, but George Katov, who worked for the Ford Company, has informed me that it would have been a costly retrofit, given the complexities of modifications once plans were put in place, production machinery ordered, and so on. The decision to modify, therefore, would have been a major and costly decision.

6. This is the problem that I have found with most books on these acts of corporate malfeasance. Naturally they are written after the fact, by investigative reporters

who are so horrified at the outcome that they tend to assume that the major actors in bringing it about begin as evildoers. They thus miss the process that transforms ordinary people into evildoers.

7. Lawyers and insurance companies play an important role in this process. Corporate leaders regard tort lawyers and personal injury lawyers as devils waiting to pounce on innocent corporate mistakes, extracting huge sums for pitiable plaintiffs. Thus they are sometimes led to deny product liability to avoid providing ammunition for legal suits. "May 24, 1974. In an internal progress report for the Dalkon Shield, Roger Tuttle (lawyer) is quoted as being opposed to removing the Shield from the market because such an action would be a 'confession of liability' " (Perry and Dawson 1985). As I understand it, those reviewing the evidence for the existence of huge settlements find them not so huge, generally reduced on appeal, and not unreasonable as a source of punitive damages on corporations whose mistakes were repeated and not at all innocent.

Lawyers participate at several other nodes in corporate decision processes after harm has been alleged. First, they counsel the corporation about how to deal with possible admissions about the harm done. The content of their counsel would be hard to study systematically; there are cases in which the advice has been to stonewall. Second, they counsel insurance companies that may be the eventual payers of claims on the manufacturing corporation. In that role, too, their advice is sometimes less than morally admirable. In the Dalkon Shield case, lawyers for both the Robins Company and Aetna, their insurers, advised denial and delay and worked the court system to produce delay (Mintz 1985).

8. The standard account of the Dalkon Shield case, for instance, was written by an investigative reporter who, struck by the eventual incredible mendacity of the participants, could not enter into their perspective. Further, a reporter, knowing the immoral end of the case, cannot see the full moral complexity of its origins.

9. In chapter 18, Willem Wagenaar points out how often disasters—to workers, consumers, or the general public—originate in bad engineering design in which safety features are minimized.

10. I am grateful to Norbert Kerr and Marilynn Brewer for bringing this analysis to my attention.

11. I do not know the authority relationship between Van Horn and Line.

12. *All My Sons*, one of Arthur Miller's earlier plays and one that I have often found powerful, concerns a wartime manufacturer of military planes who cuts corners. One of his sons, a wartime pilot, is later killed in an airplane that the father built.

13. There has been some discussion of the "death sentence" for corporations. Consider what that could mean. If the corporation is forced to go out of existence, who is harmed? Quite likely the workers, who may have been the victims of the offense, and also the stockholders. No analyst of the distribution of corporate powers assigns many powers to stockholders.

14. It is not at all unusual for a brokerage house to pay its salespersons double commissions on products that they particularly want to move out of inventory. The customer is meant to be unaware of this fact.

Chapter 2

Social Influence and the Triple Tumor Structure of Organizational Dishonesty

Robert B. Cialdini

A surprising thing happened to me several years ago, after the publication of a book I wrote for consumers. It seemed that an entirely unintended set of people became interested in it.

The book, titled *Influence,* was supposed to inform the public about the most powerful psychological pressures that cause a person to say yes to a request. In addition, it was designed to show readers how to recognize and resist the tactics of anyone who tried to use these pressures on them in an undue or unwelcome fashion. Although the book has proved more successful than I could have reasonably hoped—it is now in its third edition (Cialdini 1993)—the majority of the response has come not from those wishing to deflect influence pressures but instead from people wishing to harness them. I realized that this was the case when, shortly after publication, my phone began to ring with requests that I speak to marketing, fund-raising, or sales groups about the process of influence. Along with this realization came the recognition that there were important ethical issues to be confronted by anyone who sought to engage the influence process for profit and by anyone (including me) who sought to inform the public about that process. To consider those issues properly, it is necessary to review the approach taken in the book and the conclusions that flowed from it.

THE RESEARCH STRATEGY: ESPIONAGE

The research strategy I chose was to abandon for a time my familiar university-based laboratory orientation and enlist, instead, as a spy in the ever-raging influence wars around me. The question I wanted to address required that I get into the field where the battles were actually being won and lost. That question was, in everyday human interaction, what are the psychological factors that most powerfully push an individual to act, simply because someone else has requested it? To gather information relative to this question, I began infiltrating as many influence professions as I could get access to. I enrolled incognito in the training programs of various sales organizations and learned how to sell encyclopedias door to door, portrait photography by phone, used cars from a lot, and appliances from a showroom floor. Through inside contacts who kept my identity and intent secret, I worked for a time in a public relations firm, in two advertising agencies, and in the fund-raising departments of two charity organizations. I took a job in a restaurant to see what servers do to generate larger tips. I interviewed political lobbyists, labor negotiators, and religious cult members to learn how influence occurs in those domains. I even surveyed police bunco squad officers to find out what the con artists of our society do to generate yeses.

Through it all, I looked for commonalities, figuring that if the same principles were being used successfully in each of these diverse settings, then these principles must represent the most potent and general influences on the human tendency to comply with requests. It seemed to me that the key for a careful observer wishing to identify the major principles of influence in our society would be to examine their pervasiveness across the broadest possible spectrum of naturally occurring instances. For nearly three years, I tried to be that observer.

It was important, I felt, to resist the temptation to look for such general principles in any one specific form, time, profession, or practitioner. Instead, it was the ubiquitousness of a principle across these dimensions that would be most instructive, because, in the logic of natural selection, only effective influence principles would have been able to survive in widespread fashion within the repertoires of a variety of compliance practitioners. Consequently, the search was for overarching compliance principles—that is, those principles that (1) occurred in a multitude of versions, (2) appeared across the range of compliance professions, (3) were employable by the greatest number of compliance practitioners, and (4) had a long history of success. What I observed surprised me.

First, although it was possible to register hundreds of individual tactics, only a very few pervasive principles of influence emerged. Aside from the simple rule of material self-interest (that people prefer to get more and pay less), just six principles surfaced as consistently in use over a multitude of professions, practitioners, forms, and eras. The second surprise was how frequently targets of influence seemed to react automatically to these principles. Upon encountering one or another of them, people tend to stop considering carefully the pros and cons of their decisions and to move rather mechanically toward yes. It is now my belief that this is so because the principles can normally be relied upon to steer a person correctly when he or she is confronted with an influence attempt. These are the principles people are most likely to follow, because they are the principles that have most successfully directed their choices in the past. They work for influence agents precisely because they have usually worked for influence targets.

The last surprise was that although these pervasive principles appeared to optimize influence, they were being *used* optimally by only a fraction of those who could have benefited from them. In fact, it was possible to identify three classes of influence practitioners in terms of the degree to which they are able to engage the power of the six principles. *Bunglers* of influence regularly fumble away the chance to employ the principles, because they do not understand them or know how to harness their force. *Smugglers* of influence, on the other hand, know quite well what the principles are and how they work, but they import the principles illicitly into influence situations in which they do not naturally reside; the target therefore does not get helpful counsel from the principles as to the wisdom of complying with a request. The immediate outcome is that, typically, only one party benefits—the influence agent. In the long term, however, the influence target, who has not profited from the exchange, is unreceptive to future influence attempts by the agent. Finally, *sleuths* of influence are more knowledgeable than bunglers, more ethical than smugglers, and overall more successful than either. They approach each influence opportunity as a detective would, looking to bring to light only those principles that are an inherent part of the situation. By focusing solely on those powerful principles that exist naturally in a situation, the sleuth informs the compliance target of the genuine influence considerations present there. Of course, the more principles the sleuth can uncover and engage, the greater the chance that the target will comply. And that is as it should be, as the more principles present favor yes, the more it is in the target's interests to yield. Because the sleuth's approach tends to enhance the target's interests, it tends to do the same for the overall financial and psychological well-being of the practitioner. To illustrate, we can examine the six pervasive principles of influence in relation to the differences in the way they are used by the three types of influence agents.

THE SIX PRINCIPLES OF INFLUENCE

Reciprocation

According to an extensive review of the subject by the sociologist Alvin Gouldner (1960), there is not a single human society that does not subscribe to the rule for reciprocation, which obligates people to return the form of behavior they have received from another. Once a favor is done, even one that hasn't been requested, the recipient feels indebted and is expected to return the favor (Greenberg and Shapiro 1971; George, Gournic, and McAfee 1988). For agents of influence, this rule offers a great advantage: One person can significantly increase the chance that another will comply with a request for a favor (to buy, to donate, to vote) by providing a small favor first (Regan 1971; Berry and Kanouse 1987).

Take, for example, what has happened to many people walking through airports over the past few years. They are approached by someone who, before saying a word, gives them something—usually a flower—and refuses to take it back, describing it as a gift. Soon it becomes clear that this person is a solicitor for a "good works society" (actually a religious sect like the Hare Krishna Society) and is asking for a donation. Often, people who normally would not have been inclined to support such a group *do* make a contribution, only because they have accepted the solicitor's flower and would feel guilty about taking without giving in return. Of course, airport solicitors are hardly alone in using an initiating gift to increase the chance of a subsequent yes; witness the free address labels that come in the mail, the free inspections provided by exterminating companies, the free samples of cheese and meat given out at supermarkets.

But the airport solicitors are noteworthy in that they so clearly illustrate the smuggler's approach to reciprocation. They create an obligation that is not a natural part of the relationship between the two parties. Consequently, only they benefit, and they therefore benefit only temporarily. In a classic illustration of the smuggler-approach order of events, a successful day of trading flowers for funds at the airport is becoming rarer and rarer. Passersby who have been prior victims (or observers) of the flower scam are thereafter prepared to reject, deflect, or otherwise avoid it, assuring that the financial welfare of those who use it will be progressively undermined. It is instructive, for example, that after an initial period of success, the Krishnas have experienced severe fiscal reversals in the United States, and their formal organization (the Society for Krishna Consciousness, Inc.) has had to declare bankruptcy.

At the same time, there is no good reason for bungling away opportunities for reciprocation that are an inherent part of ongoing relationships. For instance, a person who has done a co-worker a large favor can increase the chance that the favor will be reciprocated by alluding artfully to the natural obligation that rightfully goes with such favors. Rather than responding to the co-worker's thanks with a dismissive "Oh, don't worry about it. I'd have done it for anybody; no big deal," a simple "Oh, I'm sure you'd do the same for me" would serve both parties well.

Commitment/Consistency

Social scientists have long recognized that people share a powerful drive to be consistent in their attitudes, words, and deeds (Festinger 1957; Cooper and Croyle 1984; Chaiken and Stangor 1987). For instance, if one person can get another to make a commitment (to go on record, to take a stand), the second person will experience a pressure to think, speak, and act consistently with that commitment in the future (see, for example, Howard 1990). What makes this pressure so valuable for influence agents is that the initial commitment can be quite reasonable and innocent-seeming (putting down a refundable payment to hold a piece of property or signing a petition favoring a charitable cause) and yet be very effective in stimulating compliance with much larger related requests (to purchase the property or contribute to the cause). In fact, research on a commitment/consistency tactic called the foot-in-the-door technique found that California homeowners who signed a simple petition favoring driver safety became three times more likely to agree to having a "Drive Safely" billboard erected on their front lawns (Freedman and Fraser 1966).

Certain influence practitioners smuggle such pressures into a situation by making promises designed to commit a target person to the practitioner's product. Later, with the target's commitment securely in place, some of the promises are removed, but the customer's commitment frequently remains. The low-ball tactic, used by shady car dealers, is one such ploy (Cialdini and others 1978; Joule, 1987). The customer is initially quoted an extremely low price to induce a commitment to the dealer's car. Then, just as the final papers are to be signed, something happens: The manager finds an error and disallows the deal or the used car appraiser lowers the previously estimated trade-in allowance. Remarkably, many customers purchase the car anyway on the less desirable terms, even while muttering about the dealer's tactics.

Notice how different and how much more conducive to customer satisfaction and to long-term exchanges is the sleuth's use of the commitment/consistency principle. The influence detective searches for those commitments existing within a prospect that are consistent with the strengths of the agent's product and draws the prospect's attention to the fit, letting the pressure for consistency do the rest of the work. Thus, the recent buyer of an expensive house would hardly be done a disservice by an insurance agent who pointed out the commitment to home and family that such a purchase represented and who stressed that protecting home and family through adequate insurance would be in keeping with that commitment.

Social Validation

People frequently decide what is appropriate to think, feel, and do in a situation by examining what others like them are thinking, feeling, and doing there. This simple principle of behavior accounts for a varied array of human responses. For instance, research has shown that New Yorkers use it in deciding whether to return a lost wallet (Hornstein, Fisch, and Holmes 1968), that amusement park visitors use it to decide whether to litter in a public place (Cialdini, Reno, and Kallgren 1990), that audience members use it in deciding whether a joke is funny (Cupchick and Leventhal 1974), that pedestrians use it in deciding whether to stop and stare at an empty spot in the sky (Milgram, Bickman, and Berkowitz 1969), and, on the alarming side, that troubled individuals use it in deciding whether to commit suicide (Phillips and Carstensen 1988).

One effective strategy for an influence agent, therefore, is to provide information to an influence target indicating that a lot of people just like the target have taken a desired action. When honestly portrayed, such information (honest data showing that a product is the largest selling or fastest growing in the target's age group, for example) will be invaluable to the target. Genuine evidence of this sort should never be bungled away by an influence agent, for everyone's sake. It is quite another story, however, when the information is counterfeited to give the undue impression of popularity—by marketers who lie with statistics, by TV advertisers who create phoney average-person-on-the-street testimonial commercials, by nightclub owners who create long waiting lines outside even when there is plenty of room inside, by bartenders who "salt" their tip jars with large bills at the beginning of their shifts, or by church officials who do the same before the collection plate is passed at services.

Friendship/Liking

People prefer to say yes to the requests of those they know and like. Could there be any doubt that this is the case in light of the remarkable success of the Tupperware Corporation ($2.5 million in sales per day) and their "home party" demonstration concept (Frenzen and Davis 1990)? The demonstration party for Tupperware products is hosted by a person, usually a woman, who invites to her home an array of friends, neighbors, and relatives, all of whom know that their hostess receives a percentage of the profits from every piece sold by the Tupperware representative who is also there. In this way, the Tupperware Corporation arranges for its customers to buy from and *for* a friend rather than from an unknown salesperson. The approach has been so effective that the Tupperware Corporation has wholly abandoned its early retail outlets, and the home-party idea has been copied by organizations selling everything from cookware to sex paraphernalia.

Most influence agents, however, attempt to engage the friendship/liking principle in a different way: Before making a request, they get their targets to like them. Two of the most frequently used liking tactics involve the use of praise and similarities, both of which have been shown by research to increase liking and compliance (Woodside and Davenport 1974; Drachman, deCarufel, and Insko 1978; LaFrance 1985; Locke and Horowitz 1990). For example, salespeople are commonly trained to compliment—depending on the situation—the prospect's home, children, or taste in clothes. They are trained, as well, to mention a similarity between the prospect and themselves: "Oh, really? I love camping too." Of course, the influence of compliments and similarities can be smuggled into a situation though insincere flattery and fabricated connections. But when the bases for such claims are real, an influence agent would be a bungler not to sleuth them out and bring them to the surface.

Authority

We live in a society with a regrettable tendency to worship experts; people are very willing to follow the suggestions of someone they see as a legitimate authority (Milgram 1974; Blass 1991). Because authority roles bespeak superior information and power, it makes great sense to comply with the wishes of properly constituted authorities. It makes so much sense that people do so mechanically, often when it makes no sense at all. Take as evidence the strange case of the "rectal earache" reported by two professors of pharmacy, Michael Cohen and Neil Davis (1981). A physician ordered ear drops to be administered to the right ear of a hospital patient suffering infection there. But instead of writing out completely the location "right ear" on the prescription, the doctor abbreviated it so that the instructions read, "Place in R *ear*." On receiving the prescription, the duty nurse promptly put the required drops in the patient's rectum. Obviously, rectal treatment of an earache makes no sense, yet neither the patient nor the nurse questioned it.

Because the authority principle often works so forcefully and so automatically, influence agents love to engage its power. When the sleuth's approach is used to do so, there is no problem. If an ad agency, for instance, focused its campaign on the weight of genuine scientific evidence favoring a particular headache product, everyone—the agency, the manufacturer, and the audience—would profit. Not so, however, if the agency, finding no particular scientific merit in the product, tried to pirate the impression through the use of ads featuring actors wearing scientists' lab coats or by hiring spokespersons who are identified with medical roles on TV. Under those circumstances, the agency's tactics must be considered similar to those of con artists who smuggle authority influence into a situation by counterfeiting experts' credentials.

Scarcity

As opportunities, and the items they present, become more scarce, they are perceived as more valuable (see Lynn 1991 for a review). This principle accounts for the results of studies showing that tasters rated cookies as more desirable when they were scarce rather than abundant (Worchel, Lee, and Adewole 1975), that consumers rated phosphate detergents better once their use was prohibited by the government (Mazis 1975), that college students rated their cafeteria food higher when they learned that it would not be available to them for two weeks (West 1975), and that young lovers rated themselves as more in love when their parents tried to keep them apart from their sweethearts (Driscoll, Davis, and Lipetz 1972). The scarcity principle also accounts for the actions of influence professionals who employ "limited number" or "deadline" tactics to motivate consumers. In the first instance, the customer is informed that membership opportunities, products, or services exist in a limited supply that cannot be guaranteed to last for long. In the second instance, the intent to create an aura of scarcity is the same, but it is accomplished by placing a time limit on the customer's ability to get what is offered. Targets are told that unless they make a purchase decision shortly (or immediately), they will have to pay a higher price for the item or they will not be able to purchase it at all. In one large child photography company I infiltrated, we were trained to urge parents to buy as many poses and copies as they could afford because "stocking limitations force us to burn the unsold pictures of your children within twenty-four hours."

Research in the scarcity principle has found that it works best when combined with a spirit of rivalry. We are most attracted to a scarce resource when we are in competition for it (Worchel, Lee, and Adewole 1975). One arena where this fact is well understood is real estate sales. A tactic commonly employed by sales agents to increase a prospect's ardor for a property is to inform the prospect of the existence of a rival buyer, perhaps someone scheduled to see the property and make a decision that weekend. If the information is true, the agent is acting as a sleuth to make the target aware of it; moreover, the agent would be a bungler not to do so. If it is untrue, of course, the agent would be acting as a smuggler, importing the scarcity principle into a setting where it does not naturally reside. Let's suppose that the agent chooses the smuggler's route, and let's suppose further for a moment that he or she is never caught at it, that neither the prospect nor any other client ever associates the agent with this deceptive practice. It would seem that under these conditions the smuggler's approach has paid off, both to the agent and to the realty company that employed and trained the agent. But that view is a superficial one that ignores some stiff penalties that undercut smuggler gains. In the following section, I will consider what some of these frequently unrecognized penalties might be.

THE TRIPLE TUMOR STRUCTURE
OF ORGANIZATIONAL DISHONESTY

There will never be a law against shouting "Ethics!" in a crowded board room. I believe that is so because—unlike "Fire!" yelled in a crowded theater—the term doesn't possess enough motivational power there to cause a stampede. That's not to say that, as a group, business people wouldn't prefer to be ethical. All other things equal, most would unhesitatingly choose the high road. But, except in hypothetical situations, all other things are never equal. And we often see that factors with more motivational punch— sales quotas, corporate financial health and survival, competitive concerns, career advancement—outweigh ethical choices in business decisions.

Indeed, despite a variety of contentions of the "ethics pays" sort (See Stark 1993 for a discussion of the history of ethics-as-enlightened-self-interest arguments), a look at the misdeeds, fines, criminal prosecutions, and scandals regularly reported in the business press suggests that much of the business world has not been persuaded. Instead, there remains a persistent belief that ethics doesn't pay, even in the long run (Bhide and Stevenson 1990; Labich 1992). What can a social psychologist concerned with the ethics of influence contribute to this debate?[1]

In the previous section of this chapter, I advocated the ethical use of influence principles by individuals. In the present section, I extend that advocacy to the level of organizations. My position is that *one* reason organizations should engage in honest influence practices is that the consequences of failing to do so may be much more harmful to the organization than has been traditionally recognized.[2] A brief statement of my position is this: An organization that regularly teaches, condones, or allows the use of dishonest influence tactics externally (that is, toward customers, clients, suppliers, distributors, regulators, and so on) will experience a set of costly consequences internally. Furthermore, these consequences, which I call tumors, are likely to be especially damaging, for two reasons.

First, the tumors will be malignant in nature—growing, spreading, and eating progressively at the organization's health and vigor. Second, they will be difficult to trace and identify via typical accounting methods as the true causes of poor organizational performance and profitability. They will therefore lead to expensive misguided efforts that fail to target the genuine culprits of dysfunction. The schematic in figure 2.1, which identifies these tumors and depicts the processes by which they are said to work, is described more fully in the following sections.

First, however, it is important to recognize the primary benefit of dishonest influence tactics to an organization: increased short-term profits. As the work reviewed in the first part of this chapter has documented, the unethical use of social influence pressures can produce enhanced compliance with all manner of requests. It is this engine of immediately increased profit resulting from such compliance that drives the dishonesty and renders it understandable.

Tumor I: The Costs of Poor Reputation

To the degree that an organization *systematically* engages in dishonest influence techniques toward customers, suppliers, and others outside of itself, its reputation is likely to suffer. The occasional ethical lapse is not at issue here. The real offender is the regular tendency to falsify, fabricate, deceive, dissemble, delude, or generally mislead in the process of influence, as manifest, for example, in approaches to sales management and training that focus exclusively on the bottom line. With each new instance, the likelihood rises that the dishonesty will be found out and that reputation (and

Figure 2.1 / The Triple Tumor Structure of Organizational Dishonesty

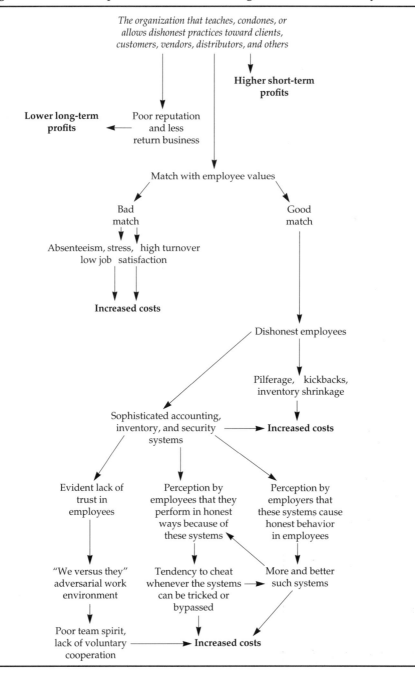

prospects for return business) will plummet. It's a matter of increasingly loaded probabilities, what we might call the "Time wounds all heels" effect.

Much has already been written about the immense value of good reputation in business and the damage to it when dishonesty is discovered (Steckmest 1982; Aaker 1991; Labich 1992; Weitz, Castleberry, and Tanner 1992). Consequently, I won't belabor the point beyond reprinting a quote from Edson W. Spencer, who was chairman of Honeywell, Inc. at the time: "The businessman who straddles a fine line between what is right and what is expedient should remember that it takes years to build a good business reputation, but one false move can destroy that reputation overnight" (Steckmest 1982, 73).

Tumor II: The Costs of Good and Bad Fits Between Employee Values and Corporate Values

In any organization, the match between an employee's values and those of the organizational culture can range from bad to good. For an organization whose culture is characterized by dishonesty toward external contacts, there will be costly internal consequences associated with both good and bad fits.

TUMOR IIA: A BAD PERSON/ORGANIZATION FIT FOR DISHONESTY. The organization whose culture encourages dishonesty in the ways its salespeople, marketers, advertising copy writers, negotiators, and others are expected to influence people outside itself can safely assume that some of its members will find the dishonesty offensive and discordant with their preferred self-concepts. Some of these people may adjust their self-concepts to align more closely to the demands of their jobs and to the values of the organization (Chatman 1991); I will have more to say shortly about the kind of price the dishonest organization may have to pay for fostering this kind of adjustment. The rest, who do not become socialized into the corporate culture, are likely to experience a set of outcomes that may also prove very expensive for the organization, but in a different way.

First, workers who feel a conflict between their own values and the expectancies and culture of the workplace are likely to experience stress (Dewe 1993). Stress in turn has been linked to increased illness (Cohen, Tyrrell, and Smith 1991), with attendant, crushingly expensive impacts on health costs and absenteeism (Cascio 1991), and poor job satisfaction (Barnett and others 1993).

Low job satisfaction, which—as one would expect—has been frequently tied to high turnover (Carsten and Spector 1987), has not shown strong connections with another factor that one would expect, job performance. Traditionally, the relationship between the quality of an employee's work and job satisfaction has been puzzlingly small (Iaffaldano and Muchinsky 1985). More recent evidence, however, suggests that the weakness of this relationship may have provided illusory comfort to organizations whose policies create low job satisfaction. Phillip Varca and Marsha James-Valutis (1993) found that the weak association applied only to workers with poor abilities, who presumably didn't possess the capacity to do good work even when satisfied with their jobs. Among highly capable employees, the impact of job satisfaction was dramatic, generating more than a 25 percent difference in performance between satisfied and unsatisfied workers. The lesson for business seems clear and notable: Factors that lead to low job satisfaction, such as requirements for dishonesty toward external contacts (Burke, Borucki, and Hurley 1992), may well lead to poor job performance among the most able workers. The company thus loses the best efforts of those whose products would otherwise reflect most positively on the firm, and it may lose the employees themselves, since the most able workers have the best opportunities to abandon the firm if they are dissatisfied; either process should grind the company down toward mediocrity.

The second of these processes—turnover—is worth a fuller look, not just because the costs to business are extreme (Cascio 1991), and frequently underestimated at that (Roseman 1981), but because it is selective. Turnover is likely to take only certain kinds of people, with good or bad consequences depending on the kind of people it clears from the system (Staw 1980). As we have already seen, a policy favoring unethical influence that leads to job dissatisfaction is likely to clear the wrong kind of people—the more able ones, who have prospects elsewhere. But there is a second damaging sort of selectivity that such a policy will foster as well, selection for dishonest employees. That is, not only will organizations socialize members to their values and try to recruit those with compatible values, they will selectively retain those workers whose values conform to the organization's.

Evidence for this tendency comes from a program of research conducted on new recruits in eight of the largest U.S. accounting firms (O'Reilly, Chatman, and Caldwell 1991; Chatman 1991). Early in their employment, the recruits filled out scales designed to assess their values; these value profiles were then matched with the values inherent in the corporate culture in their new firm. Within a year, the members of this group who had a poor initial value match with their firm scored significantly lower on measures of job satisfaction and organizational commitment. Within two years, these employees were significantly more likely to have left the company.

TUMOR IIB: A GOOD PERSON/ORGANIZATION FIT FOR DISHONESTY. When the organization's values embrace dishonesty, the same kind of mechanism can lead to dishonesty among employees and another set of untoward consequences for the organization.

Employees who have remained in a firm in part because they have been able to rationalize or excuse the immorality of cheating are prime candidates to cheat the organization as well. Thus, by selecting against workers who cannot easily participate in dishonesty and for those who can, the dishonest organization increases its exposure to a kind of damage—employee theft, fraud, and deviance—with potentially ruinous costs. For example, as early as 1981, a government legislative committee reported that in the United States 30 percent of all business losses are due to employee dishonesty, one-third of all business failures are due to internal theft, and about half of all employees admit to having stolen from their employers; most of the dishonest group showed no remorse about the thefts (Young, Mountjoy, and Roos 1981). Furthermore, there is evidence that this dishonesty exists as a trait in some people, as their deficient trustworthiness appears across a range of settings and activities (Hollinger and Clark 1983; Goldberg and others 1991).

How has American business sought to deal with the problem? Not by focusing on a potential root cause—their own dishonest dealings (Crossen 1993)—but by incurring additional costs for increasingly sophisticated monitoring, security, accounting, and inventory systems designed to prevent or identify employee wrongdoing. In 1981, spending for security was rising at about 10 percent per year, with little tangible success; according to one study of internal crime, "Despite the immense societal costs that employee crime imposes, and in spite of the adoption of the most advanced security devices and methods, the business community reports they feel that they are virtually powerless to stop the ever-increasing incidence of this problem" (Young, Mountjoy, and Roos 1981, iv). As of this writing, there is little evidence that anything has changed (Crossen 1993).

Tumor III: The Costs of Surveillance on Work Climate

Although the expense of surveillance technology is significant in itself—between 1990 and 1992 alone more than $500 million was spent on surveillance software by over 70,000 U.S. companies (Bylinski 1991; Halpern 1992)—a final set of costs, having to do with the degradation of work climate in surveilling organizations, can be significant as well.

TUMOR IIIA: EVIDENT LACK OF TRUST IN EMPLOYEES. The implementation of surveillance systems sends a clear message to those under surveillance: "We don't trust you." Such a sentiment can lead to resentment and a feeling of distrust by workers toward management (Deci, Connell, and Ryan 1989). It can also lead to an oppositional relationship, characterized by a "We versus they" orientation (Crossen 1993). This breakdown in trust and in sense of community may bring about poor organizational esprit, a lack of voluntary cooperation, and even acts of revenge or sabotage to retaliate for the implicit insult to workers' integrity that surveillance conveys. Indeed, Robert Bies and Thomas Tripp (1996, forthcoming) report that workers wreak vengeance on superiors who have insulted their sense of identity by engaging in such on-the-job actions as withholding help or support and using company resources in an unauthorized manner. These reactions are, of course, likely to spur management to new levels of surveillance technology.

TUMOR IIIB: THE UNDERMINING OF DESIRABLE BEHAVIOR.   In addition to the evidence that employees resent the "We don't trust you" message conveyed by surveillance systems, there is also evidence that they may come to believe it is justified. Such systems normally cover the behavior of all workers, the honest and the dishonest. Regrettably, research exists to suggest that practices implying an expectation of undesirable conduct may lead to more of that conduct in both groups, by producing self-fulfilling prophesies in the first case (M. J. Harris and others 1992) and self-sustaining prophesies in the second (Jussim 1991).

One problem with controls like surveillance technology is that when people perceive themselves performing the desirable monitored behavior, they tend to attribute the behavior not to their own natural preference for it but to the coercive presence of the controls. As a consequence, they come to view themselves as less interested in the desirable conduct for its own sake (for example, putting in an honest day's work for an honest day's pay and behaving honestly during that honest day's work), and they are more likely to engage in the undesirable action whenever the controls cannot register the conduct (see Deci and Ryan 1987 for a review). The result is that surveilled employees, who may now conceive of themselves as less honest, should be more willing to attempt to trick or bypass the surveillance system, sending supervisors scurrying to find even more sophisticated (and expensive) control systems.

TUMOR IIIC: THE EXAGGERATED CAUSALITY OF SURVEILLANCE.   Just as workers under surveillance come to overattribute their desirable conduct to the action of the surveillance system, so too may managers. Social psychological research has demonstrated that surveillers assume that the desirable behavior of the people they are monitoring is caused by their surveillance, even when the desirable conduct might have occurred anyway (Strickland 1958; Kruglanski 1970). This perception may help explain why surveillance systems continue to grow in popularity within business despite the fact that supervisors experience a dramatic increase in workload when such systems are installed (Chalykoff and Kochan 1989). Once the systems are in place, managers may come to see them as more effective and necessary than is the case. Once again, we can see how such a process could lead to even greater expenditures to purchase even more and "better" systems.

CONCLUSIONS

From the outset of this chapter, I have advocated an ethical approach to the influence process, arguing that, beyond moral grounds, there are sound utilitarian reasons for taking such a tack. In the second section of the chapter, I focused on what certain of those reasons—costs, for the most part—might be for business organizations otherwise tempted to teach, condone, or merely allow the systematic use of dishonest influence tactics on external contacts. Although these costs (such as decreased repeat business, low job satisfaction and performance, high turnover, employee theft, expensive surveillance mechanisms, and an atmosphere of distrust) have often been noted as severe business problems, they do not seem to have been solved in spite of the attention they have received.

One possible reason for this failure is that they have never been traced to one potential root cause, the frequent tendency of business organizations to be less than honest in their external dealings. In a recent span of ten years, two-thirds of America's five hundred largest corporations have been caught in illegal activity (Crossen 1993). A lesson, then, is that it may be wrongheaded to launch one fiscal hemorrhage (for example, increasingly expensive security systems) to stanch another (for example, employee theft). The stanching may have to be done at the self-inflicted site of the wound, with an unblinking examination of corporate dishonesty and a true commitment to end it.

ENDNOTES

1. The debate is hardly new. Compare the sentiments of Decimus Junius Juvenal— "Honesty is praised and starves"—with those of Cervantes—"Honesty is the best policy"—sixteen centuries later.

2. The emphasis on *one* here comes from my belief that there are additional reasons, based in morality, for ethical conduct.

Chapter 3

Ethical Cognition and the Framing of Organizational Dilemmas: Decision Makers as Intuitive Lawyers

Roderick M. Kramer and David M. Messick

S ocial dilemmas arise when conflicts exist between individual self-interests and the collective welfare. In organizational settings, such dilemmas can assume a variety of forms.

A major focus of research on social dilemmas over the last two decades has been on trying to understand why people cooperate or fail to cooperate in such situations (see Dawes 1980; Komorita and Parks 1994; Kramer 1991; Messick and Brewer 1983 for literature reviews). In much of the research on social dilemmas, the decision to cooperate has been construed primarily in terms of conflicts between competing rationalities. For example, it has long been appreciated that cooperative choice entails trade-offs between individual and collective interests and between short-term and long-term gains and losses (see, for example, Edney 1980; Hardin 1968; Platt 1978; Schelling 1978). Although research grounded in these conceptions has yielded important insights into cooperative choice, it is useful to consider other assumptions that might be brought to bear on our understanding of this issue. Alternative frameworks might draw attention to dimensions of decision making that have been overlooked by rational-choice models. In so doing, they might broaden our understanding of how decision makers construe social dilemmas and resolve the conflicts they pose.

A primary aim of the present chapter, therefore, is to analyze choice behavior in organizational dilemmas from the perspective of the ethical con-

---

An earlier version of this paper was presented at the Fifth International Conference on Social Justice Research, Reno, Nevada, June 26–29, 1995, as well as at the Northwestern University Conference in 1994 (see Preface). Comments from participants at those conferences are gratefully acknowledged. Conversations with Jim March, Joanne Martin, Michael Morris, Jeff Pfeffer, Phil Tetlock, and Tom Tyler contributed to the development of these ideas.

cerns to which they give rise. Construing organizational dilemmas in ethical terms draws attention to an important set of concerns driving decision making in such situations that are substantively different from those traditionally highlighted by rational-choice models. In particular, we will demonstrate how the way people construe their duty or obligation in such situations influences their choices.

"Duty," noted James Wilson (1993, 101), "exists to the extent that people are willing to honor obligations in the absence of social rewards for doing so." The question of how people perceive or define their duty and obligation in situations where there is a need for individual or collective action has attracted considerable attention from both philosophers and psychologists. We should note at the outset that our analysis of the ethical dimensions underlying choice is informed primarily by a psychological perspective, and not a philosophical one. While drawing on ethical theory, the framework we articulate here focuses on the cognitive and social psychological processes that influence ethical judgment.

We view *ethical cognitions*—defined as people's perceptions about right and wrong and about their duties and obligations—as the end product of a rather complex judgment- and decision-making process. This process influences their decisions regarding not only *whether* to cooperate but also *how much* and *when*. Our analysis of this process is based on several broad assumptions and propositions about ethical cognitions and the role they play in organizational dilemmas. First, we propose that organizational members' perceptions of their duties and obligations are heavily influenced by cognitive, motivational, and social processes that affect how organizational dilemmas are cognitively *framed*. These cognitive frames are constructed in the service of basic but powerful psychological needs and motives that influence, in turn, how decision makers process incoming information and weigh alternatives.[1]

Recent research suggests that this framing process is complex and may be influenced by a variety of distinct social-information-processing motives and goals (see, for example, Ashford 1989; Brown 1990; Kunda 1990; McGill 1989). In this chapter, we emphasize primarily self-serving goals and motives. We assume that far from being impartial seekers of such things as accurate self-assessment, truth, or rationality, people are highly motivated to maintain a perception of a privileged place in the social and organizational worlds they inhabit. To do so, we argue, they use a readily available "tool kit" of cognitive strategies and tactics with which they construct self-serving frames. These frames are used to rationalize or legitimate the pursuit of self-interest in group contexts.

In this regard, we see decision makers as intuitive lawyers, passionately advancing and defending the claims of their client, the self.[2] In their role as intuitive lawyers, people act as advocate, judge, and juror, deciding what evidence to introduce, ruling on its reasonableness, and weighing its validity. To the extent that we view people's cognitive deliberations as driven largely by motivational considerations, this intuitive lawyer can be characterized as a selective social information processor, whenever possible advancing claims regarding its own rights and duties while vigorously challenging others' claims of entitlement to contested resources. We also posit that the framing of organizational dilemmas is influenced by structural properties of the dilemmas themselves.

Specifically, we propose that the more complex the organizational dilemma, the more effectively the intuitive lawyer is able to advance its arguments and claims. Complexity creates ambiguities and equivocalities that decision makers can readily exploit (see Weick 1993). Thus, when organizational dilemmas have many facets (for example, involve complex value trade-offs along multiple dimensions and/or involve many parties representing distinct interests and constituencies), people as intuitive lawyers have more freedom in constructing their self-serving frames. In contrast, the less ambiguity and equivocality the dilemma's structural properties afford (that is, the more cut and dried the dilemma), the less cognitive room the intuitive lawyer has to maneuver. A corollary to this hypothesis is that by their very definition, most organizational dilemmas *are* complex decision problems of precisely the sort that the intuitive lawyer handles with skill and adroitness.

Before going into these ideas and processes in detail, let us take a brief look at social dilemmas, examining some of the common forms they assume in organizations.

SOCIAL DILEMMAS IN ORGANIZATIONS: AN OVERVIEW

Researchers have found it useful to distinguish between two distinct forms of social dilemmas found in organizations: *traps* and *fences*.[3] Traps arise in organizations when it is in each decision maker's own interests to engage in some form of behavior that, if repeated by many decision makers, leads to collective harm. Fences arise when people have an incentive for failing to take some action that, if taken, would be beneficial to the organization. With traps, the problem is to get people to refrain from doing something they are already doing; with organizational fences, the problem is to get people to do things they are reluctant to do because of the personal costs that individual action entails. Both kinds of dilemmas can take several forms.

Organizational Traps

RESOURCE TRAPS.   Resource dilemmas are situations in which a group of individuals shares access to a common resource pool. Each person has an incentive to increase his or her use of a shared resource. When all do so, however, the resource is overused and possibly depleted or destroyed (see, for example, Kramer 1991). One person using an office phone for personal business does negligible harm to an organization, but when everyone does so the impact is far from negligible. Similarly, a single sales person can exaggerate travel expenses by a small margin without harming the company, but when the entire sales force does the same thing the organization suffers. As these examples suggest, resource dilemmas in organizations often involve such things as employee overuse of scarce financial, temporal, human, and physical resources. Individual acts of abuse seem innocent enough, but the aggregated cost of these individual peccadilloes is sizable, especially over time.

ESCALATION TRAPS. Escalation traps are another prevalent form of organizational dilemma. In these situations, decision makers have an incentive to embark on some course of action that produces positive individual consequences in the near term but in the long term has consequences that are collectively undesirable (Brockner and Rubin 1985; Kramer, Meyerson, and Davis 1990; Platt 1980). The entrapping nature of such decisions consists in the fact that each incremental decision, in and of itself, seems to involve reasonable benefits and relatively harmless costs. Over time, however, the cumulative impact becomes unreasonable and harmful. For example, implementing a simple surveillance system in an organization may reduce immediate concerns about employee theft in a particular department. Over time, however, such systems tend to spread and become more expensive. They may also undermine trust and exacerbate the very conditions they were meant to remedy. (See chapter 2.)

Organizational Fences

There are at least four types of fences that create problems in organizations: social loafing, concealment dilemmas, missing hero problems, and symbolic dilemmas. While there is some overlap among these types, each is distinct enough to merit separate discussion.

SOCIAL LOAFING. Social loafing refers to the tendency for individuals to expend less vigor, intensity, or effort when in a group than when they are performing alone (Latane, Williams, and Harkins 1979). Social loafing is most likely to occur under circumstances where individual efforts and contributions are not identifiable and in situations where credit or blame for the performance of the group is given to the group as a whole. Committees are notorious for producing social loafing; even committees composed of talented individuals often produce shabby work, much worse than any of the members would produce on their own.

CONCEALMENT DILEMMAS.   Concealment dilemmas arise when individual incentives lead people to withhold information, even though doing so leads to collective outcomes that are less than optimal. Organizations progress and profit by developing new ideas, products, and policies that are better than those of their competitors. Units within organizations succeed by doing precisely the same thing. In many instances, progress would be enhanced if individuals or groups were to pool or share their information, but having more information than others have is an obvious advantage. Thus, individuals have an incentive to obtain information from others while at the same time concealing their own information (Bonacich and Schneider 1992).

The fate of many research consortia illustrates these dynamics nicely. The original idea behind such consortia was that by forming strategic alliances, firms could collectively make technological breakthroughs more rapidly than could any firm acting alone, and all the participating firms would benefit. Such alliances have been characterized as "learning races," because the first member to extract sufficient knowledge from the others can withdraw from the alliance, thus making a competitive race out of the cooperative arrangement (Khanna, Gulati, and Nohria 1995). Because of such dynamics, initial efforts to develop research consortia within the United States were notoriously unsuccessful.

MISSING HERO DILEMMAS.   Missing hero problems constitute a third form of organizational fence. In these dilemmas, only a single party need act to resolve or avoid a collective problem, but no individual wants to bear the costs of the necessary action (Platt 1973; Schelling 1978). A serious and recurring version of this pattern arises when employees know that one of the organization's products is defective or one of its practices is unsafe. The person who speaks up incurs the cost of being identified as a whistle-blower. Research on whistle-blowers indicates that such costs can be substantial to the individual, in both psychological stress and career damage (Glazer and Glazer 1989). Not surprisingly, therefore, many people decide it is better to remain a whistle-swallower and let someone else volunteer. It is worth noting that according to one study, a primary reason why people swallow rather than blow the whistle is not that they fear the consequences of volunteering but that they believe that reporting it will make no difference (Miceli and Near 1992). Thus, even those who perceive a duty to report what they observe may decide against doing so because of the perceived futility of doing so.

SYMBOLIC DILEMMAS.   Most of the social dilemmas that researchers have studied to date involve substantive or concrete resources like money, time, or natural resources. Some of the most valuable assets that organizations possess, however, are symbolic resources, such as their reputation, their culture, and the trust and civility that exist among their members. Qualities like an honorable reputation or a culture of civility and trust are public goods and, as such, are subject to the same risks as other public goods. People may decline to pay the price necessary to maintain them, "free riding" on the efforts of others and thus placing the existence of these assets in jeopardy. The fences surrounding symbolic resources are particularly vexing, because damage to the public good is often almost invisible or hard to assess; further, perceived responsibility for such symbolic resources is often unclear or diffuse.

From a purely formal or mathematical perspective, one can argue that there is no formal distinction between decision making in fences and decision making in traps. However, David Messick and Marilynn Brewer (1983) argued that there may be important psychological differences between traps and fences. Along such lines, research by Jonathan Baron and his associates (Spranca, Minsk, and Baron 1991) has shown that acts of omission are often perceived as less blameworthy than acts of commission. For reasons we shall explore, the harm that befalls an organization because the employees of the organization failed to do something to prevent it is less attributable to an individual or group than harm that results from an individual or group's actions. Therefore inaction will be privileged over action. This asymmetry is ironic and sometimes tragic, because many of the most serious organizational dilemmas, at least when measured in terms of their consequences, arise from collective inaction.

The fact that many of the dilemmas that individuals face are fences exacerbates the difficulties surrounding choice because of the common tendency to believe that harm caused by inaction is less blameworthy than harm caused by actions. While many participants in the studies reported by Spranca, Minsk, and Baron (1991) judged that harm that was intentionally permitted was equally blameworthy whether it involved action or inaction, those who thought that there was a difference were nearly unanimous in judging that it was worse to cause harm through action than through inaction. Extrapolating from this empirical evidence, we hypothesize that fences are, in many respects, the more dangerous and difficult of the two types of dilemmas for organizations.

As all the examples just presented make clear, choice behavior in organizational dilemmas entails difficult and painful trade-offs. Different interpretations of the implications of an organizational dilemma stem from the different characteristics of these choices, as well as the trade-offs that are perceived to be associated with them. For example, focusing solely on the payoffs to individual decision makers frames the choice in terms of rationality versus irrationality, intelligence versus stupidity, or consistency versus inconsistency. Highlighting the consequences for others, on the other hand, tends to frame the choice in terms of cooperation versus competition, altruism versus selfishness, or the group versus the individual. Finally, framing the choice in terms of temporal conflicts accentuates the tensions between the short term and the long term. Thus, while some frames make salient the desirability of immediate gratifications and pleasures, others reveal the prospect of delayed but inevitable pains and privations (see, for example, G. Hardin 1988). As a consequence, the way in which individuals frame organizational dilemmas and in turn construe the trade-offs or consequences associated with their choices plays an important role in influencing not only their willingness to cooperate but also their finer-grained judgments as to how much and when. In this respect, the decision to cooperate can be decomposed into a complex judgment about perceived responsibility (who should act), the degree of responsibility (how much any given individual should act rather than others), and matters of timing (when action should be taken). In describing how people formulate such judgments, we begin by discussing several perspectives—those of game theorists and philosophers—on the problem of cooperative choice.

GAME THEORETIC AND PHILOSOPHICAL PERSPECTIVES ON COOPERATIVE CHOICE

Many scholars have used game theory, the mathematical analysis of national strategic interaction, as a tool for analyzing and resolving ethical and moral questions about how people should behave in social dilemma situations. From Robert Braithwaite (1955) to Robert Solomon (1993), scholars have explored the common elements of game theory and ethical theory: Both game theory and ethical theory draw attention to dilemmas about social decision making, they both make normative assumptions about the reasons for choosing among alternative courses of action in such dilemmas, and they both assume more or less sentient agents who have free choice. In short, both have explored the links among sociality, rationality, and choice.

Research using the "prisoner's dilemma," which Robert Frank discusses in the next chapter, has enjoyed a special place in this discussion. It has been used to support inquiries into such opposites as cooperation and competition, egoism and altruism, loyalty and defection, and rationality and irrationality (see, for instance, Barry and Hardin 1982; R. H. Frank 1988; Gautier 1986; Mackie 1978; Rescher 1975). From the standpoint of ethical theory, prisoners' dilemmas evoke a broad spectrum of moral implications concerning people's perceptions of their rights and obligations in such situations; outcomes are framed not in terms of what is efficient but rather what is right. We will discuss these implications in terms of consequentialist theories such as utilitarianism, deontological theories, and fairness and justice perspectives.[4]

The Utilitarian Perspective

According to utilitarianism, a moral decision reflects the choice that maximizes the utilities of the concerned parties. While this theory has problems

/ 65

of implementation in many situations, in social dilemmas it does not. In any context in which the definition of the dilemma is clear, the moral choice is also clear: to make the cooperative choice, since that is the alternative that, by definition, maximizes the collective welfare. From the perspective of utilitarian theories of morality, therefore, social dilemmas represent a simple moral choice.

Note that we are not arguing that a utilitarian analysis necessarily produces a clear choice. In many real situations, especially those in which the outcomes are highly uncertain, the calculation of which option will produce the greatest expected good can be highly speculative. Instead, we are arguing that *if* a social dilemma can be clearly defined, then cooperative choice is the moral choice from a utilitarian perspective.

The Deontological Perspective

Deontological perspectives accord particular importance to the rules underlying social decisions. They therefore add a different dimension to the ethical evaluation of social dilemmas. The right to be able to make a free choice and to pursue one's own interests may seem to legitimate choosing the self-interested option in a social dilemma. Such rights must, however, be conditional on all parties' having the same right. In other words, people cannot claim a right for themselves that they simultaneously deny to others. Rights can exist only to the extent that they are consistent with all sharing that right. In this respect, deontological analyses resemble an equilibrium analysis more than the maximization analysis characteristic of utilitarian theories.

Keeping promises is often used as an example. If it is in my best interest in a given situation to break a promise that I have made, and if it is in the best interest of society as a whole, why should I not do it? A utilitarian analysis might indicate that both I and the world would be better off if I did. From a deontological perspective, however, if I break my promise when it is convenient for me to do so, I must expect that everyone might do the same. Should this be the case, the concept of a promise loses its meaning. To say "I promise" comes to mean that I will do as I say if and only if it is convenient or profitable. This is not a promise. Thus, from a deontological perspective, violating a promise is ethically wrong because a stable world in which promises are kept only if convenient is unimaginable. As rules for social sense-making and action, promises would simply not be believed or utilized.

Andrew Colman (1982) extends this type of argument to social dilemmas. He adopts a Kantian perspective based on two criteria: universalizability and reversibility (Velasquez 1992). Universalizability means that people's reasons for action should be reasons that everyone could act on in principle. This criterion captures that aspect of our moral intuition that says that we cannot make moral arguments that favor us over others. Reversibility, the second criterion, means that our reasons for actions must also be reasons that we would want others to act on, even in their interactions with us.

In the context of social dilemmas, it is clear that both self-interested motives that lead to noncooperative choice and other-regarding motives that dictate choosing the cooperative option are universalizable. We can imagine all people making choices on the basis of these motives. The self-interested choice, however, is not reversible in this context. The structure of the dilemma is such that we are not indifferent to the choices that others make; we want them to make the cooperative choice. Thus, the cooperative choice is the only moral choice, because it is both universalizable and reversible.

There are other ways to approach social dilemmas from the perspective of rights and duties. For instance, Colman (1982) interprets J. J. Rousseau's notion of the social contract as pertaining to the distinction between "the general will" (the common good) and "the will of all" (the good of each individual). The resolution is the contract in which each agrees to pursue the former at the expense of the latter, because adherence to such a contract will promote the best interests of all. The concept of a social contract resembles Garrett's (1968) proposed solution to the tragedy of the commons of "mutual coercion, mutually agreed upon." In some instances, such contracts may be implicit, more resembling a tacitly understood *psychological contract* (Rousseau 1995) rather than an explicit or legal one.

Justice and Fairness Perspectives

Theories of justice and fairness provide another perspective on ethical choice. Many of these theories adopt an essentially utilitarian perspective of economic justice. That is, they assume that if one state of affairs is preferred by everyone to another, then, in a just society, it should be chosen. This principle is one of the axioms of social choice theory (see Arrow 1951). For example, if all prefer mutual cooperation to mutual defection, then an organization is unjust (and perverse) if its decision-making procedures yield the latter rather than the former.

As will be clear by now, new game theoretic and philosophical perspectives on choice in social dilemmas have generally been concerned with the question, What *ought* people to do in such situations? Such analyses are useful in elaborating on the logical criteria that individuals *might* use when construing ethical conflicts. They suffer from an important limitation, however, in that they produce a purely normative analysis of ethical judgment and choice. In other words, they provide only a prescriptive account of ethical action and choice. While such prescriptive analyses are informative in telling us when and why one choice ought logically to dominate another, they shed little light on when and why one choice is observed rather than another in a given real-world situation. In other words, such analyses tell us a great deal about how rational, moral, or sentient beings *ought* to behave, but they offer little insight into how they actually *do* behave. Answers to this latter question must be sought in a descriptive or behavioral theory of ethical cognition, for which a social psychological analysis of choice seems particularly well suited.

A SOCIAL PSYCHOLOGICAL PERSPECTIVE ON ETHICAL COGNITION AND COOPERATIVE CHOICE

We have noted that choice in organizational dilemmas entails difficult trade-offs between individual versus collective—as well as short-term versus long-term—costs and benefits. There is considerable evidence from both laboratory experiments and historical case studies that people in organizations often have difficulty making decisions that involve such complex value trade-offs (see, for example, Abelson and Levi 1985; George 1980; Kramer 1989). Recent models of decision making portray choice in such situations as a multistage judgmental process, in which decision makers actively edit and frame incoming information (see, for example, Kahneman and Tversky 1984; Kramer, Meyerson, and Davis 1990).

Using these models as a starting point, we suggest that people's choice behavior in organizational dilemmas reflects several distinct but interrelated judgments about the perceived necessity and responsibility for and timing of action. A critical initial decision, we propose, concerns their perceptions of the necessity for action. For example, in the case of an anticipated resource scarcity, they have to answer the question, Is action really necessary? Should action be taken? Even if they decide that some sort of action is necessary, they must also decide who should take it. For example, whom do they perceive to be responsible for creating the situation and/or solving it? In collective contexts, this issue includes judgments about the apportionment of responsibility; that is, how should responsibility be divided among all the potentially culpable parties? Finally, there are questions about *when* action should be taken. These issues of timing are critical, because individuals may decide that action, even if necessary, should be delayed.

In the abstract, such questions may seem quite simple and their answers obvious. In the case of most real-world organizational dilemmas, however, they turn out to be enormously complex and problematic, for a number of reasons. First, it is often difficult, if not impossible, to determine the true nature and severity of many dilemmas. Considerable ambiguity and uncertainty exists about the state of many collective resource pools. Thus, individuals sometimes aren't even sure whether a crisis or emergency really exists. For example, considerable controversy attends the question of global warming. Does it constitute a real phenomenon, let alone an environmental crisis? Is it the result of human actions or inactions? Is there in fact a necessity for restraint or some sort of active remedial intervention? If so, how much action should be taken and when? And on whose shoulders should the responsibility for action rest? If restraint is necessary, who should take it? Should well-developed nations exercise restraint, reducing their standard of living and rolling back progress? Or should the burden be shifted to developing countries by discouraging them from technological development? Must action be taken now or can it be delayed? Doing the wrong thing now may do more harm than doing nothing at all. After all, the long-term consequences of some interventions may be worse than the cure itself. In addition, waiting may allow for the development of new technological fixes or improved solutions.

How do decision makers resolve these critical questions regarding the need for, timing of, and responsibility for action in organizational dilemmas? Conceptualizing decision makers as "intuitive lawyers," we suggest, sheds some light on these important questions. As we saw earlier in the chapter, intuitive lawyers approach these difficult questions about duty and responsibility using a variety of self-serving cognitive frames. These frames function to attenuate or mitigate their perceptions of duty and obligation. To understand how they do so, it is useful to examine briefly the motives that drive the intuitive lawyer's framing of organizational dilemmas.

The assumption that people are highly motivated to perceive accurately the social and organizational worlds they inhabit has been a prominent theme of both social psychological and organizational research over the past several decades (see, for example, Fiske and Taylor 1991; Ross and Nisbett 1991; Weick 1993). Indeed, Fiske and Taylor (1991) characterized social cognition as the study of "how people make sense of other people and themselves" (p. 19).

In light of the intuitive lawyer metaphor, this characterization is both informative and ironic, because a recurring theme of social cognition research over the past four decades is that people's attempts at making sense of themselves and others are often corrupted by a variety of perceptual distortions, judgmental biases, and cognitive illusions. Although individuals often profess the desire to achieve accurate views of themselves and the world in which they live, accuracy appears to be readily forfeited in the service of other needs and goals, including self-protection, self-enhancement, and reassurance (Allison, Messick, and Goethals 1989; Brewer 1991; Brockner 1988; Brown 1986, 1990; Goethals 1986; Goethals, Messick, and Allison 1990; Goleman 1985; Greenwald 1980; Kunda 1990; Sackheim 1983; Taylor 1989; Taylor and Brown 1988). Indeed, the belief that accuracy is the goal of human judgment itself may be regarded as a form of self-enhancing and comforting illusion.

The portrait of the self that emerges from such research is not that of a passive and neutral information processor who merely takes in the world as it is given. Rather, it implies that people are proactive and opportunistic contortionists who engage in creative processes of cognitive transformation that help them maintain a variety of positive images, including images of themselves as rational, blameless, and consistent decision makers. The intuitive lawyer metaphor thus highlights the fact that people process personal and social information selectively and strategically, developing those facts or inferences that promote their needs and interests while discounting or belittling those that run contrary to them. As intuitive lawyers, people seek to exculpate themselves from perceived responsibility when bad things happen and enhance their perception of entitlement when good things happen. And, when necessary, they vigorously challenge others' claims of entitlement and denials of personal responsibility for a collective dilemma.

The intuitive lawyer does not, however, function in a vacuum. Rather, these processes are aided by structural features and properties of organizational dilemmas that allow such cognitive contortions to occur.

STRUCTURAL FEATURES OF DILEMMAS

A central proposition in our analysis is that a number of features inherent in organizational dilemmas afford opportunities for intuitive lawyers to construe their obligation and duty in self-serving ways. These features, we argue, create ambiguity or equivocality regarding the necessity and responsibility for and timing of action or inaction. These ambiguities and equivocalities are exploited when the intuitive lawyer constructs several distinct forms of frames.

To advance this argument, it is important to point out that organizational dilemmas are characterized by at least three general properties. First, such dilemmas are multifaceted, so that there is always a multiplicity of possible perspectives on the dilemma. Second, they are inherently social. Third, in organizational dilemmas individuals typically perceive their own actions or inactions as having minimal impact on the collective outcome. Each of these critical features of organizational dilemmas influences the intuitive lawyer's framing of choice.

The Multiplicity of Perspectives

In large-scale organizational dilemmas involving numerous actors and issues, multiple perspectives on the problem are always possible. What is in the best interest of the individual decision maker is not in the best interest of the collective, and what is in decision makers' short-term interests conflicts with their long-term interests; there is a fundamental trade-off that must be made between decision makers' short-term self-interests and long-term collective considerations.

For example, most people recognize the desirability of generating revenues that can be used to further collective aims, such as the provision of critical public goods within the organization. Organizational leaders may frame such revenues as "enhancements" designed to improve the quality of work life; for the intuitive lawyer, however, they may be viewed as unjustified "taxes." Thus, whether benefits versus burdens loom large depends upon the perspective that is adopted.

The Social Nature of Organizational Dilemmas

A second feature of organizational dilemmas is that they are inherently social. This fact has at least two implications. First, because of the uncertainties and ambiguities about the true state of affairs in the organization, information about other people's behavior is a useful guide to how one ought to or might behave. The way others respond to the situation provides useful normative information and may influence the individual's interpretation of the dilemma and suggest what would be proper or justifiable conduct.

Another implication of the social nature of these situations is that people are acutely aware of how their interdependence or mutual fate governs their own and others' outcomes. As a consequence, people in organizational dilemmas are likely to have strong preferences regarding the actions of the other people involved. One of the less appreciated aspects of social dilemmas is the fact that while individual decision makers may be intensely conflicted about what they themselves should do, there is usually little conflict regarding what they want or prefer others to do.

A further implication of this feature is that individuals recognize that it is in their best interest to have others cooperate and that it makes sense to try to encourage others to do so. People are likely to view positively efforts to encourage others to cooperate. For example, they may feel that attempts to restrain others' greed and reckless behavior through the use of surveillance and sanctioning systems are both necessary and prudent. At the same time, however, they are likely to resist efforts to constrain their own choices or induce compliance, viewing such organizational actions as violating their freedom of choice and entitlement. The very same interventions and actions that are viewed as promoting responsible behavior in others are often seen as abridging one's own freedoms. (Of course, self-enhancing illusions contribute to the perception that such constraints are unnecessary for oneself, even if they are seen as essential for managing others' behavior.)

The Minimal Perceived Impact of One's Actions

A third important characteristic of large-scale organizational dilemmas is that often little connection is perceived between the behavior of a single person and the well-being of the organization as a whole. In most organizational dilemmas, the actions of a single person do not have a great impact on the collective outcome.[5] As we have noted, when one employee makes personal telephone calls from the office phone, the expense does not dramatically affect the organization's bottom line; only when many employees do it is the effect appreciable. Similarly, one person's tardiness, misuse of office supplies, impatience with subordinates, or abuse of the reputation of the organization will have but a small impact on the organization's overall well-being, but when many engage in such acts, the consequences accumulate and have large impact.

Note that even if the organization suffers from low productivity, high costs, inflated personnel turnover, and poor image as a result of such cumulative consequences, individual members cannot be held responsible. Thus, while the organization aggregates the minor misdeeds of the employees into a serious problem, each employee can justly claim, "It's not my fault (or my problem)." Moreover, individuals may feel they have evidence that their small acts of commission and omission aren't really making a discernible difference anyway; the organization always seems to endure.

At the heart of people's ability to advance their claims of innocence when an organization is harmed through the aggregated consequences of small acts is the defense that the individual has little or no direct responsibility for the outcome. After all, it would be unfair to single out any one person or group to blame. The lack of an apparent causal bond between the individual's actions (or inactions) and the collective outcome thus provides a persuasive blame shield. In this sense, people are inclined to fail to see critical path dependencies that are inherent in organizational dilemmas.

Failures to perceive such relationships do not reflect mere lack of attention or cognitive complexity. In other words, they are not simply cognitive errors and misperceptions. Rather, they reflect active, constructive perceptual and judgmental processes. We will consider these next.

THE TACTICAL TOOL KIT OF THE INTUITIVE LAWYER

We have identified a number of common or generic features of organizational dilemmas that can influence people's perceptions of whether action should be taken in organizational dilemmas, who should take it, and when. We have implied that these features provide opportunities for people as intuitive lawyers to construct self-serving cognitive frames that attenuate or mitigate perceptions of individual duty or obligation to respond. We turn now to describing in more detail just how they accomplish these goals.

As a highly selective or strategic social information processor, the intuitive lawyer is neither perfect nor randomly imperfect. Instead, each individual has a *modus operandi*, employing psychological tactics that may assume several distinct forms. We suggest that there are at least three distinct kinds of cognitive frame that intuitive lawyers use to advance their claims regarding obligations or duties in organizational dilemmas.[6] We characterize these as contextual frames, temporal frames, and identity frames.[7]

Contextual Frames

Research by Ann McGill (1989) and others has shown that decision makers' causal explanations for an event often vary dramatically as a function of the causal background adopted in the attempt to explain that event. (See also chapter 12.) Extrapolating from such evidence, we argue that decision makers construct *contextual frames* that influence the perceived causal structure of an organizational dilemma, including the perception of what and who is causing it. These frames affect, in turn, their judgments about what should be done about the problem, when it should be done, and who should do it.

Thus, contextual frames play a critical role in the intuitive lawyer's attempts to advance self-serving claims, for several reasons. First, organizational outcomes are rarely all good or all bad; there is therefore considerable latitude for framing those outcomes (see Weick 1993). In addition, the causes of a dilemma are seldom clear and singular, so there is room for creative and self-serving causal attribution (see Fincham and Jaspars 1980). These ambiguities and uncertainties can, for instance, provide an opportunity for "taking credit while laying blame" (Weiner 1971). Third, because of the complex trade-offs associated with any given course of action, the selection of a causal frame can dramatically influence which gains and losses loom large during decision making (see Kramer, Meyerson, and Davis 1990).

There are several distinct forms of contextual frames that may be particularly useful for the deliberations of the intuitive lawyer. One form of contextual framing concerns the use of "mental accounts" within which ethical choices or actions are evaluated. We propose that the perceived significance of an ethical action or inaction may be influenced by the exclusiveness (narrowness) or inclusiveness (comprehensiveness) of the mental account to which it is posted or within which it is evaluated. Research on mental accounting points out that choices can be framed in terms of relatively narrow "topical" accounts or in terms of larger comprehensive accounts.

The perceived acceptability or attractiveness of a choice can be influenced, in turn, by the particular mental account within which it is embedded or to which its costs and benefits are "posted" (Kahneman and Tversky 1984; Kramer, Meyerson, and Davis 1990; Thaler 1991). Thus, in the case of an organizational dilemma, a particular act (such as using the office phone for a personal long-distance phone call) may, when viewed by itself or in isolation, seem like a clear violation of company policy and an ethical transgression. When framed in terms of a more comprehensive mental account ("While I did make a short phone call, over the course of the year I've often worked overtime and on weekends in order to catch up on my work"), however, it may seem acceptable. By strategically framing ethical choices in terms of such larger, more integrative accounts, the intuitive lawyer can reduce or minimize the perceived magnitude of an ethical violation.

Costs and benefits, as well as actions, can be contextually framed. For instance, James Kunen (1994) has described how the cost of improving the safety of school buses is subject to framing. The cost of safety features that would reduce fire risks was estimated to be about $1,000 per vehicle. With 30,000 buses being sold each year, opponents pointed out, the total cost of adding the safety features would be $30 million, which would be borne by the nation's overburdened school districts annually. Furthermore, since only thirty passengers were dying each year, this cost would amount to at least $1 million per life saved, assuming, unrealistically, that all passenger deaths could be avoided. Framed in this way, the cost of the safety features might seem like an unacceptably high price to pay, especially since a National Highway Traffic Safety Association study had put the value of a human life at $200,000.

Proponents of requiring the safety improvements responded by pointing out that $1,000 per bus came to only $100 per year for the lifetime of a bus, which is 56 cents per bus per school day, or less than a half a cent per pupil per day. Seen in this contextual frame, the additional costs seem trivial relative to the margin of safety that would be purchased.

Another way in which decisions can be contextually framed is through comparisons or analogies with past actions or events. Richard Neustadt and Ernest May (1986) have noted that when decision makers confront decisions that entail difficult and uncertain trade-offs, they often search for relevant analogies with past decisions. Such comparisons help decision makers to make sense of an event and identify viable courses of action. And indeed, historical analogies have played a fairly prominent role in debates regarding social dilemmas. For example, calls for action and pleas for inaction have often been justified on the basis of a comparison between a contemporary resource crisis (such as the overfishing of the world's oceans) and the "tragedy of the commons" (G. Hardin 1968). Yet many scholars have vigorously disputed the validity of such comparisons, suggesting that the analogy is imperfect and misleading.

A nice illustration of the impact of contextual framing was provided during the Cuban missile crisis. When President Kennedy and his group of advisors were deliberating on how to respond to the discovery of Soviet missile installations on Cuban soil, at least one person suggested that action was necessary because inaction would signal lack of resolve and willingness to act. To advance this argument, this advisor compared the costs of inaction in the current situation to the costs associated with initial appeasements of Hitler by Neville Chamberlain (the so-called Munich analogy). Later, Robert Kennedy framed the contemplated surprise air strike as comparable to the Japanese attack on Pearl Harbor. This significant reframing moved the group away from military action.

From the perspective of the intuitive lawyer, we suggest, such historical analogies are particularly useful for the construction of causal narratives that legitimate and justify certain self-serving courses of action (or inaction, as the case may be). Thus a given organizational intervention, such as a proposal to begin rationing organizational resources, may be viewed by top management as a necessary action that will help the organization avoid bankruptcy. But it may be viewed by other employees of the organization as an attempt to create fictitious shortages in order to increase profits.

A tactic that is closely related to the strategic invocation of historical analogies concerns the self-serving articulation of different value-laden metaphors in relation to a given dilemma. As Scott Allison and Elizabeth Midgley (1994) have recently argued, not only has a bewildering array of metaphors been used to describe social and organizational dilemmas, but the particular metaphor that is used has considerable impact on how the dilemma is construed. Extrapolating from their research, we argue that the decision making of the intuitive lawyer can be influenced by the choice of metaphor for the dilemma. A metaphor such as "life on a lifeboat" may elevate concerns about protecting one's own welfare and be used to legitimate the ruthless pursuit of self-interests, while a more collectivist metaphor such as "Spaceship Earth" may be used to argue for responsible restraint (see G. Hardin 1988).

Another use of contextual framing is seen in a recent study showing how the standard outcome bias—the tendency to judge the quality of a decision by the quality of the outcome—can be completely reversed. Subjects judge those whose outcomes were positive when taking a gamble as having made better decisions than people who took precisely the same gamble and lost (Baron and Hershy 1988). The implicit reference point in this paradigm is the status quo: Did the outcome of the gamble improve or worsen things? Terry Boles and David Messick (1995) have shown that when a different reference point is made salient—namely, what *would have* happened if the second of two options had been selected—this outcome bias can be reversed, so that the person losing the gamble (and breaking even) is judged to have made a better decision than the person winning (receiving $100). The loser would have lost much more had the alternative decision been made (−$100), and the winner would have won even more ($500) had the alternative been selected. The loser's outcome, relative to the alternative (losing $100), was good, and the winner's poor. We suggest that the intuitive lawyer is clever at selecting reference points that serve his interests.

In the same way, Spranca, Minsk, and Baron (1991) offered evidence that the omission bias—the tendency to favor acts of omission that cause harm over acts of commission—is related to subjects' perception of causation. If harm is caused by some sequence of events that would have occurred whether or not a given person were present, that person should not be held responsible even if he or she could have prevented the foreseeable harm from happening. In many organizational dilemmas, the problems that the organization is experiencing are not attributable to the actions of a single party; all parties have the benefit of the omission bias. In other words, the intuitive lawyer can forcefully argue that an organization's problems would have occurred regardless of what the concerned party did.

Temporal Frames

Temporal frames are particularly important in questions regarding the *timing* of choice in organizational dilemmas. Decision makers use them to justify avoiding changing their own behavior (for example, delaying the use of restraint). Temporal framing is a complex process that involves use of the past as well as expectations and anticipations about the future. It therefore entails both retrospective and prospective forms of framing, depending on the temporal reference points that are invoked.

With respect to retrospective frames, we suggest that decision makers are skillful at using the past to justify their own behavior. Research on memory has shown that remembering is not the mechanical retrieval process that it was once thought to be, but rather an active process that reconstructs the past by weaving into it elements from the present (Kunda 1990). Thus, people's recall of past ethical behaviors tends to be quite self-serving; for example, there is evidence that people remember themselves as being fairer than others in the past (Messick and others 1985).

Prospective temporal framing can also influence perceptions of the necessity for and timing of choice. Some of the important dimensions of prospective framing emerge from the temporal distribution of outcomes (see Loewenstein & Elster 1992 for a general overview). The temporal frames used to evaluate choice in organizational dilemmas are often relatively myopic. Because of discounting, the shadow of the near future looms larger than that of the distant future. For example, the immediate loss of opportunities, pleasures, and comforts that is associated with personal restraint often exerts more influence over choice behavior than the more distant and abstract benefits that may accrue from such restraint.

Decision makers in organizations are not completely myopic, however. They are sometimes forward-looking, attempting to anticipate problems and take preemptive prophylactic measures, including delaying gratification and using self-control strategies. We suggest, however, that three forms of cognitive illusion may influence their perception of how much action is needed and how quickly. The first is the illusion of control (Langer 1975); there is evidence that people tend to overestimate their control over events. A second illusion is the illusion of invulnerability; people tend to underestimate the likelihood that they will experience many negative life events (Perloff 1983; Perloff and Feltzer 1986). Finally, people tend to be unrealistically optimistic about their futures (Weinstein 1980, 1989).

Because of these illusions of control, invulnerability, and unrealistic optimism, decision makers in organizational dilemmas may underestimate the need for immediate action and fail to take timely appropriate action. In addition, even when they eventually recognize the need to act, they may tend to view small, incremental, and relatively painless acts as adequate. There is also evidence that these individual-level illusions extend to the groups to which individuals belong (Brinthaupt, Moreland, and Levine 1991). This finding has important implications, because individuals may conclude not only that they themselves are not in danger but that their group or the organization as a whole is not in jeopardy either.

These facets of temporal framing draw attention again to the problem of trade-offs between the perceived sins and virtues (costs and benefits) of omission versus commission, which in turn influence people's preferences for action or inaction in a dilemma. Because complex trade-offs and uncertain consequences attend both short-term and long-term solutions to any organizational dilemma, it is far from obvious in most cases that one should necessarily adopt a long-term or a short-term perspective. Corporate leaders justify a policy that causes immediate harm to some, like the current downsizing of many firms in the United States, by the long-term benefit that is anticipated. It is not clear, however, that the other short-term and long-term effects of downsizing aren't worse than other remedies that might be pursued. Similarly, many executives say that they are forced to respond to short-term pressures, like having appealing numbers to put in the quarterly report, in ways that may have a detrimental impact on the long-term prospects for the firm.

Identity Frames

We noted earlier that organizational dilemmas are inherently social and that, as a consequence, people's perceptions of their obligations are often defined in social terms. Who one chooses to compare one's behavior with, for example, can clearly influence how attractive or unattractive, ethical or unethical, that behavior is. Similarly, it matters whether individuals regard themselves as members of a community or identify with the group or organization that is confronting a particular dilemma. Thus, *identity frames* are a third kind of frame that plays a prominent role in the intuitive lawyer's judgments about personal responsibility for action or restraint in organizational dilemmas.

The notion of identity framing is derived from recent work on the relationship between personal and social identity, which argues that most people are highly motivated to maintain positive and distinctive identities and that they exhibit considerable cognitive creativity and flexibility when those cherished or valued identities are threatened (Brewer 1991). A key assumption of these theories is that people possess multiple identities, which are defined by their various personal attributes as well as by the social and organizational roles they occupy.

Identity frames influence the comparative salience of these personal and organizational identities and thus govern which identity shapes action in a given context. From the standpoint of the social-information-processing goals of the intuitive lawyer, identity frames operate on two levels. First, they influence how people perceive or define themselves. This tactic has been termed *strategic* or *motivated self-categorization*. Second, they influence how people define their relationship to other members of the organization. For example, identity frames may affect which individuals and groups people use as reference points and for social comparison when evaluating and justifying their own behavior. This tactic might be thought of as a form of strategic or motivated social categorization (see Elsbach and Kramer 1994 for a fuller treatment of these two tactics).

Individuals possess membership in multiple social categories. The term *strategic self-categorization* reflects the notion that people often display considerable flexibility in how they categorize themselves, opportunistically selecting those categories that identify them in the best light in a given situation. Most accounts of self-categorization emphasize a functional interpretation of such behavior; for example, one study argues, "Variability of self-categorization allows adaptive self-regulation in terms of one's changing relationship to reality. It provides people with behavioral and psychological flexibility in that we are able to act . . . as different kinds of persons and collectivities on different occasions" (Turner and others 1994, 461). Thus, it is sometimes more or less useful in various organizational situations to categorize oneself as white, male, Christian, heterosexual, and so on. Lt. Colonel Oliver North displayed considerable cognitive flexibility in this regard when testifying at the Iran-Contra hearings, sometimes drawing attention to his role as a Marine Corps officer and employee of the Commander in Chief, while at other times invoking his duties as a dutiful husband and father to justify some expenditures and deeds.

In ambiguous contexts, small and subtle identity cues can influence how situations are perceived and how the acceptability of different choices is evaluated. Charles Samuelson and Scott Allison (1994), for instance, created a situation in which one of a group of five subjects was allowed to be the first in the group to harvest from a common resource pool. For some subjects, their role was described as that of a leader, whereas for others their role was referred to as that of supervisor. Those called leader displayed more self-restraint than those called supervisor. Apparently, the connotations of being a leader are less consistent with self-aggrandizement at others' expense than the connotations of being a supervisor. From the perspective of the intuitive lawyer, then, invoking an identity such as "merely" a manager or supervisor may allow individuals to justify overuse of a collective resource.

Strategic social categorizations serve a similarly useful function of legitimating and justifying various self-serving acts. People's perception of obligation and responsibility in social dilemmas are seldom defined in absolute terms. Rather, they are defined relative to what others have or haven't done. Thus, leaving work fifteen minutes early every Friday afternoon will seem less wrong if at least some of one's co-workers are leaving a half hour early. Indeed, one can feel virtuous for staying fifteen minutes longer than the others, even though one's still technically violating company policy and still leaving fifteen minutes before those who are working the full time expected by the organization. Through strategic social categorization, one's own actions and choices can be made to look better.[8]

People can also use this strategy to put psychological distance between themselves and others in the organization. For example, when managers confront evidence of wrongdoing by colleagues in different divisions of the firm, they can say to themselves, "This is not my problem or responsibility because the person does not report to me and is in a different division." In this case, the intuitive lawyer sheds responsibility for intervening by inventing a boundary—my division versus the other division—that separates the manager from the miscreant.

Another and somewhat more extreme reaction of this sort occurs when employees decline to act on information because their primary loyalty is to the welfare of their family. Research on whistle-blowing suggests that whistle-swallowers are often deterred from taking action by concern about the impact of such behavior on their families. In this case, responsibility to the family (a legitimate and competing basis for categorization) is used strategically to insulate decision makers from organizational responsibility.

Strategic social categorization processes can also influence how outcomes are viewed vis-à-vis their impacts on different constituencies. If by taking action one improves one's own outcomes but worsens another person's, whose outcomes should receive greater weight? There is no rule that permits us to calculate an answer to this question. As intuitive lawyers, people can be expected to place greater weight on the outcomes that pertain most directly to their own interests and less on others' interests. Moreover, if the decision has many effects, as most complex decisions do, they can identify other outcomes that have the same valence as their own and argue the importance of those outcomes to appear less self-centered. The intuitive lawyer knows, for example, that saying that a reduction in the capital gains tax will stimulate the economy and increase employment is a better moral argument than saying that it will save oneself thousands of dollars a year in taxes. As intuitive lawyers, people are therefore more likely to argue on the basis of employment and may actually convince themselves of the merit of this position in the process.

To summarize, we argue that intuitive lawyers employ psychological tactics such as strategic self-categorization and strategic social categorization primarily to manipulate their perception of duty or obligation. Although we have formulated these arguments in terms of individuals' perceptions of their duty or obligation in organizational dilemmas, it is important to note that all these same strategies can be used to increase their perceptions of entitlement and rights (see, for example, Tyler and Hastie 1991; Kramer, Newton, and Pommerenke 1993). We assume that perceptions of entitlement, in turn, often attenuate or mitigate perceptions of obligation; for example, when individuals feel entitled to scarce organizational resources because of self-serving recall of all they have done to earn them, they will feel less obligation to exercise restraint relative to others. There is a second reason, we should note, for focusing on obligations and duties, and that is what we view as a rather pervasive asymmetry in emphasis in much contemporary discourse on such matters. While much attention has been paid to the rights of individuals, the obligations of individuals (and their implications for collective rights) have been comparatively neglected (see L. M. Friedman 1990 for a thoughtful discussion). As Garrett Hardin and John Baden (1988) have noted, the destruction of Greece was at least in part "caused by men who embraced a politico-economic system that was rich in rights and poor in responsibilities" (p. xii).

ORGANIZATIONAL IMPLICATIONS

The conceptual perspective we have articulated in this chapter provides a framework for thinking about how individuals construe ethical choice in organizational dilemmas. It helps bring into bolder relief a number of considerations that previous research has tended to minimize or neglect. In particular, we think the study of ethical cognition in organizational dilemmas constitutes an important and underdeveloped area of decision research, especially with respect to choices that involve difficult value trade-offs.

We should emphasize that our use of the intuitive lawyer metaphor is intended to contrast our view of organizational decision making with several metaphors that have exerted considerable influence on this topic in recent decades. The first is that of the *intuitive scientist* (Kelley 1967). According to this view, decision makers can be characterized as more or less systematic and dispassionate information processors. A second metaphor that has exerted considerable influence on social dilemma theory is that of the *intuitive economist*. According to this metaphor, decision makers are more or less rational actors, striving to maximize their own expected utility (see Abelson and Levi 1985 for a recent review of research in this tradition). A third metaphor is that of the *intuitive bumpkin*. According to this view, people are inept decision makers whose irrational acts, misperceptions, and biases place them at the mercy of social and nonsocial forces whose complexity and subtlety frequently escape them (see, for example, Nisbett and Ross 1980). Such views emphasize that although individuals may aspire to rationality in choice, they often achieve at best a bounded or constrained rationality (Bazerman 1994; Dawes 1988).

A fourth influential metaphor is that of the social decision maker as *intuitive politician*. In this view, decision makers' choice behavior is often influenced as much by concerns about the appearance of decisions as by the content of the decisions themselves. Phillip Tetlock (1985, 1991), for example, has documented in persuasive detail how a variety of social concerns—including self-presentational motives, concerns about accountability, and the need to justify action to external audiences—exert a powerful and oftentimes corrupting influence on judgment and choice. In many respects, this intuitive politician metaphor comes close to resonating with our view of the motives and goals of the intuitive lawyer in organizations, but the two metaphors differ in one important regard. While the intuitive politician is largely outward-looking, concerned about what others think, our focus is on the *internal* audiences of the intuitive lawyer. In other words, we are interested in how people's needs to maintain a self-perception of positive identities and distinctiveness or uniqueness shape their judgment and choice.

Perhaps the closest metaphor to our view is that recently articulated by Bernard Weiner (1995), which views people as sometimes playing God in their ethical deliberations:

> Like God, [people] regard themselves as having the right or legitimacy to judge others as good or bad, innocent or guilty, or responsible or not responsible for an event or a personal plight. . . . As "fair" or "just" Gods, the defendants are permitted to offer excuses, justifications, or confessions for their actions. . . . Very closely related to this Godlike metaphor is the metaphor that life is a courtroom where interpersonal dramas are played out and where we judge one another, gather information to determine causality and responsibility, allow for self-defense, pass sentences, consider parole, and so on. (pp. 3–4)

We should emphasize that we do not regard the choice of metaphors as merely a matter of intellectual taste or disciplinary vogue. Rather, we think the particular metaphors that are adopted in decision-making research have profound implications for the empiricism such research generates. For example, most social psychology experiments on social dilemmas ask participants to decide, "How much do you *want* to take from or contribute to a common resource pool?" The form of this question implicitly, if not explicitly, frames the choice in terms of the subject's needs or preferences. This formulation largely reflects the presumptive stance of game theoretic and economic models of choice. If the same choice were framed in ethical terms, a variety of different factors and trade-offs might become salient. For example, asking "How much *should* you take from or contribute to the common pool?" brings in a very different set of concerns. Posing the question in this way moves the experimental paradigm away from a decision analytic paradigm and toward a more Kohlbergian moral dilemmas paradigm.

Which frame is better or more legitimate? There is no clear answer. The important point is that neither is neutral. Both create a certain kind of experimental demand insofar as they invoke different contextual or situated identities for study participants.

In addition to the frames made salient or suggested by the experimenter's description of the task, we need to know more about how individuals naturally or spontaneously frame such decisions in real-world settings. For example, it is not at all clear empirically that rationalistic frames dominate ethical frames in ordinary discourse and deliberations about choice within organizations. Empirical studies are needed to investigate such framing effects much more systematically and to develop a naturalistic or naive theory of framing.

Another way of assessing the utility of the intuitive lawyer metaphor is in terms of the light it sheds on the important question of why cooperation fails in social dilemmas. Research on social dilemmas documents that cooperation often fails; voluntary individual actions often fall short of providing much-needed collective goods, and voluntary restraint is often inadequate for maintaining common resource pools over time. In much of the literature, this failure has been analyzed primarily in terms of conflicting rationalities. According to such views, cooperation fails because short-term considerations dominate long-term ones, and individual rationality dominates collective rationality. These analyses imply that at the heart of a social or organizational dilemma is a certain level of choice conflict and that individuals' resolution of such conflict is driven by such things as myopia, fear, and greed. The intuitive lawyer perspective, in contrast, suggests that people may not be so conflicted about their choice as such analyses imply. Indeed, because of their impressive skills as intuitive lawyers, individuals all too easily can feel satisfied with and complacent about their own actions and inactions, sure that they are doing more than their fair share and that it is other people who are falling short in performing their duties and living up to their obligations.

Of course, the intuitive lawyer metaphor does not constitute a complete model of choice behavior in organizational dilemmas. Nor, for that matter, do any of the other models described. Because of the inherent complexity of such dilemmas, any fully developed model would quickly become ungainly. Indeed, this may be one reason why models of organizational decision making so often adopt one or another of several competing metaphors (see March 1994). It may be the case that multiple frames and metaphors are necessary to provide a sufficiently rich, multivariate understanding of choice in social dilemmas.

While the intuitive lawyer metaphor is a very useful one, it also has limitations, especially in terms of the external validity and generalizability of the model. First, in highlighting the role of defensive, self-protective, and self-aggrandizing motives, we have necessarily minimized or ignored motives relating to others. For example, much of our analysis has centered on the assumption that individuals draw a rather sharp disjunction between their rights and responsibilities. Implicitly, we have argued, rights and entitlements dominate duties and obligations. Entitlements loom large, and notions of obligation remain out of sight and out of mind. Yet we can imagine situations where concerns about duty and obligation outweigh entitlements and rights. Research on cooperation in organizations (Kramer 1991) suggests that when identification with an organization or group is psychologically salient, individuals may perceive considerable responsibility and concern for the collective welfare.

Moreover, in elaborating on the rich tool kit available to the intuitive lawyer, we might leave an impression that the ability of the intuitive lawyer to win his or her case is almost unlimited. This may be true when the case is being tried inside the head, but the intuitive lawyer will encounter more serious obstacles when claims become social. In organizations, ethical and moral deliberations are also played out in a social context, in which competing motives and pressures come into play. Accountability to others, for example, will constrain the kinds of self-serving accounts and frames that the intuitive lawyer can readily believe. Thus, a more complete model of ethical cognition in organizational dilemmas should probably posit a contingent perspective on choice (see Tetlock 1991). Such a contingent model would view organizational decision makers as acting sometimes like intuitive scientists engaged in serious attempts at understanding and problem solving, at other times like intuitive politicians concerned about appearing fair and just, and at still other times like the intuitive lawyers we have described.

CONCLUSIONS

More than forty years ago, Solomon Asch (1952) commented, "Although the facts of ethical judgment are problems for psychology, we hardly possess today a description of them, not to mention a theoretical explanation" (p. 251). Asch's observation remains surprisingly contemporary and can be applied with particular force to recent theory and research on social and organizational dilemmas. While choice behavior in such situations raises obvious and profound ethical dilemmas (see, for example, Hardin and Baden 1988), contemporary psychological and organizational theory has generally avoided any systematic exploration of these dimensions. We view the conceptual framework articulated in this chapter as a step toward addressing this neglect.

In a recent assessment of what we have learned from several decades of social science research on judgment and decision making, Philip Tetlock (1992) concluded, "The preponderance of the evidence currently favors a moderately pessimistic assessment of our skills as both intuitive psychologist and economist" (p. 334). In support of this conclusion, Tetlock summarized a large body of evidence documenting the shortcomings and fallibilities of both the intuitive scientist and the intuitive economist. Unfortunately, as we have tried to suggest here, there are many ways in which people seem all too ably equipped as intuitive lawyers. The cognitive tool kit of the intuitive lawyer provides an impressive repertoire of psychological strategies for the construction and maintenance of self-serving views about rights, entitlements, responsibilities, and obligations. In short, we have shown that decision makers, as intuitive lawyers, have ample motive, means, and opportunity.

As noted at the beginning of this chapter, recent theory and research on choice behavior in social dilemmas has, to a large extent, been formulated in terms of rationality. The framework we have advanced here attempts to reformulate such decisions in terms of identity and obligation, in which social identities and rules sometimes take precedence over considerations of rationality. Paraphrasing March (1994), we have tried to articulate here a vision of decision making in organizational dilemmas that is centered around notions of "obligations rather than expectations, of a logic of appropriateness rather than of consequences, and of a sanity of identity rather than rationality" (p. 268).

Like all metaphors, of course, the notion of individuals as intuitive lawyers highlights some features of judgment and choice while obscuring others. A rich and predictive behavioral theory of ethical cognition must incorporate elements from many such perspectives. In the final analysis, the frames and metaphors we adopt for action and inaction are hardly trivial. As George Eliot observed, "All of us get our thoughts entangled in metaphors, and act fatally on the strength of them" (quoted in Hardin 1988, 261).

ENDNOTES

1. We should emphasize that our use of the terms *frame* and *framing* is derived primarily from cognitive (Neisser 1976) and sociological (Goffman 1974) conceptions, rather than from the related but relatively narrower use of the term in recent judgment and decision-making research (for example, Kahneman and Tversky 1984).

2. The term *intuitive lawyer* has been used by a number of other researchers; see, for example, Fincham and Jaspars 1980 and Hamilton 1980.

3. A number of terms have been used to refer to such distinctions, including *give-some versus take-some* games and *public goods versus commons* dilemmas. (See Messick and Brewer 1983 for a more complete review.)

4. There are a number of other ethical theories, including ethical intuitionism, ethical relativism, and ethical egoism, that could be used to understand how individuals construe their ethical obligations in social dilemmas (See Brandt 1961 for a fuller treatment).

5. Missing hero traps (or volunteer dilemmas) might at first glance seem to constitute important exceptions to this principle. Even in those situations, however, one person does not usually completely solve the dilemma. Instead, he or she merely initiates a complex and collective problem-solving process. Thus, although a single whistle-blower may call attention to a serious problem in an organization, the solution to the problem generally requires actions and interventions by a number of decision makers throughout the organization's hierarchy.

6. Social psychological research over the past four decades has provided considerable insight into the full range of psychological tactics that might be employed in the service of the intuitive lawyer's motives and needs, including self-serving causal attributions, overly positive self-evaluation, illusions of control, constructive or self-serving social comparisons, motivated recruitment of the past, derogation of others, and unrealistically positive beliefs about the future. Because extensive treatments of these topics are available elsewhere (see, for example, Allison, Messick, and Goethals 1989; Ashford 1989; Bell and Tetlock 1989; Brown 1986, 1990; Gilovich 1991; Goethals 1986; Goethals, Messick, and Allison 1990; Greenwald 1980; Kramer, Newton and Pommerenke 1993; Kunda 1990; Taylor and Brown 1988; Tyler and Hastie 1991), our discussion will focus on three generic kinds of tactics that we feel are particularly relevant to organizational dilemmas.

7. In suggesting that these three types of frames influence ethical judgment and decision making, we should emphasize that our goal here is to illustrate how frames work rather than to lay out an exhaustive taxonomy of frames. A more complete taxonomy, and one that reflects more systematic empirical data, is clearly needed. Also, our account of framing has necessarily emphasized the motivated or strategic invocation of frames. In advancing such a functionalist account of frames, we need to make the obvious point that framing can also be in the service of other important information-processing goals, such as sense making and problem solving (see Weick 1993).

8. Strategic social categorizations exploit, among other things, the principle of perceptual contrast (see Elsbach and Kramer 1994; Taylor, Wood, and Lichtman 1983).

Chapter 4

Can Socially Responsible Firms Survive in a Competitive Environment?

Robert H. Frank

In his celebrated 1970 article, Milton Friedman wrote that "there is one and only one social responsibility of business—to use its resources and engage in activities designed to increase its profits so long as it stays within the rules of the game, which is to say, engages in open and free competition without deception or fraud" (p. 126). In Friedman's view, managers who pursue broader social goals—say, by adopting more stringent emissions standards than required by law, or by donating corporate funds to charitable organizations—are simply spending other people's money. Firms run by these managers will have higher costs than those run by managers whose goal is to maximize shareholder wealth. According to the standard theory of competitive markets, the latter firms will attract more capital and eventually drive the former firms out of business.

Of course, as Friedman himself clearly recognized, there are many circumstances in which the firm's narrow interests coincide with those of the broader community. He noted, for example, that "it may well be in the long-run interest of a corporation that is a major employer in a small community to devote resources to providing amenities to that community or to improving its government. That may make it easier to attract desirable employees, it may reduce the wage bill or lessen losses from pilferage and sabotage or have other worthwhile effects" (p. 124).

Friedman argued against using the term *social responsibility* to characterize those activities of a firm that, while serving the broader community, also augment the firm's profits. He believes that this language has great potential to mislead politicians and voters about the proper role of the corporation in society and will foster excessive regulation.

The author wishes to thank the editors and two anonymous referees for helpful comments on an earlier draft.

In the years since Friedman wrote this article, the development of the theory of repeated games has given us ever more sophisticated accounts of the forces that often align self-interest with the interests of others. For example, Robert Axelrod (1984) suggests that firms pay their suppliers not because they feel a moral obligation to do so but because they require future shipments from them.

Clearly, repeated interactions often do give rise to behaviors that smack of social responsibility. Yet as Friedman suggested, it is erroneous—or at least misleading—to call these behaviors morally praiseworthy. After all, even a firm whose owners and managers had no concern about the welfare of the broader community would have ample motive to engage in them. When material incentives favor cooperation, it is more descriptive to call the cooperating parties prudent than socially responsible.

It is also an error to assume that repeated interactions always provide ready solutions to social dilemmas and other collective action problems. Even among parties who deal with one another repeatedly, one-shot dilemmas—opportunities for cheating and other opportunistic behavior—often arise. Even a longstanding client of a law firm, for example, has no way to verify that the firm has billed only the number of hours actually worked.

In many cases, the knowledge that opportunities to cheat will arise may preclude otherwise profitable business ventures. Consider a person whose mutual fund has just been taken over by new management. She wants advice about whether to stay with the fund under its new management or switch to a different fund. She considers seeking a consultation, for a fee, from a knowledgeable stockbroker—a mutually beneficial exchange. Yet the investor also knows that a broker's interests may differ from her own. Perhaps, for example, the broker will receive a large commission or finder's fee if the client switches to a new fund. Fearing the consequences of opportunistic behavior, the investor may refrain from seeking advice, in the process depriving both herself and an informed broker of the gains from trade.

When parties to a business transaction confront a one-shot dilemma, their profits will be higher if they defect—that is, if they cheat—than if they cooperate. Yet when each party defects, profits for each are lower than if both had cooperated. In this paper, I will refer to firms that cooperate in one-shot dilemmas as socially responsible firms.

The question I pose is whether such firms can survive in competitive environments. At first glance, it would appear that the answer must be no, for if defecting were indeed a dominant strategy, then socially responsible firms would always have lower returns than pure profit maximizers. Evolutionary models pertaining to individuals have recently shown, however, that conditions often exist in which cooperation in one-shot dilemmas is sustainable in competitive environments. I will review some of this work and suggest that many of its conclusions carry over to populations of competitive firms.

EVOLUTIONARY MODELS OF ONE-SHOT COOPERATION

One of the enduring questions in evolutionary biology is whether altruistic individuals can survive. In this framework, the design criterion for each component of human motivation is the same as for an arm or a leg or an eye: To what extent does it assist the individual in the struggle to acquire the resources required for survival and reproduction? If it works better than the available alternatives, selection pressure will favor it. Otherwise, selection pressure will work against it (see Dawkins 1976, especially chapter 3).

At first glance, this theoretical structure appears to throw its weight squarely behind the self-interest conception of human motivation. Indeed, if natural selection favors the traits and behaviors that maximize individual reproductive fitness, and if we *define* behaviors that enhance personal fitness as selfish, then self-interest becomes the only viable human motive by definition. This tautology was a central message of much of the sociobiological literature of the 1970s and 1980s.

On closer look, however, the issues are not so simple. There are many situations in which individuals whose only goal is self-interest are likely to be especially bad at acquiring and holding resources. Thomas Schelling (1960) provided a vivid illustration with his account of a kidnapper who gets cold feet and wants to set his victim free but fears that if he does so, the victim will go to the police. The victim promises to remain silent. The problem, however, is that both he and the kidnapper know that it will not be in the victim's narrow self-interest to keep this promise once he is free. And so the kidnapper reluctantly concludes that he must kill his victim.

Suppose, however, that the victim were not a narrowly self-interested person but rather a person of honor. If this fact could somehow be communicated to the kidnapper, their problem would be solved. The kidnapper could set the victim free, secure in the knowledge that even though it would then be in the victim's interests to go to the police, he would not want to do so.

Schelling's kidnapper and victim face a *commitment problem*, a situation in which they have an incentive to commit themselves to behave in a way that will later seem contrary to self-interest. Such problems are a common feature of social life. Consider, for example, the farmer who is trying to deter a transient thief from stealing his ox. Suppose this farmer is known to be a narrowly self-interested rational person. If the thief knows that the farmer's cost of pursuing him exceeds the value of the ox, he can then steal the ox with impunity. But suppose that the farmer cares also about not being victimized, quite independently of the effect of victimization on his wealth. If he holds this goal with sufficient force, and if the potential thief knows of the farmer's commitment, the ox will no longer be such an inviting target.

In the one-shot prisoner's dilemma, if the two players cooperate, each does better than if both defect, and yet each individual gets a higher payoff by defecting no matter which strategy the other player chooses. Both players thus have a clear incentive to commit themselves to cooperate. Yet a mere promise issued by a narrowly self-interested person clearly will not suffice, for his partner knows he will have no incentive to keep this promise. If both players know one another to be honest, however, both could reap the gains of cooperation.

In both these examples, note that merely having the relevant motivations or goals is by itself insufficient to solve the problem. It is also necessary that the presence of these goals be discernible by others. Someone with a predisposition to cooperate in the one-shot prisoner's dilemma, for instance, is in fact at a disadvantage unless others can identify that predisposition in him and he can identify similar predispositions in others.

Can the moral sentiments and other psychological forces that often drive people to ignore narrow self-interest be reliably discerned by outsiders? A recent study (Frank, Gilovich, and Regan 1993) found that subjects were surprisingly accurate at predicting who would cooperate and who would defect in one-shot prisoner's dilemmas played with near strangers.

In our study, the base rate of cooperation was 73.7 percent, the base rate of defection only 26.3 percent. A random prediction of cooperation would thus have been accurate 73.7 percent of the time, a random prediction of defection accurate only 26.3 percent of the time. The actual accuracy rates for these two kinds of prediction were 80.7 percent and 56.8 percent, respectively. The likelihood of such high accuracy rates occurring by chance is less than one in one thousand.

Subjects in this experiment were strangers at the outset and were able to interact with one another for only thirty minutes before making their predictions.[1] It is plausible to suppose that predictions would be considerably more accurate for people we have known for a long time. For example, consider a thought experiment based on the following scenario:

> An individual has a gallon jug of unwanted pesticide. To protect the environment, the law requires that unused pesticide be turned in to a government disposal facility located thirty minutes' drive from her home. She knows, however, that she could simply pour the pesticide down her basement drain with no chance of being caught and punished. She also knows that her one gallon of pesticide, by itself, will cause only negligible harm if disposed of in this fashion.

Now the thought experiment: Can you think of anyone who you feel certain would dispose of the pesticide properly? Most people respond affirmatively, and usually they have in mind someone they have known for a long time. If you answer yes, then you, too, accept the central premise of the commitment model—namely, that it is possible to identify non-self-interested motives in at least some other people.

The presence of such motives, coupled with the ability of others to discern them, makes it possible to solve commitment problems of the sort that have been presented. Knowing that others could discern her motives, even a rational, self-interested individual would have every reason to choose preferences that were not narrowly self-interested. Of course, people do not choose their preferences in any literal sense. The point is that if moral sentiments can be reliably discerned by others, the complex interaction of genes and culture that yields human preferences can sustain preferences that lead people to subordinate narrow self-interest in the pursuit of other goals.

AN EQUILIBRIUM MIX OF MOTIVES

It might seem that if moral sentiments help solve important commitment problems, then evolutionary forces would assure that everyone have a full measure of these sentiments. But a closer look at the interplay between selfish and other-regarding motives suggests that this is unlikely (see Frank 1988, chapter 3, for an extended discussion of this point). Imagine, for example, an environment populated by two types of people, cooperators and defectors. And suppose that people earn their livelihood by interacting in pairs, where the commitment problem they confront is the one-shot prisoner's dilemma.

If cooperators and defectors were perfectly indistinguishable, interactions would occur on a random basis and the average payoffs would always be larger for the defectors (owing to the dominance of defection in all prisoner's dilemmas). In evolutionary models, the rule governing population dynamics is that each type reproduces in proportion to its material payoff relative to other types. This implies that if the two types were indistinguishable, the eventual result would be extinction for the cooperators. In highly simplified form, this is the Darwinian story that inclines many social scientists to believe that self-interest is the only important human motive.

But now suppose that cooperators were distinguishable at a glance from defectors. Then interaction would no longer take place on a random basis. Rather, the cooperators would pair off systematically with one another to reap the benefits of mutual cooperation. Defectors would be left to interact with one another, and would receive the lower payoff associated with these pairings. The eventual result this time is that the defectors would be driven to extinction.

Neither of these two polar cases seems descriptive of actual populations, which typically contain a mix of cooperators and defectors. Such a mixed population is precisely the result we get if we make one small modification to the original story. Again suppose that cooperators are observably different from defectors, but that some effort is required to make the distinction. If the population initially consisted almost entirely of cooperators, it would not pay to expend this effort because one would be overwhelmingly likely to achieve a high payoff merely by interacting at random with another person. In such an environment, cooperators would cease to be vigilant in their choice of trading partners. Defectors would then find a ready pool of victims, and their resulting higher payoffs would cause their share of the total population to grow.

As defectors became more numerous, however, it would begin to pay cooperators to exercise greater vigilance in their choice of partners. With sufficient defectors in the population, cooperators would be vigilant in the extreme, and we would again see pairings among like types only. That, in turn, would cause the prevalence of cooperators to grow. At some point, a stable balance would be struck in which cooperators were just vigilant enough to prevent further encroachment by defectors. The average payoff to the two types would be the same, and their population shares would remain constant. There would be, in other words, a stable niche for each type.

FIVE WAYS A SOCIALLY RESPONSIBLE FIRM MIGHT PROSPER

The commitment model just described shows how it is possible for cooperative individuals to survive in competitive environments. What does this model have to say about the possibilities for survival of socially responsible firms? Recall that the socially responsible firm's problem is that by cooperating in one-shot dilemmas, it receives a lower payoff than do firms that defect. In the sections to follow, I will describe five possible areas in which the socially responsible firm might compensate for that disadvantage. The first three involve the recognition of potential commitment problems that arise within firms and between firms and the outside world. The last two involve the fact that people value socially responsible action and are willing to pay for it in the marketplace, even when they do not benefit from it directly in a material sense.

By Solving Commitment Problems with Employees

Just as commitment problems arise between independent individuals, so too do they arise among owners, managers, and employees. Many of these problems, like those among independent individuals, hinge on perceptions of trustworthiness and fairness. Some examples:

SHIRKING AND OPPORTUNISM.   The owner of a business perceives an opportunity to open a branch in a distant city. He knows that if he can hire an honest manager, the branch will be highly profitable. He cannot monitor the manager, however, and if the manager cheats, the branch will be unprofitable. By cheating, the manager can earn three times as much as he could by being honest. This situation defines a commitment problem. If the owner lacks the ability to identify an honest manager, the venture cannot go forward, but if he has that ability, he can pay the manager well and still earn an attractive return.

PIECE RATES.   In cases where individual productivity can be measured with reasonable accuracy, economic theory identifies piece-rate pay schemes as a simple and attractive way to elicit effort from workers. Workers, however, are notoriously suspicious of piece rates. They fear that if they work as hard as they can and do well under an existing piece rate, management will step in and reduce the rate. There is indeed a large literature that describes the elaborate subterfuges employed by workers to prevent this from happening and numerous cases in which piece rates were abandoned although they had led to significant increases in productivity. If piece-rate decisions were placed in the hands of someone who had earned the workers' trust, both owners and workers would gain.

CAREER LOCK-IN.   Many of the skills one acquires on the job are firm-specific. By accepting long-term employment with a single firm, a worker can anticipate that the day will come when her particular mix of skills, although still of value to her employer, will be of relatively little value in the market at large. And with her outside opportunities diminished, she will find herself at her employer's mercy. Firms have a narrow self-interest, of course, in establishing a reputation for treating workers fairly under these circumstances, for a good reputation will aid them in their recruiting efforts.

But many workers will find that the firm's self-interest alone may not provide adequate security. A firm may determine, for example, that its employment base will shift overseas during the coming years, and therefore that diminished recruiting ability in the domestic market is not a serious problem. Any firm believed to be motivated only by economic self-interest would thus have been at a recruiting disadvantage from the very beginning. By contrast, a firm whose management can persuade workers that fair treatment of workers is a goal valued for its own sake will have its pick of the most able and attractive workers.

RISING WAGE PROFILES.   It is a common pattern in industrial pay schemes for pay to rise more rapidly than productivity. A worker's pay is less than the value of his productivity early in his career, and it rises until it is more than the value of his productivity later in his career. Various reasons are offered for this pattern. One is that it discourages shirking, for the worker knows that if he is caught shirking, he may not survive to enjoy the premium pay of the out years. A second rationale is that workers simply like upward-sloping wage profiles. Given a choice between two jobs with the same present value of lifetime income, one with a flat wage profile and the other with a rising profile, most people opt for the second. Whatever the reason for upward-sloping wage profiles, they create an incentive for opportunistic behavior on the part of employers, who stand to gain by firing workers once their pay begins to exceed their productivity. Given the advantages of upward-sloping wage profiles, a firm whose management can be trusted not to renege on its implicit contract stands at a clear advantage.

OTHER IMPLICIT CONTRACTS.   A firm with a skilled legal department might be able to devise some formal contractual arrangement whereby it could commit itself not to fire older workers. But such a contract would entail a potentially costly loss of flexibility. No firm can be certain of the future demand for its product, and the time may come when its survival may depend on its ability to reduce its work force. Both the firm and its workers would pay a price if this flexibility were sacrificed.

There are a host of other contingencies that might seriously affect the terms of the bargain between employers and workers. Many of these contingencies are impossible to foresee and hence impossible to resolve in advance by formal contractual arrangements. Any firm whose management can persuade workers that these contingencies will be dealt with in an equitable manner will have a clear advantage in attracting the most able workers.

By Solving Commitment Problems with Customers

A variety of commitment problems arise between firms and their customers, and at least some of these are amenable to solution along lines similar to those just discussed. Quality assurance is a clear example.

George Akerlof's celebrated paper on lemons (1970) describes a commitment problem in which sellers and buyers alike would benefit if the seller could somehow commit to providing a product or service of high quality. A variety of means have been suggested for solving this problem through reliance on material incentives. Firms can guarantee their products, for example, or they can develop public reputations for supplying high quality (see Klein and Leffler 1981).

Many forms of the quality assurance problem, however, cannot be solved by manipulating material incentives. Consider a law firm that could provide the legal services a client wants at a price the client would be willing to pay. But suppose that the client has no way to evaluate the quality of his lawyer's services. The outcome of his case by itself is not diagnostic. He might win despite having received shoddy legal help, or he might lose despite having received the best possible help. In such situations, clients are willing to pay premium fees to a firm run by someone they feel they can trust.

By Solving Commitment Problems with Other Firms

Commitment problems also arise in the context of business transactions between firms, and here too solutions that rely on character assessment often play a role.

THE SUBCONTRACTOR HOLDUP PROBLEM. Consider the familiar example of the subcontractor that does most of its business with a single buyer. To serve this buyer at the lowest possible price, much of the subcontractor's human and physical capital has to be tailored to the buyer's specific needs. Having made those investments, however, the subcontractor is vulnerable to the holdup problem; because the buyer knows that the subcontractor's customized assets cost more than they would bring in the open market, it can pay its subcontractor a price that is above the subcontractor's marginal cost but lower than its average cost. Anticipating this problem, subcontractors will be willing to invest in the capital that best serves their customers' needs only if they believe their partners can be trusted not to exploit them.

In a recent study, Edward Lorenz (1988) spelled out why material incentives are inadequate to solve the commitment problems that arise between small French manufacturing firms and their subcontractors. He described in detail how parties shop for trustworthy partners. For example, all the respondents in his sample emphasized the heavy weight they placed on personal relationships in this process.

QUALITY ASSURANCE. The problem of quality assurance arises not just between firms and consumers but also between one firm and another. Consider, for example, the relationship between a parent company and its franchisees. When a franchise owner provides high-quality service to the public he enhances not just his own reputation with local consumers but also the reputations of other outlets. The parent firm would like him to take both these benefits into account in setting his service levels, but his private incentives are to focus only on how good service affects his own customers. Accordingly, it is common for franchise agreements to call on franchisees to provide higher quality service than would otherwise be in their interests to provide. Franchisers incur costs in the attempt to enforce these agreements, but their ability to monitor service at the local level is highly imperfect. The franchiser thus has a strong incentive to recruit franchisees who assign intrinsic value to living up to their service agreements. And prospective franchisees so identified are at a competitive advantage over those motivated by self-interest alone.

MAINTAINING CONFIDENTIALITY. Many consulting firms provide services that require access to competitively sensitive information. Clearly no firm could succeed in this line of work if it acquired a reputation for making such information available to rivals. When employees leave these firms, however, their material incentives to maintain confidentiality fall considerably. In some cases, material incentives to maintain confidentiality are weakened by the fact that a number of people have had access to the sensitive information, so that it is much harder to trace the source of a leak. With these possibilities in mind, a client would be much more willing to deal with a consulting firm that is able to identify and attract employees who assign intrinsic value to honoring confidentiality agreements.

In the examples just discussed, firms compensate for the higher costs of socially responsible behavior by their ability to solve commitment problems. In addition, socially responsible firms benefit from a match with the moral values of socially responsible consumers and recruits.

By Reflecting Consumers' Moral Values

The standard free-rider model suggests that buyers will not be willing to pay a premium for products produced by socially responsible firms. For example, consumers may not like the fact that Acme Tire Corporation pollutes the air, but they are said to realize that their own purchase of Acme tires will have a virtually unmeasurable effect on air quality. Accordingly, the theory predicts, if Acme tires sell for even a little less than those produced by a rival with a cleaner technology, consumers will buy from Acme.

The commitment model challenges this account by showing that many people have come to develop a taste for socially responsible behavior. People with such a taste will prefer dealing with socially responsible firms even when they realize that their own purchases are too small to affect the outcomes they care about. Conventional free-rider theory predicted that Star Kist Tuna's sales and profits would fall when it raised its prices to cover the added cost of purchasing tuna only from suppliers who used dolphin-safe nets. Star Kist's sales and profits went up, however, not down. Any consumer who stopped to ponder the matter would know that a single household's tuna purchase would have no discernible impact on the fate of dolphins. Even so, it appears that many consumers were willing to pay higher prices in the name of a cause they cared about. There is also evidence that Ben & Jerry's sells more ice cream because of its preservation efforts on behalf of Amazon rain forests, that The Body Shop sells more cosmetics because of its environmentally friendly packaging, and that McDonald's sells more hamburgers because of its support for the parents of seriously ill children.

Experimental evidence from the "dictator game" provides additional evidence of consumers' willingness to incur costs on behalf of moral values. The dictator game is played by two players. The first is given a sum of money— say, $20—and is then asked to choose one of two ways of dividing it with the second player: either $10 each or $18 for the first player and $2 for the second. One study (Kahneman, Knetsch, and Thaler 1986) found that more than three-quarters of subjects chose the $10–$10 split. The researchers then described this experiment to a separate group of subjects, to whom they then gave a choice between splitting $10 with one of the subjects who had chosen the $10–$10 split or splitting $12 with one of the subjects who had chosen the $18–$2 split. More than 80 percent of these subjects chose the first option, which the authors of the study interpreted as a willingness to spend $1 to punish an anonymous stranger who had behaved unfairly in the earlier experiment.

Taken together, the market data and experimental evidence appear to shift the burden of proof to proponents of the free-rider hypothesis.

By Reflecting Prospective Employees' Moral Values

A fifth and final benefit that accrues to socially responsible firms is the relative advantage they enjoy in recruiting. Jobs differ in countless dimensions, one of which is the degree to which the worker contributes to the well-being of others. Consider two jobs identical along all dimensions except this one. (For example, one job might involve writing advertising copy for a product known to cause serious health problems, while the other involves writing advertising copy for the United Way.) If people derive satisfaction from engaging in altruistic behavior, it follows that if the wages in these two jobs were the same, there would be an excess supply of applicants to the second job, a shortage of applicants to the first. In equilibrium, we would therefore expect a compensating wage premium for the less altruistic job. A job applicant who wants to occupy the moral high ground can do so only by accepting lower wages. And these lower wages, in turn, help balance the higher costs of socially responsible operations.

In a recent study (Frank 1993), I attempted to quantify this advantage. The study included both experimental and empirical components; the results are described in the sections that follow.

SALARY DIFFERENTIALS IN THE CORNELL EMPLOYMENT SURVEY. Cornell University's career center recently completed an employment survey of recent graduates of the university's College of Arts and Sciences. This survey provided information on the current activities of respondents nine months after their graduation from Cornell. For those who were gainfully employed, the survey recorded information on annual salary, job title, and name and location of employer. Taking special steps to protect the anonymity of respondents, I was able to match the individual survey response forms with the college transcript of each respondent. Thus, unlike standard employment survey data sets, my data made it possible to control for the respondent's degree field as well as a rich variety of other details related to academic performance. And since almost all these data pertained to first jobs, I had access to almost as much information as did the employers who did the actual hiring.

By examining annual reports and other available records for each employer represented in the survey, I was able to categorize the employers as belonging to either the for-profit, the nonprofit, or the government sector of the economy. These categories provided at least a crude measure of the degree of social responsibility associated with the respondents' jobs, with employment in the nonprofit sector rated highest, government next, and the for-profit sector last on the social responsibility scale.

In the Cornell sample, a person employed by a private, for-profit firm earned a salary more than 13 percent larger than she would have if she were employed by government. A person working for a nonprofit firm, by contrast, earned almost 29 percent less than she would have in a government job. Thus, even after controlling for gender, curriculum, and academic performance, employees of for-profit firms in our sample earned roughly 59 percent more, on average, than did employees of nonprofit firms.

This is an enormous salary gap. Of course, the entire gap is not necessarily attributable to compensating differentials for social responsibility in the nonprofit sector. For example, some of the difference may be the result of unmeasured productivity differences between nonprofit and for-profit workers. But given the relative homogeneity of graduating classes at universities like Cornell, and given our ability to control for curriculum and academic performance, it would be difficult to maintain that unmeasured productivity differences could account for a large share of the nonprofit wage deficit. There is certainly no evidence in our data that nonprofit workers were any less motivated or capable as undergraduate students. In fact, nonprofit employees in our sample had slightly higher grade point averages than did for-profit employees. Nonprofit workers also had taken an average of almost five more science courses than had for-profit employees.

Another possibility is that dimensions of job satisfaction other than social responsibility may differ systematically between the nonprofit and for-profit sectors. At least some of these differences, however, seemed to favor the for-profit sector. For example, the average level of office space and other physical amenities in the workplace was higher in the for-profit than in the nonprofit sector, as were travel allowances and other nonsalary compensation items. Such differences suggest that the true compensation gap between nonprofit and for-profit firms may be even larger than suggested by the data.

In a second study using the Cornell data, I had a panel of second-year graduate students in a business ethics course rate the subjects' occupations and employers on a 7-point social responsibility scale ranging from least responsible (-3) to most responsible ($+3$).

Figure 4.1 summarizes the estimated compensating differentials for social responsibility thus measured. (For details on how the social responsibility measures were compressed to form the intervals shown in the diagram, see my paper.) As the figure shows, salaries fall dramatically with increases in social responsibility, even after controlling for gender, curriculum, academic performance, and sector of employment.

Figure 4.1. / Compensating Salary Differentials for Social Responsibility

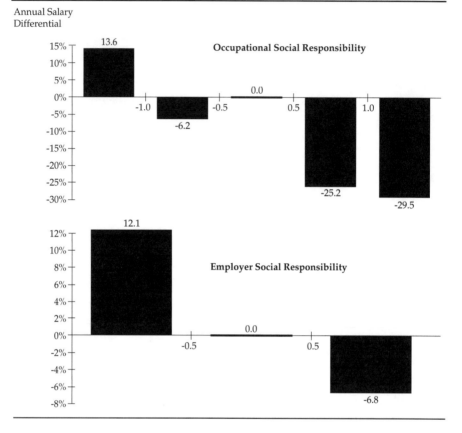

These estimates are remarkably large. As noted, they are based on frag-
mentary measures of occupational and employer social responsibility and
should for this reason be regarded as tentative. But as the sections to follow
suggest, they are broadly consistent with evidence from a variety of sources.

SALARY DIFFERENTIALS BETWEEN CORPORATE AND PUBLIC-INTEREST LAW.
Another source of evidence on the strength of unselfish motives comes in
the form of salary differentials between public-interest lawyers and corporate lawyers. When the public-interest law movement expanded rapidly in
the 1960s, the salary differences between public-interest lawyers and other
attorneys were small, on the order of only a few thousand dollars per year.
In the intervening years, however, salaries in public-interest law have risen
only modestly, while compensation in other areas of the law has mush-
roomed. As a result, there is now a very large gap between public-interest
and other legal salaries. For example, the average starting salary for public-
interest lawyers in 1987 was only $23,843, as compared with $39,847 for all

other lawyers in their first year of private practice (*The National Law Journal*, March 27, 1989, 18).[2]

The gap between starting salaries for public-interest lawyers and first-year associates in private law firms is even larger. Table 4.1 shows 1989 starting salaries for a small sample of institutions in these two categories.

At least in the case of public-interest firms in large cities, there is no indication that the lower salaries in public-interest law reflect inferior talent. Writing in the *National Law Journal*, a trade newspaper for the legal profession, Jamienne Studley (1989) reported that "well-known policy and advocacy organizations are typically deluged with excellent applicants" (p. 16). Indeed, such groups are often able to attract law review graduates from the nation's elite law schools, people who could have had their pick from among the choicest entry-level jobs in the legal profession and earned a far higher salary (see table 4.1).

FEES FOR EXPERT WITNESS TESTIMONY.   During the past several decades, a series of legislative hearings has been held concerning public policy issues related to tobacco smoke. Many of the early hearings focused on whether people who smoke cigarettes are more likely than others to contract various pulmonary and cardiovascular diseases. More recently, the hearings have focused on whether exposure to "second-hand" smoke in the environment is a public health hazard. Throughout all these hearings, there is a common pattern of expert witness testimony. On one side, witnesses associated with the American Cancer Society, the American Heart Association, the American Lung Association, and other public-interest groups testify to the effect that tobacco smoke is a significant causal factor in the health problems at issue. On the opposing side, witnesses sponsored by the Tobacco Institute and other industry groups testify that the health risks associated with tobacco smoke are either unproved or highly exaggerated. Since 1964, when the first Surgeon General's report appeared identifying cigarette smoke as a major

Table 4.1   /   1989 Starting Salaries for Private and Public-Interest Lawyers

First-Year Public-Interest Lawyers	First-Year Associates in Private Law Firms
American Civil Liberties Union, New York: $28,000	Millbank, Tweed, Hadley & McCoy, New York: $83,000
Center for Constitutional Rights, New York: $29,000	Skadden, Arps, Slate, Meagher & Flom, New York: $83,000
People for the American Way, Washington, D.C.: $25,000	Arent, Fox, Kintner, Plotkin & Kahn, Washington, D.C.: $66,000 + $2,000 signing bonus
Public Citizen Litigation Group, Washington, D.C.: $21,000	Dow, Lohnes & Albertson, Washington, D.C.: $67,000.

Source: National Law Journal, March 26, 1990.

public health hazard, there has been a growing perception that advocates of the industry's position in these hearings are morally suspect. By now it seems fair to say that a large percentage of the population shares the perception that witnesses for the public-interest groups occupy the moral high ground in the tobacco hearings.

The compensation differentials for the expert witnesses associated with the two sides reflect this perception. Almost without exception, expert witnesses for the public-interest groups appear without charge, in many cases even paying their own travel expenses. Industry witnesses, by contrast, are compensated handsomely. One source, a senior scientific research professional formerly associated with the tobacco industry, reported that the current "official" rate for industry expert witnesses was in the range of $200 to $250 per hour. This source, who asked not to be identified, also reported that because the industry has an obvious interest in keeping its official witness fees low, the actual rate of compensation in many cases far exceeds the official hourly rate. The difference is achieved in a variety of ways. For instance, witnesses might be paid at the official hourly rate for activities only peripherally related to their testimony, such as "keeping up with the literature" or attending professional meetings and conferences. Whatever the total compensation for industry witnesses may be, it is substantial by any standard, certainly far in excess of the payments received by witnesses who appear on behalf of public-interest groups (again, in most cases, these are zero).

Tobacco industry sources make no pretense that the higher fees received by their witnesses are necessitated by superior professional credentials. On the contrary, all available evidence suggests that the volunteer witnesses for the public interest groups are much more professionally distinguished than their tobacco industry counterparts. Most members of the volunteer group are active scientific researchers who hold faculty positions at prestigious universities and medical schools. Most tobacco industry witnesses, by contrast, describe themselves as affiliates of private consulting firms and do not conduct ongoing programs of scientific research. As one former tobacco industry expert witness told me, "At this point, I know of only a few academics who still testify on behalf of the industry. All the others are consultants whose scientific thought process stopped years ago."

RESERVATION PAY PREMIUM SURVEY. The final component of my 1993 study is based on a survey of the employment preferences of a sample of Cornell graduating seniors. In this survey, students were asked to consider six pairs of hypothetical job descriptions. Within each pair of jobs, the pay, working conditions, and specific tasks involved were described as being essentially the same, but the nature of the two businesses differed (for example, "write advertisements for the American Cancer Society" versus "write advertisements for Camel cigarettes"). The six pairs of jobs are listed in table 4.2.

Table 4.2   /   Six Hypothetical Career Decisions

Ad copywriter
    for Camel cigarettes
	Ad copywriter for the
	    American Cancer Society

Accountant for a large petrochemical company	Accountant for a large art museum
Language teacher for the CIA	Language teacher for a local high school
Recruiter for Exxon	Recruiter for the Peace Corps
Lawyer for the National Rifle Association	Lawyer for the Sierra Club
Chemist for Union Carbide	Chemist for Dow Chemical

Subjects were first asked which of the two jobs in each pair they would choose if each paid a salary of $30,000 per year. They were then asked how much higher the salary would have to be in the job not chosen for them to reverse their decision.[3] As expected, the overwhelming majority of subjects indicated a preference for the jobs in the right column of table 4.2.[4] The proportions choosing these jobs and the average and median pay premiums required for switching are reported in table 4.3.

The reservation pay premiums reported by these subjects are large by almost any standard. Of course, it is hard to know whether subjects would really require premiums this large when confronted with an actual opportunity to switch to a less morally attractive but higher-paying job. It is possible, for example, that people might report high premiums when asked to consider such job changes in the abstract and yet be willing to switch for significantly smaller amounts when confronted with the reality of personal budget problems. Bear in mind, however, that we saw compensating differentials on an even larger scale in the case of public-interest lawyers and their counterparts in private law firms. And even if the actual reservation premiums were only one-tenth as large as those reported by our survey respon-

Table 4.3   /   Reservation Pay Premiums for Sacrificing the Moral High Ground

	Percent Choosing	Median Pay Premium for Switching ($)	Average Pay Premium for Switching ($)
Amer. Cancer Society	88.2	15,000/yr	24,333/yr
Art museum	79.4	5,000/yr	14,185/yr
High school	82.4	8,000/yr	18,679/yr
Peace Corps	79.4	5,000/yr	13,037/yr
Sierra Club	94.1	10,000/yr	37,129/yr*
Dow Chemical	79.4	2,000/yr	11,796/yr

*Excludes one response of $1,000,000,000,000/yr.

dents, they would still constitute a highly significant feature of the contemporary labor market.

CONCLUSIONS

When a business confronts an ethical dilemma, it must incur higher costs if it takes the high road. For example, in the process of refusing to supply master automobile keys to mail-order customers he believes to be car thieves, a locksmith sustains a penalty on the bottom line. Indeed, if the morally preferred action involved no such penalty, there would be no moral dilemmas.

In this chapter, I have described five advantages that help a socially responsible firm to compensate for the higher direct costs of its actions. Three of these involve the ability to avoid commitment problems and other one-shot dilemmas. The socially responsible firm is better able than its opportunistic rivals to solve commitment problems that might arise with employees, with customers, and with other firms. A fourth advantage is that buyers are often willing to pay more for the products of socially responsible firms. And finally, the socially responsible firm often enjoys an advantage when recruiting against its less responsible rivals. Taken together, these advantages often appear to be sufficient to offset the higher costs of socially responsible action.

This claim may invite the complaint that what I am calling socially responsible behavior is really just selfishness by another name. Consider this trenchant commentary by Albert Carr, an economic advisor to Harry Truman:

> The illusion that business can afford to be guided by ethics as conceived in private life is often fostered by speeches and articles containing such phrases as, "It pays to be ethical," or, "Sound ethics is good business." Actually this is not an ethical question at all; it is a self-serving calculation in disguise. The speaker is really saying that in the long run a company can make more money if it does not antagonize competitors, suppliers, employees, and customers by squeezing them too hard. He is saying that oversharp policies reduce ultimate gains. That is true, but it has nothing to do with ethics (Carr 1968, 148).

This line of reasoning implies that any business behavior consistent with survival is selfish by definition. Such a definition, however, is completely at odds with our everyday understanding of the concept. Cooperation in one-shot dilemmas is costly in both the short run and the long run, and for that reason it is properly called unselfish. I have argued that because traits of character are discernible by others, the kinds of people who cooperate in one-shot dilemmas enjoy advantages in other spheres, and these advantages may help them survive in competition with less scrupulous rivals. It simply invites confusion to call the cooperative behaviors themselves self-serving.

ENDNOTES

1. In the version of the experiment reported here, subjects were permitted to discuss the PD game itself, and, if they chose, to make promises concerning their strategy choices.

2. One apparent effect of this growing salary gap has been a steady reduction in the proportion of law graduates accepting employment in the public interest sector. According to surveys done by the National Association for Law Placement, the percentage of law graduates taking public-interest jobs fell from 5.9 percent in 1978 to 3.0 percent in 1986.

3. The exact wording of the instructions to subjects was as follows:

   Several pairs of jobs are described on the list below. All of these jobs offer a starting salary of $30,000/year. The jobs in each pair are located in the same city, and both involve working the same number of hours each week. The actual tasks you perform in each job are essentially the same, as are all relevant fringe benefits (pensions, paid vacations, insurance, etc.). The *only real difference* between the jobs in each pair involves the nature of the employer's line of business. In one of the blank spaces provided next to each job, check the member of each pair of jobs that you would accept if you had to choose one or the other. Then in the blank space below the job you did *not* choose, write the minimum annual salary required for you to switch your job choice. To illustrate, suppose that in the first pair of jobs you choose to work for The American Cancer Society when both jobs pay $30,000/year. You should then use the blank space below the Camel Cigarettes job to indicate how high its salary would have to be for you to switch. For example, if you say $40,000, that means that if Camel paid $39,999 or less you would still choose The American Cancer Society, but that for $40,000 or more you would choose Camel.

4. On the actual survey form completed by subjects, the more attractive job for a given pair sometimes appeared on the right, sometimes on the left.

Chapter 5

Beyond the Hidden Self: Psychological and Ethical Aspects of Privacy in Organizations

Robert J. Bies

Civilization is the progress toward a society of privacy.

Ayn Rand, *The Fountainhead*

When people express concerns about privacy, it is usually in the context of "Big Brother" (Orwell 1949) and governmental intrusions into their private lives. Whether in the context of illegal governmental wiretapping and surveillance (for example, Watergate and the John Lennon case), Internal Revenue Service employees "perusing" taxpayer records (MacDonald and Tritch 1993), or the gathering of evidence at crime scenes (as in the O. J. Simpson case), privacy is an issue of central social importance.

In recent years, concerns about privacy have emerged in a new context, the work organization. As the value of information increases and new technologies emerge to gather that information (Smith 1994), there is evidence that employees in organizations are troubled about threats to their privacy (Hoerr and others 1988; H. J. Smith 1994). Surveys find that employees feel strongly that organizations ask for more sensitive information than is necessary (Harris and Westin 1979; Vidmar and Flaherty 1985). Employees have also expressed concerns about the use of video monitors in employee restrooms or locker rooms and listening devices in employee cafeterias and about the monitoring of employees to ensure that they do not spend too long in the bathroom (Bowers 1993).

There is also evidence suggesting that these concerns about privacy invasion are well founded. For example, one study of 301 businesses, large and small, reported that one in five companies routinely eavesdropped on its employees and more than 70 percent of the companies used some form of electronic eavesdropping method over a two-year period (Jacobs 1994). Another study reported that over 20 percent of the businesses surveyed reported searching employee files and e-mail messages without notifying the employees (Cappel 1993), an issue of growing legal controversy (Blackburn, Klayman, and Nathan 1993).

Concerns about privacy invasion are not limited to lower-level employees; the upper levels of management have also become the target of surveillance and privacy invasion. For example, there is evidence that Procter & Gamble officials have accessed employee medical records, monitored employee home telephone conversations, and conducted covert surveillance of top management on business trips (Swasy 1993). As a result, privacy is quickly becoming an important issue on organizational agendas (Culnan, Smith, and Bies 1994). Indeed, as Paul Saffo, of the Institute for the Future, put it: "After health care, privacy in the workplace may be the most important social issue in the 1990s" (quoted in Hoerr and others 1988, 61).

Privacy is a multifaceted issue. For example, in their comprehensive review and analysis of research on organizational privacy, Eugene Stone and Dianna Stone (1990) identify three major perspectives on privacy in the literature: privacy as *information control*, privacy as *the regulation of interactions with others*, and privacy as *freedom of control from others*. In this chapter, I will focus on the information control perspective and its implications for understanding individual privacy concerns. I recognize that there is considerable overlap among the three perspectives identified by Stone and Stone, but given the scope of this chapter I will limit my detailed analysis to concerns about information control, although implications of the other two perspectives for understanding related privacy concerns are addressed at the end of the chapter. My primary focus will be on the psychology of privacy and how organizations manage privacy issues strategically, in the process creating ethical dilemmas and paradoxically sometimes doing greater harm and undermining broader societal interests of social justice. I begin by examining the forces that have made privacy an ethical issue in organizations.

FORCES MAKING PRIVACY AN ISSUE: THE ORGANIZATIONAL AND ETHICAL CONTEXT

Imagine that you have just been named the Chief Executive Officer (CEO) of a Fortune 500 consumer products company that has, until recently, been very successful in the competitive global marketplace. In fact, the reason you have been appointed to this position is to turn around the company's fortunes so that it regains global excellence. From previous experience, you know that motivating and managing the company's multicultural work force to achieve high performance will be one of the keys to your success. But, as you also remember from your wise organizational-behavior professor, creating a high-performance organization is no easy task. Organizations are collections of people with different backgrounds and motives, and without "perfect information" about what motivates them to work cooperatively as a team and achieve high performance, your task of turning the company around will be extremely challenging, if not impossible.

One night you lie awake, wrestling with what you should do to turn the company around. Falling back on your Jesuit education in high school and college, you pray to your guardian angel: "If only you could help me get perfect information about every person who works in the company. With perfect information I could motivate them to excellence and go down in history as one of the great global business leaders."

Just as you finish your prayer, a mystical figure appears and speaks thusly: "I have heard your prayer and have come to answer your request. Since you are familiar with the Jesuit perspective, you know that you will be asked to make a choice. So let me present you with two alternatives."

Alternative 1: As per your prayer, you will have perfect information about each and every one of your employees. You will know *everything* about them, including their life histories and knowledge of all their innermost thoughts, fears, hopes, and dreams. You will know what motivates them, what makes them "tick."

You interrupt, saying with great delight, "Oh, thank you, thank you." But the mystical figure responds, "I am not finished describing the alternative." The angel continues,

Not only will you have perfect information about the employees, the employees will know *everything* about you, too. They will know every aspect of your life history, and they will know every one of your innermost thoughts, fears, hopes, and dreams—including your thoughts and feelings about them. Indeed, they will know what motivates you, what makes you "tick."

"Wait one cosmic minute. I'm not so sure I want everybody to know everything about me." The mystical figure responds, "Well, then, listen to the second alternative."

Alternative 2: Instead of perfect information, you will have no information about any of your employees. You will know *nothing* about them and their life histories. Your employees' innermost thoughts, fears, hopes, and dreams will be a "black box"; you won't even know what they think or feel about you. But, at the same time, you will be completely hidden to them. They will never know anything about you. They will not know any of your innermost thoughts, fears, hopes, and dreams—or how you think or feel about them. Neither of you will know what motivates or what makes the other "tick."

You interrupt again: "But this is not fair, this is not real. Life is not like that." And the mystical figure responds, "Have you forgotten your Jesuit education so quickly? First, you know that life is not fair. And second, reality is socially, sometimes cosmically, constructed. Remember, you called me, so quit complaining. Choose one." You begin to fear and tremble, pondering the two alternatives.

As the CEO, which alternative would you choose? Which world would you prefer to live in? Your answer to that question will reveal your fundamental attitude toward privacy. You may be leaning toward one alternative or the other. For example, you know that there are increasing pressures on organizations to gather more information about employees and consumers in order to compete effectively in the global marketplace; in addition, new technologies have emerged enabling organizations to collect such information rather easily (Smith 1994). Such pressures can make Alternative 1 look quite appealing. Yet, on the other hand, you know that there are social and moral expectations about what types of personal information should be available to others. Such a moral recognition makes Alternative 2 an ethically appealing alternative. If you feel a tug and pull between the two alternatives—if you are on the horns of the dilemma, so to speak—it is because there are merits to each alternative.

At the core of the dilemma is this issue: Individuals want to protect the hidden self—a wall demarcating private and public spheres of life—while organizations would like the individual employee to be a more transparent self. Privacy emerges as an organizational and ethical issue because of a fundamental tension and competition between the organizational and individual interests (Schein 1977).

The Organization's Interests

The pressures on organizations to gather information about their employees is growing as the value of information increases (Culnan, Smith, and Bies 1994; H. J. Smith 1994). For example, to create a high-performance organization, managers need accurate and in-depth information about employees for a variety of purposes, including hiring and performance appraisal. In addition, managers need reliable and accurate information about the products made by employees to assure the quality of the goods before they reach the marketplace. There is therefore increasing pressure to monitor employee performance.

Additional pressures facing organizations increase the demand for information about employees. For example, there is evidence that organizations are experiencing growing antisocial behavior, such as employee theft (Greenberg 1990) and workplace violence (Bies and Tripp 1996, forthcoming). These problems are costly and increase the need for surveillance of employee activities. At the same time, rising medical and health care costs are motivating efforts targeted at more in-depth screening of job applicants and monitoring of current employees and their behaviors on and off the job. Finally, organizations are bombarded with requests from other organizations for information on current and former employees for job reference checks, credit checks, and security checks (Bies and Tripp 1993).

In the face of all of these pressures, technologies have emerged to enable organizations to gather the information more easily and often unobtrusively (H. J. Smith 1994). Computerization has made it easier to collect and store data about employees, and with the advent of new and expanded telecommunications capabilities (for example, wide-area networks), it is much easier to share data about employees (H. J. Smith 1994). Finally, there have been technological advances in monitoring devices, such as one that electronically counts word processor keystrokes (Reynolds 1993) and the more esoteric "active badge"—a computer in the shape of a clip-on identification card— that tracks an employee's every movement (Coy 1992), allowing more information about the employee to be gathered.

The Individual's Interests

The right to privacy—or the "right to be let alone" (Warren and Brandeis 1890)—is a right valued and cherished by most citizens. While there are some cross-cultural differences in sensitivity to the right of privacy (Hiramatsu 1993), most people view privacy as an essential right. For example, one survey reported that 75 percent of respondents believe individuals have a basic right to privacy (Harris and Westin 1979). In a more recent study, 79 percent of the respondents expressed a similar belief (Harris 1991).

There is growing empirical evidence of a belief on the part of employees that a right that we attach to our citizenship, such as privacy, is not forfeited upon entering the workplace (Bies 1993). It is a simple and fundamental moral expectation (Culnan, Smith, and Bies 1994), part of a social contract governing the employer-employee relationship (Bies and Tripp 1995; see Donaldson and Dunfee 1994 for a more extensive discussion of social contracts). Indeed, employees expect their privacy to be protected as part of this contract (Bies and Tripp 1996, forthcoming), and when the contract is violated, employees are increasingly taking legal action (Bies and Tyler 1993) and winning (Blackburn and others 1993)—signs that we may be witnessing the growing belief "that the rights we attach to citizenship in society—free expression, privacy, equality, and due process—ought to have their echo in the work place" (Westin, quoted in Hoerr and others 1988, 68).

Thus, at the same time that organizations increasingly need to gather extensive and in-depth information about their employees, employees have a moral expectation for privacy. In the context of these competing interests, it is important to understand what aspects of organizational procedures and practices cross the line and violate an individual's privacy zone.

WHEN PEOPLE PERCEIVE AN INVASION OF PRIVACY: LOSING CONTROL OF PERSONAL INFORMATION

Control of information about oneself has become the dominant perspective and definition of privacy used by organizational researchers (for example, Bies 1993; Stone and Stone 1990; Westin 1967) and other social scientists (for example, Goffman 1959; Jourard 1966). According to this perspective, "Individuals have privacy when they are able to manage or control information about themselves and the subsequent impressions that others form of them. . . . Through this limiting of self-disclosure the individual prevents others from acquiring complete and accurate information about his or her past, current states, or future intentions" (Stone and Stone 1990, 354).

Empirical research has identified the following information control factors that can influence how individuals perceive privacy concerns: authorization of information disclosure, advance notice of information gathering, selection procedures used in information gathering, relevancy of information used in decision making, target of information disclosure, and intrusiveness of information-gathering procedure. In addition, the outcome associated with information disclosure has been found to influence privacy perceptions. An overview of the key findings associated with each factor follows (see Stone and Stone 1990 for more comprehensive literature reviews).

Authorization of Information Disclosure

One kind of information control is granting permission or authorization to others to have access to personal information. When a person grants permission to the organization or another individual to disclose personal information to a third party, it is reasonable to expect the person to be less likely to perceive an invasion of privacy than if such permission has not been granted. And in fact, two studies found that when individuals gave permission for disclosure of information from their personnel files (Fusilier and Hoyer 1980) or permitted the disclosure of personal information for a job promotion decision (Tolchinsky and others 1981), they were less likely to perceive an invasion of privacy than when they had not given such authorization. A recent study found that people express moral outrage about the invasion of their privacy when another party discloses secrets or personal information without permission (Bies and Tripp, in press).

Advance Notice of Information Gathering

Providing advance notice prior to any decision or testing procedure should allow individuals time to make any changes in their personal behavior necessary to pass the test. Advance notice therefore gives individuals a greater ability to control information about themselves and thus should influence perceptions of invasion of privacy. A study of blue-collar employees found that their attitudes toward testing for illegal drug use were significantly less negative when employees were provided advance notice of drug testing than when they were not (Stone and Kotch 1989; Stone, O'Brien, and Bommer 1989).

Selection Procedure for Information Gathering

In any testing procedure, but particularly one dealing with the detection of drug use, there is always the issue of who must take the test and how that selection process occurs. The type of selection procedure used could result in a perceived invasion of privacy. For example, a random selection procedure would fail to meet the criterion of reasonable suspicion that is associated with due process, as would testing all individuals. Reasonable suspicion, based on the availability of evidence suggesting actual drug use by an individual, is an important criterion for people; it is legitimated by the U.S. Constitution (in the Fourth Amendment, for example). The intrusion of the government into individual, private matters without reasonable cause has always been a serious concern for United States citizens (Culnan, Smith, and Bies 1994).

Two studies provide support for this line of reasoning. In one survey (Masters, Ferris, and Ratcliff 1988), only 30 percent of respondents agreed that random testing for drugs was acceptable, while almost three-quarters of the respondents found testing acceptable when there was reasonable suspicion of drug use. In a study with employees of a chemical company (Stone and Bowden 1989), random testing of job applicants was perceived more negatively than either testing all applicants or limiting testing to those suspected of drug use.

Relevancy of Information Used in Decision Making

Organizations gather information about their employees for a variety of purposes, such as hiring and performance appraisal. Whether such information gathering is viewed as an invasion of privacy may depend on the relevancy of the information to the stated purpose of data collection (Stone and Stone 1990). That is, information that appears unrelated to a decision should increase perceptions of privacy invasion (Simmons 1968).

Several studies of organizational hiring practices support this line of reasoning. Bernard Rosenbaum (1973) found that job applicants viewed requests for some types of information (for example, family background and management of one's finances) as less relevant to the decision at hand, and thus a greater invasion of privacy, than requests for other types of information (such as personal history and interests). Similarly, M.B.A. job candidates viewed questions about their marital status and whether they were going to have children as an invasion of privacy (Bies and Moag 1986). Surveys of U.S. respondents (Harris and Westin 1979) and Canadian respondents (Vidmar and Flaherty 1985) found that employer requests for some types of information (for example, home ownership and financial status) were viewed as less relevant to a hiring decision and thus perceived to be an invasion of privacy, a finding supported by field research on United States employees (Tolchinsky and others 1981) and employees from multinational companies (Woodman and others 1982).

Target of Information Disclosure

A key determinant of self-disclosure is the identity of the individual to whom one might disclose the information (Jourard 1966). The disclosure of information to outsiders or strangers or to individuals who are antagonistic may be perceived as a greater invasion of privacy than a disclosure of the same information to insiders or acquaintances, or to those who share one's interests. In other words, the target of information disclosure should influence perceptions of invasion of privacy.

Three studies have examined these effects. Woodman and others (1982) found respondents much more concerned about the disclosure of information to people outside the organization than about disclosure of the same information for the internal uses of the organization. Similarly, Tolchinsky and others (1981) found that subjects reported greater invasion of privacy when the disclosure was external than when it was internal. Finally, Tom Tripp and I (in press) have found that the disclosure of personal confidences and secrets by a third party to one's "enemies" or "antagonists" was perceived as an invasion of privacy by employees.

Intrusiveness of the Information-Gathering Procedure

The view of privacy as information control is not limited to such matters as the relevancy of information, or authorization of disclosure and selection procedures. In addition, as Virginia Schein (1977) argues, one must consider the psychological impact of the procedures for gathering the information. If the procedure is too psychologically intrusive to the individual, the information gathering may be perceived as an invasion of privacy.

Two studies support this line of reasoning. In one study (Stone, O'Brien, and Bommer 1989), people were more likely to accept a job offer if job applicants were not directly monitored when providing a urine sample for drug testing. In a survey of private and public sector employees (LeRoy 1990), over 75 percent of respondents reported acceptance of drug testing in the workplace "under controlled conditions where the individual's privacy is protected" (p. 167).

Outcome of Information Disclosure

A favorable outcome can influence the extent to which employees perceive an invasion of privacy (Stone and Stone 1990). Individuals appear to perform a cost/benefit analysis in assessing their outcomes as the result of providing sensitive information (Thibaut and Kelley 1959). From such an analysis, a positive net outcome should be less likely to result in the perception of invasion of privacy than would a negative net outcome.

Empirical evidence suggests the existence of an egoistic bias in privacy perceptions (Bies 1993). Marcelline Fusilier and Wayne Hoyer (1980) found that subjects who received a positive outcome (job offer) as a result of an extensive and sensitive information disclosure perceived that disclosure as less an invasion of privacy than did those who received a negative outcome (no job offer). Tolchinsky and others (1981) found that when individuals received favorable consequences (job promotion) there was less of a perceived invasion of privacy than when they received unfavorable consequences (no job promotion). Stone and Kotch (1989) found that blue-collar employees viewed drug testing more negatively when detection of drug use resulted in the discharge of the employee than when the employee was referred to an assistance program (a more favorable outcome by comparison).

Thus, there are a variety of aspects of organizational procedures and practices that can lead people to perceive that their privacy has been violated. At the same time, however, there is consistent evidence of an egoistic bias that may lessen these privacy concerns. Given that perceived privacy violations can pose serious legal, economic, and social repercussions for the organization (Culnan, Smith, and Bies 1994), privacy emerges as a strategic issue of importance for organizations. How organizations anticipate or respond strategically to privacy concerns or violations is the focus of the next section.

MANAGING PRIVACY: STRATEGIC RESPONSES AND DILEMMAS

Organizations do not respond immediately to privacy concerns raised by employees. On the basis of extensive research across a variety of industries, Jeff Smith (1994) has observed a three-phase cycle of organizational responses to these concerns. These phases are *drift, threat,* and *reaction.*

In the drift phase, top management essentially abdicates responsibility for managing privacy to lower- and midlevel managers to craft their own practices, if any. If a privacy matter is raised, it is handled on an ad hoc basis by the manager. In the second phase, the organization perceives a threat to its legitimacy, resulting from its practices of gathering or using personal information about employees. This threat often takes the form of negative media publicity, employee litigation, or legislative scrutiny. In the final phase, privacy has become a strategic issue, and top management engages in a forceful reaction. Typically, efforts are made to codify existing practices and create new formal procedural safeguards and regulations to protect privacy.

This approach to managing privacy—drift, perceiving a threat, reacting with formal procedures and practices—corresponds to key dimensions of the *legalization* process (Sitkin and Bies 1993). Legalization is the "diffusion of legalistic reasoning, procedures and structures to sustain or enhance the legitimacy of the organization . . . with critical internal or external constituencies" (Sitkin and Bies 1993, 346). Legalization has emerged as the dominant strategic response made by organizations to privacy issues (Culnan, Smith, and Bies 1994). The new procedural safeguards that are enacted usually reflect employee concerns about information control (Bies 1993; Culnan, Smith, and Bies 1994). For example, the requirement of employee permission, as in a release form, is an increasingly common organizational practice. Other information control factors such as advance notice and relevancy of information are becoming quite common.

Managers have found legalization to be the most convenient way to balance organizational interests (for example, legal liability, and company reputation) and individual interests (that is, information control). It is, however, an approach that can also create organizational and ethical dilemmas and paradoxical consequences. One dilemma and one paradox are illustrative.

THE CONFIDENTIALITY DILEMMA.   In response to employee litigation and legislative mandates, organizations have developed rules and procedural safeguards about the type of information they can gather and the manner in which they can gather it from prospective and current employees (Bies 1993). These rules and safeguards can protect the individual's interest of privacy, which is important, and protect the organization's legal liability, which is also important.

Yet these privacy rules and safeguards, representing a well-meant attempt to protect both the rights of individuals and the interests of organizations, can create what I call *the confidentiality dilemma*. For example, should an airline be able to ask a prospective pilot about any previous drinking problem before offering that person a job because airline passengers and employees may be put at serious risk if the drinking problem returns? On the other hand, if the pilot is a recovering alcoholic, should a history of drinking carry a lifelong stigma that destroys that person's career and livelihood? These questions go to the heart of the confidentiality dilemma. On the one hand, protecting individual privacy may not be organizationally sensible and may create new legal and ethical problems for the organization; on the other hand, the absence of privacy safeguards may be extremely unfair to the individual.

THE JUSTICE PARADOX.   Legalization and the creation of strict procedural safeguards and regulations can also impede the broader social goal of achieving equality and social justice. For example, as Virginia Schein (1977) observed, "Privacy regulations may conflict with requirements for equal employment compliance, which call for increased data collection, longitudinal research, and the need for common identifiers" (p. 161). Therein lies the *justice paradox* (Sitkin and Bies 1993). Specifically, organizations create rules and procedural safeguards to control access to personal information about prospective and current employees—a central privacy concern of many individuals. But paradoxically, such procedural controls can make it very difficult to determine whether broader interests of social justice such as affirmative action and equality of opportunity are being pursued actively and according to the law. Determining systemic biases requires in-depth personal information that may be off-limits because of the privacy regulations. The justice paradox is thus a situation of law without justice (Bies and Sitkin 1993).

ANY WAY OUT? From the attempt to balance interests and the resulting dilemmas and paradoxes, the question emerges, What to do? One response is that while formalized procedural safeguards and establishment of rights for individuals are important (Selznick 1969), the new legalistic structure and practices must be implemented wisely and fairly (Bies 1993; Folger and Bies 1989; Tyler and Bies 1990). In other words, structure must not dominate but must be informed by wise decision makers who attempt to balance the rights-based concerns of individuals with the organizational interests of efficiency and control. Or, as one executive has stated, "Where do you draw the line? That's the question. It takes good judgment and a sense of fair play" (Bob DeGennaro, quoted in Zalud 1989, 40).

WHY STUDY PRIVACY?

Why study privacy? The answer is that in the brave new world of organizations, new privacy issues will emerge and privacy concerns will be raised over a wider domain of organizational activities. Whether they involve people's reactions to new technologies (for example, the active badge) or to the increasing surveillance of their work performance, privacy issues will abound. Indeed, in any encounter involving the gathering or exchange of information, privacy and confidentiality issues will likely be central.

A few issues worthy of empirical study deserve mention. One issue is the egoistic bias and how that bias is elicited in social situations. The extant research suggests that people are willing to accept privacy invasion if they receive personal benefit. Given this finding, the question of how to make the "benefits" of privacy invasion salient to the individual emerges as an important empirical (and strategic) issue. Empirically, one could examine framing effects on perceptions of privacy invasion (Bies, Tripp, and Neale 1993).

Another important variable would be the social account (Bies 1987) or justification given for the privacy invasion.

Other areas for fruitful research include identifying the social cognitive and organizational factors that inhibit or facilitate privacy's becoming a strategic issue on top management's organizational agenda. Another important research question involves how managers attempt to "do justice" with privacy dilemmas—that is, how they attempt to balance competing employer and employee interests.

Even broader privacy issues can be studied. Privacy is not just information control; it has another key aspect, *interaction control* (Altman 1975; Sundstrom, 1986). According to the interaction control perspective, "Privacy is achieved by controlling the amount of contact that one has with other people" (Stone and Stone 1990, 355). Two key interaction control factors that can influence privacy perceptions in the workplace include personal space (Hall 1966; Sommer 1969) and architectural aspects of the office setting (Oldham and Brass 1979; Sundstrom, Burt, and Kamp 1980).

The interaction control perspective becomes important as we move into the era of the "boundaryless organization." For example, with the introduction of its "virtual office," Chiat/Day Advertising has refashioned its work environment by eliminating individual desks and fixed, private work areas (Garland 1994). While there may be organizational benefits to the new social architecture, it may also raise issues of privacy for both employees and clients.

Interaction and information control factors can be present simultaneously, raising new privacy questions for research. For example, as employees gain access to the information superhighway and become "connected" to the job at home, they will lose control over communications, which can be sent to them continually, at all times of the day or night. Such intrusions can be viewed as the invasion of privacy (Bies and Tripp, in press). And what makes the situation more intriguing is that organizations have the capability to know whether one has opened one's e-mail or responded to other electronic communications. In other words, in the virtual office, privacy may be virtually lost.

Beyond these empirical questions, there are ethical questions. Is the invasion of personal privacy morally acceptable, and if so, on what grounds? But to raise this question challenges the core assumptions of management theory and practice, which William G. Scott and D. Kirk Hart (1979) refer to as the *organizational imperative*. The organizational imperative is based on a primary and absolute proposition—"Whatever is good for the individual can only come from the modern organization" (p. 43)—and the related secondary proposition—"Therefore, all behavior must enhance the health of such organizations" (p. 43). These assumptions justify total intrusion into people's lives, invasion of their privacy, and total control of their actions. In other words, the core assumptions of modern management theory are totalitarian.

I propose that privacy become a new core assumption for management theory and practice as a moral challenge to the totalitarian assumptions (see Bies 1987; Bies and Moag 1986). In this new core assumption, an individual has an "inviolate personality," and to invade a person's privacy is to violate that person's "independence, dignity and integrity" (Bloustein 1964, 971). This new core assumption will not only generate new and important empirical questions on privacy but also will be the motivation for an ethical crusade to "increase the respect of all . . . for the essential values of human life" (Beaney 1966, 271).

Chapter 6

Judge Not, Lest . . . : The Ethics of Power Holders' Decision Making and Standards for Social Judgment

Stephanie A. Goodwin and Susan T. Fiske

It takes no special training to discern sex stereotyping in a description of an aggressive female employee as requiring 'a course in charm school.'
Price Waterhouse v. Hopkins, 1 S. Ct. 1 1989, 1793

Ann Hopkins's lawsuit against the accounting firm of Price Water-house highlighted the potential for powerful decision makers to misuse social categories and their corresponding stereotypes. In this case, ultimately reviewed by the U.S. Supreme Court, the senior partners had denied Ms. Hopkins a partnership in the firm, claiming that despite her exemplary work record she was unqualified for partnership because she was not feminine enough. The wording of the Supreme Court's response to *Price Waterhouse v. Hopkins* (1989) embodied a fundamental assumption in our culture: People should be evaluated on the basis of their individual characteristics without regard to their social group. Decisions that violate this egalitarian assumption are considered both unethical and illegal: "We are beyond the day when an employer could evaluate employees by assuming or insisting that they matched the stereotype associated with their group" (pp. 1790–91).

Despite our egalitarian expectations and the laws that endorse them, prejudice and discrimination persist, with important consequences for women and minorities. Employment statistics reflect enduring barriers that not only prevent members of these groups from entering the work force but also limit

The writing of this version of this chapter and the work of Stephanie Goodwin were supported by National Institute of Mental Health Grant 41801 to Susan Fiske. The chapter is based on the doctoral dissertation of Stephanie Goodwin. The authors wish to thank Icek Aizen, Paula Pietromonaco, Jacques-Philippe Leyens, Vincent Yzerbyt, Don Operario, Theresa Claire, and two anonymous reviewers for their comments on earlier drafts.

the earning potential and advancement of those members who are employed. Discrimination in the workplace is a consequence of complex social factors, such as the structure of relations, education, socialization, and individual factors, such as personality characteristics and cognitive processes. Although research into these important variables has yielded substantial insight into the problem, the role of the powerful individual as decision maker has been largely ignored (Dépret and Fiske 1993; Fiske 1993a). Ironically, we will argue, decisions to hire and promote often rest on the shoulders of powerful individuals who may be vulnerable to stereotyping their subordinates. Because powerful people control important outcomes, their potential susceptibility to unethical decision making demands attention, especially in light of the societal presumption that their decisions *ought* to be guided by egalitarian standards. At this time, the field lacks a theory addressing the role of such standards in the decision processes of those who hold power.

In this chapter, we consider how powerful decision makers evaluate those for whom they control certain outcomes. Paying particular attention to the role of standards in ethical decision making, we take a social/ cognitive perspective that focuses both on *how* powerful decision makers think about subordinates (that is, their cognitive processes) and *why* they adopt these cognitive styles (their underlying motivations and goals). We propose that those who evaluate others generally monitor their judgment strategies, engaging in a pragmatic process that tells them when it is appropriate to judge others. This process, which operates parallel to the formation of impressions of others, involves comparisons in which people determine whether or not they have violated their internal (for example, personal values) and their external (for example, cultural norms) judgment standards. When these judgment standards have been sufficiently met, people experience a heightened sense that they are able to judge; that is, their *perceived ability to judge* increases. Power holders, we will argue, are most likely to feel able to judge when both their judgment strategies and their expressed judgments are consonant with their stereotypes about subordinates. In meeting these particular judgment standards as they form impressions, the powerful are vulnerable to stereotyping and unethical decision making.

We begin by outlining the Continuum Model (CM) of impression formation (Fiske and Neuberg 1990), a theory of how people think about and form impressions of others. Applying this model to powerful individuals clarifies how the powerful person's motivation to maintain power influences the propensity to stereotype. Key to the analysis is the recognition that people may not always be ready, willing, and able to judge one another when asked to do so (Leyens, Yzerbyt, and Schadron 1994). According to their Social Judgeability Theory (SJT), which uniquely considers the standards people use when judging others, people's judgments must meet certain requirements before they will feel confident enough to judge. Applying SJT's tenets to the CM leads to our proposed Judgment Monitoring Model, which delineates a role for judgment standards in impression formation. The chapter concludes by hypothesizing ways to encourage ethical decision making in light of the model.

Before we continue, it is important to clarify the definition of power as *outcome control*. Social psychologists have often confounded power with other common correlates, such as social influence, prestige, and status (for reviews see Cartwright 1959; Dépret and Fiske 1993; Ng 1980). Our definition of power, in contrast, rests on the nature of the interdependence in any given relationship (Dépret and Fiske 1993). According to this definition, people who have asymmetric control over the resources (that is, over the desired social or economic outcomes) of others are powerful, whereas those who depend on them for outcomes are relatively powerless. This definition resolves traditional confusion with the correlates of power and enables us to quantify power differentials between individuals in power relationships. Although power is not a one-way street (both members of a dyad may control distinct resources for one another), this chapter restricts attention to situations in which one powerful individual has asymmetric, disproportionate control over the resources desired by another.

THE CONTINUUM MODEL: HOW PEOPLE FORM IMPRESSIONS

The goal of this chapter is to clarify both how powerful people think about their subordinates and why they do so in the particular way that they do. The Continuum Model of impression formation (Fiske and Neuberg 1990) addresses how people in general think about others when forming impressions. Importantly for this discussion, the theory addresses not only the cognitive processes (the "how") but also the motives and goals that underlie different impression formation strategies (the "why"). Research supporting this theory has been integrated into a theory of how powerful individuals may be motivated to stereotype their subordinates (Fiske 1993a; Goodwin and Fiske 1995).

Overview of the Model

The CM (figure 6.1) is a cognitive/motivational approach that posits, as its name implies, a continuum of strategies available when people are forming impressions—that is, when they are functioning as *perceivers*. These strategies range from effortless category-based strategies to more effortful attribute-based or individuating strategies (Fiske and Neuberg 1990). According to the theory, whether perceivers categorize or individuate is contingent on their motivations and cognitive resources. When motivation and

Figure 6.1 / Simplified Version of the Continuum Model

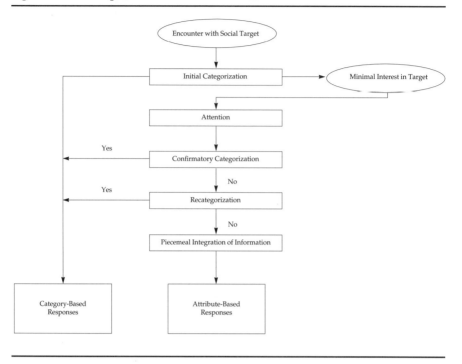

Source: Adapted from Riley and Fiske (1991) with permission.

cognitive resources are low, as when people are disinterested or too busy to attend (see Gilbert 1989; Gilbert, Pelham, and Krull 1988; Macrae, Milne, and Bodenhausen 1994), they engage in less effortful, category-based processing, attending to information that fits their initial categorization and processing the information in simpler ways (Erber and Fiske 1984; Fiske and others 1987; Neuberg 1989; Neuberg and Fiske 1987; Pavelchak 1989; Ruscher and Fiske 1990; Ruscher and others 1991). This process leaves the perceiver to rely, by default, on category-consistent or stereotype-confirming information; perceivers do not process information that could alter their stereotypic expectations, and therefore they have no alternative information on which to base their impressions. When cognitive resources are available and people are motivated to form accurate impressions, however, they move along the continuum to more effortful individuation strategies, attending more to information that may counter their initial categorizations, and processing the information in complex ways. Individuating attention strategies do not ensure that people will make nonstereotypic judgments; people may still recategorize or reinterpret inconsistent information to make it consistent with their expectations. Unless they attend to information that counters their expectations, however, they cannot make nonstereotypic judgments.

Symmetric and Asymmetric Interdependence

Motivation to individuate can stem from the nature of the outcome dependency relationship (that is, the interdependence) between the perceiver and the person being perceived (Erber and Fiske 1984). When people perceive their outcomes to be contingent on the behaviors of another person, they become motivated to form an accurate impression of that person; doing so affords prediction and control of their own outcomes. In some situations, the interdependence is *symmetric*; parties contribute equally to their joint outcomes and thus have equal power over outcomes. For example, co-workers on a joint project are likely to be motivated to form accurate impressions of one another, because doing so enables them to adjust their efforts appropriately to complete the task at hand. Empirical research finds that outcome dependency (e.g., working together to attain a joint aim) increases attention to category-inconsistent information, increases complexity of thinking about that information, and leads to more variable, individuated impressions (Erber and Fiske 1984; Neuberg and Fiske 1987; Ruscher and Fiske 1990).

In other situations—a supervisor hiring a new employee, for example—the interdependence is *asymmetric*. One person has the power to control the outcome for the other—the supervisor either hires or doesn't hire the applicant—and does not perceive the other to control his or her own outcomes (though in fact the potential for the employee's behavior to control outcomes may be there). The focus of this chapter is on understanding how people with asymmetric outcome control (that is, the powerful) judge their subordinates. Research in support of the Continuum Model has recently addressed power in terms of asymmetric outcome control.

Drawing on the model and the definition of power as resource control, Susan Fiske (1993a) proposed a tripartite theory of power and stereotyping. According to the Power-As-Control (PAC) model, power holders may be (1) unmotivated, (2) unwilling, or (3) unable to individuate their subordinates. First, in the absence of any outcome dependency on the powerless, the powerful have no implicit motivation to expend mental energy individuating their subordinates. Unmotivated to attend to unexpected information, they ultimately rely on their default categorizations of subordinates. Second, personality differences in dominance may lead to similar stereotyping processes. The propensity to seek control over others may make power holders particularly unwilling to individuate those they control. Third, the powerful typically have heavy demands on their time and attention. They may therefore be unable to attend to subordinates because they lack the necessary cognitive resources. Fiske further asserted that power and stereotyping are mutually reinforcing; because stereotyping constrains the stereotyped subordinates to specific behaviors and roles, it enables the powerful to confirm their expectations, maintain the status quo, and maintain their control over others (see also Jost and Banaji 1994).

In 1995, we elaborated on the assumption that power and stereotyping are mutually reinforcing and extended the PAC model (Goodwin and Fiske 1995). We argued not only that power holders may be unmotivated to individuate but that they also may be particularly motivated to *confirm* their stereotypes actively by paying attention to stereotype-confirming information. To test the argument, we developed an employment review paradigm in which half the participants believed they had some control (30 percent) over decisions to rehire student interns, while the remaining participants believed they had no outcome control (0 percent). All participants evaluated alleged application materials that included comments presumably provided by former co-workers. In reality, these fictitious co-worker comments consisted of equal numbers of trait-descriptive sentences pretested to be consistent and inconsistent with the applicant's ethnicity. Results supported the two separate sets of predictions. First, powerful subjects gave less attention to stereotype-inconsistent information than did nonpowerful subjects, thereby effortlessly stereotyping subordinates by default, as noninterdependent perceivers in previous CM research have done. Second, unlike previous studies in which attention to stereotypic information remained constant across motivational conditions, this study found that powerful subjects gave more attention to stereotype-confirming information, effortfully stereotyping subordinates by design, than did nonpowerful subjects. Thus, power holders stereotyped subordinates in both effortless and effortful ways.

To test the PAC model's unwillingness hypothesis, the study was replicated using individual differences in the predisposition for dominance rather than power as the variable (Goodwin and Fiske 1995). We preselected participants high and low in dominance and placed them in the same experimental context. Procedures were the same as in the previous study, except that the amount of control participants believed they might have remained ambiguous. Paralleling the previous pattern of effects, high-dominance perceivers used effortful stereotyping strategies, in comparison with their low-dominance counterparts. More recently, these attention strategies characteristic of stereotyping-by-default and stereotyping-by-design have been replicated in a second paradigm in which participants were part of a power hierarchy, evaluating information about superiors, subordinates, and resource-irrelevant others (Goodwin, Fiske, and Yzerbyt 1995). In the laboratory hierarchy, power holders' motivations to stereotype were supported by the pattern of overall attention as a function of role. Perceivers paid significantly less attention overall to the resource-irrelevant person, but statistically equivalent overall attention to the superior and the subordinate. At a general level, given that perceivers are motivated to individuate superiors (in order to predict their own outcomes), it seems they are equally motivated to stereotype their subordinates. More specifically, the patterns of relative attention to stereotype-confirming and -disconfirming information replicated the original employment evaluation study, with the powerful increasing attention to confirming information and decreasing attention to disconfirming information relative to the powerless.

On a more optimistic note, it seems that power holders *can* engage in a somewhat less stereotypic strategy when they are motivated to feel responsible for their subordinates' outcomes (Goodwin and Fiske 1995). Half the power holders in the first employment evaluation paradigm were primed to feel responsible for others prior to evaluating subordinates. These high-responsibility subjects completed the Humanitarian-Egalitarian Values Scale (Katz and Haas 1988), which specifically primes internalized egalitarian values (for example, "A good society is one in which people feel responsible for one another"). The remaining subjects completed a control questionnaire. The priming manipulation had the intended effects of increasing perceived responsibility during the decision-making task and of erasing the stereotyping-by-design process. Power holders who felt responsible did not give more attention to stereotype-confirming information, as did their counterparts who were not so motivated. Feeling responsible did not increase attention to counterstereotypic information, however. Stereotyping subordinates by default was therefore unaffected by power holders' feelings of responsibility for those they controlled. Although the responsibility manipulation was only partially successful at eliminating stereotype-based processing, these findings strongly suggest that some type of judgment standards (such as personal values) may influence how power holders view their subordinates. We will now consider what these values and standards may be and how they may operate in the social judgment process.

SOCIAL JUDGEABILITY THEORY AND JUDGMENT STANDARDS

Experimental explorations of social judgment have, with few exceptions, relied upon techniques that virtually demand that participants make judgments (for example, rate a person on a number of trait dimensions) but have failed to consider whether subjects feel comfortable or confident doing so. In everyday life outside the laboratory, people refrain from making social judgments unless they feel entitled to do so, thus providing anecdotal evidence of the existence of judgment standards. Recent evidence from inside the laboratory supports this possibility (Yzerbyt and others 1994; Schadron and Yzerbyt 1991). When asked to make judgments but *given the option not to judge*, subjects are more likely to indicate that they cannot judge in the absence of individual attribute information (Schadron and Yzerbyt 1991). That people feel more able to judge when they have more information is not terribly shocking, but it appears that even the mere belief that one has information is enough to enable one to judge (Yzerbyt and others 1994). In a series of cleverly designed studies, participants who were initially unwilling to judge targets because of a lack of information were subsequently led to believe that they had received "subliminal" target information during a separate task. In fact, the task was bogus, and the participants had not learned anything about the targets. Nevertheless, when participants merely *believed* they had received individuating information, they made more extreme judgments and they were more confident in those judgments.

These data underscore the central theme in Social Judgeability Theory: People need to feel able to judge before they will do so. SJT argues that people follow certain judgeability rules that enable them to meet certain levels of adequacy when making judgments. When judgment strategies meet these proposed levels of adequacy, perceivers feel more confident to judge and consequently may make more extreme judgments. We will argue that SJT's adequacy levels may be viewed as global standards for judgment strategies, or *global judgeability standards*.

Defining Characteristics of Judgeability Standards

Before elaborating on the global judgeability standards and the more specific standards that underlie them, it is important to delineate clearly what we mean by judgeability standards. In lay terms, a standard is a criterion for comparison. In broad terms, one can think of social judg*ment* standards therefore as comparison criteria for evaluating other people. Social judge*ability* standards are another kind of social judgment standard. More specifically, they are the expectations about judgment strategies that act as criteria for making or expressing judgments (Leyens, Yzerbyt, and Schadron 1992; Leyens, Yzerbyt, and Schadron 1994; Schadron and Yzerbyt 1991).

It is important to note that we are not referring to what other social cognition theorists have called judgment standards when they refer to the benchmark comparisons perceivers use for anchoring individual trait judgments (Biernat and Manis 1994; Biernat, Manis, and Nelson 1991; Higgins and Stangor 1988). An example of such a benchmark might be knowing that "most salespeople are outgoing" and using this knowledge as a ruler for measuring the extroversion of a particular salesperson. In contrast, social judgeability standards serve as criteria for the validity of making a judgment at all, regardless of which rulers are cognitively handy. You may know that your sales manager, Christine, is somewhat extroverted at the office, but if you feel this is not enough evidence to conclude whether or not she is generally outgoing, you may be hesitant to make a judgment about her extroversion.

Judgeability standards differ for those judgments that are actually expressed and those that are privately held. One may meet the standards to conclude confidently to oneself that another person has a particular trait (for example, incompetence) but encounter other standards that prevent the expression of that judgment (you should not say such things about the boss). Thus people may think certain judgments but not express them. Unfortunately, in the absence of other methodological techniques, one must rely primarily on what people are willing to express in order to ascertain when they feel able to judge. In response to this methodological issue, SJT theorists have argued for a link between the ability to judge and judgment confidence. Judgment confidence is correlated with judgment extremity (Clark and Rutter 1985; Devine 1989a; Zelasny 1990) and judgment polarization (Devine 1989a). Extrapolating from these findings, one can argue that confidence is likely to be correlated with perceived accuracy and judgment response times, though evidence is still forthcoming on these methods. Thus, perceived ability to judge, as manifest in judgment confidence, has consequences not only for the qualities of expressed judgments but also for the ability to express a judgment at all.

The term *standard* connotes that the criteria people use are not arbitrary and changeable but instead are relatively stable over time. Although it is possible that some standards exist only for the duration of a particular interaction, the criteria of interest here—social judgeability standards—are relatively intransient rules that permit perceivers to judge. This is not to say that all judgeability standards apply to all situations. Judgeability standards vary in their generalizability across situations. Some are more clearly applicable across a variety of social contexts (for example, having enough information), whereas others are likely to be specific to particular settings (for example, having a role, such as manager, that sanctions making judgments). The bottom line is that people follow a number of relatively universal judgeability standards, some global and some more specific, when determining if they can make social judgments.

Adequacy Levels and Global Judgeability Standards

SJT posits four levels of judgment adequacy, which are considered here as global judgeability standards: *reality, integrity, culture,* and *theory.* By adequacy, the authors of the theory mean that a judgment must serve certain purposes, needs, and goals in order to be adequate. When a judgment cannot be made or expressed in such a way as to serve these global requirements, people refrain from judging.

REALITY. Perhaps most familiar to social psychologists is the global standard to make a judgment that adequately fits reality; this standard reflects perceivers' attempts to make sense of available information. Much of the research on social cognition explores just how people come to feel able to judge, given particular information about another person (Leyens, Yzerbyt, and Schadron 1992). For example, trait integration theories are concerned with how people consider and weight individual pieces of information during impression formation (see, for example, Anderson 1981; Asch 1946; for recent reviews of the literature, see, for example, Fiske 1993b; Fiske and Taylor 1991; Higgins and Bargh 1987; Jones 1990; Kunda 1990; Snyder 1992; Zebrowitz 1990). A clear pattern emerges in the research: Perceivers are constrained by the nature of available information when making social judgments. Perceivers recognize that there is a reality "out there" to be considered when making social judgments, a reality that must be integrated with prior beliefs and expectations but that cannot be entirely denied. Consequently, perceivers' final judgments reflect a global *reality-matching* judgeability standard and typically do not deviate wildly from the actual data with which they are presented (Kunda 1990).

INTEGRITY. At the adequacy level of integrity, SJT argues that people make social judgments that fit their own individual identities ("I'm the kind of person who is fair") and their social group identities ("I am Irish Roman Catholic"). Consequently, people avoid making judgments that can threaten these identifications. For example, Leyens and Yzerbyt (1992) found what they termed an *in-group overexclusion effect*; people required more evidence to confirm that a target was a member of their own group than to exclude the target as an out-group member. In accord with Social Identity Theory (Tajfel 1969) and Self-Categorization Theory (Turner 1987), they found that falsely identifying a target as an in-group member was more threatening than mistakenly identifying someone as an out-group member (see also Omoto and Borgida 1988). The effect has been replicated in an idiographic paradigm using subjects' own individual self-views (Yzerbyt, Leyens, and Bellour 1993). Thus the need to protect identities is not limited to those of one's social groups but extends to individual, idiosyncratic self-descriptions as well.

CULTURE. People are likely to be guided by cultural norms regarding social judgments and therefore to have a global *cultural-fit* judgeability standard. As an example, the earlier-mentioned research that suggests a judgeability standard for being informed (Yzerbyt and others 1994) is likely to reflect a cultural norm ("Don't judge a book by its cover") not to make hasty and unfounded judgments based on group membership (Blanchard, Lilly, and Vaughn 1991; Darley and Gross 1983; Quattrone and Jones 1980). Social roles may similarly imply judgeability standards about whom, how, and when to judge. People may feel more or less generally entitled to judge depending on their role and whether they are accountable to others (Tetlock 1992). Cultural judgeability standards are likely to become internalized; such a standard is the Judeo-Christian biblical proverb alluded to in the title of this chapter, "Judge not lest ye be judged." People who adhere to this tenet could be less willing to make judgments, at least publicly, because doing so would violate an expectation of their social group (that is, their religious affiliation) and possibly their own self-views.

THEORY. Theoretical adequacy refers to whether a person's naive explanatory theories are adequate for explaining the behavior under consideration. Perceivers have different types of theories to explain, for example, why people hold attitudes on different issues (Leyens and others 1995). Thus, if asked why a person holds a particular attitude toward affirmative action, the perceiver might answer that it is because of a personality characteristic such as dominance, because of socioeconomic factors such as education or income, or perhaps because of biological factors such as gender and age. Perceivers normally associate specific types of explanatory theories with specific attitude issues (for example, sociological theories with attitudes toward communism), but these theories may not necessarily be cognitively active at the time of judgment. Jacques-Philippe Leyens and others (1995) found that people felt more confident to judge when there was a match between the perceiver's cognitively active explanatory theory and the theory normally associated with the attitude issue. A mismatch, however, led people to refrain from judging. This finding suggests a global *theoretical-fit* judgeability standard that enables perceivers to maintain broad causal explanations during social judgment.

Judgeability Standards

This preliminary yet compelling evidence supports the types of judgment adequacy levels presented in SJT (Leyens, Yzerbyt, and Schadron 1992, 1994). People adhere to certain global criteria to gain a sense of perceived ability to judge when faced with a social judgment situation. At another level of analysis, these four global judgeability standards reflect perceivers' strivings to maintain a view of the social world that is both realistic and consistent with their beliefs and expectations. These global standards are analogous to threads in a fabric representing perceivers' broader expectations about the social world as well as their desires to predict and control that world. When perceivers make judgments that do not meet these global judgeability standards, the threads may loosen or fray and the integrity of the fabric is jeopardized. Thus, perceivers may be highly motivated to maintain consistency between their judgment strategies and their judgeability standards in order to maintain the integrity of their own expectations about the social world.

Although these global judgeability standards provide a framework for understanding the motives of perceivers making social judgments, they are not specific enough to answer our questions about the standards that guide power holders' decision-making processes. As we have noted, these global standards reflect a myriad more specific values and standards that may or may not be accessible in particular social contexts. Meeting the cultural-fit standard, for example, may require simply having more information in one context or having a particular kind of information in another. To extend our cloth analogy, the threads of global judgeability may be made of many different kinds of fibers that vary in substance, having different textures and hues for different perceivers or social contexts. We now consider the substance of these threads for power holders—that is, the standards that are likely to be accessed by the powerful.

POWER HOLDERS' STANDARDS

In considering specific judgeability standards that guide power holders' judgment strategies, it is helpful to consider the origins of some standards most relevant to ethics and values: the expectations of groups and the broader culture, the expectations of other important individuals, and expectations about the self. With reference to these sources of judgeability standards, two basic questions loom over the perceiver: (1) "Are my judgment strategies consistent with what is expected?" and (2) "Is this the judgment I am expected to make?"

Expectations of Groups and Cultures

The norms, roles, and expectations imposed by larger social groups and the culture as a whole should imply social judgeability standards. Roles, as an example, may dictate not only who is allowed to judge (for example, Supreme Court justices) but how they are supposed to do it (on the basis of the U.S. Constitution and not their individual beliefs) and what constitutes a reasonable judgment (one that complies with the spirit of the Constitution as opposed to one that is consonant with current political ideology). Scripts, established procedures for judging, may similarly imply judgeability standards. To the extent that people view their routines for making judgments as valid (for example, checking past politically sympathetic precedents), they may feel more entitled to judge.

Culture and social groups contribute directly to power holders' perceived ability to judge and also to the salience or availability of various standards that indirectly influence this perceived ability. First, power holders, unlike most social perceivers, are in socially sanctioned positions to judge others (Fiske 1993a; French and Raven 1959; Leyens 1983). Being a personnel manager, for example, *requires* making social judgments in the course of executing the role (for example, selecting candidates for interviews and hiring personnel). This unique position to judge others should have a direct effect on power holders' perceptions that they are entitled to judge (that is, their perceived ability to judge). To the extent that power holders' judgments are heavily scripted or routinized, their already heightened perceptions of entitlement may be further augmented. A generally high sense of perceived ability to judge may lead power holders to view their own prior expectations (including their stereotypic beliefs) as particularly valid and justified. If prior expectations are viewed as valid bases for judgment, the powerful may fail to seek out or attend to information that counters these expectations. Even if some attention is paid to subordinate information, if it is coupled with an adequate theory for explaining subordinates' behaviors the powerful could make decisions based on irrelevant or insufficient information. This process would explain the stereotyping-by-default attention strategies of power holders observed in the research on impression formation discussed earlier in the chapter (Goodwin and Fiske 1995).

The beliefs and expectations of social groups are also likely to influence power holders' judgment strategies via the salience of expectations about social groups. To the extent that social groups become salient—that is, they become perceptually prominent—and their associated stereotypic beliefs therefore become more cognitively accessible, these expectations are increasingly likely to influence power holders' judgments. For example, the salience of gender, ethnicity, and age factors in the work force will make stereotypic expectations about members of these groups more accessible for powerful decision makers to utilize. Moreover, stereotypes about particular social groups are substantially linked to cultural and organizational power hierarchies. Men and women, for example, are culturally stereotyped into roles and occupations that differ with regard to power (for example, Anglo men are more often expected to hold power). Thus, to the extent that a particular social group characteristic, such as gender or ethnicity, is associated with a particular power role (powerful versus powerless), these cultural expectations will set the tone for power holders' judgments.

Expectations of Other Individuals

The beliefs of other important individuals are an obvious source for judgeability standards. Whenever people perceive that their judgments will be evaluated by others, accountability and self-presentation concerns are likely to arise, in turn making others' expectations more salient and accessible. Phillip Tetlock and his colleagues (Tetlock, Skitka, and Boettger 1989) have argued that accountable perceivers adopt one of three coping strategies, corresponding to three judgeability standards (Tetlock 1992), that have consequences for information processing and judgment expression. When the views of the audience are readily available and people have no prior commitment to a particular judgment, they can adopt *acceptability standards;* they can simply accept or express the views of the audience. If, however, uncommitted perceivers find themselves accountable to an unknown audience, they adopt the standards of a *rational and fair decision maker* and engage in preemptive self-criticism, attending more to, and thinking more complexly about, available information. Finally, when feeling accountable but already committed to a particular judgment, people adopt *rationalizing* judgment standards and engage in defensive self-bolstering, attending to information that supports their judgment and defending their views from possible attack.

Given that people may adopt these three different standards when they feel accountable to others' expectations, one could argue that the standards of the rational and fair decision maker are most likely to lead to ethical decision-making strategies. Yet, given the power holders' likely perceptions that their own opinions are particularly valid, it is arguable that power holders are vulnerable to adopting rationalizing judgment standards, attending more to information that supports prior expectations. This process would account for their tendency to stereotype by design, increasing their attention to stereotypic information about subordinates (Goodwin and Fiske 1995).

Should power holders find themselves uncommitted to a particular judgment or unable to express their own judgments without threatening their own outcomes, adopting acceptability standards may similarly lead to stereotype confirmation. If, for example, a third party controls the power holder's own outcomes (for example, job security), the cost of countering that third party's expectations may be too high. In this case, the power holder may simply follow the standards expected by the third party. At this point, the power holder's perceptions about the third party's expectations are crucial. If the perception is that the third party expects fair and rational decision making, the power holder should follow more ethical decision strategies. If, however, the perception is that the third party has biased expectations about the decision-making task (for example, "Men cannot be secretarial staff"), then less ethical strategies will be used.

Beliefs and Expectations About the Self

The self is a rich source of judgeability standards. The values of parents, partners, and paycheck signers are likely to become internalized over time, as are the values of broader social groups and one's own culture (for a review of such self-standards, see Higgins 1989). When these values are linked to evaluations of self-worth, they have consequences not only for self-esteem but also for affect and motivation (Higgins 1987). One's self-concept as a judge is probably related to individual differences in cognitive processing styles. For example, differences in the general need to come to a decision—openness versus closure—whether situationally induced or a trait characteristic of the individual, have consequences for how people process information (Kruglanski 1989; Neuberg and Newsome 1993). These needs can become associated with internalized expectations about how one makes decisions and are therefore likely to be related to internalized judgeability standards. People with a high need for general openness may see themselves as the kind of people who make judgments more carefully or who are more responsible, and thus they might require more information before feeling able to judge. Conversely, people who have a high need for general closure may view themselves as not wasting time, as being decisive ("An expert doesn't need much time"). Similarly, people with a high self-monitoring style (Snyder 1984), who are especially concerned with what others think of them, may be more vulnerable to adopting acceptability judgment standards, because doing so fits their own ideas about how they ought to make judgments ("I ought to take the views of others into consideration"). Finally, individual differences in the need to evaluate are likely related to how people view themselves when making social judgments (Jarvis and Petty, in press). People with a lower documented need to evaluate could be less interested in making social judgments and therefore spend less time judging or possibly avoid making such judgments altogether.

To the degree that power holders internalize their power roles and accompanying cultural expectations about powerful people, their desire to maintain power should increase. Power holders who identify strongly with their power roles should be motivated to protect these roles and their expectations about power relations and hierarchies. Social group identifications such as gender, ethnicity, and age also may be central to the self and may motivate the powerful to defend these identities via different judgment strategies. If power holders see themselves in a particular way, they may not only try to make judgments in a way that fits their self-definitions (for example, attending only to expectancy-confirming information) but may also be more or less willing to accept or express a particular judgment. So, for example, people who define themselves as white-supremacist may evaluate not only members of other ethnic groups less carefully but may be unwilling to accept or express certain types of judgments about these people (that is, that nonwhites are equally competent as whites), because changing these expectations would threaten existing power roles. Conversely, those who see themselves as nonracist are more likely to evaluate others carefully and refrain from expressing judgments that threaten views of themselves as fair-minded egalitarians (Devine 1989b; Devine and Monteith 1993). The effects of priming responsibility as an antidote to power holders' stereotyping processes reflect the potential for such a process to occur (Goodwin and Fiske 1995).

Social Judgeability Theory and the PAC Model

To recap, the motivational pressures for power holders to confirm stereotypic expectations are clear in light of the specific judgeability standards they presumably employ in order to meet global judgeability standards. First, power holders are vulnerable to relying more confidently on their own prior beliefs, thereby enhancing their sense of entitlement to judge and perhaps allowing them to judge with less information. Second, even if power holders are held accountable for their judgments, high confidence in judging others may encourage rationalizing judgment standards; conversely, perceived threats to power may encourage adopting acceptability standards that could similarly lead to stereotyping. Finally, identification with specific power roles and social group memberships associated with power roles encourages judgment strategies that protect existing power structures; stereotyping subordinates allows the powerful to maintain the status quo. Thus, the specific strands that constitute power holders' global judgeability standards are spun with fibers that encourage stereotyping subordinates and allow the powerful to feel confident in doing so.

The judgeability standards employed by the powerful mesh well with the PAC model's hypotheses regarding power holders' impression formation strategies, which likewise predict motivational pressures to confirm stereotypes about subordinates. Recall that the PAC model predicts that power holders' lack of resource dependence, lack of attentional resources, and possible lack of interest, coupled with a motivation to maintain power, will lead the powerful to stereotype subordinates. Given the empirical evidence that power holders engage in stereotype-based attention strategies in line with the PAC model and the nature of power holders' accessible judgeability standards suggested by SJT, a merging of these two perspectives is warranted. The chapter's goal in integrating these two theories is to address the specific processes whereby perceivers meet judgeability standards during impression formation, and thus to clarify how these standards function at a cognitive level.

JUDGMENT MONITORING

Today's social cognition theorists view the social perceiver as motivated to be "good enough" to meet the demands of social life (Fiske 1992). Being "good enough" implies that people are able to monitor, consciously or not, whether they are able to come to a judgment (for a review of conscious/nonconscious processing, see Uleman and Bargh 1989). Pragmatically, it makes sense for people to recognize, at some level, when they have met sufficient conditions to make a judgment; failure to do so could lead people not only to make inappropriate or premature judgments but also to overexpend valuable cognitive resources (such as the capacity to concentrate).

In line with this reasoning, we propose a parallel judgment-monitoring process that operates throughout the various stages of social judgment. The function of this self-regulation process is twofold: first, to enable perceivers to follow the implicit rules for making social judgments (that is, judgeability standards), and second, to alert perceivers when judgeability standards have been violated, so that they may correct their judgment strategies and avoid potentially negative consequences, such as the loss of desired social or material outcomes.

The judgment monitor compares judgment-related cognitions and behaviors against internally accessible or externally salient standards. The process essentially involves a simple check of whether standards have been met or violated. Whenever the process encounters an inconsistency between judgment beliefs or behaviors and an active standard, perceivers sense they are less able to judge. The sense ability to judge is manifest as a sense of knowing or certainty in making a judgment (see Clore 1992; Chaiken, Liberman, and Eagly 1989). The degree to which people feel able to judge is likely to depend on the importance they place on the accessible standards; the more important a standard is, the more influence it will have on perceived ability to judge.

Coping with Inability to Judge

When people sense that they are less able to judge, they make use of certain coping strategies. A certain minimal threshold of ability to judge is likely to exist, however, below which perceivers feel completely unable to judge. How they cope with an inability to judge should reflect the urgency of making a judgment (that is, whether a judgment must be made at all), the availability of cognitive resources, and their motivation to resolve inconsistencies between standards and judgment beliefs and strategies.

When the situation does not demand an immediate judgment, perceivers may simply refrain from judging, privately and publicly. In a situation where a judgment must be made or expressed or there is motivation to raise the ability to judge to a high enough level for a judgment to be made, perceivers have several options for responding. First, people who feel unable to judge may resist making extreme judgments and express moderate or ambivalent judgments. This "nonjudgment" response is unlikely to improve one's ability to judge, but it may ease concerns or feelings of anxiety elicited by having to judge under uncertainty. Non-judgment behaviors may be most likely to occur in constrained social interactions (for example, laboratory experiments or brief encounters) when people have either less time, fewer cognitive resources, or less motivation to respond to inability to judge.

A second strategy for perceivers who are unable to judge is to increase their cognitive efforts and either change the relative importance of the standard in question—that is, put more weight on another standard that has been or can easily be met—or change strategies or beliefs in accord with the standard. To illustrate changing the relative importance of standards, graduate students asked to evaluate a potential new faculty member may not feel legitimately entitled to judge because of their social role, but they may decide that they are nevertheless able or qualified to judge because they have more than sufficient information to do so. Or one can retain the importance of the standard and change one's behavior. If, for example, the salient standard is to make an informed decision, then the perceiver who feels unable to judge can seek more information before coming to a decision. These two types of strategies require considerable cognitive resources and at least a minimal motivation to become able to judge. Hence, these strategies are unlikely to occur under cognitive constraint such as high demands on attention and time pressure or when motivation is low as in noninterdependent, transient interactions.

Failure to meet a judgeability standard is likely also to have affective consequences that detract from one's overall sense of ability to judge (Devine and Monteith 1993; Higgins 1987). Should these affective responses be strong enough, they may affect consequences for perceivers' abilities to process information and their willingness to express their judgments publicly. Strong affective responses may create a distraction or lead people to focus on themselves instead of on their judgments (Salovey 1992). When people become too self-focused, they become less able to process other task information (see, for example, Mackie and Worth 1989; Vallacher and Wegner 1987). Such an affect-induced mental busyness may prevent people from using strategies to improve judgeability, leaving them "frozen" and unable to judge.

Awareness of the Monitoring Process

The judgment-monitoring process most often operates subconsciously; perceivers are unaware that they are using judgeability standards. For example, personnel managers probably do not realize consciously that knowing the applicant's gender makes them feel more confident about selecting interviewees, but they are probably more hesitant in making such decisions before they know this piece of information, even if it is not strictly relevant. Sometimes, however, people *can* become aware of the standards and of their role in judgment. Accountability, for example, could obviously make people aware of the standards that they use to make judgments. When people feel accountable, they may consciously consider exactly what is expected of them ("What does the CEO want me to do?") and the consequences for failing to meet those expectations ("I might not get that promotion"), recognizing that they feel more or less able to judge and perhaps even why they feel that way.

Another possibility for increasing the conscious awareness of one's ability and its role in making judgments is through cues in the situation that, either directly or indirectly, indicate judgeability criteria. People may become aware of judgeability standards as a consequence of feelings of inability to judge created by such cues. For example, directly asking people to judge someone solely on a group label (for example, "What do you think about women?") may cue a judgeability standard because the situation is so unusual and blatantly violates current Western egalitarian gender norms. If people are asked to do essentially the same task but in a less direct manner

("Please rate this female manager"), they may feel equally unable to judge but they may not be so aware of why they feel that way.

Finally, heightened affective reactions to unmet standards may alert perceivers to the origins of their discomfort and the nature of the failed standard. Particularly negative feelings are likely to motivate perceivers to determine why they feel as they do and lead to recognition of judgeability standards (Salovey 1992).

Regardless of whether a standard becomes conscious, its accessibility, salience, and relative importance predict its role in the judgment process and in the perceived ability to judge. Standards that are more easily accessible are more likely to influence the judgment process. Similarly, if there is little perceived consequence for failing a standard in a particular situation, people may give less importance to meeting the standard when determining if they are able to judge.

STAGES IN THE JUDGMENT PROCESS

Referring back to the CM (figure 6.1), one can conceive of the judgment process as having four general stages: (1) a precategorization and categorization phase in which social constructs are activated and applied to a judgment target, (2) the concurrent and subsequent activation of motives and goals, (3) information gathering and cognitive processing, and (4) the making or expressing of a judgment.

Judgeability standards and perceived ability to judge can directly and indirectly influence each stage of the judgment process. Moreover, the relationship between these constructs is dynamic and recursive; changes in both may occur during the judgment process and as a consequence of the process itself. Stringent judgeability standards may alter perceived ability to judge, and conversely, perceived ability may alter which standards become active. Finally, any direct effects of standards on perceived ability to judge at one stage in judgment may have indirect effects on subsequent stages. Thus, a standard that activates a particular categorization can subsequently have indirect effects on motivation, processing, and the final judgment. The following sections address several possible direct effects of standards and perceived ability to judge at each of the four general stages of judgment.

Precategorization and Categorization

Before one even encounters a target for judgment, specific judgeability standards to maintain cultural fit or self-integrity may chronically prime one's explanatory theories and consequently affect one's beliefs about the judgment task or target and one's strategies for making judgments. When a judgment target is encountered, these primed constructs will have consequences for how one categorizes that target. For example, a person who feels threatened by members of a particular ethnic group may have defensive judgment strategies that are chronically active; these strategies facilitate the activation and application of particular group categorizations. Similarly, one's role or the environment can prime specific judgeability standards and their corresponding explanatory theories. Consider a corporate manager who, at work, is primed to think of others in terms of their work-related roles (for example, secretary, plant maintenance worker, administrative assistant) and therefore is more likely to categorize people in ways that are consistent with those roles, as opposed to using other category labels that are not work-related (for example, parent, little league coach, community volunteer). The work-related category labels are not only more salient because of the environment but also more accessible because of the perceiver's role. It is more pragmatic for managers to apply work-related categories because these categories are more relevant to the judgeability and judgment standards that managers use.

People who feel less able to judge before categorization may choose different categories or subcategories and apply them more hesitantly when making initial categorizations. For example, Devine and Monteith (1993) have argued that low-prejudiced people may actively inhibit automatic stereotype-based responses in an effort to avoid the negative affective consequences of violating their internalized nonprejudicial standards. Over time, people who practice such inhibitory responses may learn to override their initial categorizations in favor of identifications that are more consistent with nonprejudiced beliefs.

Motivation and Goals

Defensive motives, cultural norms, or the need for prediction and control can motivate goals of either accuracy or directional (biased) processing goals (Kruglanski 1989; Kunda 1990; Snyder 1992). These goals have consequences for the attentional strategies used in the following judgment stage, when information is gathered and interpreted. This link between global judgeability standards, relevant goals, and attention can explain, for example, why perceivers attend to negative information, discount it, and make positive judgments about people who may in turn evaluate them, such as a dating partner (Fiske and others 1995; Stevens and Fiske 1995). Judging a potential evaluator may elicit motives to form a positive impression in order to maintain self-esteem and thereby meet the global self-integrity standard. Thinking of an evaluator in positive terms may fulfill the self-integrity standard either by permitting the hope that the evaluator will reciprocate with a positive evaluation or by predicting a positive interaction with the evaluator.

Conversely, perceived ability to judge may influence motives and goals. For example, people who from the outset feel quite capable and confident in judging may be vulnerable to using less effortful cognitive strategies because these strategies seem "good enough" to meet their current judgeability standards. Unless some event or feature of the situation activates a standard that lowers perceived ability, there is no perceived need, and hence no motivation, to expend extra effort on judging the target.

Information Gathering and Cognitive Processing

Judgeability standards and perceived ability to judge will directly affect perceivers' desire for and attention to information. Two primary characteristics of information are central to determining whether a person will attend to it, depending on that person's distinct goals; first, whether the information is positive or negative, and second, whether or not it is consistent with primed or accessible categorizations. For example, when sizing up the new boss (a likely evaluator), people may fulfill their goals to form positive impressions by selectively attending to positive or category-consistent information that allows maintenance of initial positive expectations, while simultaneously avoiding negative or inconsistent information that threatens positive expectancies. In general, perceivers find negative information more informative and consequently show an attentional preference for negative rather than positive information (Skowronski and Carlston 1989). Attention to positive information is likely to reflect a motivation to protect a positive expectancy. With regard to information consistency, research indicates that accuracy goals elicit attention to inconsistent information (Fiske and Neuberg 1990), whereas other goals may be met by attending to positive or consistent information (Goodwin, Fiske, and Yzerbyt 1995; Ruscher and Fiske 1990; Stevens and Fiske 1995), negative information (Goodwin, Yzerbyt, and Fiske 1994)—or no attention at all, if the goal is to make a quick decision because the target is not particularly relevant (Goodwin, Fiske, and Yzerbyt 1995). Attention to consistent information and attention to inconsistent information appear to be independent processes, driven by distinct motives and goals (Goodwin and Fiske 1995). If perceivers' processing goals are thwarted because of the type of information available to them (for example, someone seeking positive information finds only negative), they should feel less able to judge.

When perceived ability to judge is high during information gathering, perceivers should feel able to judge with less information. Conditions that lessen ability to judge during this stage, in contrast, may subsequently increase information search, if information is believed to be available and if time permits. Perceived ability to judge may operate therefore as a gatekeeper in the information gathering and processing stage, determining when and if perceivers exit the stage to make a judgment.

Making a Judgment

Accessible standards may prevent or encourage expressing one's judgment. For example, no matter how much information one has mulled over, and regardless of one's private certainty in a judgment, judgeability standards may preclude the public expression of certain negative judgments about others, such as employers or in-laws. Accessible standards may thus directly inhibit expression of some judgments and mandate the expression of others, as when perceivers adopt acceptability standards and tell people what they want to hear.

In natural settings, people who are unconstrained by time or information limitations can reach the judgment stage by choice. People can cope with inability to judge in unconstrained situations by simply waiting until more evidence is available or by not expressing a judgment at all. Many situations, however, require people to judge within time and information constraints. Personnel managers, for example, rarely have the luxury of postponing their judgments for long but instead must make many decisions rather quickly and with what little information is contained on an application form. The issues surrounding situational constraints are highly relevant to laboratory experiments in which perceivers most often reach the judgment stage by consequence of the experimental design and are essentially forced to make a judgment. Theoretical assumptions that perceivers are ready to judge may not be accurate and may lead to results with low generalizability outside the lab.

CONCLUSIONS FOR JUDGMENT MONITORING AND ETHICAL DECISION MAKING

Recall that power holders are wont to confirm their stereotypes because of (1) their unusually high sense of entitlement to judge, which in turn can lead to overconfidence in and overreliance on prior expectations and beliefs; (2) their propensity to adopt rationalizing standards and defend prior expectations, coupled with a vulnerability to perceive and adopt biased expectations on behalf of third parties who may control their outcomes; (3) their motivations to protect power and social role identifications; and (4) their lack of interdependence with subordinates. The Judgment Monitoring Model (JMM) suggests that reducing perceived ability to judge and promoting rational and fair decision-making standards are the primary routes to curbing power holders' propensities to stereotype. Such social changes are likely to be most effective at the organizational and individual levels, rather than the cultural level. Western cultures arguably already hold high cultural expectations that power holders be egalitarian, yet the legal system is jammed with discrimination cases that belie power holders' failure to adhere to these cultural standards. The answer to unethical decision making, in our view, lies with the organizations and institutions that bestow outcome control on specific individuals and with the individuals who must ultimately wield that control. We will briefly consider what organizations and individual power holders can do to encourage ethical decision making (for other reviews of organizational and individual responses to stereotyping, see Fiske and Glick 1995; Eberhardt and Fiske 1995).

Organizational Remedies

FOSTER AN EGALITARIAN CLIMATE.   The primary role of organizations in promoting ethical decision making lies in creating, sustaining, and enforcing a climate of rational and fair decision-making standards. This goal can be accomplished in several ways. Perhaps above all else, organizations must make ethical judgment standards salient. Management, for example, can make people aware of expectations to adhere to ethical standards by setting examples across all levels of power within the organization. People throughout the hierarchy must follow the same decision-making standards. Active and intense recruiting and promotion of members of all social groups sends a message to members of the organization that egalitarianism is not only valued but practiced. Direct education, such as formal explanation of expectations for fair decision-making practices, is also beneficial in increasing the salience of egalitarian decision-making standards. Finally, maintaining a professional environment should make these standards salient as well. For example, discouraging unprofessional behaviors such as telling ethnic or sexual jokes communicates the message that stereotyping will not be tolerated.

The organization also has a role in maintaining standards for fair decision making by establishing monitoring systems to prevent or respond to violations of these expectations. The mere existence of such systems has the added bonus of highlighting the value of these standards to the organization. The costs of violating ethical standards must be made clear. Making power holders' outcomes dependent on their own egalitarianism will increase their desire to adhere to these standards, even if they do not personally believe in them. For example, highly dominant or highly prejudiced power holders might adopt ethical standards in order to protect their own outcomes and control. Thus, severe sanctions should be in place and be utilized to inhibit individuals from using less ethical decision-making standards.

INCREASE THE AVAILABILITY AND USE OF APPROPRIATE INFORMATION. Organizations should establish guidelines and routines for decision making that maximize the availability of relevant information while reducing the availability of irrelevant information. For example, some job application forms request personal but not necessarily job-relevant information about an applicant (for example, interests in athletic activities or hobbies), presumably as a means of better understanding the person's personality. Such information may inadvertently provide power holders with irrelevant information that biases their decision making, however. Making power holders explicitly aware of how such irrelevant information may bias their decisions should help to reduce their reliance on such information during decision making.

Although guidelines and routines will provide important structure for decision making, organizations should also recognize that power holders are vulnerable to relying on specific routines as a source of judgment confidence. Thus, emphasis should be placed on treating each decision as unique, so that power holders do not simply go through the required motions and feel over-confident in their decisions simply because they have done so.

INCREASE POWER HOLDERS' INTERDEPENDENCE.   Increasing power holders' perceived or actual interdependence with subordinates should increase their use of ethical decision-making strategies. Organizations can structure power hierarchies in a way that emphasizes teams rather than individuals, while de-emphasizing the power holders' role in controlling outcomes. Communications within the organization can emphasize that power holders are dependent on subordinates for achieving their own goals and rewards. Power holders who recognize that their own promotions hinge on the productivity of their employees, for example, should be motivated to form more accurate impressions and therefore should be more likely to engage in ethical decision-making strategies.

Increasing interdependence among the powerful and the powerless may have the additional benefit of reducing both the "us versus them" mentality of management relations and power holders' generally high sense of expertise when making decisions. To the extent that power holders perceive themselves as similar to the powerless, their tendency to see themselves as uniquely qualified to make decisions may decrease, leaving them feeling less able to judge. According to the Judgment Monitoring Model, this perception should encourage more effortful and perhaps more ethical decision making, assuming that power holders are also encouraged to be fair decision makers.

Individual Remedies

STRUCTURE DECISION MAKING TO ENCOURAGE THE USE OF ETHICAL STAN-DARDS.   Individual power holders can take many actions to structure their decision making to improve their chances of making ethical decisions about subordinates. First, individuals must recognize the need to have ample time and cognitive resources when evaluating others so that they can attend to information about a judgment target. Given ample time and ability to evaluate, the decision maker should seek out all relevant information about a target, recognizing the influence of irrelevant information. For example, knowing that a job candidate is from one's own hometown may positively bias one's opinion, but it is irrelevant to whether or not that candidate is right for the job. Finally, power holders should also be aware of situational factors that may bias their decision making. For example, if a personnel director spends the lunch hour in casual conversation that includes telling jokes about women or minorities, these conversations will likely prime stereotypes about these groups that could affect later decisions. Being aware of such influences can enable the power holder to structure the decision-making process to minimize the effects of such factors.

RECOGNIZE AND RESPOND TO BIASED REACTIONS.   Perhaps the most difficult task for the powerful decision maker is to recognize biased reactions during decision making. Power holders should recognize that gut reactions can be a consequence of prior beliefs and expectations, including stereotypes, and thus that they may lead to unethical decision making. Awareness of rationalizing behavior is also of importance. For example, discounting information may be a sign of defensive information processing ("Well, that woman was successful in school only because she enrolled in easy courses") and should signal decision makers to the possibility of rationalizing a biased decision. The powerful decision maker must also recognize fears of loss of power and how those fears may operate to bias judgment.

Becoming aware of these biases may not necessarily prevent unethical decision making—individuals may not be able to overcome these biases on their own—but it will allow them to monitor and respond to potentially unethical judgment strategies. Even assuming the most ethically motivated power holder, there will nevertheless be situations in which third parties, situational forces, or personal biases lead the powerful astray into unethical decision making. When power holders recognize they have engaged in biased decision making, it is important that means be available to remedy the biases. One possibility is to seek the opinions of other people uninvested in the decision outcomes. This process could be informal, such as asking a friend, or a formal component of the organization. When choosing people from whom to solicit advice, it is important to consider the vested interest those others may have in the decision outcomes. For example, if an individual power holder fears making a biased decision because of feeling threatened by the competence of a particular subordinate, it probably would not be wise for the power holder to seek advice from a spouse who could also have outcomes indirectly at stake in the decision. The key is to seek advice from people who can provide another point of view with minimal pressures for biased decision making.

Weaving It All Together

The JMM of impression formation proposed here is a first attempt to understand how people use standards when making social judgments in everyday life. The model is promising in that it illuminates several possibilities for alerting powerful decision makers of their vulnerability to less-than-ethical judgments of subordinates. It emphasizes that the social perceiver is not condemned to relying on stereotypic responses but instead has control over reactions to and decisions about other individuals. Ultimately, a better understanding of how judgeability standards operate may lead not only to reducing power holders' vulnerability to unethical decision making but also to increasing the ethical distribution of outcomes in society.

Chapter 7

Social Categories and Decision Making: How Much Differentiation Do We Need?

Myron Rothbart and Robert Mauro

Individuals and organizations base their decisions, to a greater or lesser extent, on variables believed to correlate with criteria they wish to predict. The problem is that we do not seem to be particularly good at either isolating the correct predictors or knowing how much weight to place on those predictors (see Brehmer 1980). In the absence of certainty about relevant predictors, individuals and organizations alike fall back on the use of stereotypes, with all the attending shortcomings of that approach. The use of race as a predictor in decision making is particularly vexing, because it raises basic questions about the validity of our perceptions, the meaningfulness of race as a causal variable, and the long-term effects on our society of using race (as opposed to more differentiated variables) as a predictor.

The goal of this chapter is to explore the issue of accuracy in our perception of groups, with particular reference to the use of race as a predictor of behavior. Since the emphasis in this book is on the implications of such behavior for business ethics, our focus will be on organizational decisions, rather than on the less formal and more casual uses of race by individuals, although the two are not unrelated. We begin our discussion with an examination of Walter Lippmann's ideas about the relation of stereotypes to public policy and end with an examination of the institutional use of race as a predictor in drug searches and parole decisions. Lippmann examined the triangular relations among reality, perception, and behavior and noted that how we structure our perception of reality affects our behavior, which in turn can affect the realistic basis of our perceptions. That any of the three points of the triangle can influence, and be influenced by, any of the others could be taken as the motif of this chapter.

This research was supported in part by the National Institute of Mental Health Grant MH40662 to the first author.

REALITY AND ITS REPRESENTATION

Walter Lippmann, in his seminal work *Public Opinion,* addressed what he called the "triangular relationship" of the "scene of action," the "human picture," and the "human response to that picture working itself out upon the scene of action" (Lippmann 1922). To restate this concept less eloquently, Lippmann was interested in (1) the relation between social reality and our interpretation of that reality, (2) the nature of our behavioral decisions based on those interpretations, and (3) the effect of those decisions on social reality itself. Lippmann had a keen interest in psychology and his book posed some important questions. One of the most significant issues he raised is the correspondence between reality and the representation of reality.

> For the real environment is altogether too big, too complex, and too fleeting for direct acquaintance. We are not equipped to deal with so much subtlety, so much variety, so many permutations and combinations. And although we have to act in that environment, we have to reconstruct it on a simpler model before we can manage with it. To traverse the world men must have maps of the world. Their persistent difficulty is to secure maps on which their own need, or someone else's need, has not sketched in the coast of Bohemia. (p. 4)

In this passage one can recognize a number of ideas that were to become pervasive in psychology half a century later. Probably most important is the idea of information reduction and its relation to action (see Simon 1989). As Lippmann noted, the goals of the observer are inextricably linked to the complexity of the representation. Our internal representation is a simplified map of external reality, with just enough complexity to allow us to "traverse the world." In short, our simplified view of the external world is "good enough" to enable us to get where we want to go. Although we are allowed to sacrifice fidelity for simplification, there is a danger in allowing too much discrepancy between image and reality, as in a map that includes the coastline of a landlocked country. It is unlikely that simplification would result in this error of commission, but it is highly likely that simplification would result in significant errors of omission, failing to include landmarks that "ought" to be included by some criteria of fidelity.

We think of Lippmann's view as pragmatic, because he judged the adequacy of a mental representation by the quality of outcomes resulting from decisions based on the representation, rather than by the degree of match between representation and reality. Lippmann's view appeals to us, for a number of reasons. First, it recognizes the important simplifying function of stereotypes (among other forms of representation). Second, and perhaps most important, it ties motivational and cognitive processes together by linking the representational level of complexity to the observer's goals. To take the map metaphor further, the level of detail needed in a map to guide one by auto from Eugene, Oregon, to San Francisco, California (a distance of 550 miles), would be minimal; one would need probably just the freeway exits for Interstate 5 and the location of rest stops and gas stations. For a 15-mile backpacking trip through the Three Sisters Wilderness Area in the mountains of Oregon, however, one would require a detailed topographic map showing such features as streams and rock outcroppings to determine a route that avoided steep and difficult terrain.

Lippmann's pragmatic view of stereotypes is compelling but ultimately unsatisfying. Mental representations may be "good enough to get us what we want," but the simplification that results from stereotyping, particularly of out-groups, may result in outcomes that are unnecessarily impoverished, both for the observer and for the object of stereotyping. Taking a simple view of others, one that lacks "subtlety" and "variety," may have severe disadvantages or costs that may be fully as consequential as sketching in the coastline of Bohemia. How much discrepancy is tolerable between social reality and our representation of that reality? Lippmann's answer, we assume, would be that as long as we can "traverse the world" to our satisfaction, the discrepancies are inconsequential. The problem, of course, is that we might be considerably more satisfied with the consequences if we acted on the basis of a more complex (and veridical) image of the world; conflicts that we might view as inevitable might have been avoided with a different view of our adversary. One wonders, for example, to what degree our involvement in the Vietnam conflict was guided by a simple classification system that placed countries in a free world–communist world dichotomy, leaving little room for the subtlety and variety of a Vietnamese movement that was primarily nationalistic and secondarily communist in character (see, for example, Karnow 1983).

THE ACCURACY OF STEREOTYPES

Although some of the earliest experimental psychologists defined their task as identifying the mathematical relation between physical reality and psychological response, more modern psychologists have been chary of using reality as a criterion, particularly when that reality concerns social objects. We can measure the physical intensity of illumination in foot-candles, but what is the comparable unit of measurement for assessing the "reality" of extraversion in college fraternities? Despite the reluctance to use social reality as the criterion for assessing the accuracy of social perception, recent research on the accuracy of social stereotypes (Judd and Park 1993; Judd, Ryan, and Park 1991), as well as on the basic mechanisms of stereotype formation and change (Rothbart and Lewis 1994), suggests that stereotypes constitute a domain of social perception in which the mental representation is far less complex than the social reality being represented.

Before attempting to identify sources of inaccuracy in our impressions of groups, however, we offer a caveat. We are not attempting to consider all possible sources of influence on the stereotyping process. Our focus will be on cognitive processes, in which the motivation to disparage out-group members is apparently absent. Clearly, there is no shortage of theories describing the "irrational" components of intergroup hatred (for a recent interesting example, see Deutsch 1990), but that is not the focus of our example. We are making the benign assumption that even when malevolent intention is absent, it is often difficult to form accurate impressions of human groups.

There are at least four areas in which it is possible to identify important discrepancies between perception and reality. The first three pertain to stereotypes in general, and the fourth is more specific to stereotypes associated with racial or ethnic groups.

Exaggeration or "Idealization" of the Group Impression

Rather than representing the group by an average, there is a tendency to give disproportionate weight to the extreme examples of the category (Rothbart and others 1978).

Indeed, stereotypes can be thought of as caricatures, in which distinctive features are exaggerated. Individuals appear to remember caricatures better than the faces upon which the caricatures were based and even to misremember faces as caricatures. In a recent study on facial caricature (Mauro and Kubovy 1992), individuals were shown faces having distinctive features, such as a long nose or narrow eyes. Later, subjects were again presented with versions of these faces in which the distinctive features were either unchanged, exaggerated, or minimized and they were asked to identify which faces were previously shown. Subjects were more likely to identify the exaggerated face than the unchanged face as having been originally presented.

Scott Lewis (1990) found a parallel result in the domain of physical stereotypes. Lewis presented subjects with computer-drawn faces in a concept formation task, in which subjects had to learn to place each face into an "A" or a "B" category. For any given subject, the faces differed on a particular feature (for example, width of nose) but did not differ on other features. After the category-learning phase, subjects were asked to reconstruct on the computer screen a "typical" face from each category. Subjects were allowed to adjust all the facial features until the face "looked right," and it was possible to compare subjects' constructions of the critical and noncritical features with the actual mean of the presented features. Lewis consistently found that subjects' representations of the "typical" face were displaced in the extreme direction. That is, for the group that was characterized by a wide nose, the face constructed by the subject included a nose wider than the average of the noses presented for that group. The Lewis data on aggregated judgments directly parallel those of Mauro and Kubovy (1992) on single faces.

The research cited above, conducted in experimental settings, allows us to compare the stimuli actually presented to the subject with the subject's mental representation of those stimuli. Assessing accuracy is more difficult when we compare subjects' judgments about a target group with the "reality" of the target group—usually the target group's judgments about itself. For example, during the Vietnam War, Dawes, Singer, and Lemons (1972) advertised in a campus newspaper for self-described hawks and doves and asked each subject to write attitude statements that accurately described the positions of hawks and doves. These statements were then given to the appropriate groups (attitude items written to describe hawks were given to hawks, and items written to describe doves were given to doves), and subjects were asked to indicate whether the item was "accurate," "too mild," or "too extreme." In general, statements written to describe either group (hawks or doves) were rated as too extreme. That is, there was a tendency to see both groups as more extreme then they really were. However, the tendency to polarize the attitudes of a group was much greater when the attitude statements were written by out-group members (hawks describing doves, and doves describing hawks) rather than by in-group members. Using self-ratings as the criterion for accuracy, then, there was a pervasive tendency to perceive the attitudes of groups as unrealistically extreme, and the degree of polarization was greatest when judging the attitudes of outgroups.

One criticism of this study is that the self-described hawks and doves who answered an ad in the campus newspaper may actually have been less extreme than the hawks and doves in the general population. Recall that the research subjects were not judging other subjects in the experiment but hawks and doves in general. Improving on this paradigm, Judd and his colleagues (1991) asked engineering majors and business majors on the Boulder campus to make a number of judgments about each group on both trait and attitude items and also asked the subjects to indicate their own positions on the same items. These subjects, were not volunteers but were systematically chosen to be representative of the two campus populations. Although the results were somewhat complex, they generally paralleled earlier findings; there was a tendency to overestimate the extremity of all groups, and this tendency was particularly pronounced in judgments of the out-group. Other research (for example, Judd and Park 1993) on the accuracy of perceptions of Democrats and Republicans also generally support this pattern of findings.

Perceptions of Variability Within the Group

The research described in the previous section focuses on the accuracy of judgments about the central tendency of a group. It indicates that people's judgments are systematically displaced in the direction of idealization or extremity. That is, images of a group are more extreme than are warranted by the attributes of the members that make up the group. Another issue concerns the accuracy of judgments of intra-group variability, the amount of perceived variation around the central tendency. A number of studies have confirmed the finding that greater estimates of group variability are made by those who are members of the category than by judges outside the category (for example, Park and Judd 1990; Park and Rothbart 1982). Differences between in-group and out-group may be irrelevant to issues of accuracy, however, since in principle in-group judges may perceive more variability than actually exists or out-group judges could perceive less variability than exists. The only study we know of that examines the accuracy of variability judgments is Judd et al. (1991), which shows again that all judges underestimate variability (on one of the measures), and that the degree of underestimation is greater for out-group than for in-group judges. Thus we now have evidence that the idealization process both displaces the central tendency and underestimates the variability that exists within the category.

Perceptions of Group Membership: "Goodness of Fit"

A third source of inaccuracy is somewhat more speculative but is related to the previous two sources of inaccuracy. There is reason to believe that people's stereotypic beliefs, once established, become insensitive to disconfirming information. The rationale for this prediction is related to the finding described earlier that our images of groups are more extreme than is warranted by the characteristics of the members who make up these groups. Over time one would expect image and reality to converge, so that as people accrue more and more experience with group members, the perception becomes more accurate, but this does not occur.

Several studies (Rothbart and John 1985; Rothbart and Lewis 1988) have argued that a critical issue in stereotype change concerns the dynamic relation between the group and the members who make up the group. Although an experience with a group member whose attributes strongly disconfirm the stereotype should in principle generalize to and alter the image of the group, this frequently does not happen. Instead, atypical members are often not perceived to be group members, and their attributes fail to generalize to the group as a whole. The same attributes of group members that make them disconfirming of the stereotype also make them a poor fit to the category and unlikely to be thought of as group members (Rothbart, Sriram, and Davis-Stitt 1996).

In short, the same arguments that led Eleanor Rosch (1973, 1978) to think of group membership as graded with respect to "natural kind" categories apply as well to social categories. Psychological membership in a category is not "all-or-none," but is graded in terms of "goodness-of-fit" between the attributes of the category and the attributes of the category member. A logical member of the category who is a poor fit to the category may not be thought of as a category member at all. Thus, those group members who most disconfirm the category are more likely to be dismissed as nonmembers, exceptions, or "special cases" than to be integrated into the stereotype (see Hewstone and others, in press; Johnston and Hewstone 1992; Kunda and Oleson 1994). The implication of this argument is that disconfirming exemplars are functionally isolated from the stereotype, allowing the stereotype to remain insulated from disconfirming information. Ironically, then, the more discrepant the stereotype is from the exemplars that constitute the category, the more likely the exemplars are to be dismissed as atypical deviations from the category.

One of the clearest predictions from this research is that stereotypes should be more stable over time than is warranted by the evidence available to the perceiver. We know of no study that allows such a comparison, but a longitudinal study (Rothbart and John 1993) showed an extremely high level of test-retest reliability of social stereotypes in college students over a four-year period, from freshman to senior year. Averaging over fourteen different target groups, the test-retest reliability, computed across over forty traits per group and a four-year period, was .92, compared with .96 for a one-week test-retest period with an independent sample. Given that the four-year college experience is, for many subjects, the first time that they are exposed to ethnic minorities, gays, and lesbians (some of the target groups included in the study), this level of stability seems extremely high.

The theoretical underpinnings of Rothbart and John's argument have also found support in the laboratory. In a series of experiments by Rothbart and his colleagues, subjects judging the attributes of a category gave greater weight to exemplars with good fit to the category than to those with poor fit, even when they were judging geometric shapes (Rothbart and Lewis 1988); subjects were more likely to generalize from an individual to a group in proportion to the goodness of fit between the individual and the stereotype of the group (Rothbart and Lewis 1988). As subjects acquired new information about a category member, the strength of the association between the category and the exemplar increased when the information tended to confirm the stereotype but decreased when the information disconfirmed the stereotype (Rothbart, Sriram, and Davis-Stitt 1996). Subjects also had more difficulty retrieving information about atypical than about typical exemplars of a category (Rothbart, Sriram, and Davis-Stitt 1996). Thus, the longitudinal data, as well as the laboratory research, lends support to the idea that stereotypic beliefs are insufficiently sensitive to disconfirming information.

The Special Case of Racial Attribution

A fourth source of error concerns attributional processes more specific to racial stereotypes. Although stereotypes are formed on almost every conceivable basis, there may be reason to believe that racial stereotypes have special status. We make this argument not on the basis of the physical attributes of race (the Nazis treated Jewishness as a racial attribute but acknowledged substantial overlap in physical attributes of Jews and Aryans), nor on any scientific meaning that might be ascribed to racial concepts, but on the social concept of race. Indeed, there is little scientific basis for a concept of race; there are no clear distinctions between race and ethnicity, and physical differences may or may not be a marker of race. Yet the concept is ubiquitously used by individuals, by governmental agencies, and in scientific research.

The notion of race, we suspect, is related to the concept of *essentialism*— the belief that members of a race have some fundamental property or properties in common with one another that make them different from all others (see Allport 1954). Race has two important properties of an essentialist concept: (1) it is unalterable—individuals who are members of a racial category are thought of as always being in the category—and (2) it has "rich inductive potential"—that is, knowledge of category membership is *perceived* to be predictive of a broad array of attributes and behavior (see Rothbart and Taylor 1992). It is worth noting that racial concepts are likely to be viewed as "natural kinds," meaning that even though physical appearance is thought to reflect some deep, underlying essence, the absence of physical differences does not negate "racial" qualities (consider the Nazi's view that a Jew who looks Aryan is still a Jew).

In our view, racial concepts may serve as a magnet for the attribution process in several ways. First, attributions to race may occur when there is no correlation between race and behavior—illusory correlation. A considerable amount of research has been done on illusory correlation in stereotyping by David Hamilton and his colleagues (Hamilton and Sherman 1989). This research shows that the co-occurrence of distinctive behaviors (for example, antisocial behaviors) with distinctive individuals (for example, members of racial minorities) lead them to be perceived as "going together," even though there is statistical independence between behaviors and group members.

There is also a second type of illusory correlation that may occur with racial minorities. Individuals are more likely to learn and use differentiating information about a person when that person is an in-group rather than an out-group member (Park and Rothbart 1982). For example, a white observer who reads a story about a white person engaged in child abuse is likely to search for (and find) differentiating information about the perpetrator that may "explain" his or her behavior—the abuser was unemployed or an alcoholic. If the white observer reads the identical story but with a black rather than a white perpetrator, the reader is unlikely to seek out or remember differentiating information about the abuser. Thus people are likely to make differentiated, individualistic attributions for in-group members' behavior but group-level attributions for out-group members' behavior. It may be difficult to say which is the correct or incorrect attribution, but it is quite possible that behaviors more appropriately attributed to an individual are erroneously attributed to the entire out-group.

A second kind of attributional error occurs because a behavior is attributed to race that would more appropriately be attributed to correlates of race, such as poverty or minority status (see Zadowski 1948). This distinction may appear to be a subtle one, but the implications are often not subtle. There is a major difference between attributing behavior to an unalterable, "essential" quality of the self and viewing the behavior as a product of, or an adaptation to, a powerful environment. Some behaviors may be more appropriately attributed to minority status, where they represent adaptations to powerlessness; other behaviors may be more specific to a particular cultural history or educational and employment opportunities; and still other behaviors may reflect the rewards and punishments associated with peer group members.

INDIVIDUAL AND ORGANIZATIONAL USE OF RACIAL STEREOTYPES

Despite the many potential sources of error in people's perceptions of groups' stereotypes (including racial stereotypes) clearly influence the judgment and decisions of both individuals and organizations (see, for example, Lewin and Grabbe 1945; Sagar and Schofield 1980). The question remains whether these stereotypic images, with all their inaccuracy, are nonetheless "good enough" to allow us to "traverse the world." Although one can ask this question for both individuals and organizations, the answers may be different for the two parties.

In private life, the apparent costs of relying on an inaccurate stereotype are quite small—an ashen look, a few embarrassing moments in conversation. The costs in lost opportunities may be objectively large, but these costs are often obscure. If one rarely interacts with members of an ethnic group because they are mistakenly believed to share noxious tastes in art, food, music, or lifestyle, one may be denied many of the experiences that could enrich one's life, but it is difficult to appreciate the costs of not doing what is not done.

Compared with the costs incurred by individuals in their private lives, the real and apparent costs of relying on inaccurate stereotypes in making professional decisions are much greater. For example, employers who do not hire members of an ethnic group because they mistakenly believe that members of that group are unreliable or dishonest deny the organization the benefit of potentially good employees and deny the group the benefits of economic gain.

The set of factors relevant to making professional decisions also differs from and is much smaller than the set of factors relevant to making private choices. Individuals choose their friends on the basis of a host of idiosyncratic factors, and observers are hard pressed to question the rationality of those choices in all but the most abusive relationships. Businesses, however, are expected to base decisions on a more restricted set of criteria. Ultimately, the rational business person must justify all decisions in terms of the benefits that are expected to accrue to the firm.

Since 1964, discrimination by race in most employment contexts has been illegal in the United States. Title VII of the Civil Rights Act of 1964 (as amended by the Equal Employment Opportunity Act of 1972 and the Civil Rights Act of 1991) prohibits employment discrimination against individuals on grounds of race, color, religion, sex, or national origin, by state and local governments and private employers with more than fourteen employees, and it prohibits discrimination by labor unions, employment agencies, and all agencies of the executive branch of the federal government. The large number of lawsuits for alleged racial discrimination in employment and hiring that continue to be brought each year, however, suggests that many employers continue to rely on race or factors associated with race in making business decisions. The goal of this chapter is not to analyze the legal or ethical issues raised by racial discrimination in the workplace but to explore the rationality of considering race in making professional decisions.

When is it rational to consider race in making decisions? The answer to this question depends on several factors: first, the costs of making different types of errors; second, the strength of the relations between race and the criterion, between relevant factors (other than race) and the criterion, and between race and these other relevant factors; and finally, the time frame and scope of the decision maker. We will consider each of these issues in turn.

The Costs of Making Errors

Any employer hiring new workers will inevitably make mistakes, and the results of this selection process can be displayed in a two-way table (see table 7.1).

The rational decision maker attempts to maximize the number of good employees hired (true positives, in the vernacular of the statistician) and poor employees not hired (true negatives) relative to the number of good employees that are not hired (false negatives) and poor employees that are hired (false positives). However, the costs of making poor decisions and the

Table 7.1 / Outcomes Associated with Hiring Decisions

	Reality	
Decision	Good employee	Poor employee
Hire	Hit (true positive)	Miss (false positive)
Don't hire	Miss (false negative)	Hit (true negative)

benefits of making correct decisions will vary, depending on the situation. In some situations (for example, entry-level assembly-line work) rejecting potentially good employees may incur few costs to the organization. When there is a large supply of satisfactory potential workers, missing a few good candidates may be a relatively minor loss. However, when the supply of potential employees is small (for example, when a firm is searching for someone to fill a high-level technical or managerial position), the costs associated with failing to hire a good employee are more substantial. Other factors in addition to the supply of workers affect the costs of making the different types of errors. For example, the search process itself may be quite costly; if a firm is searching to fill a given number of positions, the more candidates who are screened and incorrectly rejected, the greater the costs to the firm.

The relative costs of making the different errors (false positives and false negatives) and the benefits of making the different types of correct decisions (true positives and true negatives) will determine the decision rule. A rational employer with a large supply of potential employees may reject all minority applicants if there is even a weak association between ethnicity and job performance because it may seem preferable to reject a large number of well-qualified applicants than to do anything that would increase the risk of hiring a bad employee. Another employer facing the same weak association between ethnicity and job performance but having a more limited applicant pool might attach less weight to an applicant's race—or even ignore race—rather than incur the costs of making many incorrect rejections.

The Strength of Relations Between Variables

No matter what the decision rule, a rational employer will strive to make the best possible prediction of job performance at the lowest possible cost. Because gathering information may be costly in time and resources, the real-world decision maker will probably limit the search. In this case, the most efficient types of variables to consider are those that are highly predictive of job performance, relatively uncorrelated, and cheap to measure. The predictor variables need not be causally related to the criterion; they need only predict the criterion.

As we have noted, there are many psychological mechanisms that encourage people to believe that race is an important predictor when it is not. Without access to carefully conducted research, determining the true effect of race in any situation is quite difficult. Rational decision makers may be tempted to consider race in making decisions even when the association between race and the criterion is weak because race is often easy and inexpensive to measure. Compared with the other measures of an applicant that an employer could gather, such as academic preparation, previous experience, and recommendations, race is inexpensive to determine (in most cases), hard to distort, and very reliable. Ease and reliability of measurement cannot compensate for lack of predictive power, however, and the predictive power of race is often overestimated.

Even when statistical information is available, it is frequently difficult to determine the true effects of race. On the surface it would appear that determining whether race is related to job performance would be a simple matter. Assuming that one had experience with both white and minority workers, one could simply compare the job performance of both groups. Yet workers are not selected at random. Observed differences between groups of workers could be a function of the selection process rather than of racial differences (in statistical terms, a sample selection bias). For example, a sales manager may note that white sales representatives outperform African American sales representatives and conclude that whites are superior sellers. However, the sales representatives may have been hired by a personnel manager who did not select at random from the pool of applicants. For example, the personnel manager might have interpreted assertiveness in blacks as hostility and avoided hiring assertive blacks, while assertiveness in whites might have been viewed positively as showing signs of drive and commitment. Because assertiveness is important in making sales, the bias in selecting assertive whites and nonassertive blacks could create an apparent racial disparity.[1]

In addition to difficulties in assessing the unconfounded relation between race and a criterion, decision makers must confront an additional problem. They must determine not the simple correlation between race and performance, but rather the effect of race on performance when the effects of other factors are taken into account.[2] Without access to carefully crafted research, this is an exceedingly difficult task. For example, in many parts of the country, race and performance in school are substantially correlated. Academic performance is frequently related to job performance. In these circumstances, race may be related to job performance because it is correlated with academic performance; but, knowing that race is related to job performance and that academic performance is related to job performance, an employer might decide that a minority applicant with a poor scholastic record is a doubly poor risk. This in effect doubles the negative weight assigned to poor academic performance when predicting the job performance of minority applicants. Once the applicant's academic performance is known, however, knowledge of the applicant's race adds little or no predictive power. Indeed, in cases like this, minority status may be a positive factor. That is, a white with a poor scholastic record may be a worse bet as a worker than a minority-group member with a similar record. The minority applicant may have had to work harder against greater obstacles to achieve the same record as the white. In terms of correlations, although there may be a negative simple correlation between minority status and job performance, when the effects of other factors are taken into account, the effect of minority status may be positive. To estimate the effect of race correctly in situations like this requires considerable statistical sophistication and access to information not normally available to the business decision maker. In principle, a more accurate prediction could be made by ignoring race than by estimating its true effect from the zero-order correlation.

THE DRUG COURIER PROFILE.   The case of the drug courier profile provides an interesting example. Since 1974, law enforcement agencies in the United States have utilized a behavioral and circumstantial profile of a drug courier to aid them in determining who should be scrutinized for possible involvement in the transportation of illicit drugs. Originally devised by a single Drug Enforcement Agency agent in Detroit for screening passengers on commercial aircraft, the profile has been modified for use by highway patrols in screening motorists. In this context, police officers compare the characteristics of motorists stopped for traffic violations with the characteristics of drug traffickers as indicated by the profile. When the officers believe the match is sufficiently strong, they attempt to search the vehicle for drugs. Legally, a match to the drug courier profile is not considered sufficient "probable cause" to allow the police to search a vehicle without consent, so the officers must obtain the motorist's consent to search the vehicle. This is rarely an issue, since virtually all motorists give consent.

In the only study to date to evaluate the drug courier profile, Mauro (1994) observed that the race of the motorist appeared to affect the search decisions of (some) police officers in Oregon. Of the vehicles for which consent to search was requested, 48 percent were occupied by Hispanics, whereas 27 percent were occupied by whites. Of the vehicles for which consent to search was not requested, only 14 percent were occupied by Hispanics; white motorists occupied 49 percent. These statistics in themselves do not demonstrate racial bias. It is possible that Hispanics could be more than three times likely to be transporting illegal drugs than whites. However, searches of Hispanics were successful in only 20 percent of the cases; searches of whites were successful in 30 percent of the cases. Furthermore, statistical models of these data indicate that being Hispanic *does not* increase the likelihood that a motorist is transporting drugs once other profile characteristics are taken into account.[3]

Why, then, do at least some officers apparently overestimate the strength of the relation between race and drug trafficking? A clue can be found in the content of the profile. The items constituting the profile can be divided into four groups: suspicious behaviors (such as traveling under an alias, being extremely nervous), suspicious travel (such as going to or coming from a source or distribution area for narcotics), suspicious possessions (such as carrying a concealed weapon or large quantities of cash in small denominations), and suspicious personal history (such as having a criminal record). In the study area, many of these items—such as traveling to or from a source area for illicit drugs (such as Los Angeles or Mexico) and being extremely nervous when contacted by the police—are correlated with being Hispanic. Although these items are predictive of trafficking in illicit drugs, once they are taken into account, Hispanics are no more likely to be carrying drugs than other motorists. The officers who acted as if race was predictive of drug trafficking (in this study only a few did) treated "Hispanic" as if it were an additional profile item. This caused them to spend hours engaged in fruitless searches. In fact, had the officers ignored race and relied solely on the factors in the drug courier profile (and used a moderately conservative decision rule), they could have made hundreds more successful searches.

This is not to say that race should never be considered in making any professional decision. For example, if race is predictive of job performance and that information is properly integrated with other available factors, then our decision maker should consider the applicant's race. Not considering an individual's race under these circumstances would result in predictions that are not as accurate as they could be. The federal parole guidelines provide a case in point.

FEDERAL PAROLE GUIDELINES.   For decades, parole decisions were made on a strictly qualitative, case-by-case basis. The prison record of each inmate eligible for parole was reviewed and the inmate interviewed. As might be expected, this process led to large discrepancies in the way similar cases were handled. In 1972, the federal parole system began a large-scale project designed to address this problem. Federal parole boards now use an actuarial system that sets the appropriate ranges of time to be served by different classes of inmates. Parole boards may depart from the ranges provided, but it is rare. In one follow-up study, researchers observed that 84 percent of the parole boards' decisions followed the guidelines (Hoffman and Stone-Meierhofer 1977).

The range of time an inmate must serve is determined by the inmate's score on two scales (see table 7.2): one measures the seriousness of the

Table 7.2 / Guidelines for Parole Decision Making: Customary Total Time Served Before Release (in months)

Offense Characteristics: Severity of Offense	Offender Characteristics: Parole Prognosis (Salient Factor Score)			
	Very Good (9–11)	Good (5–8)	Fair (4–5)	Poor (0–3)
Low (such as minor theft)	6–10	8–12	10–14	12–18
Low moderate (such as possession of small quantities of drugs)	8–12	12–16	16–20	20–28
Moderate (such as possession of moderate quantities of drugs with intent to sell)	12–16	16–20	20–24	24–32
High (such as organized vehicle theft)	16–20	20–26	26–34	34–44
Very high (such as robbery)	26–36	36–48	48–60	60–72
Greatest (such as kidnapping)	40–55	55–70	70–85	85–110

offense and the other the likelihood of success on parole. The latter scale is a composite based on nine variables. Inmates gain points on this scale for not having prior convictions, for not having been previously incarcerated, for not having previously violated parole, for not having stolen a car in the current crime, for not having engaged in forgeries (one point each), for having reached the age of 18 (one point) or 26 (two points) before their first crime, for not having a prior history of opiate or heroin abuse (one point), and for having a history of employment or school attendance for at least six months out of the last two years prior to conviction (one point) (see Gottfredson, Wilkins, and Hoffman 1978).

These factors were selected in a quasi-empirical fashion. First, all of the data routinely available about inmates were assembled. Then, several of the variables that the oversight board determined were unethical to consider— such as age and race—were eliminated. The variables used to form the "salient factor score" were selected from the remaining variables. After a preliminary set of guidelines was created, some variables (namely, education and family ties) found to be predictive of success on parole were eliminated and others (car theft, forgeries) were added. The result is a scale designed not to produce the best possible prediction but only to produce the best possible prediction given the permissible variables. In other studies (for example, Petersilia and others 1985), age and race have been found to be significant predictors of success on parole and probation, even when the effects of numerous other predictors are taken into account. Thus, the present federal parole guidelines may be criticized for being demonstrably unfair. That is, there are inmates who in all likelihood would be good parole risks who serve longer sentences because the federal parole board uses a predictive system known to be less accurate than it need be.[4] The officers deciding whom to search for illicit drugs made more efficient decisions when they ignored race and relied on more individualized information (such as the behavioral profile indicators). For the parole board, the situation may be different. There may not be additional variables that once taken into account would make reliance on race unnecessary or counterproductive.

However, even in cases like these it may be unwise to base decisions on race. Once the long-term consequences of a decision are considered, there may be both pragmatic and ethical reasons not to rely on race.

Time Frame and Scope of the Decision

When evaluating the consequences of decisions, it is important to consider Lippmann's "triangular relation" between reality, interpretation, and behavior. A decision may have consequences far beyond its immediate context and may substantially affect the larger social environment. Thus far, we have assumed that the business decisions being made have no effect beyond the firm and the individuals involved. This is probably a good approximation of the effect of the decisions made by small businesses acting in isolation. However, decisions of large corporations or of many small businesses acting in concert may substantially affect their environment. In this case, it is important for decision makers to consider the impact of their decisions on that environment.

For example, it may be in the best interest of every firm and every member of the society to live in a society where social and economic inequality is not based on race. Making decisions based on race, even when they reflect racial differences existing at the moment, may serve to perpetuate those differences and carry racial divisions into the future. On this basis, the federal parole board could argue that its decision not to base parole on race is not only ethical but rational because it supports the long-term goal of building a society in which minorities are not more likely to be bad parole risks. In business, this tension between short- and long-run goals may create a social dilemma. In the short run, each decision maker may be better off considering race in making business decisions, but if all decision makers do so, the differences between the races are continued and the result is an environment that is less beneficial for society (and presumably business) than it could have been. It may be better to be "unfair" and to tolerate inefficiencies in the short run in exchange for a fairer and more efficient future.

Unfortunately, the prognosis for solving such social dilemmas through voluntary action is not good (cf. Messick and Brewer 1983). When there are real racial differences, a business may not be able to incur the short-run costs of ignoring race. Executive officers may find it necessary to ignore the long-run benefits to survive in the short run. To solve this type of social dilemma, we may need to rely on "mutual coercion, mutually agreed upon." Equal opportunity laws may be necessary to compel us to do what is in our own best interests.

CONCLUSIONS

In sum, the tendency to simplify our impressions of groups is not limited to individuals but is common to organizations as well. By using race as a categorical predictor, we may be giving race too much weight, either because the true relation between race and the criterion is smaller than the perceived relation, or because race has in effect already been included by the use of correlated variables.

Three hundred years of slavery and discrimination in America are not without their effects, and there are cases where race, as a categorical predictor, does predict a criterion of importance. In some cases there may be causally relevant, individuating predictors that may be used instead of race to increase our predictive efficiency without perpetuating existing inequalities. Even when these predictors do not exist it may be unwise to base decisions on racial differences. Although, in the short run, ignoring race may lead to less accurate predictions and increased costs, the cost of perpetuating or magnifying existing racial inequalities may be even higher.

ENDNOTES

1. In some cases, better performance by a minority group may be indicative of discrimination against this group at an earlier stage in the selection process. For example, it may be that black workers outperform white workers because, to be hired at all, the blacks had to display qualifications greatly in excess of those possessed by the whites.

2. In statistics, this is the problem of multicollinearity. The task of predicting performance may be viewed as a problem in estimating the effects on performance of several highly correlated predictor variables. When the predictors are highly correlated it is impossible to isolate the effect of a single variable. One can only estimate the effect of the predictor in a model in which the other variables are taken into account.

3. We do not know what is the real association between race and drug trafficking on the highways patrolled by these officers, nor can it be easily determined. To properly determine the characteristics of highway drug couriers, a random sample of motorists would need to be stopped and searched. However, motorists cannot legally be stopped at random and the police cannot afford the time to search every vehicle stopped for a traffic violation. We can only examine the product of the decisions to stop for a traffic violation and to seek consent to search. It is possible that Hispanics are disproportionately involved in drug trafficking.

4. In reality, the parole guidelines are not as inaccurate as they might have been. Some of the variables added belatedly (such as the car theft factor) are correlated with the excluded factors. Of course, this may have produced the worst of all possible situations: a prediction system that is demonstrably less accurate than it could be (because important predictors are missing) and that is unethical (because it is based on a scale that includes proxies for variables that the designers believe should not be considered).

Chapter 8

In-Group Favoritism: The Subtle Side of Intergroup Discrimination

Marilynn B. Brewer

Although people tend to think in terms of dichotomies and bipolar distinctions, bipolarity may actually be a relatively rare natural phenomenon. The distinction between *hot* and *cold* is one instance of a truly bipolar dimension. Since cold is literally the absence of heat, reducing heat increases cold, and cranking up the heat makes things less cold. The reciprocal relationship is perfectly negative.

For many years, psychologists and social scientists have represented positive/negative evaluations and affect as bipolar concepts analogous to hot and cold. The implicit assumption has been that the more positive one's orientation toward an object or idea, the less negative, and vice versa. In order to improve attitudes, one could either increase positive evaluations or decrease negative evaluations, with the same effect. This assumption has been incorporated into our measuring instruments. Endorsement of a positive belief and rejection of a negative belief are treated as equivalent positive responses; similarly, rejection of positives is scored as equivalent to endorsement of a negative. By definition, then, net attitude is a bipolar construct; the more positive endorsements there are, the less negative is the overall attitude.

Recent research on both behavioral and neurological levels has begun to challenge this bipolar representation (Abelson and others 1982; Cacioppo and Berntson 1994). Evidence is accumulating that positive and negative evaluative processes represent different, independent systems that may or may not be reciprocally activated. As this new conceptualization takes hold, the nature of attitude measurement is changing as well. Bipolar scales are giving way to new classification systems in which positive and negative evaluations are assessed separately and overall attitudes are represented in terms of the convergence or conflict between positive and negative evaluations.

If positive and negative affect are two separate substrates of behavior, then we cannot assume that decreasing negative evaluations of a social object necessarily increases positive affect toward that same object. When expressed attitudes vary, across time or across persons, it becomes appropriate to ask where the *locus* of the variation lies—whether it reflects variation in positive evaluation, negative evaluation, or both. This distinction has implications for understanding the nature of intergroup attitudes and behavior. In this chapter, I will elaborate this idea of identifying the locus of intergroup prejudice and consider its implications for antidiscrimination policies and practices in business settings.

INTERGROUP DISCRIMINATION: A RECONCEPTUALIZATION

Discrimination is operationally defined as differential treatment or outcomes associated with social category membership. In many policy-relevant contexts, this means differences in treatment accorded to members of one's own membership group (in-group) and that accorded to members of an out-group. Net discrimination is, by definition, the difference in outcomes received by the in-group (I) relative to those of the out-group (O). But like any other difference score, the difference $(I - O)$ can vary either because of variation in favorability toward the in-group or because of variation in negativity toward the out-group.

Conceptually, one can represent this distinction by imagining an absolute standard of fairness (S), against which both I and O can be evaluated. Differences between I and O could then take three different forms, reflecting three different types (or locus) of discrimination (see figure 8.1). The first type represents discrimination *against* the out-group; the out-group is treated unfairly, while treatment of the in-group is indifferent (unbiased) with respect to the fairness standard. In other words, discrimination is driven by greater activation of *negative* evaluative processes for the out-group than for the in-group. The second form reflects discrimination *for* the in-group, where treatment of the in-group is biased in a positive direction and treatment of

Figure 8.1 / Forms of In-Group/Out-Group Discrimination

Type 1	$I = S$
	$O < S$
Type 2	$I > S$
	$O = S$
Type 3	$I > S$
	$O < S$

the out-group is indifferent. This form of discrimination is driven by differences between in-group and out-group in activation of *positive* evaluative processes. Finally, a third form of discrimination involves differential treatment in favor of the in-group and against the out-group. This is the form associated with (actual or perceived) zero-sum situations, in which gains for the out-group are seen as being achieved at the expense of the in-group. In this case, activation of positive and negative evaluations is reciprocal.

I will argue here that discriminatory outcomes derive from all three of these forms and that the locus of discrimination differs in different cases or at different times. Further, I argue that understanding which form of discrimination is operating is important for policy making, because the psychology underlying the three forms of discrimination differs fundamentally. Although the end result is the same in terms of relative standing of the in-group and out-group, knowing the locus of the differential has significant implications for documenting and changing discriminatory behavior.

Most policies and regulations regarding discrimination on the basis of gender, ethnicity, and sexual orientation implicitly assume Type 1 discrimination. The state-of-mind criterion for conviction in a discrimination case is *intent* to discriminate *against*. Evidence is amassed to document that the claimant has been treated or judged more negatively than standards of equality or fairness would dictate. The assumption is that if negative orientation toward the out-group can be reduced, discrimination will be eliminated. But if discrimination is of Type 2, these efforts may be misplaced. Treating the out-group more fairly does not necessarily eliminate positive biases that favor the in-group. And a great deal of social psychological research now suggests that it is Type 2 discrimination that underlies much differential treatment of in-group and out-group members. A few illustrations follow.

Locus of Prejudice: In-group Positivity Versus Out-group Negativity

The most direct evidence for in-group positivity effects comes from a series of experiments by Samuel Gaertner and John Dovidio, who used various measures of cognitive processing to assess the locus of racial prejudice in white college students (Gaertner and Dovidio 1986; Gaertner and McLaughlin 1983). These methods were designed to measure independently both negative and positive feelings about blacks relative to whites.

One experiment, for instance, used a procedure designed to measure the strength of association between two words. Highly associated word pairs (for example, *doctor-nurse*) produce faster responses in a word recognition task than do unassociated word pairs (*doctor-butter*). Gaertner and McLaughlin (1983) used such a word association task to assess the relative strength (speed of recognition) of associations between racial terms (*black* and *white*) and various positive and negative words (for example, *smart*, *clean*, or *lazy*, *stupid*). Consistently in these and other reaction-time experiments, the researchers have found that the response to negative words is not affected by the pairing with *black* versus *white*, but responses to positive adjectives are significantly speeded up when preceded by the word *white* compared to the response time following *black*. Further, additional research indicates that whites who consider themselves low in prejudice make a conscious effort to suppress negative affective reactions to black stimuli but show no suppression of differential positive affect toward white stimuli. Apparently this more subtle in-group positivity is not consciously recognized as a form of prejudice.

Asymmetries in Positive and Negative Allocations

Much of the experimental research on in-group bias has been conducted in the context of the so-called minimal intergroup paradigm (Brewer 1979; Tajfel 1970). In this paradigm, participants in an experimental session are divided into two social categories on the basis of some arbitrary distinction (for example, overestimating or underestimating the number of dots in a visual display). Results have demonstrated again and again that this categorization alone is sufficient to motivate differential judgments, evaluations, and behavior toward other individuals as a function of whether they belong to the in-group or the out-group.

The original studies using the minimal intergroup paradigm (Tajfel and others 1971) documented in-group bias in the form of preferences for allocation of outcomes to an in-group compared to an out-group member. Individuals were asked to make choices among an array of alternative allocations of prize monies to be given to a member of the in-group category and a member of the out-group category. (Self-interest was presumed not to be a factor in these allocations, because the allocator did not benefit in any way from the choices he or she made.) Paired outcomes such as the following were presented; the top value represents the outcome to be allocated to an in-group member and the bottom the value to be given to the member of the out-group category:

15	14	13	12	11	10	9
8	9	10	11	12	13	14

Typically in these choice situations, subjects rejected the options that came closest to equal allocation (12–11 or 11–12) and preferred an allocation that benefited the in-group member more than the out-grouper (for example, 14–9 or 13–10). This pattern of decisions has come to be labeled *in-group favoritism*. Note, however, that it is not possible to tell from such choices whether the subject is motivated to give the in-group member *more* than a fair share or to give the out-group member *less*.

Further research on allocation biases has demonstrated that the degree of in-group favoritism expressed is moderated by whether positive or negative outcomes are being allocated (see, for example, Hewstone, Fincham, and Jaspars 1981; Mummendey and others 1992). By way of example, consider this simplified choice for allocating positive outcomes:

	Options	
	A	B
In-group member	+3	+4
Out-group member	+3	+1

In this form, the dominant choice is option B, the one that benefits the in-group, rather the equality distribution, even though total allocations are lower with choice B. Preferences change, however, if the choices are transformed so that negative allocations are involved as in the following:

	Options	
	A	B
In-group member	−1	+1
Out-group member	−1	−3

In this case, subjects are more likely to prefer choice A, the one that minimizes the amount of harm distributed. Apparently, when benefits to the in-group can be obtained only at the expense of losses or harm to the out-group, they are less acceptable than benefits to the in-group that do not appear to make the out-group worse off.

Further, the choice of B over A is rated as more "morally justified" in the case of positive allocations than in the negative allocation case (Blanz, Mummendey, and Otten 1994). Such framing effects provide evidence that the discriminatory behavior that results in in-group bias is motivated by favoritism to the in-group rather than negative intent toward the out-group.

In-group/Out-group Differences in What Is Judged to Be Fair

In-group favoritism is particularly pernicious when it alters one's perception about the rules of fairness that should be applied when decisions about merit are being made. This perceptual shift is well illustrated by the results of an experiment by Sik Hung Ng (1984) using the minimal intergroup paradigm. After participants had been divided into arbitrary social categories, they had the opportunity to observe teams made up of one in-group and one out-group member performing a cooperative task. Teams were rewarded according to the total number of items produced by the two persons combined. Across conditions, participants observed either a situation in which the in-group member outperformed the out-group member in contributing to the total product or one in which the out-group member produced the greater contribution.

After viewing the performance outcomes, participants were asked to make a decision regarding the allocation of the team reward to the two team members. When the out-group member outproduced the in-group member, subjects were more likely to choose an *equal* allocation principle; when the in-group member was the higher performer, they were likely to choose an *equity* principle through which the in-grouper received more of the allocation. Further, the extent of overallocation to the high producer was significantly greater when that contributor was an in-group member than when the same performance differential was observed between two persons who were not categorized by an in-group/out-group distinction. Apparently, the threshold for application of the equity/merit principle is affected by whose merit is being judged.

Attributional Ambiguity: Who Deserves Help?

Another line of research relevant to the assessment of intergroup discrimination has investigated decisions about whether or not to help another individual under conditions of uncertainty. For instance, one factor that makes intervention in a potential emergency ambiguous is the presence of other bystanders who could also offer help or assistance. The diffusion of responsibility created by the presence of others reduces the probability that any one individual will decide to help (Darley and Latane 1968). To test the effect of this ambiguity on cross-racial helping, Gaertner and Dovidio (1977) designed a laboratory experiment in which white participants thought they were participating in a study of ESP. Participants were assigned to serve as "receivers" to a "sender" who was located in another room. The sender (actually an experimental confederate) was either white or black (as indicated by a facial photograph provided to the actual subject). Some subjects participated believing that they were the only receiver present during the experimental session. Other subjects believed that there were two other receiver-subjects present in separate rooms.

During the course of the ESP "transmission" trials, an apparent emergency was staged. The sound of falling chairs was transmitted through the intercom, and the sender was heard to cry out, followed by prolonged silence. The behavior of interest was whether the subject decided (during a three-minute period) to get up and leave the cubicle in order to come to the aid of the sender.

When the subject believed she was alone with the victim, there was no difference in response to the black or white sender. Fully 88 percent of the subjects stood up to help, and the speed of responding was equivalent for both in-group and out-group victims. When the subject believed that others were present, however, and thus responsibility to intervene was potentially diffused, a significant race-of-victim effect emerged. In this condition, 75 percent decided to help when the sender was believed to be white, but only 37 percent stood up to intervene when the sender was believed to be black. Further, subjects showed more physiological arousal (as indexed by change in heart rate) in response to the emergency involving a white victim, but less physiological response when the victim was black and responsibility was diffused.

The results of this and other experiments by Gaertner and Dovidio demonstrate that whites do not deliberately *avoid* helping blacks; when help is clearly called for, whites and blacks are treated equivalently. But when there is ambiguity in the situation—when they are making a judgment call about whether or not help is warranted—then the threshold for giving help is lower when the one needing help is an in-group member, rather than an out-group member.

Attributional Ambiguity: When Is Negative Behavior Justified?

An effect known as the *intergroup attributional bias* refers to the finding that positive behaviors by an in-group member are more likely to be attributed to the person's disposition ("He's a nice person") than are those same behaviors when performed by an out-group member, and that negative actions by an in-group member are more likely to be attributed to external reasons ("The heat was getting on his nerves") (Hewstone 1990).

In a recent experimental test of the intergroup attribution bias with arbitrarily designated in-group/out-group categories, Joseph Weber (1994) found that the nature of the bias depends on the ambiguity of justification for the observed behavior. When another individual was observed to exhibit an unambiguously altruistic act (helping an out-grouper when help was not required), attributions for the behavior were not affected by in-group or out-group membership. The helpful behavior was attributed to dispositional factors (helpfulness, generosity) whether the actor was an in-grouper or an out-grouper. When the actor was observed to *refuse* to help in the same situation, however, category membership significantly affected attributions for the behavior. When exhibited by an in-group member, this ambiguous negative behavior was seen as more clearly caused by the situation (that is, as justified by the circumstances) than was the same behavior from an out-group member.

This finding is one illustration of a general *leniency bias* in favor of in-groups. In-group and out-group members are equally likely to be given credit for unambiguously positive actions and to be blamed for unambiguously negative ones. When possible external justifications are present, however, in-group members are less likely to be held accountable or blamed for negative behaviors or for failures to do something positive. As in the case of deciding whether to give help, biases in favor of the in-group with respect to justifying negative behaviors appear only when the situation is ambiguous.

The rule appears to be, when judgments are uncertain, give an in-group member the benefit of the doubt. Coldly objective judgment seems to be reserved for members of out-groups.

The Person/Group Discrimination Discrepancy

Subtle in-group favoritism provides one possible explanation for a puzzle in the research literature on perceived discrimination. In surveys of discrimination felt by members of disadvantaged groups, a significant discrepancy is found between the degree of discrimination that is reported for the group as a whole and the degree of discrimination reportedly experienced by the individual. This discrepancy was first noted by Crosby (1982) in research on relative deprivation among women in the workplace. Repeatedly Crosby found that women perceived high levels of deprivation for women compared with men in salaries, raises, promotions, and other working conditions. When asked about their personal experiences, however, most women reported little or no discrimination. This same discrepancy between perceived levels of discrimination at the personal versus group level has since been found among members of many disadvantaged groups (Taylor and others 1990).

Although there may be many psychological reasons why individuals report little personal discrimination, the discrepancy between discrimination at the level of the group and at the level of individual experience is what would be expected if most discriminatory outcomes are indirect rather than direct. Relative disadvantage may not always be the cumulative effect of discrimination against individuals in the disadvantaged group. It can also result from the cumulation of leniency biases that benefit members of the advantaged in-group but are absent in judgments and decisions affecting out-group members. Because these practices occur under ambiguous circumstances and involve the *absence* of benefits, rather than the *presence* of overt discriminatory acts, they are likely to be invisible to those who are ultimately disadvantaged by their discriminatory effects.

TYPE 2 DISCRIMINATION IN THE WORKPLACE

Conscious perception of discrimination brings us to the implications of subtle in-group biases for business ethics. In the day-to-day operations of any business organization, there are multiple decision-making situations that parallel the decision tasks studied in the social psychology experiments reviewed in the previous section. Selection and merit reviews are particularly vulnerable to positivity biases and the leniency effect identified in social psychological research. Preferential selection of women and minorities is often criticized on the grounds of fairness. Such criticisms reflect the assumption that the default selection would *not* be preferential, an assumption that is contradicted by evidence of in-group bias. Conscious preferential selection of out-groupers may be the only available antidote for preferential selection of in-group members at the unconscious level.

Subtle in-group preferences also come into play in the many situations in which mentoring activities are at stake. The decision whether to invest in nurturing and mentoring a newcomer into an organization is essentially a subjective judgment about that person's future potential, in many ways parallel to the decision about who deserves help. As the studies described earlier demonstrated, such decisions are significantly influenced by the attributions made about ambiguous behaviors. When a newcomer makes a mistake or demonstrates ignorance of prevailing practices, it makes a great deal of difference whether that mistake or ignorance is attributed to inexperience or to lack of ability. The in-group attributional bias and the leniency effect suggest that, in many cases, the benefit of the doubt will go to newcomers who are classified as in-group members, whereas out-groupers are more likely to be judged on the basis of current performance.

I do not mean to suggest that all (or even most) cases of intergroup discrimination are of Type 2, rather than Type 1 or Type 3. Certainly there are groups and individuals for whom discrimination is motivated by hate or fear of the out-group rather than preference for any particular in-group. Discrimination that is driven by in-group favoritism may be more pervasive, however, than is commonly thought. In an early review of the in-group bias literature (Brewer 1979), I concluded that enhanced in-group preferences are inherent in the process of differentiating in-groups from out-groups. In-group/out-group categorization results in reducing the perceived differentiation between the self and members of the in-group, rather than increasing differentiation between the self and the out-group. Later experimental studies by Gaertner and his colleagues (Gaertner and others 1990) have confirmed this view of group formation as a process that brings in-group members closer to the self.

Subgroup Differentiation and Discrimination

Although in-group favoritism provides a basis for discrimination that is psychologically different from out-group prejudice, one could reasonably question the role of in-group preferences in accounting for the major forms of discrimination that result in different outcomes for the white majority in the United States and the distinct minorities such as African Americans and Asian Americans. Until recently, at least, there was little evidence that "white" represents a social category with which most Euro-Americans strongly identify. Instead, the salient social identities of whites appear to be associated with more distinctive categorizations, such as ethnic origin, religion, or occupation.

Thus, the idea that a motivation to benefit whites underlies discriminatory outcomes for nonwhite minorities is not intuitively compelling.

This absence of a strong in-group identification on the part of a white majority is consistent with a theory of in-group formation that is based on the individual's need to achieve a balance between inclusion and distinctiveness (Brewer 1991). According to this theory, in-group attachment and loyalty should be limited to relatively small, distinctive social categories. In-group favoritism and associated biases are then restricted to these small social groupings and not extended to large, majority categories such as white Americans. (For instance, when my grandmother, who was born in Sweden, became a naturalized U.S. citizen, she consistently voted for political candidates with names like Johnson, which she regarded as "nice, Swedish names." Given the nature of Chicago politics in the 1950s, more often than not she was probably voting for an African American politician, but that was certainly not her intent. On the other hand, she would not have voted *against* a candidate just because he was black, nor for someone just because he was white. But she would vote for someone just because she thought he was Scandinavian.)

This limitation on the extent of in-group favoritism is not inconsistent with aggregate effects that favor whites over nonwhite minorities, however, given certain broad conditions. If most in-group identities are racial *subgroups* (for example, white ethnic groups or religious denominations or occupational categories that are white-dominated) and if initial resources and power are differentially distributed between whites and nonwhites, then subgroup favoritism will cumulatively benefit whites more than nonwhites, even if the society eliminates the negative biases that may have produced the power differentials in the first place. In this case, it is not that the bases of discrimination differ between minority and majority subgroups but that the power to *implement* discriminatory preferences is differentially available.

A particularly interesting example of the escalating effects of in-group preferences is provided by a recent study by Westphal and Zajac (1995), who examined board of directors appointments and salary decisions of 413 Fortune 500 companies from 1986 to 1991. Based on their analyses, the researchers concluded that when a firm's incumbent chief executive officer is relatively powerful, new directors are likely to be demographically similar to the CEO, whereas when the board is more powerful than the CEO, new directors resemble the existing board members. Further, greater similarity between the CEO and the board predicts more generous CEO compensation packages.

Implications for Antidiscrimination Policies

The idea that discrimination based on in-group favoritism is psychologically different from discrimination based on out-group hostility has pervasive implications for how antidiscrimination policies might be worded and implemented. Current policies rest on the assumption that discrimination will be manifest in unfair practices that directly *dis*advantage minorities and deny them access to objective or impartial evaluation and judgment. Thus, the search for evidence that discrimination exists focuses on how minorities themselves are treated, looking for cases where qualified minorities have been denied opportunities or resources commensurate with need or merit (see Messick 1994). Rarely is treatment of majorities scrutinized to the same degree in a search for evidence of unwarranted leniency, benefit of the doubt, or special favors that exceed the objective merits of a particular case. Yet these practices, if selectively applied, leave minorities at the same disadvantage they would experience under Type 1 discrimination, while decision makers can legitimately deny "discriminatory intent" as it is now conceptualized.

In many ways, the current attempts to drive out anti-out-group discrimination may have backfired on us. By making decision makers highly conscious of negative biases, we may have instigated scrupulous attention to objective assessments and standards of practice that are applied without exception to minority cases. In effect, then, minorities may be denied the potential *benefits* of sympathy-based judgment calls or bending over backward that are still available in many cases to non–minority group members. If, as I argue at the beginning of this chapter, positive and negative discrimination are potentially independent of each other, eliminating negative biases does nothing to increase positive behaviors toward out-groups nor to eliminate positive biases that benefit in-group members more than out-groupers.

Type 2 discrimination creates a real policy making dilemma. Reframing discriminatory intent in terms of benefits conferred rather than harm done parallels the distinction between nondiscrimination and affirmative action as bases of antidiscrimination policies. It is one thing to commit to removing *dis*advantage, quite another to commit to removing advantage. The difference in public acceptance of the philosophy of nondiscrimination versus that of affirmative action underscores the difficulties faced by policy makers in this arena. But if our goal is to eliminate the cumulative effects of discriminatory treatment based on social category membership, then we have to start by first understanding where the discrimination is located.

Chapter 9

Managing Work Force Diversity: Ethical Concerns and Intergroup Relations

Tom R. Tyler and Maura A. Belliveau

How can groups maintain their cohesion and the ability to function effectively when they have internal conflicts of interest or of values? When there are disagreements within a group about the distribution of rewards, resources, or opportunities, social mechanisms for bridging those differences are crucial. Our discussion will focus on two mechanisms through which contemporary organizations facing increasing work force diversity can be effectively managed. These two mechanisms are *procedural justice* and *superordinate identification*. Each suggests a distinct managerial approach to maintaining group cohesion in the face of identity and interest conflicts.

The effective management of diverse interests is becoming a central question not only in management but in law and politics. The key to the success of both the procedural justice and superordinate identity mechanisms in diversity management is that they facilitate the acceptance of differences in identities and interests while also reinforcing a shared concern for fair treatment and overarching organizational interests. These strategies differ from the traditional American model of assimilation, in which the management of diversity involved efforts to develop and maintain a common set of cultural values and to discourage subidentities. Ethnic and cultural groups within American society are increasingly rejecting the assimilation model and encouraging respect for their distinct cultures in a mosaic or "salad bowl" society. Our concern is with the viability of such an organization.

Can such mosaic models function effectively? One vision of the future posits increasing struggle between the advantaged and disadvantaged, a grim world of conflict between narrowly defined special interest groups. Another vision focuses on the development of mechanisms for bridging groups and their distinct interests and identities. Research suggests that such mechanisms exist.

PROCEDURAL JUSTICE

An important finding of psychological research exploring people's reactions to third-party efforts at resolving disagreements among people and groups is that people focus upon issues of procedural justice when evaluating their experiences. Consider a dispute between two parties, mediated by a political official. People might evaluate their experience through how much they win or lose (outcome favorability). They might also evaluate their experience by assessing whether what they receive is fair (distributive justice). Both of these evaluations derive from the outcomes of the conflict. Finally, people might focus on how dispute is resolved. Studies suggest that this procedural focus actually dominates people's assessments of their conflict resolution experience (see Lind, Tyler, and Huo 1994). Hence, third parties can gain acceptance for their decisions by making them in ways that people will regard as fair. In the sections that follow we will show how a procedural justice approach functions in several areas of diversity and conflict.

Bridging Across Economic Interests

One type of conflict is between people whose economic interests conflict. An example of such conflict is found in the case of policies of gender-, race-, and ethnicity-based preferential treatment intended to increase job opportunities for members of targeted groups. Americans typically think of the economic marketplace as providing equal opportunity for everyone (Kluegel and Smith 1986) and may therefore oppose government intervention into and regulation of labor markets. It was posited, however, that judgments about fairness should influence their willingness to accept redistributive policies. Members of both targeted and nontargeted groups should defer to justice issues and support the redistribution of resources when they believe that economic markets are distributively unfair.

This issue will be considered on two levels. The first involves the acceptance of the personal consequences of employment policies on one's own career (Belliveau 1995). For example, while organizations can implement affirmative action programs without the support of white male (that is, nontargeted) employees, positive interaction between groups, as well as the numerical representation of women and minorities in the workplace, may be enhanced when white males accept or endorse such measures. The second level involves broader support for public policies at the societal level. On each level the influence of judgments about the favorability of policies can be related to judgments about their fairness.

First, consider reactions to organizational policies designed to promote distributive justice (Belliveau 1995). Most field research on affirmative action addresses the attitudes of randomly sampled individuals employed by a variety of organizations whose implementation of affirmative action is not ascertained. In these studies, neither the subjects' actual exposure to affirmative action nor their career outcomes under the policy are typically known. In contrast, Maura Belliveau (1995) explored the influence of procedural justice and self-interest (or outcomes) on feelings about affirmative action by examining the attitudes of employees at all levels in two large municipal fire departments in California whose implementation of affirmative action in entry-level hiring differed.

Both organizations were experiencing rapid gender and racial integration. In Fire Department 1, the affirmative action program in entry-level hiring was voluntary. In Fire Department 2, a court-mandated system of racial/ethnic and gender quotas had been used in making entry-level hiring decisions since 1985, and other hiring cohorts had been affected by litigation since 1980. In both departments, affirmative action implementation at the promotional level was voluntary. The two organizational samples were combined, and this merged sample was used in the analyses to follow.

Belliveau (1995) explored employees' attitudes toward affirmative action (specifically, preferential treatment) as a function of type of policy implementation, employee demographics, career outcome favorability, procedural and distributive fairness judgments, racial attitudes, and stratification beliefs (beliefs regarding the status of minorities in American society). More than four hundred employees at all hierarchical levels in the two organizations completed surveys, describing their demographic background, personal career experiences, judgments of the fairness of their organization's hiring and promotional procedures, racial attitudes, beliefs about the causes of inequality between minorities and nonminorities, and attitudes toward affirmative action. Judgments about the outcome favorability, distributive fairness, and procedural fairness of affirmative action policies were measured with regard to two career stages: entry-level hiring and promotions. Separate analyses were performed using as the dependent variables (1) attitudes toward affirmative action in entry-level hiring and (2) attitudes toward affirmative action with regard to promotions, and independent variables corresponding to career stage.

Regression analyses included variables controlling for organization (voluntary versus mandated implementation), race/ethnicity, gender, education level, political affiliation, organizational tenure, rank, favorability of the subject's hiring (or promotional) outcomes, distributive fairness (use of merit in hiring/promotional decisions), racial attitudes, stratification beliefs (that is, perceptions of the causes of outcome inequality between minorities and nonminorities [Kluegel and Smith 1986]), and assessments of the procedural fairness of hiring and promotion procedures. Measures of procedural fairness included overall evaluations of procedural justice in entry-level hiring and promotions and organizational openness in decision making.

Results of the analyses confirmed the hypothesized view of the effect of procedural justice on affirmative action attitudes. Even accounting for employee demographics, type of procedural implementation, and the favorability of personal hiring outcome, procedural fairness significantly influenced employee endorsement of affirmative action in entry-level hiring and promotions. Interestingly, although the effect of procedural implementation (voluntary versus mandated) on attitudes toward affirmative action at the entry level was nonsignificant, analyses of each organizational sample revealed stronger procedural justice effects among the firefighters exposed to the voluntary plan (Fire Department 1) than among those in the organization undergoing court-mandated entry-level integration (Fire Department 2).[1] The results imply that the greater the disjunction between process and outcome in affirmative action implementation, the greater the influence of procedural fairness judgments on attitudes toward the policy. Nonetheless, it is noteworthy that procedural fairness significantly influenced affirmative action attitudes even in the organization where mandated quotas were in place. Overall, procedural justice concerns were stronger with regard to evaluations of affirmative action in initial hiring than in promotions.

In contrast, concerns with societal-level distributive unfairness (belief in discrimination as the primary source of outcome inequality) and organizational-level distributive justice (use of merit) were greatest at the promotional level. With regard to entry-level hiring, the perception that distributive principles such as equity (rewards proportional to skills or inputs) were being upheld or compromised was unrelated to affirmative action attitudes, but the same was not true with regard to promotional affirmative action. In this case, employees' responses indicated that the perceived use of merit in making promotional decisions was critical to support for affirmative action. Firefighters' responses suggested that leveling the playing field at the entry level by giving greater weight to characteristics other than merit is acceptable but that merit criteria must be given primary consideration if promotional preferential treatment is to gain acceptance.

In addition to examining the influence of procedural and distributive justice, Belliveau (1995) also tested an alternative model, the self-interest view of affirmative action endorsement. This model proposes that personal outcomes influence attitudes toward the policy. Therefore, white males who do not receive positive career outcomes should have especially negative attitudes toward affirmative action, and women and minority employees who obtain favorable career outcomes should have particularly positive evaluations of affirmative action. In this study, self-interest was measured by asking all firefighters to rate the favorability of the outcomes of their initial hiring and most recent promotional opportunity.

Self-interest judgments influenced attitudes toward affirmative action at the entry level, but personal outcome favorability failed to influence endorsement with regard to promotions. The absence of support for the self-interest perspective at the promotional level is noteworthy. Given the powerful outcome measures used in this study, it is hard to argue that self-interest was not fully captured. Furthermore, results showed the significant effect of procedural justice on affirmative action attitudes, even when personal outcome favorability was included in regression models. This evidence of an independent effect of procedural justice is difficult to reconcile with a self-interest perspective. Presumably, if personal outcomes are accounted for, along with demographic proxies for self-interest (that is, race/ethnicity and gender), procedural fairness should exert no independent influence on affirmative action attitudes.

Also, as Belliveau (1995) notes, self-interest theories suggest that stronger outcome effects would be expected with regard to endorsement of affirmative action at the promotional level rather than entry level. This is because entry-level hiring decisions are one-time outcomes. By virtue of their presence in this study's sample, all individuals received objectively positive entry-level hiring outcomes. Since both the promotional and entry-level outcome favorability measures used here are subjective, respondents could (and some did) rate their entry-level hiring decision as relatively unfavorable because of disputes or budgetary constraints that delayed their being hired.

In contrast, for white males, a negative promotional outcome is likely to be seen as part of a repeated game (a game played over time, with many opportunities to win or lose). Non-minority male players in such games might react particularly negatively to an unfavorable career outcome because they may see race and/or gender as a significant factor in organizational decisions and their own race and gender as immutable. Given such a situation, it might be expected that the traditionally robust procedural fairness effect will evaporate and career outcomes will explain attitudes toward affirmative action policies (Belliveau 1995).

This proposition was tested by examining the significance of personal outcome favorability in promotional decision making on attitudes toward affirmative action at the promotional level. Although the main effect of racial/ethnic minority status was highly significant, the effect of personal outcome favorability at the promotional level was not. Furthermore, the interaction of minority group membership and promotional outcome favorability was also nonsignificant, indicating no differences between racial/ethnic groups on the basis of promotional outcomes received.

Of course, one could argue, as some self-interest theorists do, that outcomes underlie procedural justice judgments and therefore outcome effects on affirmative action attitudes are indirect. To test this possibility, Belliveau (1995) explored the relational (Tyler and Lind 1992) and self-interest antecedents of procedural justice judgments. Relational antecedents refer to judgments about the treatment received from authorities. Three aspects of treatment are distinguished within the relational model: neutrality, trustworthiness, and status recognition. Neutrality refers to lack of bias, honesty, and the use of facts in making decisions. Trustworthiness refers to having benevolent motives. Status recognition refers to treating people with dignity and respect. If people feel that the authority or organization with which they are dealing uses neutral procedures, has benevolent intentions, and treats them with respect and dignity, then a relational model suggests that they should feel that they are receiving procedural justice. In contrast, a self-interest model suggests that people link judgments about the fairness of procedures to their ability to control directly or indirectly the outcome of those procedures. For example, people think that procedures that allow them to make arguments to sway the third-party decision maker are fairer.

Again, the dependent variable was assessed with regard to two career stages: entry-level hiring and promotions. Results show that both relational factors and personal outcome favorability influenced entry-level procedural fairness evaluations in most models, but only relational factors affected judgments of organizational procedural fairness at the promotional level. Overall, Belliveau's (1995) findings provide strong support for a procedural justice rather than self-interest interpretation of affirmative action attitudes, and a relational versus self-interest view of procedural justice judgments. While self-interest theories suggest that procedural justice effects should be weakest and outcome effects strongest at the promotional level, where the metaphor of a repeated game seems most apt, this study's results clearly disconfirmed this view.

These procedural justice findings are especially striking because fire-fighters have a very low turnover rate. In other words, their organization's policies are likely to have long-term implications for their careers. In addition, the measures of outcome favorability in this study were particularly strong, making it likely that any outcome effects that existed would be detected. Furthermore, this particular population pursues employment and promotions within a civil service system involving many formal rules. The effect of relational factors in this context demonstrates the ubiquitous role of interpersonal treatment in judgments of organizational justice. Finally, this study assessed the influence of distributive fairness at both the societal and organizational levels on affirmative action attitudes and showed that distributive concerns play an important role in determining policy support, particularly at the societal level.

Willingness to endorse public policy among individuals who do not stand to benefit can also be explored on a more abstract level. Heather Smith and Tom Tyler (in press) examined the influence of judgments about the fairness of the market—that is, of distributive injustice (African Americans receive poorer outcomes from the market) and procedural injustice (economic markets discriminate based on race)—on white support for policies that redistribute economic resources. Their study is based on interviews with 352 white respondents randomly chosen from the San Francisco Bay area.

Their findings indicate that judgments of both distributive and procedural injustice in markets encourage support for redistributive policies. Those respondents who regarded market outcomes as unfair were more likely to support the intervention of Congress into the market. In addition, those who regarded market procedures as unfair were more likely to support the intervention of Congress into the market. Finally, there was an interaction; those respondents who regarded both outcomes and procedures as unfair were especially likely to support Congressional intervention.

The findings outlined in this section suggest that conflicts of interest between the advantaged and the disadvantaged can be bridged. The key lies in the power of judgments of injustice in economic markets to motivate support for public policies aimed at employment practices (Belliveau 1995; Smith and Tyler, in press) and the power of judgments about the fairness of policies such as affirmative action to shape reactions to them (Belliveau 1995; also see Lea, Smith, and Tyler 1994; Nacoste 1990). These findings are optimistic and suggest that conflicts of interest need not adversely affect organizations.

Bridging Across Ethnic Diversity

A second aspect of the need to manage conflict effectively occurs across ethnic differences. As America develops an increasingly diverse work force, disputes will increasingly occur across ethnic and cultural boundaries, as people with differing cultural values are required to seek common solutions to policy issues. Can procedures effectively bridge such differences?

Tom Tyler, Allan Lind, and Yuen Huo (1994) studied employee/supervisor conflicts among 305 employees at the University of California at Berkeley. They recruited subjects through ethnic staff associations to create a diverse sample of employees strongly associated with their ethnic subgroups. The sample was 18 percent African American, 22 percent Chicano/Latino, 43 percent Asian American, and 17 percent white. Employees were interviewed about a recent experience with a supervisor in which they discussed disagreements about work tasks, tried to resolve problems, or otherwise tried to deal with work-related or personnel issues.

The situation found in their study mirrors that found nationally. Most white employees had white supervisors (79 percent). Of the minority employees ($N = 233$), most ($N = 147$, 63 percent) also had white supervisors. Hence, a variety of the employee-supervisor interactions involving minority employees were cross-ethnic. In such situations, when conflict occurs across ethnic boundaries, a key concern is whether people will continue to focus on issues of procedural justice or whether they will focus on the favorability of their outcomes, making it difficult for leaders to find a solution acceptable to all parties. The findings of the study suggested that procedural justice remains important when the conflict occurs across ethnic boundaries.

The data from the previously outlined study of policy-level reactions to affirmative action (Smith and Tyler, in press) can also be used to examine whether ethnicity influences the weight that people put on procedural justice in deciding whether or not to accept decisions made by third-party authorities (in this case Congress). Analysis of their data suggests that there are no such significant ethnicity effects. Lind, Huo, and Tyler (1994) similarly found that affect following the use of various types of dispute resolution procedures was strongly linked to procedural fairness, not to outcome favorability, among students of varying ethnicities and gender who were asked to discuss recent interpersonal disputes.

The findings outlined strongly support the argument that procedures can bridge differences in interests and ethnic backgrounds. The success of a procedural strategy for bridging differences, however, depends on more than a common willingness to accept decisions reached via a fair procedure; it also requires that people in different groups—whether separated by cultural differences or differences in values, experience, or interests—agree on common criteria for evaluating the fairness of decision-making procedures. If such criteria do not exist, the parties to conflict will not be able to agree on a single fair procedure and accept its outcome.

In a study of people's personal experiences with legal authorities, Tyler (1988) examined the criteria used to define the meaning of procedural fairness. He did not find either demographic or ideological differences. Tyler (1994a) further examined this issue in a study of reactions to congressional decision making. His findings indicated that ethnicity did not influence the criteria used to evaluate the fairness of congressional procedures. He failed to find ethnic, gender, or income differences in the basis of judgments about the fairness of congressional decision-making procedures in two experimental studies that manipulated voice and neutrality by presenting decisions made by a committee that allowed or did not allow testimony (voice) and did or did not include people representing all sides of the issue (neutrality). Nor did he in a survey that explored naturally occurring variations in voice, neutrality, and other criteria of procedural justice. Further, Lind, Tyler, and Huo (1994) found that disputants in the United States, Hong Kong, and Germany placed similar weight on issues of neutrality, trustworthiness, and status recognition when defining the meaning of a fair procedure.

The finding that procedural preferences and evaluations are generally unaffected by ethnicity is ironic, since recent efforts to deal with questions of multi-ethnicity and multi-culturalism have focused on procedural issues. The Commission of the California Supreme Court on the future of the California courts (Dockson 1993), for example, advocates that the cultural experience of the disputants should be taken into account when the procedures for resolving disputes are determined but rejects the argument that cultural values should be taken into account in the judgment of conduct or determination of punishment—that is, when distributive justice is determined. Such procedural accommodations may prove to be minimal, since the members of different ethnic groups share very similar psychologies of procedure. On the other hand, efforts to deal with the substance of various cultural values may be a formidable task, since research finds larger differences in the views of people of varying ethnicity about distributive justice (Tyler and Smith, in press).

American society has a history of stability in its institutions and unity in its cultural values. The European intellectual heritage defined American conceptions of institutional authority, and white male values have dominated the exercise of authority in law, politics, management, and even the family. Within that context, managing diversity seems like an unimportant issue. Diversity has been managed by assimilating the members of other groups into the dominant culture.

Increasingly, the assimilation model is becoming less adequate for thinking about organizations. The American polity is becoming diverse in both ethnic and cultural terms, and subgroups are increasingly unwilling to abandon their own cultural backgrounds and values to join one common culture. But while the movement toward a mosaic model of society may have many benefits, it intensifies stresses on those authorities who are responsible for formulating common policies. Such strains will occur more and more often within managerial settings as managers are asked to accommodate to the interests of varying groups. It will be increasingly necessary for management to find ways to bridge such differences in the exercise of authority.

If America's diverse work force is effectively managed, diversity can be a distinctive and valuable aspect of the business community that gives America an edge over more ethnically and culturally homogeneous business cultures, such as those of Japan and Germany. America can profit from its diverse character (Gentile 1994). On the other hand, if work force diversity is ineffectively managed, it can be a source of widespread worker dissatisfaction and hostility and can fuel intergroup competition and conflict. In other words, the future does not need to be a period of conflict between the advantaged and disadvantaged. Instead, social relations can be managed in ways that draw strength from diversity.

The findings we have outlined give cause for optimism. They suggest that organizational authorities can bridge differences in values and interests, holding diverse groups together. One key to effectiveness is the perception by employees that managers are using fair procedures for decision making.

Unfortunately, recent changes in managerial practices seem to encourage the deterioration of feelings of fairness in dealings between employees and their supervisors. One change is the move toward contingent workers, temporary employees who are not accorded organizational membership and who, conversely, do not feel organizational loyalty. Increasingly, workers are being told not to develop organizational loyalties but instead to play the field by moving opportunistically from company to company.

Bridging Across Value Differences

As we have noted, conflicts of values may be even more difficult to resolve than conflicts of interest, since people's values are moral or ethical in character and are difficult to compromise. As with conflicts of interest, one mechanism that can potentially bridge value conflicts is procedural justice. Parties who disagree about the desirable outcomes of a conflict or the policies they would like to see enacted may be able to agree about how policy decisions should be made. Making decisions following those procedures may legitimize the outcome of the decision-making process, leading all parties to accept the outcomes. This procedural justice hypothesis, proposed by John Thibaut and Laurens Walker (1975), has been widely supported in studies of the willingness to accept third-party decisions in the resolution of personal conflicts dealt with by legal, political, and managerial authorities. Several studies extend the test of procedural justice to people's reactions to policy-level value conflicts.

This issue is examined in an area that has recently seen considerable value conflict—national abortion policy. In *Roe v. Wade*, the United States Supreme Court ruled that women have a legal right to make their own personal decisions about whether or not to have an abortion. This decision was contrary to the views of many Americans. The Supreme Court is a "legitimate" legal institution, however, whose decisions ought therefore to be deferred to and obeyed (if not personally agreed with) (for discussions of legitimacy, see Tyler 1990, 1993). If the Court has such deference, then it can bridge value differences, setting a policy followed by all members of society.

The data we present is from a survey of 502 randomly chosen respondents within the San Francisco Bay area (Tyler and Mitchell 1994). Those respondents were interviewed over the telephone after the Clarence Thomas hearings, but prior to its recent abortion decision (that is, *Casey*).[2]

In the survey, 38 percent of respondents did not support the doctrine of free choice articulated in the *Roe v. Wade* abortion decision, although a higher percentage supported abortion in special circumstances (for example, only 22 percent opposed abortion when the baby was likely to have a serious birth defect, and only 10 percent when the woman's life was in danger). Hence, a subset of respondents were faced with a legal doctrine that differed from their personal moral views. Moral judgments about abortion were linked to social background (religion, race) and social ideology. They were also independent of views about the legitimacy of the Supreme Court.

Bridging moral differences requires a legitimate social authority. The interviews suggested that in general terms the Supreme Court was viewed as such a legitimate authority. Seventy-one percent of respondents felt that the Court should be allowed to "declare acts of Congress unconstitutional," 78 percent that the Court does its job well. Similarly, only 3 percent felt that we should get rid of the Court, and only 23 percent agreed that "if the Court makes decisions that people disagree with, it should be abolished." Interestingly, the one area most directly relevant to the abortion issue—whether the Court should have the power to make abortion decisions—yields the most problematic information. Sixty percent of respondents did not feel that the Court should have this power.

As a generally legitimate authority, the Court could potentially override differences in morality and bring the differing groups together on abortion. To do so does not require that people be persuaded—that is, that they change their attitudes. A value consensus is not required. What is needed is general deference to the legitimacy of the Court's decision. Deference involves willingness to empower the Court to make abortion decisions and a sense of obligation to obey such decisions once they are made.

In a test of the ability of the Court to bridge value differences, the influence of institutional legitimacy on empowerment and obligation was examined. The findings indicated that both empowerment and obligation were more strongly influenced by institutional legitimacy than by either agreement with past abortion decisions (that is, *Roe v. Wade*) or evaluations of the morality of abortion. This influence should be distinguished from attitude change. The legitimacy of the Court was unrelated to attitudes about abortion. People deferred to the Court if they viewed it as a legitimate institution, but their views about the morality of abortion did not change. Hence, no value consensus was obtained.

These findings suggest that having legitimate authorities facilitates holding societies together in the face of value conflicts. Legitimate authorities can bridge differences and gain deference from both sides of a conflict, because people feel an internalized obligation to defer to and obey the decisions of legitimate organizational authorities. This finding suggests the importance of understanding the antecedents of legitimacy.

What Influences Views About the Legitimacy of Authorities?

Our examination of the antecedents of legitimacy focuses on judgments about the actions taken by authorities. Three judgments are considered: agreement with decisions, judging the decisions made to be fair, and judging decision-making procedures to be fair.

An analysis of the influence of these three judgments about the Supreme Court on the legitimacy of the Court suggests that only procedural judgments shape evaluations of the legitimacy of the Court. Further, procedural judgments have the dominant influence on empowerment and feelings of obligation. The robustness of this influence is shown by a subgroup analysis that divided respondents into subgroups depending on whether they respected the Court and whether they agreed with past abortion decisions. Even among those respondents who had lower levels of support for the Court and who disagreed with its past abortion decisions, procedural justice shaped empowerment. Hence, irrespective of their own views, people deferred to the authority of the Court, if it made decisions fairly. Legitimacy has a procedural base. Agreement with decisions has strikingly little influence on legitimacy, empowerment, or obligation. So procedure is the central basis for bridging value differences.

The finding that procedure is the basis of legitimacy accords with a broader analysis of the psychology of legitimacy in legal, political, managerial, and familial settings (Tyler 1994b). That analysis suggests that legitimacy is generally responsive to procedural, not outcome, concerns. This finding is equally true of the legitimacy of authorities at the local and national levels.

We can move beyond showing that procedural justice is important and examine the psychology underlying procedural influences. Psychologists have proposed two models of the psychology of justice. One, the instrumental model of Thibaut and Walker (1975), suggests that people are concerned about having direct or indirect influence over the outcomes of their dealings with third-party authorities. The second, the relational model of Tyler and Lind (1992), suggests that people are concerned about their status with the group or society. They value information suggesting that they are accepted, respected members of the organization or society the authorities represent. As we have noted, three aspects of treatment influence such judgments: the neutrality of the authorities, their trustworthiness, and the respect and dignity of their treatment of others, reflecting the status recognition of those others in the organization or society.

The influence of these varying aspects of authorities can be compared in the context of people's evaluations of the Supreme Court. Such an analysis indicates that relational judgments dominate procedural justice and legitimacy. In contrast, control judgments have little influence. This finding is central to the argument that procedures can bridge differences, since relational judgments are at best linked only loosely to the outcomes of procedures.

The findings outlined are correlational in nature. Hence, the centrality of procedure to legitimacy cannot be disentangled from the possibility that both procedural justice judgments and legitimacy evaluations are linked to a general affective orientation toward authorities. To test that possibility Tyler (1994a) measured respondents' general feelings toward authorities, then presented them with vignettes in which procedures varied in fairness and outcomes varied in degree of agreement with the views of the respondents.

Two experiments were conducted, each on an independent sample of 502 respondents. In each case, respondents were presented with a vignette describing decision making by Congress. Two vignettes were used, each presented to different people. In the first vignette the issue involved was federal funding of abortions; in the second, support for educational training programs for the disadvantaged. The dependent variable was willingness to vote for a member of Congress involved in making the decision. In both studies, procedural justice manipulations—descriptions of fair or unfair decision making—influenced legitimacy (as indexed by willingness to vote for the member of Congress). These influences are especially important because they occur when the possible effects of prior views about Congress are controlled for.

These findings suggest that authority is effective for noninstrumental reasons. It is legitimacy, not agreement, that shapes empowerment and obligation. It is procedural justice, not outcome judgments, that shapes legitimacy. And it is relational, not instrumental, judgments that shape procedural justice. At each level the social bond between people and authorities is central to the ability of authorities to bridge differences among group members.

The importance of legitimacy as a characteristic of organizational authorities is rather ironic in that the legitimacy of organizational authorities is at a low level in comparison with earlier periods. In fact, the decline in the legitimacy of legal, political, managerial, religious, and other authorities is a striking American national trend (Lipset and Schneider 1983). Thus the emerging nature of authority relations within American society most requires legitimacy and feelings of obligation at a time when such feelings are minimal. Further, changes in the structure of institutions seem to be encouraging the deterioration of legitimacy, not its reinvigoration.

SUPERORDINATE IDENTIFICATION

A second mechanism through which groups can bridge differences is the development of superordinate identifications that span ethnic and value differences. Studies that draw from the ideas of social identity theory find that people who identify with their larger community are more likely to behave in ways that reflect concerns about overall community welfare (Tyler and Dawes 1993; Tyler and Degoey, in press). It is important to distinguish superordinate identification, which develops from social identity theory, from superordinate goals, which develop from realistic group conflict theory. The focus is on the definition of self and self-identity, not the definition of self-interest.

Do superordinate identifications encourage actions on behalf of other group members? Smith and Tyler (in press) tested this suggestion in the context of the psychology underlying support for redistributive economic policies among white respondents. Smith and Tyler distinguished between two types of judgments about Congress: instrumental and relational (Tyler and Lind 1992). Instrumental judgments reflect beliefs about the degree to which Congress makes policies that benefit the respondent. Relational judgments reflect beliefs about the degree to which Congress is neutral, trustworthy, and respectful of citizen rights.

Two subgroups of respondents were identified: those who identify more strongly with America than with their own ethnic group and those who identify more strongly with their own ethnic group than with America. Within each subgroup, regression analysis was used to examine the influence of instrumental and relational judgments about Congress on willingness to endorse Congressional policies that advantage minorities in the marketplace.

Among those white respondents who identify with America, relational judgments but not instrumental judgments influenced policy endorsement. If respondents felt that Congress was neutral and trustworthy, they supported its policies, irrespective of whether those policies favored them. Among those white respondents who identified more strongly with their ethnic group than with America, the primary judgments about Congress that shaped support for Congressional policy were instrumental judgments. In other words, this latter subgroup was concerned with the influence of policies on their own and their own group's interests.

Finally, we can test the possibility that these two mechanisms interact. Tyler and Degoey (in press) did so in the context of citizens' willingness to empower government authorities to make water conservation rules during a drought. Their study was based on a sample of 402 randomly chosen people in the city of San Francisco, who were interviewed during the 1991 water shortage. The concern of the interviews was with the antecedents of (1) people's willingness to empower government to make and enforce rules governing the use of water, and (2) people's feelings of obligation to obey government rules once those rules were created.

The findings of the study indicate that both procedural justice and superordinate identification with one's community influence willingness to empower authorities. Procedural fairness has a main effect on support for authority, while the influence of identification is more complex. Identification interacts with procedural justice. Those who identify with their community (as indexed by pride) place greater weight on procedural justice when making judgments about support for authority and place less weight on decision satisfaction.

CONCLUSIONS

As societal strategies for dealing with diversity, procedural justice and superordinate identification have the valuable attribute of allowing societies to effectively bridge differences in values and interests. This finding offers encouragement that multi-cultural societies are possible. John Rawls (1993) has raised concerns about the viability of diverse societies, noting that historically it has rarely been possible "for there to exist over time a just and stable society of free and equal citizens, who remain profoundly divided by reasonable religious, philosophical, and moral doctrines" (p. 4). The historian Arthur Schlesinger (1992) has expressed similar doubts. The findings outlined in this chapter, however, give reason for optimism. They suggest that diversity need not create unbridgeable gaps within a society or organization.

The findings suggest that the effectiveness of authorities is linked to the judgment that the authorities make policy decisions fairly. Hence, the ability of authorities to bridge differences flows from procedural legitimacy, which develops out of the formal structures and informal characteristics of authority that groups create to facilitate resolving conflicts. While procedural justice research has focused on the formal structures of authority, research suggests that such judgments are also shaped by the manner in which authority is implemented (Tyler and Bies 1990). Hence, both formal structures and sensitivity to interpersonal aspects of justice represent ways to bridge differences among group members. If authorities act in ways that people regard as fair, they will receive deference.

Further, the findings support a relational perspective on authority that further supports the viability of a procedural justice strategy. They indicate that judgments about procedural justice are distinct from instrumental judgments about outcome favorability or control. Instead, they are linked to broader judgments about authorities and their behaviors—for example, to assessments of neutrality, trustworthiness, and standing.

The studies described also show the potential value of social identification. Although emotional bonds among the members of organizations have been recognized as important, their potential role in binding groups together has not been emphasized in recent discussions of diversity.

> Part of the problem is the tendency to think of community only in political terms, so that communities not based on political organization are ignored. Consequently we only look for political solutions to social ills. The rich variety of communities and social practices which exist independently of the political process and which contribute greatly to human welfare tend to be discounted in academic kinds of analyses. (J. C. Smith 1986, 362)

The findings outlined here reinforce the idea that organizational ties are an independent influence on people's reactions to organizational authorities.

Thus procedural justice and social identification are mechanisms that accommodate and protect diversity, rather than trying to suppress or co-opt it, by allowing differences to be valued and maintained within a shared overall perspective. As such, they are strategies important to the future of an increasingly diverse America. It is important to note, however, the larger questions posed by the changes that are predicted for American society, questions about the gains and losses associated with different forms of social organization.

The traditional form of American society was based on one dominant culture, the European tradition, embodied in white male values. As people with other cultural traditions came to America, they were encouraged to abandon their own cultural values and assimilate into American society. Education was regarded as a mechanism for assimilation into the dominant culture.

The American twist on an assimilation model is the definition of a private sphere of life, distinct from state authority. In that private sphere of religion and personal ideology, people do not need to assimilate. For many this meant keeping up cultural traditions within the home or in religious and social groups but accepting American values in public settings such as law and politics and in work settings.

Of course, the assimilation model does not define the totality of frameworks that can lead to a single dominant set of social values. An alternative model is the consensus model, in which the members of various ethnic or cultural groups discuss their value differences and reach some consensus about the appropriate social values to define their society. This model differs from the assimilation model in that the various cultures involved all contribute to the social values of the society; groups do not defer to the values of other groups.

Another alternative model, which is becoming increasingly important within American society, is what we called at the beginning of this chapter the mosaic or salad bowl model. In that model, different groups within society coexist, each group maintaining its own identity and values. Those ethnic and cultural values are then bridged at a public level through unifying authority structures. This model puts greater strain on public authority structures, since it is expected that those structures will be responsive to diverse cultural values.

Consider the example of bilingual education. Traditionally it was expected that all students would learn English. While accommodations were made to those children from other countries on an ad hoc basis, the normative framework indicated that learning English was the appropriate behavior for people in American schools. Increasingly, immigrant groups have disputed this normative framework. In California, for example, Chicano/Latino groups have demanded bilingual education as a right, rejecting the idea that their children learn to conduct their public lives in English. To the extent that societies accommodate to such pressures, the problems of creating generally acceptable policies increase.

The purpose of this chapter is not to compare these various approaches to dealing with diversity. Rather, it is to suggest two general mechanisms that can help organizations, communities, groups, or societies handle issues of diversity. These mechanisms function to enhance the ability of authorities to gain acceptance for their decisions.

ENDNOTES

1. Both the mean and variance of judgments of procedural fairness in entry-level hiring were actually greater in Fire Department 2, suggesting that this difference between organizations is not due to restricted range of ratings by members of Fire Department 2 relative to Fire Department 1.

2. The percentages reported have been statistically adjusted to reflect the parameters within the population (Tyler and Mitchell 1994).

Commentary

The Business Ethics of Social and Organizational Processes

Thomas Donaldson

The preceding nine chapters discuss many ethical issues, but they may be conveniently grouped into three categories. The papers in the first category examine how individuals and organizations can unintentionally slip into unethical behavior—for example, how they can slowly succumb to stereotyping in decision making or to self-destructive attempts to manage appearances. Those in the second category speak to the economic advantages of ethical behavior—for example, how companies can recognize the costs of misbehavior and the payoffs for ethical behavior. Those in the third category identify many negative group tendencies that stem from group features such as diversity, size, or complexity.

Not accidentally, these categories all deal with what ethicists call the *empirical*, rather than the *normative*, side of ethics. The authors, who are all social scientists, treat things the way they *are*, not as they *ought* to be. In other words, they are accustomed to examining the *is* of ethical behavior, rather than its *ought*. The implications of their work for normative insight, however, lie close at hand, because much of the motivation for writing even an empirical article on ethics usually is normative; what *is* the case turns out to be terribly important for what *ought* to be the case. For example, the fact that nations often demonize adversaries and go to war without sufficient cause (something that *is* the case) has implications for how people should respond to the presumed slights of other nations (something that *ought* to be the case). Each of the nine papers in part 1 isolates facts with normative relevance for business.

I have taken my task, in turn, to be to address at least many of the normative implications of the articles in this section. I want in particular to examine the implications for corporate structure and managerial decision making. In isolating these implications, I will use two normative models widely discussed in the business ethics literature, the *social contract* model and the *stakeholder* model. Referencing these two normative models will make it easier to draw the normative implications from the various empirical studies.

In the business ethics literature, both stakeholder theory and social contract theory emerged during the past fifteen years. Both may be classified as
neoclassical theories, in the sense that they diverge substantially from the
classical theory of business ethics associated with either microeconomic theory or the economically inspired views of writers such as Milton Friedman
(1970). To say that they are neoclassical means that they expand the normative obligations of the firm, and of individual business persons, beyond that
of making a profit. Both hold that business people possess duties not only to
stockholders but to other individuals and groups, including people who are
neither customers nor employees (Freeman 1984). Stakeholder theory identifies stakeholders as persons or groups who have legitimate interests in procedural and/or substantive aspects of corporate activity and adopts the normative position that the interests of such stakeholders are of *intrinsic value*
(Donaldson and Preston 1995). That is, each group of stakeholders merits
consideration for its own sake and not merely for its ability to further the
interests of another group, such as shareholders. While the various proponents of stakeholder theory defend different versions of it, all hold that managers have obligations to consider the welfare of many corporate interest
groups, and all reject the classical or stockholder-only perspective (Carroll
1989).

Social contract theory, much like stakeholder theory, views a firm's
responsibilities as extending beyond the satisfaction of the single con-
stituency of the shareholders. Yet unlike stakeholder theory, it does not limit
itself to the firm or business organization, and can apply as well to individuals as to firms (Donaldson 1982). Nor does it classify corporate constituencies
as stakeholders. Instead, it derives a business's responsibilities from the
implicit social contracts that exist in economic communities—that is, among
companies, industries, nations, economic systems, and cultures (Donaldson
and Dunfee 1995). So, for example, employees of Johnson & Johnson may
be seen to have entered an implicit agreement to work for the goals
expressed in the company's famous "Credo."[1] Or, in a still broader sense,
people in democratic/capitalistic cultures may be seen to have entered into
an implicit agreement that allows private, for-profit corporations to exist and
to enjoy certain privileges such as limited liability and unlimited longevity.
In turn, this agreement holds corporations responsible for assuming certain
broad social duties such as paying taxes and providing efficient use of
resources (Donaldson 1982). Even particular industries or professions may
be seen to reflect implicit agreements. The assumptions about what constitutes professional ethics for attorneys or what constitutes misleading advertising on Madison Avenue may be reflected in implicit (and sometimes even
explicit) agreements within the legal profession or the advertising industry
(Donaldson and Dunfee 1994). The fact that an implicit agreement exists does
not necessarily convey the moral rightness of the agreement. Neighbors may
have entered into an implicit agreement to refrain from selling houses to

members of minority groups. But such an implicit agreement would be "illegitimate" (Donaldson and Dunfee 1994). When, however, a given agreement is compatible with fundamental and widely understood ethical norms, social contract theory credits it with the ability to represent and specify the authoritative ethical norms of the community in question.

What happens when we view the findings of the articles in this section from the perspective of these two normative theories of business ethics? Do we find implications for modern managers? I will consider these questions piecemeal with respect to each of the three categories of empirical conclusions found in the articles. Again, these categories are the following:

1. The way in which individuals and organizations unintentionally slip into unethical behavior, as when they slowly succumb to stereotyping or self-destructive attempts to manage appearances;

2. The economic advantages of ethical behavior—that is, the costs of corporate misbehavior and the payoffs of ethical behavior; and

3. The negative tendencies associated with group features such as diversity, size, or complexity.

SLIPPING INTO UNETHICAL BEHAVIOR

Many of the authors show a keen eye for detecting ethical self-deception and moral stumbling. John Darley, for example, reveals how organizations follow a syndrome, first refusing to admit publicly, then later being forced to cover up, actions that at first seemed innocent. Taking the much discussed case of B. F. Goodrich as an example, he notes that "individuals within the organization can lose sight of the fact that individuals may be harmed while fulfilling the other goals of the corporation or bureaucracy."

Some normative implications of Darley's work are obvious. The lure of being caught up in the classical rather than the stakeholder conception of the corporation depends in part on the normative credibility of working exclusively for the benefit of profit and the shareholders; the classical conception provides an excuse for attending single-mindedly to the interests of a single entity (the firm), something people would never attempt to excuse in their private lives. As John Ladd and others have noted, we would generally be less offended by the celebrity who advertises a product she never uses than by the private citizen who recommends to her neighbor a product that she has never tried. The myopia that accompanies the transference of the organization's goals to the individual within it, a phenomenon that drives much of Darley's analysis, could never occur without the rationalization that comes by way of the "classical" normative conception of the corporation. In this sense, the act of covering up in the B. F. Goodrich brake scandal is cut from the same cloth as other less dramatic but still harmful actions. The CEO who undertakes a bloody restructuring to raise the rate of return on equity by a tiny amount for shareholders usually is relying heavily on the classical conception. Such an action could never be taken from a stakeholder or social contract perspective.

Nonetheless, while stakeholder theory implies special responsibilities for corporate managers, it says nothing about how to discharge those responsibilities (Ladd 1970). Even people who adopt a stakeholder perspective can be prey to ethically distorting influences. The work of Stephanie Goodwin and Susan Fiske shows that we must keep the limits of any normative theory in mind—at least when such theories are considered as psychological correctives. As these authors note, powerful people in organizations often slip into stereotyping behavior, even as powerless employees can slip ethically by attending overmuch to the organizational hierarchy. Using Social Judgeability Theory and the Continuum Model, Goodwin and Fiske stress how individuation and categorization are dependent upon many variables other than normative attitudes. In turn, the organization must be seen as more than a collection of individual minds with normative perspectives. It should be seen, instead, as a microculture where structural factors contribute to perceived standards of judgeability (such as the lack of representation of certain social groups within the management hierarchy).

Entire organizations, and not only the individuals within them, can slip unwittingly into unethical behavior. Focusing on the issue of privacy, Robert Bies identifies organizational responses to privacy issues and describes how these organizational responses sometimes create ethical dilemmas that paradoxically result in greater harm than good. Legalization has become the dominant strategic response, but rules designed to force privacy can lack sensitivity to subtle negative consequences. Should an airline be able to ask a prospective pilot about a previous drinking problem before offering that person a job? Even efforts to eliminate discrimination can be sabotaged by well-meaning rules that enforce privacy. Some discrimination elimination may, ironically, require information curtailed by rules instituted to protect privacy and safeguard minorities.

If, as many normative theorists have argued, implicit social contracts are important for understanding business ethics, then it becomes necessary to understand *how* people make such contracts, what weaknesses such contracts have, and what consequences follow from them. A well-known and pernicious force in shaping the implicit agreements that inform collective behavior is stereotyping. Here too, we can unwittingly slip, in part because stereotypes sometimes have predictive value. Myron Rothbart and Robert Mauro explore sources of error in perceptions of groups, especially of racial groups. Are there disadvantages or costs associated with having a simple view of the world, one that lacks complexity? The literature on social contract theory identifies one disadvantage as neglecting the conflict between some implicit social agreements (for example, that African American males are more likely to engage in criminal behavior) and key "hypernorms" such as nondiscrimination that render many implicit social contracts "illegitimate." Rothbart and Mauro seem to agree. They note that "three hundred years of slavery and discrimination in America are not without their effects, and there are cases where race, as a categorical predictor, does predict a criterion of importance." Nonetheless, they suggest that despite documented instances of institutional predictions involving, for example, race in police drug searches and parole decisions, predictors other than race can often be found and should be used. Rothbart and Mauro's normative views even lead them to say that even when nonracial predictors are absent, "it may be unwise to use them since the long-run aggravation of racial inequalities may be worse."

Marilynn Brewer's essay on polarization has implications for the process through which social contracts are generated. Here, too, slips are common. Even communities that collectively eschew discrimination *against* minorities may inadvertently slip into a prejudice *in favor of* fellow community members, with outcomes that are just as disastrous for minorities as discrimination. Evidence is accumulating that positive and negative evaluative processes represent different, independent systems that may or may not be reciprocally activated. Even if whites favor only their particular ethnic groups and not all whites, the aggregate effects favor whites over nonwhite minorities. These effects can occur when most in-group identities are racial subgroups (white ethnic groups, religious denominations, or occupational categories that are white dominated), and when initial resources and power are differentially distributed between whites and nonwhites. In this instance, subgroup favoritism will cumulatively benefit whites more than nonwhites even if the society eliminates the negative biases that may have produced the power differentials in the first place.

THE ECONOMIC ADVANTAGES OF ETHICAL BEHAVIOR

What are the practical consequences of managers' adopting one of the two neoclassical normative theories discussed above? Does a CEO's adopting stakeholder theory or social contract theory lower profits and harm investors? Or does the opposite happen? In short, does corporate ethics pay? These questions, discussed frequently by both academics and practicing business people, are empirical, not normative, questions. One might, for example, defend either of the neoclassical theories while at the same time believing that, in contrast to the classical theory, they dramatically lower corporate profits. Or one could defend them believing that they dramatically raise corporate profits. Normative justification can, and often does, proceed independently from factual states of affairs.

Nonetheless, the economic consequences of ethical attitudes in business are of pressing importance. For if managers believe that being ethical pays, or at least that it does not sink a corporation's finances, then they will be more likely to adopt neoclassical normative views of the firm.

Both Robert Cialdini and Robert Frank offer empirical analyses consistent with what has been called the *instrumental* version of stakeholder theory. The instrumental version establishes a framework for examining the connections, if any, between the practice of stakeholder management and the achievement of various corporate performance goals. The principal focus of interest in instrumental stakeholder theory has been the proposition that, other things being equal, corporations practicing stakeholder management will be relatively successful in conventional performance terms, such as profitability, stability, and growth (Donaldson and Preston 1995).

Therefore, the empirical analyses by both Cialdini and Frank bolster claims for instrumental stakeholder theory. Cialdini's "triple tumor" reveals the financial costs to companies of organizational dishonesty. The costs of poor reputation, of conflict between employees and corporate values, and of surveillance all hit companies at the bottom line. Similarly, Frank shows that firms can prosper by solving commitment problems with employees, customers, and other firms, even as they enhance their ability to recruit employees on more favorable terms and gain customer support. Clearly, many managers otherwise sympathetic to a stakeholder or social contract approach have refused to embrace such a view because they believe that doing so would damage their company's profitability and, in turn, violate their duty to shareholders. Therefore, the work of Cialdini and Frank can, by showing the empirical links between ethics and corporate success, bring these fence-sitters to the neoclassical normative side.

NEGATIVE GROUP TENDENCIES ASSOCIATED WITH GROUP DIVERSITY OR GROUP SIZE AND COMPLEXITY

As noted earlier, Goodwin and Fiske's article suggests that managers may adopt a neoclassical normative vantage point yet still succumb to psychological forces with unethical consequences. In a similar vein, Kramer and Messick show that even the size or complexity of organizational dilemmas may shape ethical illusions, thus baffling even well-intentioned and reform-oriented managers. The ways that individuals construe their duty or obligation in organizational dilemmas influences their choice of behavior. They argue that various features of organizational dilemmas to a large extent create the cognitive opportunities for the "intuitive lawyer" to construct self-serving frames. In contrast, the more cut and dried a dilemma is (the less ambiguity and equivocality its structural properties afford), the less cognitive room exists in which the intuitive lawyer can maneuver. This too, has implications for implementing stakeholder or social contract theory. Behaving ethically in organizational contexts means more than having the right intentions; one must attend to the shape of organizational dilemmas and attempt to reduce the negative tendencies they generate.

One key implication of social contract theory is that ethics in economic behavior need not be monolithically derived. The theory explicitly provides normative validity to diverse moral perspectives and assumes that it is healthy, within certain limits, for different communities to embrace different ethics. It follows that persons from different ethnic and cultural backgrounds, even when they are members of the same organization, need not have a common denominator in their views. How can such diversity be managed in large organizations? In step with social contract theory, Tom Tyler and Maura Belliveau tend to presume the validity of normative pluralism in their analysis of empirical issues associated with diversity. Diversity, the authors note, has been managed historically by assimilation, but increasingly, this model seems inadequate. Subgroups are becoming less and less willing to abandon their own cultural identity. Yet while the move toward a mosaic model of society may have many benefits, it intensifies stresses on those authorities who are responsible for formulating common policies.

Tyler and Belliveau's work has many implications for how social contract theorists should harmonize diverse cultural and ethnic identities in the modern workplace. Some strategies are better in coping with diversity—and by implication fulfilling the vision of social contracts—than others. Belliveau earlier found that procedural fairness judgments, not career outcomes, explained attitudes toward affirmative action implementation. A key antecedent to effectiveness is that employees view managers as using fair procedures for decision making. Even as legitimacy of authority is key to bridging value differences in a nation's legal system (for example, the authority of the Supreme Court is crucial in bridging value differences about U.S. law), so legitimacy of authority can be key to bridging value and racial differences in the corporation. And, as with the Supreme Court, an important foundation for managerial authority can be *procedure*. Legitimacy in business, just as in the courts, can have a procedural basis.

A second mechanism through which groups can bridge differences, according to Tyler and Belliveau, is the development of superordinate identifications that span ethnic and value differences. People who *identify* with their larger community are more likely to act in ways that support it. The focus is on the definition of self and self-identify, not the definition of self-interest. Procedural justice and social identification are mechanisms that accept and protect diversity, rather than trying to suppress or co-opt it, by allowing differences to be valued and maintained within a shared overall perspective. For corporations, the questions implied by those ideas are obvious. Can corporations develop methods of bringing employees to a greater identification with the corporate whole—for example, through joint stock-holding plans or participative management mechanisms? If so, the work of Tyler and Belliveau suggests that successful management of the cultural mosaic will be made easier.

CONCLUSIONS

The papers examined in this section share a thoroughly empirical bent. Nonetheless, they carry strong implications for normative research and, in particular, for the two prevailing normative theories of business ethics. Each of the three themes from the papers intersects with questions of stakeholders and social contracts.

The theme of individuals and organizations slipping imperceptively into unethical behavior holds implications for the normative view of the firm. The articles show how the temptation is greater, and the self-deception stronger, when employees and managers are caught up in the classical rather than the neoclassical conception of the firm—a conception that prescribes activity exclusively for the benefit of profit and the shareowners and not for other stakeholding constituencies. The articles also clarify the limits of any normative theory, whether classical or neoclassical, at least when such theories are considered as psychological correctives. The right ideas about ethics are not by themselves sufficient to ensure an adequate level of moral behavior. Finally, the theme of slipping into unethical behavior is shown to have implications for the shaping of the shared ideas about ethics that characterize the "social contracts" of economic communities. Understanding how stereotyping and positive/negative evaluation process influence collective moral attitudes is crucial for people who wish to improve those attitudes.

The remaining two themes also show normative relevance. The papers discussing the economic advantages of ethical behavior hold positive implications for the acceptance and implementation of social contracts and stakeholder approaches by exhibiting the empirical links between ethics and economic success. While the normative theories do not require economic success, their compatibility with traditional firm objectives removes a roadblock to their practical implementation and acceptance. Finally, the papers that discuss the negative group tendencies associated with group features such as diversity, size, or complexity contribute to understanding the role of normative ideas such as procedural justice in improving the modern workplace.

ENDNOTE

1. Johnson & Johnson's "Credo" is a list of priorities held by the company. They emphasize the welfare of the customer and of Johnson & Johnson employees as well as the financial well-being of the shareholder. Most large U.S. companies have such lists of shared values, although managers regard them with varying degrees of seriousness.

RISK, REASONING, AND DECISION MAKING

Chapter 10

Do No Harm

Jonathan Baron

Ethics, including business ethics, is often seen as a kind of constraint, like the law. When we desire to do something, first we must ask whether it is unethical. Even if it is the best thing to do, the ethicist, like the lawyer, can tell us that we shouldn't do it. For example, it is "unethical" for doctors to inform someone that her lover is infected with HIV. In some states, it is also illegal.

Ethical systems based on constraints imply an asymmetry between action and inaction. They hold us responsible for harms that we cause through action but not for harms that we fail to prevent. More specifically, they hold us responsible for *all* harms that we cause through action but only for *some* harms that we fail to prevent. Codes of ethics for business, medicine, law, psychology, and so on do contain positive obligations that are contingent on certain relationships, such as that between a practitioner and a client or a buyer and a seller.[1] But these obligations are limited. They can be seen as the result of certain social conventions, which create expectations. I expect my doctor to look at my blood-test results before filing them, although I would not expect another doctor who happened to see them lying on the table to inform him or me of any problems. My expectation is a consequence of what it means to be a doctor in my culture. The law of torts recognizes such expectations. I can sue my doctor for failing to alert me to a condition that needs attention, but I can't sue someone else for the same thing. It is important here that he agreed to be my doctor; if he fails in his role, he has broken a promise. The promise is not explicit but is contained in the definition of the role. In sum, the positive obligations that stem from ethical codes are almost always contingent on voluntary promises and agreements. Likewise, in business, almost all positive obligations arise from contracts, even if the contracts are only implicit.

This research was supported by National Science Foundation grants SES91–09763 and SBR92–23015.

This kind of constraint-based ethical system can be contrasted with simple utilitarianism. Simple utilitarianism holds that moral obligations depend on expected consequences; we should always choose the option that yields the best expected consequences overall. We are free to consider all sorts of consequences in making this judgment, including the effects of our choices on the choices of others, but utilitarianism makes no distinction between acts and omissions. For example, a utilitarian approach to life-sustaining medical therapy would maintain that decisions should be based primarily on a judgment of whether it is better on the whole for the patient to be dead. If we judge that it is, and if the outcome is in our power to control, then it does not matter whether our decision is to initiate therapy, to withdraw therapy that has already been initiated, or to kill the patient (painlessly). Of course, when we actually consider the effects of our choices on others and the possibility of error, these distinctions may turn out to matter. But they do not matter in themselves. They matter just in case they affect the expected consequences.

In this paper, I want to do the following: (1) sketch the utilitarian view of acts and omissions; (2) report and review some results about this distinction; and (3) discuss the implications of what I take to be this incorrect understanding of the distinction, for a number of moral issues.

A UTILITARIAN VIEW

I take the fundamental moral question to be about the advice we give each other about what to do, what choices to make.[2] We give this advice in a variety of ways. We teach our children and students about right and wrong. We express judgments about particular cases. We gossip. We mete out punishment and reward. Expressions of judgment and the assignment of punishment and reward are themselves actions that have other consequences aside from advice giving, so we cannot take them as fundamental. We may, for example, not punish a woman who takes cocaine while pregnant even if we think this is a horrendous act, just because we do not want to discourage other mothers from seeking treatment.

But what advice should we give? What should be the content of morality? The standard way of answering this question in modern philosophy is to consult our moral intuitions—that is, our judgments about cases and principles. The assumption here is that somehow we have come to make the correct judgments. We may err occasionally, but we can catch these errors by detecting inconsistencies with other judgments and reflecting on them. We reason in the manner of judges, finding precedents and principles and applying them to the cases before us, until we feel that we have it right.

Against this view, I claim that these intuitions are systematically biased. If we apply this method, we will get the wrong answer. To evaluate my claim, we must *put aside our intuitions* and try to figure out what advice we would give without them. We can do this because our moral intuitions are not the only things we value. They are limited to the values we have for the behavior of people, independent of their own values for outcomes.[3] We can put aside our moral intuitions and still be left with other reasons to give advice, primarily our concern for other people's values for outcomes, their own utilities, reflected in our altruistic concern. If we think this way, we will decide that the act/omission distinction itself is irrelevant except when it affects consequences, because it is the consequences that matter. If, on the other hand, we consult our moral intuitons, many of us will conclude that the distinction is relevant whether it affects consequences or not, and our intuitions will lead us to produce worse consequences than if we attended to consequences only.[4]

Defining morality in terms of advice giving helps us reconstruct morality after putting aside our intuitions. Ordinarily, we can give advice because of our own particular values. I can advise you to do the things that I like to see you do. For example, if I am against public nudity, I can rail against nude beaches. But why should you listen? It is clearly *my* values that motivate it. The kind of advice that you might follow is what springs from altruistic values, from my interest in seeing that the objectives of others are satisfied. If you see my advice as coming from such values, you have two reasons to follow it: your own interests and your own altruism. In sum, the effective advice that we have reason to give must stem from our interest in seeing the objectives of others satisfied.

Advice that stems from such values does not distinguish among the means by which the objectives of people are achieved, unless, of course, these means have effects of their own on what people value. In that case, it is not the means themselves that matter but the effects, effects that we would value no matter how they were brought about. Any other advice that I give is necessarily an attempt to impose my own values on people who do not necessarily share them. For example, consider a vaccine that prevents some disease but has side effects that are as bad as the disease although less likely to occur than the disease itself. My all-things-considered judgment is that people's values for health are better served if the vaccine is used than if it is not used. If I were a government official in charge of approving the vaccine, I should approve it, and if I were anyone else I should support its approval. If I oppose approval because I have a strong intuitive moral rule against causing harm through action (vaccinating) but no equivalent rule against causing harm through omission (failing to vaccinate), then I am going against my best judgment of how the objectives of others are best satisfied. I am following my rule without regard to what other people value (and without regard to any altruistic concern I have to see that their values are satisfied), so I am imposing my moral intuitions on people to their overall detriment.

Satisfaction of values is what I mean by *consequences*. The view I just sketched thus helps to define this difficult term. Of course, I have put aside a number of issues, such as how to consider probabilities, how to measure degree of value satisfaction, or utility, and how to aggregate utility across individuals and over time. For present purposes, one can finesse such questions by relying on simple holistic judgments of expected consequences, as in the case I just gave. In that case, one can simply assume that since no one knows who the victims are, everyone has the same utility for health versus disease, so the fewer sick people the better.

It is possible, of course, to develop moral systems for particular social groups, such as families, nations, or religions. Some philosophers have taken that approach, regarding morality as setting up background conditions for national government. Traditional civic morality, in which loyalty to country is a virtue, can appeal to citizens whose decisions affect each other primarily. Moral advice for limited groups, however, cannot expect to find an audience outside the group. More importantly, such limitations are arbitrary, since groups can be defined in many ways. Utilitarians have traditionally argued that morality concerns all people—indeed, all sentient beings (Singer 1982). There is a role for group loyalty in utilitarianism, but not as a fundamental justification. It is something that must be justified by appeal to the greater good of all.

HOW UTILITARIANS HONOR THE ACT/OMISSION DISTINCTION

Although utilitarians do not distinguish acts and omissions when consequences are otherwise held constant, they do recognize situations in which, as a general rule, the distinction should be honored *because of* the consequences. I think that all these situations can be subsumed under the concept of lines of authority. Social custom, convention, and law dictate that certain decisions are to be made by certain people. We say that these people are "responsible" for the decision. At one extreme, national governments are responsible for certain decisions about their citizens. At the other extreme, individuals are responsible for certain decisions about their own lives. In the middle, decision-making authority is allocated in complex ways within institutions like corporations. Social groups may differ, of course, in how they assign such responsibilities.

If someone violates these lines of authority by doing something in someone else's domain, the whole system of responsibility allocation is thereby weakened. Other people will be tempted to step across the same line. For example, at the national level, the United Nations' invasion of Somalia in 1992 created a precedent that was seen as weakening the power of national governments. Of course, Somalia had no such government, but many other nations could be described in the same terms without too much exaggeration. On the individual level, health professionals sometimes override the expressed desires of a patient on the grounds that anyone who expresses such desires (for example, against treatment for an easily treatable condition) is incompetent to decide. In doing so, they weaken the "autonomy" of individuals, the authority that people are granted for making health decisions for themselves. Finally, at the middle level, if one member of a company reports a problem occurring in another division, the lines of authority for dealing with similar problems are weakened, even if the report helps to solve the problem. As the Bhagavad Gita puts it, "Better one's own duty, though void of merit, than to do another's well . . . Perilous is the duty of other men" (3:35).

Notice that these good acts—helping the people of a desperate nation, treating a sick patient, helping another division—have bad side effects. Omitting to perform such helpful acts does cause harm, but it causes less harm than if these side effects were absent. Thus, these otherwise harmful omissions become excusable or even desirable because of their side effects. Harmful acts, by contrast, have no such compensating benefits. We are thus led to an asymmetry between acts and omissions. The asymmetry results from the conflicts that would arise if two people were responsible for the same decision, when one person intervenes and takes an action that someone else should have taken. A second thing to notice about this utilitarian analysis is apparent in the examples. The bad effects of going outside the line of authority are just bad effects to be weighed against other effects, not absolute prohibitions. Thus, intervention into the affairs of other nations, violations of individual autonomy, and reporting problems in another division are sometimes justified. Moreover, in some cases the bad effects are not so bad. Arguably, some lines of authority *should* be weakened. Laws against child abuse may weaken the authority of parents over their children, but this kind of authority we do not need. If such laws weaken parental authority more generally, that may well be a price worth paying.

Against such arguments, the slippery-slope argument is often raised. Yes, it may be best in this case to violate the lines of authority, but that will set a precedent toward other such decisions, which will go too far. One answer to this slippery-slope argument is that the slope slips both ways. Allowing parents to beat their children, allowing people to starve because they have no government, and allowing people to die because they refuse helpful treatment, all in the name of preserving the lines of authority, can lead to further callousness, indifference, and suffering. Perhaps the best precedent is to make the best decision. On the other hand, there may be cases where a clear line must be drawn to avoid a particular kind of temptation that would make one slope more slippery than the other, such as rules against nepotism.

In sum, the utilitarian view makes a distinction between acts and omissions just in those cases in which social practice establishes lines of authority that yield good consequences in the long run, but the distinction thus made is not absolute and can be overridden.

THE "DO NO HARM" HEURISTIC

In research in the area of ethics, many subjects distinguish between harms caused by acts and those caused by omissions, and the conditions under which they do so seem to have little to do with the utilitarian arguments just advanced. In particular, many results are difficult to justify in terms of lines of authority, and subjects do not typically bring up this argument.

For example, in one study (Ritov and Baron 1990) Ilana Ritov and I examined a set of hypothetical vaccination decisions. In one experiment, subjects were told to imagine that their child had a ten-in-ten-thousand chance of death from a flu epidemic. A vaccine could prevent the flu, but the vaccine itself could kill some number of children. Subjects were asked to indicate the maximum overall death rate for vaccinated children at which they would be willing to vaccinate their child. Most subjects answered well below nine per ten thousand. Of the subjects who showed this kind of reluctance, the mean tolerable risk was about five out of ten thousand, half the risk of the illness itself. The same results were found when subjects were asked to take the position of a policy maker deciding for large numbers of children. When subjects were asked for justifications, some said that they would be responsible for any deaths caused by the vaccine, but they would not be (as) responsible for deaths caused by failure to vaccinate. When subjects were asked to consider the desires of those affected by their choice, the bias was largely eliminated (Baron 1992). This bias correlates with mothers' resistance toward DPT vaccination, which may produce death or permanent damage in a very few children (Asch and others 1993).

Other studies (Ritov and Baron 1992; Spranca, Minsk, and Baron 1991) have indicated a general bias toward omissions over acts that produce the same harmful outcome. In one study (Spranca, Minsk, and Baron 1991), for example, subjects were told about John, a tennis player who thought he could beat Ivan Lendl only if Lendl were ill. John knew that Ivan was allergic to cayenne pepper, so, when John and Ivan went out to the customary dinner before their match, John planned to recommend to Ivan the house salad dressing, which contained cayenne pepper. Subjects were asked to compare John's morality in different endings to the story. In one ending, John recommended the dressing. In another ending, John was about to recommend the dressing when Ivan chose it for himself, and John, of course, said nothing. Ten out of thirty-three subjects thought that John's behavior was worse in the commission ending, and no subject thought that the omission was worse. In this case, one might appeal to lines of authority, and some subjects did so, saying, for example, "It isn't John's responsibility to warn Ivan about the cayenne. It's Lendl's responsibility to ask." Most subjects in this case and others, however, simply appealed to the action-omission distinction directly: "John did not *recommend* the dressing." "Choosing to do nothing isn't really immoral." "John doesn't plant the seed, he just lets it grow."

Ritov and I found that this asymmetry between action and omission is typically found only for bad outcomes—that is, outcomes that are worse than the outcome produced by another option (Baron and Ritov 1994). We may thus think of omission bias—the tendency to consider harmful acts to be worse than equally harmful omissions—as caused by the use of a heuristic rule against causing harm (relative to the foregone option) through action. Hence the characterization of the results as a rule against *"doing* harm" as opposed to "bringing harm about." This heuristic is not always absolute, although some people may think of it that way some of the time.[5]

People seem to apply this do-no-harm principle to groups as well as to individuals, even when they themselves judge the utilitarian consequences to be worse. Jurney and I presented subjects with six proposed reforms, each involving some public coercion such as compulsory vaccination and tort reform involving elimination of lawsuits (Baron and Jurney 1993). Most subjects judged the reforms to be beneficial on the whole, but many of *these* subjects said that they would not vote for the reforms. Grounds for opposing such beneficial proposals included *unfairness* in the distribution of costs or benefits and *harm* to some people despite benefits to others. In one study, 39 percent of subjects said they would vote for a 100 percent tax on gasoline (to counter global warming), but 48 percent of those who would vote against it thought that the tax would do more good than harm on the whole. Subjects would thus make non-utilitarian decisions, by their own judgment of consequences. Of those subjects who would vote against the tax despite thinking that it would do more good than harm, 85 percent cited the unfairness of the tax as a reason for voting against it, and 75 percent cited the fact that the tax would harm some people.

Another study (Baron 1995) obtained further evidence for the do-no-harm principle applied to groups. Subjects were asked to put themselves in the position of a benevolent dictator of a small island consisting of equal numbers of bean growers and wheat growers. The decision was whether to accept or decline the final offer of the island's only trading partner, as a function of its effect on the incomes of the two groups. Most subjects would not accept offers that reduced the income of one group by more than a small amount in order to increase the income of the other group by a much larger amount. The same subjects judged the small reduction that they rejected to have less effect on the losers than the gain would have on the winners. In another study in the same series, many subjects would not recommend a vaccine that would reduce death rates a great deal in one group while increasing them a little in another group of the same size. The same subjects favored the vaccine more if both groups were affected equally, although the overall improvement was the same. The test to determine who was in which group was not available, so nobody would know which group they were in.

Subjects do not always distinguish between acts and omissions. The percentage of subjects showing this omission bias in various studies depends on the scenario and ranges from zero (in unpublished data, where the omission is failing to prevent a crime after planning it with another person) to over 90 percent (Baron 1992, Experiment 1, where failing to shoot one prisoner leads to the death of three others). Given this variability, it is difficult to argue that omission bias is a necessary part of our moral system. Like most heuristics that produce biases, the do-no-harm heuristic is not always used; people often think like utilitarians too. Heuristics of this sort are thus unlike optical illusions that everyone sees; they are, rather, simply rules that compete with other rules (Baron 1994).

The individual and situational factors that govern this variability are largely unknown, but a few studies have attempted to isolate them. One study (Haidt and Baron 1995) found that role relationships affect the judged seriousness of harmful omissions. For example, in one omission, a person selling a car fails to mention a potential problem to the buyer. Subjects judged this omission to be worse when the buyer is a friend rather than a stranger. When the seller actively lied about the problem, subjects judge the infraction to be almost equally bad regardless of who the buyer was. It seems that relationships such as friend or relative create responsibility similar to that created by a line of authority. Notice, however, the difficulty of finding a beneficial institution or practice that is harmed by omitting to tell a stranger of the defect. One could argue that the institution or practice is that of "caveat emptor," but the asymmetry of information argues that the responsibility should, in a case like this, be on the seller. In the terms of Guido Calabresi (1970), the seller is the "least-cost avoider" of harm.

Another study (Baron and Miller 1994) examined cultural differences in judged seriousness of harmful omissions. Our subjects were college students in the United States and India. We used a scenario in which a person needed a bone-marrow transplant, and one person, the donor, was one of a relatively small number of compatible individuals. Indians were more likely to say that donation was morally required, even when the needy person was a stranger "on the other side of the world" from the donor. This finding agrees with other work showing that Indians see moral obligations where Americans do not see them (see, for example, Miller, Bersoff, and Harwood 1990). Indians and Americans were, however, sensitive to different manipulations of the basic scenario. When the needy person was the donor's cousin, Americans thought that the obligation to donate increased considerably. Many expressed outrage at the thought of not donating to one's own kin. Indians were less affected by family relationships. Indians were, however, more affected by proximity and requests. When the needy person lived in the same town or when he specifically requested a donation, Indians thought that obligation increased. Americans were less affected by these factors.

The most direct test of the act/omission distinction in this study was a comparison of two cases involving advice. In one case, a friend says nothing to the donor, knowing that the donor would donate only if the friend advises him to do so. In the other case, a friend advises the donor not to donate, knowing that the donor would follow whatever advice the friend gives. Both Indians and Americans thought that the friend's behavior was worse in the second case.

These scenarios revealed another cultural difference of some interest. Americans were more concerned with individual autonomy, the line of authority by which each person is responsible for her own decisions. Twenty-five percent of the Americans, versus 12 percent of the Indians, referred to the donor's autonomy when asked to justify their responses to these items (for example, "It's the person's decision so the friend shouldn't intervene"). By contrast, 62 percent of the Indians, but only 21 percent of the Americans, referred to the friend's positive responsibility to give advice ("If a friend needs advice it is because he is uncertain. A true friend would not play on insecurities but encourage him to do what is good").

The American concept of autonomy is part of a culture concept of individual rights. When Americans engage in moral discussions with other nations about human rights, they may do well to consider the fact that other cultures do not have quite the same concept. The idea of paternalism, of breaking the line of authority of individuals over themselves, may be more acceptable elsewhere. For utilitarians, this is indeed a contingent matter. If the ideal of autonomy is important to a culture, outsiders should be hesitant to weaken that culture's way of functioning. But if a culture gets along without it, it is not a fundamental moral concept that anyone needs to impose on them. The question of where to draw the line between paternalism and autonomy is a difficult one, and Americans may well be at one end of a continuum of answers.

AN EXAMPLE: FREE TRADE

Responsibilities to foreigners or those outside one's ethnic group are a major issue in the world today. Increasingly, problems of environmental externalities and of fairness in the distribution of goods require international solutions. Such problems include overfishing, refugees from violence and scarcity, destruction of forests and the species that inhabit them, the ozone layer of the atmosphere, population growth, food production, water resources, and possibly the release of greenhouse gases. These considerations argue for more skepticism about the lines of authority of nation states and greater responsibility for foreigners. Of course, utilitarians have always considered foreigners to be morally equal to compatriots, but the lines-of-authority argument has limited the obligations owed to them.

In this context, attitudes toward responsibility to foreigners are of some interest. I consider here only the question of obligation to help. I put aside those cases—all too common today—in which people contrive various justifications to inflict active harm on those outside their ethnic or national group.[6]

One context in which responsibility toward foreigners arises is that of trade. Reduction of trade barriers against poor countries is one way to promote their development. If the reduction is reciprocal, then it becomes politically feasible. Reduction of trade barriers does not interfere with the national lines of authority of those who are helped. It is a national decision with a positive externality (effect on others not making the decision). Of course, this is a complex issue. Even if a given trade agreement is a net improvement, we might do more good by holding out for a better agreement.

My hunch, however, is that some of the opponents of the recent North American Free Trade Agreement (NAFTA) held basically non-utilitarian intuitions about the act/omission distinction and the obligation to foreigners. Although they would have judged that the consequences of NAFTA were better on the whole and that no better agreement was feasible, were it not for these intuitions, they opposed it because they did not want to be a party to harming some people in order to help others, or because they felt no moral responsibility to help Mexicans and other foreigners. When challenged with utilitarian arguments, these opponents may have come to believe that a better agreement was possible or that NAFTA was in fact harmful on the whole, but this was not the source of their original opposition.

I report here two questionnaire studies. One questionnaire was given to forty-four university students in the weeks just before the U.S. Congress voted on NAFTA in late 1993, and one was given to fifty-three students in the weeks just after the vote. These questionnaires examined both the act/omission distinction and the question of responsibility to foreigners. The questionnaires were similar, so I here provide the questions from both, interleaved, numbered 1 for the first questionnaire and 2 for the second, followed by the responses.

1. Do you think that the U.S. should accept NAFTA? (yes 12%, uncertain 78%, no 10%)
2. Do you think it was good that the U.S. accepted NAFTA? (yes 40%, uncertain 40%, no 21%)
1. How do you think that NAFTA would affect jobs in the U.S. and Mexico? (help both 10%, hurt both 23%; many subjects answered separately for the two countries)
2. How do you think NAFTA will affect jobs in the U.S. over the long term? (more jobs 32%, uncertain or no effect 40%, fewer jobs 28%)
2. How do you think NAFTA will affect jobs in Mexico over the long term? (more jobs 75%, uncertain or no effect 21%, fewer jobs 4%)

Attitude toward NAFTA (in the first question) was correlated with beliefs about its effect on U.S. jobs ($r = .53$ across both studies, $p = .000$) but not at all with beliefs about its effect on Mexican jobs ($r = .03$).

2. How do you think NAFTA will affect total jobs in both countries combined over the long term? (more jobs 54.7%, uncertain or no effect 36%, fewer jobs 9%)

1. Suppose that a trade agreement would cause 10,000 job losses in the U.S. but prevent 11,000 job losses (by giving more business to exporters). It would have no other economic effects. Would you favor such an agreement? (yes 69%, no 31%)

2. Suppose that a trade agreement would cause 10,000 job losses in the U.S. but prevent 11,000 job losses in the U.S. over the same time period. (The jobs would be of the same type.) The agreement would have no other economic effects. Would you favor such an agreement? Why or why not? (In this case and all other cases, imagine that there is no doubt about these predictions.) (favor 60%, oppose 21%)

Opposition to this hypothetical agreement correlated with opposition to NAFTA across both studies.[7] This result suggests that some of the opposition to NAFTA was based on the do-no-harm heuristic. Even those who may have otherwise admitted that NAFTA would increase employment in the United States were reluctant to hurt some people in order to benefit others.

Most justifications for "oppose" responses showed clear evidence of the do-no-harm heuristic: "No, because you would be giving someone else a job at your expense. Everyone has a fair share to their jobs." "No, because 10,000 jobs would be lost even though 11,000 would be saved." "No, because you still lose 10,000 jobs!" A few answers showed a simpler form of omission bias, in which the default was favored in the absence of a very strong reason to change: "No. It basically cancels itself out, so what's the point?" "You would only save 100 jobs [sic]." One response was procedural: "No. It is not fair for anyone to lose their jobs over a trade agreement that the government enacts without first getting input from the general public."

Several subjects tried to rationalize their responses by adding information not stated in the question, such as the possibility of better agreements or the possibility that the prevention of 11,000 job losses was uncertain (although the loss of 10,000 was certain): "[No] because of the job losses. . . . There are other ways of dealing with the problem." "I don't support job losses for any reason. I would much sooner find another way to prevent the 11,000 jobs from being lost." "No, because 10,000 job losses is no comparison to 11,000 *prevented* job losses. There is no guarantee that that 11,000 would lose their jobs." Adding the stipulation that the results should be taken as given did not remove these responses.

2. Suppose that a trade agreement would cause 10,000 job losses in Mexico but prevent 11,000 job losses in Mexico over the same time period. (The jobs would be of the same type.) The agreement would have no other economic effects. Would you favor such an agreement? (favor 57%, oppose 24%)

Although most subjects saw this item (given only in the second study) as a repetition of the preceding item, five subjects opposed the change because they did not want to do anything that would affect Mexico: "No. Mexico is of no concern." "No. I'm a U.S. citizen, not a Mexican citizen."

1. Suppose that a trade agreement would cause job gains in Mexico and job losses in the U.S., and no other effects. The gains in Mexico would be ten times the losses in the U.S. The jobs in question would mean just as much to the Mexican workers as to the U.S. workers. Would you favor such an agreement? (yes 16%, no 84%)

2. [identical question] (favor 28%, oppose 70%)

Responses to this item correlated with opposition to NAFTA in the first question ($r = .28$, $p = .006$). Most of the opposition came from outright, admitted, nationalistic bias: "No, because U.S. jobs are being taken away from the U.S. workers and more people will be unemployed in the U.S." "No, because we should not enter an agreement where we lose jobs." "Absolutely not. The purpose of American government is to provide protection . . . for its citizens. While the reasoning may sound selfish and isolationist, American economic policy should protect American workers. . . . Any sacrifice of American workers, no matter what the benefit in Mexico, cannot be accepted. We must still protect ourselves and not always try to be the world's policemen and guardian." "No, because, for me, Americans are far more than ten times more important than Mexicans."[8]

A few subjects raised more general questions of fairness: "No—there should be an equal gain by both countries involved in the agreement or some gain by both countries. . . ." "No, because one country would benefit while another suffers." "No. I don't think it is just to offer so many jobs to one country's people at the expense of another. . . ."

A few other subjects raised questions of responsibility: "No . . . because they should be responsible for their own jobs." "No, it's not the U.S.'s responsibility to provide jobs for Mexico." "No, because the U.S. can't afford to lose no more jobs. They need to help themselves." Such arguments are more easily understood as applications of a simple heuristic of limited responsibility than as an application of the utilitarian argument for national lines of authority.

Subjects who favored the agreement usually did so on utilitarian grounds: "Thinking globally, or about the *whole* picture, yes, the agreement would be better. This is because more people would have jobs." "Yes. Here I see the larger continent or world a general welfare unit. . . ." A few of these subjects, however, favored the agreement because of side effects such as reduced immigration from Mexico to the United States.

1. Do you think that such an agreement would be better on the whole? That is, would it be better on the whole to have such an agreement or not? [In the first study, subjects who favored the agreement in the preceding item were told not to answer this question and all subsequent ones.] (better 34%, worse 54%)

2. Do you think that such an agreement (creating ten Mexican jobs for every U.S. job lost) would be better on the whole? (yes 45%, no 32%)

Attitude toward this item (in study 2) was considerably more positive than attitude toward the agreement in the preceding question about whether subjects would favor the agreement.[9] Many of the nationalistic subjects were therefore admittedly nonconsequentialist in their nationalistic bias.

Most subjects who said no took "better on the whole" to mean "better for both nations": for example, "I think it would be better for the Mexicans, who would have a major increase in the employment rate and probably a boom in their economy. However, I don't think it would benefit the U.S. at all. So I don't think it would be better on the whole." Those who thought the agreement was better on the whole were about equally divided between those who simply referred to the greater number of jobs and those who referred to beneficial side effects. Some subjects (counted as neither agreeing nor disagreeing) were unwilling to make a holistic judgment based on a loss to some and a gain to others: "Would be better for who? It would be better for the families with the additional income, but what about the families where the job was lost?" "Maybe for the Mexicans it would benefit but for us we would be at a loss."

A couple of responses mentioned other moral issues such as fairness and responsibility: "Yes. Mexico is in need of a boost in the economy more than the U.S. Helping one's neighbor that is in need, especially when you have more than enough yourself, is being compassionate." "No, because the U.S. through Capitalism created a strong country. By creating ten jobs in Mexico at the expense of one U.S. job is allowing a weaker form of government to exist and sponge off a stronger one."

1. Do you think that it would be morally better to accept such an agreement or reject it? (accept 47%, reject 37%)
2. [identical question] (accept 45%, reject 41%)

The response to this question in study 2, like that to the preceding "better on the whole" question, was more favorable toward the agreement than was the response to the initial question about the agreement itself ($p = .005$, Wilcoxon test). Subjects' initial responses to the agreement (in which 10 Mexicans gain jobs for every U.S. loss) therefore went against their own moral judgments as well as against their judgments of overall consequences. These two judgments (morality and consequences) did not always agree, but they did not differ consistently in one direction or the other.

Most subjects who thought morality favored the agreement based their judgment on the total number of jobs in both countries: for example, "Morality demands that we accept such a deal. Any other course of action would suggest that an American's desires are up to ten times more important than a Mexican's." Subjects had a great variety of reasons for thinking that the agreement was immoral, however: "Accepting it would be insensitive to the suffering of those who would lose their jobs." "For me, it wouldn't be morally better because I would feel responsible for the loss of jobs to hardworking Americans." "[I would] reject it because, although you may be helping others with the creating of more jobs, you would hurt the ones who have lost jobs, which is wrong." "Of course it would be morally better to help ten Mexicans at the expense of one American, but I think that this country has a duty to look out for the interests of its citizens first." "Reject. We must look out for the U.S.A. first." "We should look out for ourselves." "Mexicans are losing nothing but gaining jobs. Americans are losing jobs but gaining nothing. Fair, right? WRONG!" "[I would] reject it because, by accepting it, problems would be created in the U.S. (more unemployment)." "Absolutely not. . . . The U.S. was created by U.S. citizens. They have a moral right to exist for themselves and not be an altruistic sacrifice for any and all people with wants." Notice that some of these reasons referred to role-specific obligations of a presumed decision maker rather than overall consequences.

No justifications simply asserted that U.S. citizens counted more than Mexicans. (Nor did any justification clearly say this in response to the previous question.) It appears, then, that nationalistic bias is morally based on role-specific obligations of citizens and political leaders rather than on inherent moral worth. Some subjects gave answers for both roles: for example, "In terms of the constituents you represent, no. In terms of the world . . . [I] accept it." Political leaders may well have a line of authority that requires them to look out for their constituents first, but it is more difficult to see why citizens, as individuals, should also have this commitment. If they do, who looks out for international externalities? People may transfer the lines-of-authority argument from political leaders to the citizens who elect them.

Some subjects avoided answering this question, often taking a relativistic stance toward morality: "Depends on which side you're on." "I do not feel that there is a moral judgment to be made on such a policy. However, morally, for all mankind, it is an almost rhetorical question. Of course, one would think that you must accept it. However, tell that to the American worker who worked hard all of his life and now cannot provide for his family since his job was given to a 19-year-old Mexican. The Lord Jesus asks us to give of ourselves, but I don't think He would ask me to shoot myself in order to provide someone with a heart transplant. So, therefore, although it may seem as if there is, I don't believe that there is a moral judgment to be made in such a situation."

> 1. If you were living in a third country, neither Mexico nor the U.S., would you favor the agreement or oppose it? (76% favor, 3% oppose)

The strong approval of the agreement here supports the view that most opposition is role specific.

1. Suppose that the jobs created were in Ohio and the jobs lost were in Pennsylvania. There would be ten times as many jobs created in Ohio as were lost in Pennsylvania, and no other effects. (favor 66%, oppose 26%)

2. Suppose that all the jobs created were in one state of the U.S. and all the jobs lost were in another state of the U.S. There would be ten times as many jobs created as lost, and no other effects. (accept 62%, reject 32%)

These questions were designed to encourage subjects to rethink their answers to previous questions. Most rejected the parallel to the international agreement: "The boundaries between states are very different than borders between countries." One subject accepted the parallel: "This agreement would hurt Pennsylvania, but it would greatly help the economy of the whole country, so I would support it. I realize the implications of this last question, and it makes a valid point: If different countries could work together and look out for the benefits of the whole world, as the states of America are united, then everyone would benefit."

Opposition was based on the do-no-harm principle and on fairness: "I would oppose it. . . . I don't think one should gain from the loss of others." "Oppose it. The job employment should be dispersed." "Things have to be kept *even*." "It wouldn't be fair for the state with the job losses while the state with the job gains flourished." "It doesn't seem fair to put one state in jeopardy for the benefit of another."

2. Suppose that all the jobs created and all the jobs lost were in the same state of the U.S. There would be ten times as many jobs created as lost, and no other effects. Would you favor such an agreement or oppose it? (accept 81%, reject 11%)

The remaining opposition was based mostly on the do-no-harm principle: "Oppose it because it would hinder some people."

IMPLICATIONS

I have argued that people would adopt a sophisticated form of utilitarianism, one that takes account of existing social arrangements, if they were not biased by prior moral intuitions. These intuitions are themselves approximately utilitarian in many situations. Many of them are based on principles that were invented, I think, to deal with particular bad consequences. But the principles may have applied to the case at hand and not to other cases. Thus, an injunction against harm does not apply to cases in which harm is justified by greater good, from a utilitarian perspective. And respect for the lines of authority of individuals or national governments may be unwarranted or misapplied in some situations, such as trade agreements.

This argument has two kinds of implications for the topic of this book, about which I have said very little so far, namely ethics and business. First, some of the opposition to government programs that are good for business is based on non-utilitarian intuitions of the sort I have discussed. Free trade is an example. Many people are reluctant to harm some in order to help others, and any kind of change does just that. Similar arguments could be made about other changes that would affect business, such as basing risk regulation on an analysis of costs and benefits.

Second, the lines-of-responsibility argument may be overused by those inside of corporations, just as it is overused by their opponents. Corporations faced with demands to be more socially responsible in one way or another often argue that it is not their responsibility to do good but rather to make a profit for their shareholders. From a utilitarian point of view, the stockholders are indeed relevant, but they are not the only ones affected by corporate policies. When necessary, their interests may be sacrificed for the greater good of others, although, obviously, not so much as to cause greater harms (such as weakening the overall confidence of investors).

Of course, too much sacrifice will induce the stockholders to bail out. The long-run sustainability of the corporation must also be considered, as well as the more general willingness of investors to invest at all, and these considerations make us worry more about the stockholders than we would if we were assured of eternal corporate life and investor confidence. And if the corporation is doing good by satisfying peoples' true values (rather than, say, satisfying addictions that go against these values), it is better for the corporation to grow, so that it can do more good. For a utilitarian, however, these are considerations that can be balanced against other considerations, such as the benefit to others. On the other side of the balance are factors like corporate reputation (Orts 1995). These factors can make corporate altruism worthwhile in the long run, even at the short-run expense of the stockholders.

A good example of all these points is the pharmaceutical industry. This industry—through research, development, and marketing of products—has done enormous amounts of good. It has also suffered from lawsuits against some of its most beneficial products, those given to healthy people, such as birth-control products and vaccines. Many of these lawsuits were, arguably, based on non-utilitarian intuitions related to the distinction between acts and omissions (Baron and Ritov 1993). For example, the makers of the Salk polio vaccine were never sued for failing to prevent polio, but the makers of the Sabin (oral) vaccine were sued many times for causing it, even though the total risk was smaller with the Sabin.

It is difficult to second-guess the extent to which the industry has lived up to its responsibility. It is true that research and development have decreased on birth-control products (Djerassi 1989), vaccines (Huber 1988), and especially medicines useful for treating or preventing diseases of the world's poor (Gibbons 1992). How much of this reduction was necessary to preserve long-term financial strength is difficult to judge. On the other hand, we have seen some outstanding examples of corporate altruism, such as the donation of a treatment for river blindness by Merck, which realized that the millions of people who could benefit were simply too poor to pay (Hanson 1991).

Some would argue that utilitarian reasoning is dangerous, even if it is correct, because it goes against simple rules of ethics. I'm not sure those rules are much followed anyway. If the other arguments I have made here are correct, then a utilitarian analysis would be useful both for those in corporations and those outside of them in dealing with the problems of the world.

ENDNOTES

1. I distinguish morality and ethics. Morality concerns the basic principles by which we justify our decisions to each other. Ethics concerns more limited, culture-specific codes that play a similar role. Ethics is ultimately justified by morality, but it also takes into account the facts about institutions and their function in a given society.

2. I have presented this argument at greater length in Baron (1993).

3. I use the term value in the sense that Keeney (1993) and Anderson (1993) have used it, and I use the terms *goals, interests,* and *objectives* for the same concept. These are not mere desires but rather desires that we endorse and accept as criteria for the evaluation of states of affairs.

4. Similarly, people who consult their intuitions will decide that rights and duties can override consequences. Usually, honoring rights and duties will lead to the best consequences, so the issue does not come up. When it does not, we must ask where the authority of these intuitions comes from, for following them harms people by bringing about worse consequences than could be achieved otherwise.

5. Baron and Ritov (1994) discussed the relationships among omission bias, harm avoidance, loss aversion, and norm theory.

6. I suspect, however, that part of the problem here is the result of similar non-utilitarian understandings of punishment and retribution, as well as of self-deception about one's own goodness and the badness of others.

7. The correlation ($r = .27$, $p = .018$) remained significant ($p = .003$) when the U.S.-jobs item was partialled out.

8. This response, and a couple of others like it, remind me of Rabbi Yaacov Perrin's statement in his eulogy for Dr. Baruch Goldstein, who was beaten to death after killing forty Palestinian worshipers: "One million Arabs is not worth a Jewish fingernail" (*New York Times,* Feb. 28, 1994). Of course, that is an extreme view on the continuum of nationalistic sentiment.

9. This was significant at $p = .002$ (Wilcoxon test), counting both increased agreement, from 28 percent to 45 percent, and reduced disagreement, from 70 percent to 32 percent.

Chapter 11

Behavioral Decision Theory and Business Ethics: Skewed Trade-offs Between Self and Other

George Loewenstein

B ehavioral decision theory studies the trade-offs people make when they decide between options or courses of action. For example, someone choosing between jobs might trade off a high salary in one job against the high prestige of another job; for someone considering a risky prospect, such as starting a business, there would be a trade-off between certainty and expected value; and in intertemporal choices the typical choice is between earlier smaller rewards and later larger rewards. Behavioral decision theory also helps us to understand ethical decisions that involve trade-offs. My focus is on managerial decisions involving trade-offs between a manager's personal well-being and that of others.

Business decision making often calls for trade-offs between the well-being of the decision maker and that of others. The decision to blow the whistle on unsafe working conditions, for example, may result in the loss of one's job, but failure to do so may harm those exposed to the unsafe conditions. The desire to keep one's job is clearly consistent with self-interest; the desire to benefit another person is often termed *altruism*.[1] Altruism can be expressed formally by assuming that individuals' utilities depend not only on their own consumption (S) but also on that of others (O): $U = U(S, O)$. Altruism is said to exist when the partial derivative of U with respect to O is positive—that is, when utility increases with increasing payoffs to "other" or decreases with increasing costs borne by "other." Altruism is distinct from situations in which people care about others' outcomes only because they influence their own—that is, $U[S(O)]$, with $S'(O) > 0$.

A second, somewhat controversial, feature of behavioral decision theory is its attention to *errors* in judgment and choice. Unlike economics, which

The author wishes to thank Jon Baron, Eloise Coupey, and Karen Jenni for helpful comments.

214 /

assumes that people behave optimally, subject to constraints, behavioral decision theory describes human decision making with all its blemishes and warts. Proponents of the focus on error argue that errors are more interesting than "normal" behavior and that the best way to understand the norm is often to study deviations from it. This is especially true when it comes to studying ethical aspects of decision making. How many readers would make it to the second chapter of a book on ethics that trumpeted the ethical behavior of managers, and how much light could such a treatise shed on the determinants of unethical behavior? Ivan Boesky has more to tell us about business ethics than Ben and Jerry.

Fortunately, at least for ethics commentators, managerial behavior provides a virtually inexhaustible source of seemingly skewed trade-offs between personal well-being and that of others. Many examples are so notorious that they have become virtual code words for callousness: the Pinto, Johns Manville, DES, and the Dalkon Shield, to name a few. In each of these cases, a cohort of managers knowingly imposed egregious harm on an unknowing group of customers or workers for the purpose of making a profit. The question such cases raise is how such large groups of people could have deliberately traded relatively minor enhancements in their own material well-being for others' lives and/or livelihoods. I believe that behavioral decision theory, together with the allied disciplines from which it borrows, offers at least part of the answer to this question.

Behavioral decision research, I will argue, paints an extremely bleak picture of the possibilities for altruism in general, and managerial altruism in particular. The research I discuss in this chapter suggests several different reasons why managers' trade-offs between their own and others' well-being are likely to be skewed to the point where they put very little weight on the effect of their decisions on other parties, except insofar as those effects have repercussions for their own well-being.

First, considerable research points to the fact that altruism is generally a weak force in human behavior except, perhaps, in a relatively small subgroup of the population. Moreover, altruistic sentiments tend to be highly transient and ephemeral, at times surging to absurd proportions but at other times displaying an appalling feebleness. Second, it is especially easy to discount negative consequences to others when those who experience the consequences are statistics rather than known persons—a condition that is frequently satisfied in managerial decision making. Third, people are generally much more sensitive to incentives that are immediate than to those that are delayed. The fact that the impact of managerial decisions on managers themselves is generally much more immediate than their impact on others produces a further reduction in concern for others. Fourth, people typically evaluate trade-offs by comparing them with other trade-offs they have recently made or accepted. Thus, skewed trade-offs between self and other that might be unacceptable if introduced in their entirety, may well be accepted if the decision is broken down into a series of small steps. This pattern is exacerbated when decision making takes place in insulated groups whose members use one another as points of reference. Fifth, people possess a remarkable ability to mislead themselves about the nature of the trade-offs they face—to rationalize that what benefits them also benefits (or does not hurt) others—and also to minimize their own responsibility for any adverse outcomes that occur. Finally, people underestimate—or are entirely oblivious to—the impact of many of these factors on their own decisions and, as a result, do not develop defenses against them. After reviewing research supporting each of these assertions, I discuss the possibilities for motivating ethical behavior and describe by way of contrast an example of how to ensure *un*ethical behavior—the case of the "independent" auditor.

THE WEAKNESS OF ALTRUISM

Recent empirical investigations of altruism have found it to be a surprisingly weak force in human decision making. There is no reason to believe that managers are exceptions to this rule; quite the opposite, as I will argue.

The weakness of altruism is evident in research on *social utility functions*, which specify an individual's well-being as a function of payoffs to that person and to other parties. In one study (Loewenstein, Thompson, and Bazerman 1989), we presented subjects with scenarios in which they and another party received money from the sale of jointly owned property or had to divide costs stemming from liability arising from such property. We found very little evidence of altruism; subjects' satisfaction with the outcome of the transaction rarely increased with the other party's payoff, and in many cases it declined substantially. This finding held true even when we described the relationship between the parties in very favorable terms. Rather than altruism, what we observed was a powerful loathing for coming out below the other side. This research suggests that altruism is a relatively minor force in human affairs when compared, for example, to the distaste for being "one-down."

Similar conclusions have been reached in research on experimental games. For example, in the "ultimatum game" (Güth, Schmittberger, and Schwarze 1982), two subjects are paired off; one is assigned the role of "divider" and the other is assigned to be "chooser." The divider is asked to split a fixed amount of money (for example, $10) between the two players. The chooser then decides whether to accept or reject the proposed split. Neither person gets any money if the chooser rejects the offer. Although traditional game theory predicts that dividers should offer minimal amounts and choosers should accept them, dividers in fact typically offer the other subject more than a trivial amount, favoring most often an equal split, such as $5/$5.

Early accounts of the ultimatum game attributed the behavior of dividers to altruism; it postulated that dividers give up part of the "pot" because they care about the well-being of choosers. Results from a closely related game, however, cast doubt on this explanation. The so-called "dictator" game (Hoffman and others, in press; Bolton, Katok, and Zwick, in press), is just like the ultimatum game except that the chooser must accept the split and therefore has no power to punish the divider. In the dictator game contributions are far lower than in the ultimatum game. Thus, consistent with the findings from research on social utility, it appears that dividers in the ultimatum game offer nontrivial amounts because they are worried that choosers will reject small amounts as unfair. This worry is well founded, since choosers often do reject inequitable offers, sacrificing personal gain to punish unfair dividers.

There are some exceptions to the general rule of weak altruism, not only across persons[2] but within them. Most people experience periodic surges of pity and concern for others, and at these times might even be willing to sacrifice on their behalf.[3] Such fluctuations, however, are probably relatively uncorrelated with the objective desirability of altruistic behavior. For example, a few weeks before writing this paper, when the massacre in Rwanda was taking place, I went to see a movie in which a boy who is somewhat older than my son is hit by a car and later dies. Later that night it struck me that my emotional response to the fictitious boy in the movie was stronger than my reaction to the slaughter of hundreds of thousands of Rwandans.

STATISTICAL VICTIMS

In the research on the ultimatum game discussed earlier, subjects have a sense that they are playing the game with another specific individual, even though that person's identity is not revealed. In contrast, the people who will be adversely affected by many business decisions cannot specifically be identified at the time the decision is made; they are so-called statistical victims. Many commentators have lamented the public's tendency to show more concern for identifiable victims than for statistical victims.

Karen Jenni and I (Jenni and Loewenstein 1994) recently conducted research to test the validity of the *identifiable-victim effect* and to attempt to understand its underlying cause. Besides confirming that such an effect indeed exists, our research points to three major differences between statistical and identifiable victims that contribute to their differential treatment.

The first difference is the greater amount of information people have about identifiable victims. Given modern media coverage, when an identifiable person is at risk of death, a great deal is known about them almost immediately. For example, people see the school picture of a small girl who is trapped in a well, hear interviews with her tearful parents, and watch desperate attempts to rescue her. This information, necessarily unavailable for statistical victims, increases empathy for the identified victim.

Second, in situations with identifiable victims, all or almost all of the people at risk can usually be saved, whereas actions to save statistical lives generally save only a small portion of those who are at risk. People care much more if half of a group of twenty will die than if .01 percent of a group of one hundred thousand will die (Ritov and Baron 1990). Four (out of an identifiable group of four) whales trapped in the ice elicit international concern and costly rescue efforts, but hundreds of otherwise unidentified whales that will be caught in fishermen's nets are barely worthy of mention. Our empirical research suggests that this *reference group effect* is the single most important cause of the differential treatment of statistical and identifiable lives.

Third, identifiable victims are certain to be injured or to die if action is not taken, but statistical risks are probabilistic, so there is some possibility, however small, that no one will die. This factor seems to be a minor contributor to the discrepant treatment of statistical and identifiable victims.

Clearly, in most cases of business decision making, and especially those involving top management, the people who are adversely affected are not only anonymous to the decision makers (as in the ultimatum game) but are statistical in character. Smokers who eventually contracted lung cancer, workers and their families who died of asbestos poisoning, drivers and passengers who were incinerated in Pintos, and women who suffered high rates of infertility and miscarriage as a result of DES were all statistical victims from the perspective of the responsible managers at the time that the relevant decisions were being made. Specific victims couldn't be identified (and thus identified with) at the time the relevant decisions were made; it was thought that only a small fraction of groups exposed to the products would be affected; and there was some possibility, however small, that no one would be adversely affected.

IMMEDIACY OF EFFECTS

In most business decisions, some of the consequences are felt immediately by the decision maker, whereas payoffs or consequences for others are typically delayed. Time delay is yet another factor that might cause decision makers to place undue weight on consequences to themselves relative to others. Considerable research has shown that people (and animals) place greater weight on outcomes that are immediate than on those that are delayed—a phenomenon commonly referred to as *time discounting*. People are disproportionately influenced by rewards and costs that are immediate or imminent. Because consequences to self are typically more immediate than those experienced by others, time discounting exacerbates the discrepancy in concern for consequences to self and others. For example, the whistle-blower is in danger of immediately losing his or her job, but the benefits resulting from blowing the whistle (or the costs of not doing so) are delayed.

The combination of delay and uncertainty seems to be especially pernicious, not only when it comes to managers imposing costs on others but also in people's behavior toward themselves in the future. In many of the standard examples of suboptimal individual decision making—for example, overeating, smoking, or failure to wear seat belts—the costs of changing one's behavior are immediate, but the benefits are both delayed and probabilistic. Given that people expose themselves to such risks, is it surprising that managers expose other people to similar types of risks? The Safeway supermarket chain may have adulterated its meat, mixing new meat with old and washing spoiled meat in order to sell it as new, but I ate a full rack of ribs for lunch the other day at the local house of grease, then barbecued a steak for dinner (both actions with delayed and uncertain consequences). The Ford Motor Company cynically sold Pintos with exploding gas tanks to increase profits, but for years I saved money by driving a rusty death trap (which I then sold to my neighbor's son). Executives of cigarette companies concealed evidence about the dangers of smoking but, while possessing the knowledge, they themselves smoked at a very high rate. The dictum to "do unto others as you would do unto yourself," even if followed religiously, might have little impact on the behavior of the executives of Safeway, Ford, and the cigarette companies.

Time delay and uncertainty are typically treated separately in the decision literature. Roger Brown (1986), however, argues that they can usefully be viewed as two dimensions of a more general construct that could be termed *immediacy*, which would also encompass attributes such as physical proximity and various forms of sensory contact. In general, people care more about immediate, certain, identified victims who can be seen, smelled, touched. Brown illustrated the effect of immediacy—broadly construed—by reanalyzing the results from the famous Milgram shock studies (Milgram 1974). The original Milgram shock studies demonstrated that a large fraction of relatively average people could be induced to administer what they believed were extremely painful and potentially hazardous shocks to another person (the victim) in response to verbal prodding by an experimenter.

Milgram ran twenty-one variations of his experiment, and Brown showed that the rank ordering of these conditions according to the percentage of subjects who administered the maximum level of shock could be predicted perfectly on the basis of the immediacy of the experimenter (who exhorted the subject to administer the shocks) and the victim. Shock rates were highest in the baseline condition in which subjects were in the physical presence of the experimenter but the victim was in another room. Rates declined when the victim was moved into the same room, declined further when the subject had to hold down the victim's arm to deliver the shock, and declined to virtually nil when the experimenter was absent.

Unfortunately, managers' trade-offs between their own and others' well-being typically occur in circumstances that approximate the baseline condition in the Milgram experiment (the experimenter is physically present and the victim is not), in which shock rates were at a maximum; the impact of managers' decisions on themselves is generally far more immediate in all senses of the term than the impact on other parties.

ADAPTIVE TRADE-OFFS

Trade-offs, or the awareness of trade-offs, between self and other often change over time. For example, during the early stages of development of products such as cigarettes, asbestos, or DES, the executives responsible for producing and selling the products probably were not aware or only dimly aware of their hazardous qualities. Thus, they thought that the profit they were earning was at the expense of only minimal risks to their customers; awareness of risks emerged gradually.

Such a gradual unfolding of hazards to the public would not be problematic if managers evaluated risks and returns in terms of absolute levels. At a certain point, executives would simply decide that the product was too dangerous to sell to consumers, and they would take the product off the shelves. But human judgment is generally more sensitive to change than to absolute levels. A clever experiment conducted by Amos Tversky (1969) illustrates the hazards of making decisions on the basis of changes rather than levels.

Tversky presented subjects with a series of choices between simple gambles offering a chance of winning a small amount of money. For each choice, one gamble always paid $.25 more but had a 1/24 smaller chance of winning. For example, the first choice was between $4.00 with probability 11/24 and $4.25 with probability 10/24; the next choice in the series was between $4.25 with probability 10/24 and $4.50 with probability 9/24. The probabilities of winning those gambles were not presented numerically, but as spinners (like a wheel of fortune) with a certain fraction shaded black. If the spinner landed in the black area, the subject won the amount specified by the gamble. Probably because they could not visually detect the difference between the probabilities of adjacent gambles, most subjects opted for the higher payoff–smaller probability gamble from each of these choices. Thus, presented with a series of stepped choices, subjects aggregated responses pointing to a preference for the last gamble in the series ($5.00, 7/24) over the first ($4.00, 11/24). When Tversky presented subjects with a direct choice between these two gambles, however, a majority of subjects stated a preference for the $4.00, 11/24 choice. This experiment shows that people can arrive at very different outcomes depending upon whether they are presented with a single large choice or a series of smaller incremental choices.

Many instances of unethical behavior seem interpretable in these terms. People often violate their own moral precepts in a series of small steps; they are "led down the garden path." Thus, in the famous Milgram experiments, subjects were not asked at the outset to administer a potentially lethal shock but were given a series of requests to increase the voltage marginally. Having given someone a 100-volt shock, one finds it difficult to justify stopping at precisely that point rather than acquiescing to the experimenter's request to increase the voltage again by a small amount. Similarly, R. J. Lifton (1990) argued that it was the incremental character of ethical decay that made it possible for German doctors to become active killers, even though they had taken the Hippocratic oath to do no harm. He described a process whereby doctors were first present when euthanasia took place, were later asked to add their signature to a document, still later were asked to supervise a mercy killing, and so on, to the point where many actually administered lethal injections to eugenically "undesirable" persons.

This failure to notice step-by-step degradation of ethical standards is likely to be exacerbated when managers are imbedded in insulated groups, as is common. It is well established that people in groups tend to compare attitudes and opinions among themselves and that such social comparisons can have an important formative impact (see, for example, Asch 1951; Myers and Lamm 1976; Janis 1972). Just as a rude comment from a shopkeeper would be more noteworthy in Atlanta than in Manhattan, behavior that is extreme with respect to the standards of the general population will appear much less so in a group context if all members of the reference group change together. Choices that appear unethical to outsiders may seem perfectly justified to a group of managers.

THE HUMAN CAPACITY FOR RATIONALIZATION

People are not objective information processors. One of the most important nonobjective influences on information processing is self-interest, which poses yet another impediment to incorporating concerns for or about others in business decisions. It is by now well established that people tend to conflate what is personally beneficial with what is fair or moral. For example, David Messick and Keith Sentis (1979) asked subjects to specify the "fair" rate of pay for two people (self and other) who had worked at the same task, one for ten hours and one for seven. The person who worked seven hours was always paid $25; subjects were asked how much the person who worked ten hours should be paid. When told that it was the subject who had worked seven hours and the other person had worked ten, a large number of subjects advocated strict equity or piecework wages—$25 for each worker—as fair. When told that the other person had worked seven hours and the subject had worked ten, however, subjects tended to advocate a fixed hourly wage, resulting in a higher payoff for themselves, as fair.

In studies by Roth and Murnighan (1982), pairs of players bargained over one hundred chips that determined their chances of winning a monetary prize (for example, thirty-seven chips gave a 37 percent chance of winning). One player's prize would be $20 and the other's prize would be $5. Notice that there are two ways to split the chips "equally"; one can give fifty chips to each, giving them equal chances of winning, or one can give twenty chips to the $20-prize player and eighty chips to the $5-prize player, equalizing the expected dollar winnings). When neither player knew the prize amounts, they agreed to divide the chips about equally. When the players knew the prize amounts, however, they tended to hold out for the distribution of chips that favored themselves, producing a higher rate of disagreement.

In my own work with Linda Babcock, Sam Issacharoff, and Colin Camerer (Babcock and others 1995; Loewenstein and others 1993), we have presented subjects with diverse materials from a lawsuit resulting from a collision between an automobile and motorcycle. Subjects are assigned the roles of plaintiff and defendant and try to negotiate a settlement. If they are unable to settle, the amount paid by the plaintiff to the defendant is determined by an impartial judge who has read exactly the same case materials. Before they negotiate, we ask subjects to predict the judge's ruling, and we offer a monetary reward for accuracy. Nevertheless, plaintiffs' predictions of the judge's award amount are typically substantially higher than defendants'.

Recent research by Chris Hsee (1994a) points even more directly to the prevalence of rationalization. Hsee exposed subjects to decisions involving a trade-off between instrumental attributes (those that are easy to justify) and affective attributes—for example, the choice between two job candidates, one of whom is more competent, the other more physically attractive. Hsee found that when both attributes were defined precisely, people generally opted for the candidate stronger on the instrumental attribute—in this case, the more competent candidate. If provided with an excuse for hiring the more attractive candidate, however, such as a remote possibility that the more attractive candidate is in fact more competent, people used the excuse to justify hiring the more attractive candidate.

All this research shows that when there are competing norms of fairness, subjects will tend to select as relevant those that materially favor themselves. In addition, when there is ambiguity about the consequences of alternatives, people will be able to rationalize taking the option they personally prefer as opposed to the one that is normatively or ethically more justifiable. Since the consequences of business decisions are typically highly ambiguous, these types of rationalizations are likely to be very common in business decision making.

A second form of ambiguity that is pervasive in business settings probably contributes to self-serving judgments and to the undermining of ethical behavior by managers. This is the ambiguity of who is *responsible* for a particular outcome. People seem to be quite adept at relieving themselves of responsibility for harming another person, as illustrated by the very high rates of maximum shock delivery (90 percent) in a variant of the Milgram experiment in which the subject did not actually pull the switch that delivered the shock but carried out an operation that was ostensibly necessary for the shock to be delivered (see Sabini and Silver 1982). As in this experiment, many people in businesses perform functions that are necessary for a particular project to be completed, but few perform functions that are sufficient for its completion, so that any consequences can be traced purely to their own actions. In business and other institutional settings, as Sabini and Silver (1982) note, "The relation between an individual's action and the rules and commands of an organization obscures personal responsibility" (p. 65).

FAILURES OF SELF-PREDICTION

The final nail in the coffin of managerial altruism is the tendency to underestimate the influence of the factors just discussed on one's own behavior. In principle, people may want to behave in a fashion that reflects a substantial weighting of others' welfare, but in practice their failure to recognize the force of these factors may undermine their ability to do so.

For example, people underestimate the influence of immediacy on their decisions. The failure to predict the impact of immediacy is well illustrated by an oft-cited study by Christensen Szalanski (1984). He interviewed expectant mothers about their desire for anesthesia during childbirth. A majority of women expressed a preference for natural childbirth until after labor began, at which point a majority shifted in favor of anesthesia. Apparently, the women were unable to anticipate the severity of or the motivating quality of the pain they would experience, as if they did not somehow fully empathize with their future (in-pain) self. Interestingly, this was also true of women who had given birth previously, suggesting that the lack of empathy also extended to their past (in-pain) self. The tendency to underestimate the effect of immediacy can also explain why the results of the Milgram shock experiment are so surprising to people. When subjects were presented with a description of the Milgram experiment but not told about the final result, most predicted that only a very small fraction of subjects would administer high levels of shock and that they themselves would not (Milgram 1974). People seem to underestimate the impact of the experimenter's immediate presence.

People also underestimate the effect of adaptation on their own behavior. For example, a robust finding in behavioral decision research is that when people are endowed with an object, they are typically very resistant to giving it up—far more so than one would expect on the basis of their desire for the object in the first place. This *endowment effect* is typically explained on the basis of adaptation (to possession) and *loss aversion* (the aversion to losing what one has). My own research on the endowment effect (Loewenstein and Adler 1995) shows that people are unable to predict that they will become attached to objects once they possess them. Thus, they seem to underestimate the effect of adaptation on their own behavior. In the context of business decisions, this research suggests not only that managers will adapt to the status quo, perhaps influenced by their peer group and by a series of small changes, but also that they will be unaware of the adaptation they have undergone.

Finally, people seem to underestimate their own powers of rationalization. In the studies of the legal dispute discussed earlier (Loewenstein and others 1993; Babcock and others 1995), we paid plaintiffs and defendants for the accuracy of their prediction of the judge's ruling; the fact that this motivation had no effect on the predictions is consistent with the conclusion that the self-serving bias is unconscious and nondeliberate. Moreover, in one set of studies we informed subjects about the bias before they gave their predictions of the judge's award; we also asked them to predict their opponent's prediction of the judge's award. Telling them about the bias had no impact on their own predictions of what the judge would do, but it did change their prediction of their opponent's prediction; subjects informed of the self-serving bias believed the result and thought that their opponents would exhibit the bias but that they themselves were somehow immune to it.

In each of these cases, failure to appreciate the effect of a particular factor is likely to leave managers vulnerable to it. Unaware of or doubting the effect of immediacy, adaptation, and rationalization, managers exposed to situations in which these factors are operative, although confident in the belief that they will not be affected, are likely to succumb to these forces.

POSSIBLE SOLUTIONS

Early social thinkers such as Adam Smith and Thomas Hobbes were impressed by the power of human empathy and altruism but nevertheless concluded that these tendencies were not sufficiently powerful to ensure socially constructive behavior. Smith argued that the desire for personal gain was a much more reliable force with which to motivate socially beneficial behavior, while Hobbes believed that the coercive force of strong government was needed to rein in human behavior. The research I have reviewed supports their skepticism concerning the possible role of altruism in social life.

Probably the best way to encourage behavior that benefits other people is to provide a personal incentive for doing so. To a great extent such incentives are built into daily life. For example, there is a strong *reciprocity norm*; acts that benefit others are often paid back in some form, and moreover, as the ultimatum game demonstrates, people are often willing to sacrifice their own well-being to punish people they feel have harmed them or treated them unfairly. Thus, people have built-in behavioral responses that motivate others to treat them fairly (see Frank 1988).

The legal system is also designed, if not to encourage generosity toward others, at least to discourage the imposition of egregious harm on others. To the extent that legal behavior is also ethical behavior, fear of sanctions is undoubtedly a major contributor to the latter. Finally, social norms and the sanctions that result from violating them are probably an important source of behavior that takes others into consideration. For many people, managers included, loss of reputation or social standing is as much to be feared as any material penalty. Thus, people's personal constitutions and the institutions and norms that prevail in society are all arranged in ways that reduce the necessity for personal altruism.

Whether or not it is necessary or even socially desirable to promote individual altruism is an unresolved (and probably unresolvable) question. To the extent that one wants to do so, however, the foregoing discussion suggests several ways to encourage business managers to consider the concerns of others and the impacts that their decisions may have. First, managers should be in close contact with the people who are affected by their decisions, making these people "identified" and "immediate." Second, measures should be taken to prevent managers from forming an insulated subgroup, in order to minimize the chance that group norms will deviate substantially from societal norms. Ideally there should be a periodic introduction of new personnel into the ranks of any group of managers. New people will not only see any incremental changes that have occurred in the aggregate but will take time to adapt to the evolved norms of the management subgroup in which they are placed. Third, steps should be taken to keep people out of situations in which they are faced with temptation and in which the various factors that undermine altruism are operative. With respect to this third point, it may be informative to examine a case in which precisely the opposite occurs—the case of so-called independent auditors.

HOW TO GUARANTEE UNETHICAL BEHAVIOR: THE CASE OF AUDITING[4]

In theory, auditors are supposed to represent the interests of external users of financial statements, such as stockholders, potential stockholders, financial advisers, underwriters, and potential creditors. Auditors are paid by the company they audit, however, who can hire or fire them at will. Moreover, auditors often socialize with the management of the company they audit. The American Institute of Certified Public Accountants (AICPA) acknowledges the pressures on auditors but argues that personal integrity is sufficient for objectivity. Rule 102 of the AICPA (1988) code of professional ethics states,

> In the performance of any professional service, a member shall maintain objectivity and integrity, shall be free of conflicts of interest, and shall not knowingly misrepresent facts or subordinate his or her judgment to others.

The AICPA (1988) seems to feel that such integrity can be maintained by exhortation alone:

> Members should accept the obligation to act in a way that will serve the public interest, honor the public trust, and demonstrate commitment to professionalism.

In light of the points I have raised, this standard can be seen as entirely unattainable for most people. First, the people who will be hurt by any misrepresentation of information are statistical. Many of them might lose a small amount of money; it isn't clear who will do so; and there is some chance that no one will be adversely affected by a minor misrepresentation. In contrast, the auditor is likely to be intimately acquainted with those who would be hurt by a negative ("qualified") opinion on an audit. Second, the negative consequences of a qualified opinion are likely to be immediate—loss of the client's friendship, likely loss of the contract, and possible unemployment— whereas the effects of a false negative (an unqualified report where qualification is merited) are likely to be delayed in time. Third, auditors form an ongoing working relationship with the organizations they audit, and any deterioration in the audited company is likely to unfold gradually. Auditors may unknowingly adapt to small changes year after year in the company's financial practices. Fourth, financial records are inherently ambiguous, so it is very easy for an auditor to rationalize arriving at a judgment that is consistent with self-interest rather than with the actual financial figures. In sum, if one wanted to create a business setting that would virtually *guarantee* unethical behavior, it would be difficult to improve on the existing case of independent auditing.

CONCLUSIONS

Every generation would like to believe it is more civilized than the last, but inevitably there comes a moment of truth. As recent events in Bosnia and Rwanda show, our generation enjoys no exemption. In the aftermath of each period of mass cruelty and murder, a soul-searching follows in which people ask themselves how human beings could have done these things to one another. Their answers are as diverse as intellectual thought itself: mob psychology, toilet training, authoritarian family structure, a "death instinct," capitalist greed, obedience. The purpose of this chapter has been to consider what insights behavioral decision theory and allied subdisciplines have to offer on the age-old question of "man's inhumanity to man" and, more specifically, on the behavior of managers.

In light of the behavioral decision theory research, I believe, the prevalence of unethical business behavior poses no puzzle whatsoever. The paradox in search of explanation, if any, is the relative infrequency of such behavior. The key to business ethics does not lie in altruism.

ENDNOTES

1. The exact definition of altruism has been debated endlessly. For example, some writers would exclude from altruism situations in which people help others because they feel good as a result of doing so. Distinctions are also commonly made between "genetic" altruism and "psychological" altruism. I define altruism simply as the weight placed on others' costs and benefits relative to one's own in decision making. This definition does not count as altruism situations in which people help others because they expect to be compensated in some material fashion.

2. There probably are some "true" altruists in the population. Indeed the research on social utility functions and dictator games, as well as studies of behavior in the prisoner's dilemma and in social dilemmas, suggests that a subgroup of the population—perhaps 20 percent—may be noncontingent altruists. Although such people deserve commendation, their aggregate influence is probably relatively small.

3. Much of the social psychology literature on altruism and helping behavior has focused on the issue of how to elicit or inhibit such pity and concern and on the exact mechanism by which concern leads to actual helping behavior (see, for example, Batson and others 1991; Cialdini and others 1987).

4. This section borrows from an unpublished term paper by Kimberly Morgan, "Auditors' Perceptual Biases: A Threat to Independence" (University of Pittsburgh, Katz Graduate School of Business).

Chapter 12

Responsibility Judgments and the Causal Background

Ann L. McGill

Questions of business ethics commonly arise after some negative event has occurred—for example, when a product does not perform properly, when an employee is injured on the job, or when an explosion occurs at a factory, killing workers and neighbors. In such cases, business ethics may be considered in terms of causal judgments. That is, people may approach the question of ethics in decision making by first asking what caused the event and who is to blame. Hence, a complete analysis of business ethics requires an understanding of how people form causal explanations and how these explanations are related to judgments of blame and responsibility.

To understand the link between causal explanations and responsibility judgments, it is necessary to consider what people mean when they specify something as "the" cause of an occurrence. This question is especially intriguing when one notes that a host of factors may be related to an occurrence. For example, a train may derail because of the speed at which it was traveling, the weight it was carrying, the age and maintenance of the track on which it was running, the experience of the engineer, the manner in which it was loaded, the condition of the brakes, and so forth (see Hilton and Slugoski 1986). Further, while people may be aware of all or most of these factors, they rarely specify all the factors they know to be related to an event in devising a causal explanation for the occurrence. Instead, they tend to base their explanations on one or two select factors (Einhorn and Hogarth 1986; Hilton and Slugoski 1986; McGill 1989, 1990a, 1991; Mill [1872] 1973). For example, people might state that "the train was traveling too fast" or "it was overloaded" as explanations for the derailment, even though they may be aware that other factors contributed to the accident.

Recent research indicates that the factor selected is determined by how people specify the event to be explained (Einhorn and Hogarth 1986; Hastie 1984; Hilton and Slugoski 1986; Mackie 1974; McGill 1989, 1990a; see also Hart and Honore 1959). In particular, research suggests that in devising an explanation for an occurrence, people compare the occurrence—called the *target episode*—with some contrasting case in which the event did not occur. This contrasting case is the *causal background*. The factor selected as the basis of the causal explanation is a distinguishing feature between the target episode and the contrasting causal background (McGill 1989). For example, in devising an explanation for the train derailment, people might compare the accident (the target episode) with an earlier time when the train was moving along fine (the contrasting causal background). In this comparison, the event to be explained is the *change* in the performance of the train (Hastie 1984) and some distinguishing feature between the time when the accident occurred and when it did not occur. For example, the engineer's speeding around a bend might be a plausible explanation for the occurrence. More static features of the train—such as the amount of weight it was carrying or the quality of the tracks—would not be plausible explanations for the occurrence. Although these features may be understood to have contributed to the accident, they cannot account for the train's change in performance. Hence, they lack *explanatory relevance* for the causal background adopted (Hilton 1990).

Central to this view of causal reasoning is the contention that the same target episode may be compared with different causal backgrounds. For example, one might compare the train that derailed (the same target episode) with another train that also went speeding around the bend but did not derail (a competing causal background). In this comparison, the event to be explained is the *difference* in the performance of the two trains under similar conditions. Speeding around the bend lacks explanatory relevance in this case because this feature is common to the target episode and the contrasting causal background. Instead, distinctive features of the train that derailed—such as the amount of weight it was carrying or the experience of its engineer—are relevant. Thus, people may provide different explanations for an occurrence depending on the causal background adopted. For example, people riding on the train, enjoying an uneventful trip until the surge of speed around the bend, might blame the engineer for the accident, whereas investigators familiar with the practice of speeding around the bend might blame management's decision to load the ill-fated train beyond proper limits.

SELECTION OF A CAUSAL BACKGROUND

A growing body of research has established the influence of the causal background on people's causal explanations for events, including illness (McGill 1991), job and task performance (McGill 1989, 1993), choice (McGill 1989, 1990a, 1991), and product failure (McGill 1990b). More recent research has addressed the origins of the causal background, exploring factors that influence the adoption of one type of comparison case rather than another.

Expectation Versus Feature Mutability

Recent research suggests two possible origins of the causal background. One line of research suggests that people may adopt the usual or expected case as the causal background (Hesslow 1983; Hilton and Slugoski 1986; McGill 1989). Support for this hypothesis derives from research on spontaneous causal reasoning indicating that people search for causal explanations for events that depart from the usual or expected state of affairs (Weiner 1985), thereby rendering the usual or expected state the natural choice as causal background.

Daniel Kahneman and Dale Miller's (1986) norm theory provides a competing characterization of the causal background. According to this theory, each episode suggests its own comparison case. That is, instead of retrieving the expected case from memory to serve as the causal background, people *construct* the contrasting case piecewise from features and the target episode. The comparison case shares some features with the target and differs from it on other features. The key ideas behind this characterization are "that the mental representation of a state of affairs can be modified in many ways, that some modifications are much more natural than others, and that some attributes are particularly resistant to change" (pp. 142–43). The unchanged (shared) features between the target and the comparison case are referred to as the *immutable* features of the episode, and the features that differ as the *mutable* features. Hence, the rules that govern mutability guide the construction of the causal background.

An important difference between these two characterizations of the causal background concerns the sensitivity of the comparison case to the features of the target episode. The implication of the view that people adopt the usual or expected case as the causal background is that the features of the causal background should not vary depending on the features of the target episode. Instead, the characteristics of the background are the features of the prototypical case. By contrast, the implication of norm theory is that features of the causal background are derived from the features of the target episode, sharing those features that were perceived as immutable and differing on those features that were considered mutable.

A recent study was conducted to explore whether the causal background adopted appears to depend on features of the target episode or whether it appears to be selected independently based on its own merits as the usual or expected state of affairs (McGill 1993). The experimental context for this research concerned explanations for the failure (success) of a young man or a young woman at a task. Subjects were asked to rate the degree to which they preferred to compare that individual with young men versus young women who succeeded (failed) at the same task.

230 /

Two different types of tasks were described. Traditionally male-oriented tasks (for example, shooting pool, driving an obstacle course, negotiating a lower price of a car) were perceived as usually accomplished by men, whereas traditionally female-oriented tasks (for example, sewing, typing, quieting a crying infant) were perceived as usually accomplished by women. The usual or normal comparison case in this context would thus depend on the task. For example, if the causal background does not depend on the features of the target episode but is instead chosen on its own merits, then subjects should prefer to compare the individual who failed with young men who succeeded for the male-oriented tasks and with young women who succeeded for the female-oriented tasks, irrespective of the gender of the actor.

By contrast, if the causal background is constructed from the target episode, then the preferred comparison may depend on the gender of the actor. This hypothesis derives from recent research that suggests that people may perceive the genders to differ in degree of mutability. Specifically, findings suggest that people may perceive the gender male to be less mutable than the gender female (see, for example, Eagly and Kite 1987; Gilligan 1982; Hall 1987; McClelland 1975; J. B. Miller 1976; D. T. Miller, Taylor, and Buck 1991; Tannen 1990). That is, people are less likely to imagine a male actor to have been female than they are to imagine a female actor to have been male. Hence, differences in perceived mutability suggest that different comparison cases may be preferred depending on whether the individual who failed is male or female.

Results of the experiments support this view. Specifically, the findings indicated that subjects preferred to compare male actors with other males regardless of the task (that is, whether male-oriented or female-oriented) or outcome (success or failure), thereby identifying explanations based on individual characteristics of the man in question. Comparison cases chosen for female actors varied, however, with task and outcome. Subjects preferred to compare a female actor with other women (1) when the female actor succeeded, regardless of task orientation, suggesting explanations that address how the successful woman differs from other women, and (2) when the female actor failed at a female-oriented task, suggesting explanations that address individual shortcomings of the woman who failed. Subjects preferred, however, to compare the female actor who failed at male-oriented tasks with men—not women—who succeed, suggesting explanations in terms of gender.

Thus, differences in the chosen comparison suggest different explanations for the performance of men and women. For example, men fail because of individual shortcomings, whereas women fail because they are women, at least on traditionally male-oriented tasks. Results of this research are therefore consistent with the prediction of norm theory that people construct the causal background by varying the more mutable features of the target episode.

/ 231

The Influence of Culture and Perspective

Recent research has examined additional factors that may influence the causal background adopted and thus may affect assessments of blame and responsibility (McGill, in press). Research on attribution theory suggests that the perspective of the judge may influence the causal background adopted. Such research has focused on differences in the use of internal attributions (attributions to factors within the entity, such as stable traits of the actor, the entity being the person or thing central to the occurrence) versus external attributions (attributions to factors outside the entity, such as characteristics of the situation). Results of studies conducted in Western cultures indicate that in general internal attributions are used more often than external attributions (Ross 1977), but that relative preference for these attributions may vary with the perspective from which the occurrence is considered. In particular, a large body of research indicates that observers tend to attribute an individual's behavior to stable trait characteristics of the actor, whereas actors are more likely to attribute their behavior to situational factors (see Watson 1982 for a review).

Causal background theory suggests that these different patterns of attributions may not reflect preferences for internal versus external attributions per se but rather may reflect differences in the causal background adopted. Specifically, research on the divergent perceptions of the actor and observer suggests that observers tend to compare the actor's behavior with the behavior of other people in the same situation (and so identify distinctive characteristics of the actor as explanations for the event), whereas actors tend to compare their behavior in the target situation with their behavior in other situations (and so identify distinctive characteristics of the situation as explanations for the event [Einhorn and Hogarth 1986; Kahneman and Miller 1986; McGill 1989]). Findings indicate that actors and observers will make similar attributions when the comparison to be adopted—that is, across situations versus across people—is made explicit (McGill 1989). Thus, the effect of perspective on the use of internal versus external attributions appears to derive from the adoption of competing causal backgrounds.

This effect of perspective may, however, be moderated by culture. Cross-cultural research in attribution theory has revealed both similarities and differences across cultures in patterns of attributions. Garth Fletcher and Colleen Ward (1988), reviewing this literature concluded that some fundamental features may in fact be universal. Nevertheless, evidence suggests that subjects in non-Western cultures make greater use of external attributions (Cha and Nam 1985; Cousins 1989; Dalal, Sharma, and Bisht 1983; Jahoda 1982; J. G. Miller 1984; Shweder and Bourne 1984).

Like differences in perspective, cross-cultural differences in attributions may derive from the comparison case adopted, with subjects in non-Western cultures showing greater inclination to compare across situations than across entities. That is, use of situational versus trait attributions may derive from the causal background chosen and not from the nature of the attributions themselves.

How Culture May Affect the Comparison Case Adopted

In addition to the empirical results I have reported, there is theoretical support for the effect of culture on preference for comparison across situations versus entities. Specifically, the dimension of individualism/collectivism, which is known to vary significantly across cultures, may influence the type of comparison adopted. Broadly speaking, individualism, which is characteristic of many Western cultures, reflects a self-orientation, whereas collectivism, which is characteristic of many Asian cultures, reflects a group or social orientation (Hofstede 1980; Triandis, McCusker, and Hui 1990). Recent research suggests that this dimension may embody a variety of distinctions such as degree of concern about the effects of one's actions on others, extent of sharing of material and nonmaterial benefits, and degree of feeling involved in the lives of others (Hui and Triandis 1986).

Of particular relevance to the present research is the distinction between the independent and interdependent construals of the self, which corresponds to the individualist/collectivist distinction. For cultures emphasizing the independent construal of the self, "there is a faith in the inherent separateness of distinct persons. The normative imperative of this culture is to become independent from others and to discover and express one's unique attributes" (Markus and Kitayama 1991, 226).

By contrast, cultures emphasizing the interdependent construal of the self focus on the extent to which human beings are connected to one another:

> Experiencing interdependence entails seeing oneself as part of an encompassing social relationship and recognizing that one's behavior is determined, contingent on, and, to a large extent, organized by what the actor perceives to be the thoughts, feelings and actions of others in the relationship. . . . The interdependent self also possesses and expresses a set of internal attributes, such as abilities, opinions, judgments, and personality characteristics. However, these internal attributes are understood as *situation specific*, and thus as sometimes elusive and unreliable. (Markus and Kitayama 1991, 227, emphasis added)

These competing construals of the self imply different types of comparisons. In the independent construal, "thinking of individuals has the effect of focusing on individual differences and hence heterogeneity" (Triandis, McCusker, and Hui 1990, 1018). By contrast, for cultures emphasizing the interdependent construal of the self, "specific social situations are more likely to serve as the unit of representation than are attributes of separate persons" (Markus and Kitayama 1991, 232). This focus on situations may result because the behavior of people in collectivist/interdependent cultures is constrained to a greater extent by the demands of the situation compared with individualist/independent cultures (Jahoda 1982). Hence, those with interdependent selves are less likely to compare across individuals and are more likely to compare across situations.

A recent study was conducted to evaluate the effect of perspective and culture on the adoption of competing causal backgrounds (McGill, in press). Subjects in this study were asked to rate possible causal explanations for the poor performance of a firm. Specifically, subjects were asked to rate components of the firm's marketing strategy as possible causal explanations of the firm's poor showing. Stimuli were constructed so that components of the strategy either differed over time (corresponding to a comparison across situations) or across firms (corresponding to a comparison across people). Subjects were also asked what course of action should be adopted to correct the problem in the future.

Perspective was manipulated by instructing subjects to consider the occurrence (the firm's poor performance) either from the perspective of a manager of the target firm or from that of a manager of a competing firm. In the light of research on differences in the perceptions of actors versus observers (Einhorn and Hogarth 1986; Kahneman and Miller 1986; McGill 1989; see also Jones and Davis 1965), it was hypothesized that the former perspective would foster a firm-centered orientation, so that changes in the performance of the firm over time would become salient, whereas the latter perspective would foster a competitor-centered orientation, in which case differences in the performance of the target firm and that of its competitors would be salient.

It was hypothesized, however, that the effect of this manipulation of perspective would be stronger for subjects from individualist cultures than for subjects from collectivist cultures. This hypothesis was based on research described earlier showing that for subjects from collectivist (interdependent) cultures, comparisons across situations had greater perceived relevance than comparisons across entities, whereas for subjects from individualist (independent) cultures, the pattern was reversed. To test this hypothesis, the study was conducted in both the United States, a highly individualist country, and Thailand, which is a highly collectivist country (see Hofstede 1980; Komin 1991; see also Weisz 1991). The expectation was that Thai subjects would be less willing than American subjects to compare across firms, preferring instead to emphasize differences over time, regardless of management perspective.

Results of the experiment support the effect of culture and perspective on the comparison case adopted. Specifically, the findings indicated that subjects who were instructed to evaluate the occurrence from the perspective of a manager of the target firm favored explanations that addressed changes in the firm's strategy from years in which the firm performed well to the present year. By contrast, subjects who were instructed to evaluate the occurrence from the perspective of a competing firm favored explanations that addressed differences in the target firm's strategy compared with that of the competing firm. Results indicated, however, that the effect of perspective was moderated by culture; Thai subjects, who represented a collectivist/interdependent culture, were less likely to adopt comparisons across firms than American subjects, who represented an individualistic/independent culture. Findings indicate that managers' different explanations for poor company performance and different preferred remedies to correct the problem depended on the comparison they adopted.

IMPLICATIONS FOR ASSESSMENTS OF BLAME AND RESPONSIBILITY

Prior research suggests a correspondence between people's causal explanations for an occurrence and their beliefs regarding how a problem should be corrected (Belk, Painter, and Semenik 1981; Belk and Painter 1983; McGill, in press) and who should be held accountable (Folkes 1984, 1988; Hamilton 1980; Weiner, 1980—but see McGill 1990b). Hence, findings that people's causal explanations vary as a function of the causal background adopted have important implications for responsibility judgments.

Management Perspectives

In particular, these findings suggest systematic differences in assessments of blame and responsibility depending on management perspective. For example, managers of a firm in which some accident has occurred are more likely to focus on changes over time—that is, event-specific factors that occurred in the period leading up to the accident—whereas managers of competing firms may identify systems and procedures, distinctive to the target firm, that created an atmosphere conducive to accident.

For example, managers of the company whose train derailed might identify the action of the engineer who sped around the bend as the cause of the accident. Management response to the accident might therefore be to fire the engineer and to send memos to all employees reminding them to be very careful, not to speed, to follow safety regulations, and to stay alert. Managers of the target firm might even note that the train was overloaded compared with other trains in their line. In this case, management might fire the midlevel manager responsible for freight that day and again send around a memo reminding freight employees of company policies regarding loading limits. It is unlikely that management would assume any responsibility for the accident or make changes to existing systems and policies, arguing that most of their trains do not derail and that the train in question was running along fine until the engineer exceeded speed limits.

By contrast, outside observers who compare the train that derailed with trains on other companies' lines that do not derail might suggest very different explanations. These observers might note that engineers in all companies often become distracted and exceed speed limits; that employees are sometimes fatigued, hung over, or emotionally distracted by events in their personal lives; and that printed company policies are commonly ignored in favor of actual day-to-day practices. In other words, these observers might take as given the imperfections and variability of human behavior and instead look to differences in the systems and practices created by one firm versus another in minimizing the number of accidents.

These observers might therefore blame management for not installing systems to prevent speeding or overloading, such as automatic warning sirens or checks on the amount of weight loaded per car. Comparison across firms might even reveal management practices that fostered employee violation of company policy, such as reward systems that placed greater emphasis on output than on safety—for example, systems that might encourage engineers to speed and freight clerks to overload trains in order to achieve a bonus or to make a quota. People adopting comparisons across firms might therefore hold management accountable for the accident, viewing employees' mistakes and policy violations that led up to the accident as part of the ordinary and expected failings that all firms must address in creating safe and effective systems.

Differences in the comparison adopted may explain recent debate regarding who should assume responsibility for the *Exxon Valdez* accident in which a tanker spilled thousands of gallons of oil into Prince William Sound, in Alaska. The events leading up to this accident are generally agreed upon; the captain, who was known to drink, left a lower-ranking sailor to pilot the ship, which went off course and ran aground. Despite agreement regarding how the event occurred, parties disagree regarding management responsibility. Some argue that the fault is with the captain and, in particular, with his decision to leave the bridge that evening. Such a belief is a natural outcome of comparing across time; the question seems to focus on identifying factors that made the difference between the trip in which the accident occurred and other trips taken by Exxon vessels—some even under the command of this same captain—in which no accident occurred. Others argue that responsibility rests with Exxon management for allowing a man with a drinking problem, whose judgment was therefore suspect, to captain a vessel. This belief may derive from a broader comparison that considers whether the policies of Exxon were more likely to produce an accident than those of other companies.

Differences in the comparison adopted also suggest different explanations for the alleged practice of Sears Automotive employees of charging customers for unnecessary repairs. Depending on the comparison adopted, one might hold the individual employees responsible. Specifically, if one were to compare those employees who overcharged customers with those who did not, one might blame the dishonesty of the individual employees. By contrast, if one were to compare the operation at Sears with operations at other firms not known for overcharging customers, one might identify management practices at Sears that encouraged such dishonesty.

A policy that favors explanations at the systems level—that is, management policies versus individual actions—has the desirable characteristic of taking into account the ordinary, predictable failings of human beings. Systems that are certain to work only if employees never get sleepy, distracted, depressed, desperate for money, hung over, or angry and intent on hurting someone are bad systems. They are accidents waiting to happen. Hence, it seems desirable in evaluating questions of business ethics to encourage broad comparisons that look beyond the narrow set of events leading up to accidents and problems. (See Willem Wagenaar's related discussion of causal analysis and safety in chapter 18.)

One concern with this approach, however, is that it may produce a gradual erosion of a sense of individual responsibility. That is, if systems are built to take into account human failings and managers are held responsible for tragedies because they did not engineer around a broad range of employee action, then the role of the individual in producing or preventing events is minimized. Employees who drink on the job, pay little attention to the task at hand, childishly exact revenge on customers and the firm, or otherwise perform poorly may be freed of responsibility for tragedies because these behaviors are treated as normal and expected. Therefore, the choice of comparison adopted must also reflect societal desires regarding individual responsibility and dignity. One solution to this problem may be to distinguish questions of responsibility at the individual level and at the systems level and to adopt separate standards for each level of analysis. Thus, one may compare across people or systems depending, respectively, on whether one is interested in judging the propriety of the employee's actions versus the quality of the firm's safety procedures.

Cultural Differences in Assessment of Responsibility

Cross-cultural differences in the comparison adopted add another layer of complexity to the already challenging task of evaluating the decisions of firms engaged in international enterprises. For example, Thomas Donaldson (1989) has recognized the ethical dilemma raised when a firm from one country with its own standards of operations—including, for example, plant safety, hiring and promotion, and product testing—conducts business in a country with less stringent standards of operations. Should the firm be held to the standards of its own country or only to those of the host country?

Similarly, one must consider which comparison case should be adopted in evaluating the causes of events across cultures. Should managers adopt the comparison suggested by their own culture, or should managers adopt the comparison suggested by local judges? Sensitivity to differences in the causal backgrounds adopted by people from different cultures may also alert managers to possible conflict regarding causal explanations for events. For example, events that might appear to be unfortunate but unavoidable accidents when evaluated in light of one comparison (for example, across situations) may appear the result of negligent and culpable actions in light of another comparison (for example, across systems and procedures).

The Role of Mutability in Judgments of Responsibility

There are also important implications in the findings that people may not adopt the usual or expected case as the causal background but may instead construct the causal background by varying the more mutable features of the target episode. In particular, these findings suggest that similar events may produce different causal explanations and therefore different responsibility judgments, depending on the specific features of the target episode.

While a general theory of mutability is lacking in the literature, studies suggest a list of features that vary in degree of mutability. As I have noted, studies suggest that the genders male and female differ in perceived mutability, with the gender male perceived to be less mutable than the gender female. Hence, in imagining alternatives to events, people may imagine female actors to have been men more frequently than they imagine male actors to have been women. Thus, an accident at one firm in which some of the actors were women may be perceived as having been caused by the presence of women in sensitive positions, suggesting women as inadequate or easily corrupted decision makers. By contrast, a similar accident at a firm in which the principal actors are men would not be explained in terms of gender. For example, people may explain a plane crash involving a female pilot in terms of her gender, possibly with an appeal to stereotypes involving the inability of women to perform under pressure, while they would not explain a crash involving a male pilot in terms of his gender, despite other readily available stereotypes involving male tendencies to show off or to rebel against rules and regulations.

Other factors identified in the literature as differing in perceived mutability include temporal order (D. T. Miller and Gunasegaram 1990), the character of an event as exceptional or routine (Kahneman and Tversky 1982), and the prominence of an actor in a story (Lerner and Miller 1978). Specifically, people appear to perceive later events in a sequence to be more mutable than earlier events, exceptional events more mutable than routine events, and focal actors in a story more mutable than background actors. Responsibility judgments may follow these lines of feature mutability. For example, people may blame recent events, such as hiring of new employees, changes in policy, or shifts in environmental conditions, more than earlier events for negative outcomes. Further, they may blame exceptional actions more than routine actions.

This focus on the recent and the exceptional may prevent people from identifying the persistent, central, and enduring causes of events. More generally, Kahneman and Miller (1986) have noted the perverse effect of evaluating alternatives relative to constructed norms, suggesting that "judgments of a stimulus evaluated in isolation will tend to be dominated by features that are not the most central" (p. 141). That is, in constructing alternatives to an event, people are more likely to vary marginal details of the event than more central features. These marginal details are then distinctive between the target episode and the constructed background and, therefore, more likely to be identified as causal explanations than are the central features of the event. Thus, people may explain negative social events such as rape in terms of details associated with a specific incident—for example, the woman's decision to walk a different way home from work—and not in terms of enduring societal characteristics that make rape frequent and familiar. Only by comparing societies in which rape is common with those—perhaps imagined—in which rape is rare is one likely to identify those "routine" factors that produce such tragedies. Unfortunately, research on feature mutability and its role in constructing alternatives suggests that such broad comparisons are less likely than those involving small details.

A similar effect can be seen in causal explanations and responsibility judgments for accidents, incidents of product failure, employee illness, and other negative events associated with conducting business. People may explain those events by referring to recent and exceptional events leading up to the occurrence rather than by considering the stable and familiar practices of the firm. Yet it may be precisely those familiar practices that are enabling negative events to recur; separate instances, each with its own distinctive and potentially distracting details, may share the same underlying cause. The types of comparisons needed to identify such causes, however, may seem extreme, unrealistic, and even a bit subversive to those individuals accustomed to constructing alternatives around the more mutable features of an event.

Finally, the finding that focal actors are perceived to be more mutable than background actors raises the concern that causal explanations—and hence responsibility judgments—may vary depending on how the event is framed. Specifically, changing the story so that different actors are in the foreground may shift perceptions about who caused the event and who is to blame (Lerner and Miller 1978). More generally, background effects in causal judgment imply that blame and responsibility for events may be easily deflected simply by suggesting other plausible comparison cases against which to view the event. This fluidity of judgment is especially distressing in an era in which "spin control" and other efforts to frame events for maximum personal advantage have risen to high levels of sophistication.

Without standards for the types of comparisons that should be adopted in particular circumstances, there may be little consistency in judgments of blame and responsibility, and those people who are most effective in establishing the causal background may be able to control public assessment of blame. In the following section, therefore, I suggest a possible framework for constructing a normative theory of the causal background.

STANDARDS OF COMPARISON: A NORMATIVE THEORY OF THE CAUSAL BACKGROUND

Germund Hesslow (1983) proposed five kinds of comparisons that people frequently make: (1) comparison with the *temporally normal* case—the object in question at an earlier time; (2) comparison with the *statistically normal* case—the usual or most common case; (3) comparison with the theoretical ideal; (4) comparison with a moral ideal; and (5) comparison with the subjectively expected case. The choice of which of these five comparisons is employed depends on the purpose of the judgment. The following paragraphs evaluate the first four of these comparisons in devising a normative model of the causal background. The fifth comparison—the subjectively expected case—is not suited to a normative model of comparison in that it varies with the particular expectations of the judge and the individual circumstances of the event.

The temporally normal case may be employed to identify the proximate cause of an event—for example, the engineer's speeding around the bend. Such a comparison may address the actions or events just preceding an occurrence and so identify those factors that, if omitted, would have prevented the problem. Such a comparison does not, however, identify enduring causes that allow these events to occur repeatedly, nor does such a comparison identify differences in systems and practices that make one firm more likely to have problems than others.

By contrast, the statistically normal case may be used to evaluate the target episode in comparison with existing, accepted practices. Such a comparison may identify ways in which the firm's behaviors, including its enduring systems and practices, differ from those of competing firms. In this respect, the statistically normal case may be most useful for questions of negligence on the part of management and employees. Comparison with the statistically normal case does not, however, identify practices that although common, are nevertheless morally wrong or painfully inefficient. For example, such comparison would not identify "normal" hiring practices that exclude women and ethnic minorities. Nor would such a comparison identify unsafe practices that are common in an industry. For example, most commercial aircraft do not have on-board radar that is able to pinpoint the location of dangerous wind shear, although such radar is both available and recommended by pilots.[1]

240 /

Two other types of comparison cases—comparison with the theoretical ideal and comparison with the moral ideal—may be employed to identify inadequacies in existing practices and sources of moral responsibility for events. The theoretical ideal suggests what is possible. Hence, comparison with this ideal may suggest avenues of improvement in practices beyond what is common or statistically normal. By contrast, the moral ideal suggests what should be done relative to a moral code. Comparison with the moral ideal suggests causes of events in terms of right and wrong. To apply such a standard to an entire industry would therefore require agreement regarding the nature of the moral ideal, difficult to achieve in a pluralistic community in which many different religions and moral codes are represented. Thus, the moral ideal may be applied most effectively on an individual basis in which judges apply their own standards to their own actions.

An important question for future research concerns how people resolve competing standards or conflicts between causal judgments. This question is especially relevant when judgments of blame or responsibility are addressed through litigation. For example, a jury may be asked to assess degree of liability of a manufacturer in a case involving product failure, employee injury, or damage to the environment. In such a case, lawyers for each side may try to persuade the jury to adopt the background that favors their client. Specifically, lawyers for the plaintiff may suggest comparisons in which actions of the defendant are distinctive and hence are possible explanations for the event. By contrast, lawyers for the defense may suggest comparisons in which factors that are unrelated to the defendant are distinctive, so that the defendant is left blameless.

For example, in a case of product failure, lawyers for the plaintiff may compare the unsatisfactory or unsafe performance of the target brand with the superior performance of other brands in similar usage situations, a comparison that may suggest that the problem was caused by a distinguishing feature of the target brand. By contrast, lawyers for the manufacturer may compare their brand's poor performance in the target situation with superior performance of the same brand in different usage situations, a comparison that may suggest that the problem was caused by misuse of the product by the customer (McGill 1990b).

Alternatively, lawyers for the defense may attempt to undermine the plaintiff's case, not by suggesting alternative explanations for the poor performance of the product but instead by suggesting that poor performance in the target usage situation was not unusual and so requires no explanation or blame (Einhorn and Hogarth 1986). This strategy would involve comparison of the target brand's performance with the similarly poor performance of other brands in the usage situation. This approach may be less successful than suggesting alternative explanations for the event, depending on the jury's willingness to accept the premise that familiarity of the problem somehow excuses responsibility for specific instances.

/ **241**

Although prior research on causation in the law has recognized the complexity of these issues (Hart and Honore 1959), future research may examine preference for types of comparisons under different circumstances. Such areas for study might include legal versus ethical judgments, judgments involving different parties to disputes (for example, businesses versus households), and judgments across different cultures. This research may also address the extent to which adoption of a background reflects conscious deliberation and hence is open to persuasion and to what extent the process is automatic and therefore less easily affected through argument.

CONCLUSIONS

Prior research has suggested that causal explanations for an occurrence vary as a function of the causal background adopted. More recent findings have suggested that the background adopted depends in turn on factors such as management perspective, culture, and perceived mutability of events. Causal explanations and related judgments of responsibility and blame may therefore depend on characteristics of the judge and the circumstances under which the event is considered, and similar events may receive different evaluations depending on these superficial, easily varied factors.

This chapter has proposed a possible framework for a normative theory of the causal background, identifying different types of comparison cases and suggesting which types of comparison should be adopted depending on the purpose of the judgment. Future research is needed to refine this framework, to propose additional types of comparisons, and to expand the descriptive model of the causal background, with particular attention to identifying factors influencing people's choice of comparison cases.

ENDNOTE

1. It should be noted that although the temporally normal case may commonly involve analysis at the individual level (that is, comparison with the firm but across time) and the statistical norm analysis at the systems level (that is, across firms within a period of time), as implied by the examples in the text, these levels of analysis are not implicit in the type of comparison. For example, one may adopt as the temporally normal case another train that passed along the same track just before the train that derailed, a background that would allow comparison across systems. The statistically normal case may also be specified to allow comparison within the firm rather than across firms—for example, when "normal" is interpreted as normal for this firm. More generally the statistical norm suffers in that the relevant population is not specified; the norm may vary depending on whether one is considering what is normal for the firm, the industry, the region, or the nation.

Chapter 13

Ethics as Hypothesis Testing, and Vice Versa

Joshua Klayman

How is it that people come to be doing unethical things? This is obviously one of the fundamental questions of interest to those who study ethics. I approach this question from an outsider's perspective, as someone who studies cognitive processes of reasoning and judgment. I believe that unethical behavior is closely tied to cognitive processing, particularly with regard to how people change, or fail to change, their ideas.

It is intriguing to note how many different ethically troubling situations are linked in some way to processes of change and resistance to change. In chapter 1 of this book, for example, John Darley talks about how new organizations "stray into" wrongdoing. This imagery conveys the idea that people and organizations do not deliberately set out to engage in unethical practices, but rather have trouble extricating themselves. Manufacturers and users of asbestos, for example, thought for a long time that asbestos was a harmless—indeed, a beneficial—product. When it turned out to be dangerous, however, it was difficult for them to change their patterns of use.

Robyn Dawes, in chapter 16, addresses the ethical issues involved when people representing themselves as experts do not, in fact, deliver anything of value to their clients. He proposes clinical psychology as an example, but similar allegations have been made about astrologers, naturopaths, and mutual-fund managers. For the most part, these practitioners are not deliberate charlatans but professionals who set out with a sincere belief in their ability to help others, a belief they share with their customers. Ethical questions arise when neither practitioners nor customers are swayed by evidence that the purported expertise is worthless. I would speculate that people and organizations are much less likely to engage in fraudulent, hazardous, or damaging actions when the harm is anticipated at the outset than when it is discovered after the activities are in place.

Many ethical problems also seem to involve gradual commitment to a course of action, rather than any sudden leap, as George Loewenstein points out in chapter 11 and John Darley in chapter 1 (see also Brockner 1992; Heath 1995; Staw and Ross 1989). The implication is that people will do bad things if you can get them there with only minute, hard-to-notice changes; then you can trust them to stay where they have gotten. An intuition along these lines may underlie the different moral status people give to acts of commission and acts of omission, as noted by Jonathan Baron (see chapter 10). Acting in a way that changes things for the worse is noteworthy and highly culpable, but failing to take actions that could change things for the better seems more commonplace and less culpable.

Why is failure to change such a recurring theme? Logically, people don't often choose to do things that society frowns upon or that they themselves frown upon. Thus, it is reasonable to expect that many ethical dilemmas arise when people start out doing something that they believe is appropriate and acceptable but that subsequently turns out to have a bad side they didn't foresee. Violations of ethics happen, then, when people fail to stop engaging in a behavior they never would have set out to engage in to begin with.

To escape from unethical behavior requires two kinds of change in beliefs. One is to change from thinking that what you are doing is good to thinking that it is not. The second is to change from believing that the current way of doing things is superior to all others, to believing that at least one alternative course of action is better. Both kinds of changes in belief may be difficult to make, especially in ethically ambiguous situations.

Why are people resistant to change in such situations, despite the fact that they face both internal conflict and social censure? Processes of hypothesis development—processes by which people generate, test, and revise their beliefs—play a critical role. At the same time, other forces—such as cultural context, social sanctions, and motivations toward self-preservation—are also important in getting people to engage in ethically dubious behaviors and in keeping them from quitting. Although my focus in this chapter is on the cognitive elements, I also discuss some of the connections between these social and motivational forces and hypothesis development.

COGNITIVE PROCESSES AND RESISTANCE TO CHANGE

The concept of *perseverance of beliefs* or *confirmation bias* is familiar to most social and cognitive psychologists: There is a general tendency for people to maintain and defend their beliefs in the face of contradictory information. Behind this general tendency, however, there is actually a rather complex system of different processes and phenomena (see Klayman 1995). The following are four basic cognitive processes that I believe are implicated in problems of ethical behavior.

Positive Test Strategy

The first process concerns how people search for information to test whether their hypotheses are correct. People have a general tendency to perform *positive hypothesis tests* (Klayman and Ha 1987). That is, they test a hypothesis largely by trying what they think will work. Thus, personnel managers tend to hire people they think will perform well in the position; manufacturers test market products they think will be profitable; and creative staff in ad agencies work up ideas they think their director—and ultimately their client—will like.

Positive testing is not the same as confirmation bias, however. People who try what they think will work may be fully prepared to revise their ideas if they fail. Indeed, positive testing is often a very effective way to find out where current ideas are wrong (Klayman and Ha 1987). Positive hypothesis testing can have the effect of leading people to hold overly narrow hypotheses, however (Klayman and Ha 1989). That's because positive hypothesis tests are good only for finding false positives—things you thought would work but don't. They are useless for finding false negatives—things you didn't think would work but do. The result can be a narrow but safe rule for whom to hire, what to test market, and which creative ideas to develop.

Figure 13.1 provides a graphic representation of this process. The space inside the rectangle represents the universe of possibilities—the people you could hire, the products you might develop, all the ideas you could have for an ad campaign. At the onset, you have a hypothesis about the subset of this universe that will work, represented by the area enclosed by the solid line. Meanwhile, there is, beyond your knowledge, the true set of all things that will work, shown by the shaded area.

Let's say that you are charged with developing a profitable new car model for the upcoming year. You hypothesize that what will work this year is a small car that is cute, but not classy. You ask your design people to work up some ideas along those lines (shown by the circles numbered 1 in the figure), and you test them in consumer focus groups. Some of the ideas seem to catch on (the 1s in the shaded area); others don't. You then try to figure out what was wrong with the subset of designs that you thought consumers would like but they didn't. You devise a new hypothesis about what works—one that rules out the bad designs but includes the good ones (the area within the dashed line). That might be, say, "small, cute cars *that cost less than $10,000.*" In a second round of testing, you try out some more models that fit the revised scheme (the 2s in the figure). Once again, you find that some work and some don't, and you revise your idea to exclude the bad designs while retaining the good ones, say "small, cute cars under $10,000 *that are also very light and thus economical to run*" (the area within the dotted line). In a third round of testing, you try more of these and find that every one you test works well. You are now convinced that you have found the best formula. Yet outside the dotted line there is a large shaded area representing other designs that could also be profitable. For example, consumers this year might be looking more generally for sensible cars at a good price. They might be willing to pay more for a better-built small car, or for a somewhat larger

Figure 13.1 / How Positive Hypothesis Testing Can Produce Overly Narrow Hypotheses

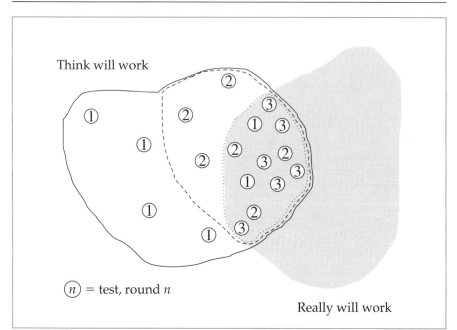

Note: The shaded area represents those instances that possess a target property, for example, those that will work. The area enclosed by a solid line represents an initial hypothesis about what will work. Small circles represent tests of the hypothesis. After round 1 of testing, the hypothesis is revised to include only the area bounded by the dashed line. After round 2, the hypothesis is revised to the area bounded by the dotted line. In round 3, all tested instances work, so no further revision takes place.

model that was still economical to run. With positive testing alone, you can never discover that you have identified only a small subset of all potentially successful designs.

The picture of pure positive tester in this example is usually an exaggeration. However, even a general tendency to favor positive tests can lead to difficulties in hypothesis testing. This was demonstrated in a study (Klayman and Ha 1989) in which students were given variations on the rule-discovery task invented by Peter Wason (1960). In that task, the experimenter tells the subject something like this:

> I have in mind a rule that generates sets of three numbers, called "triples." The triple [2, 4, 6] is an example that fits the rule. You try to figure out the rule by proposing other triples, and for each triple you propose, I'll tell you whether that triple fits or does not fit the rule.

246 /

We made up eighteen different problems like that, some using numbers and some using the names of cities around the world. The first column of table 13.1 shows the initial triples given as examples. The next column indicates the typical initial guesses that subjects made in response to the example. The next three columns show different generating rules used by the experimenter to classify triples. Some of these rules were designed to be broader than subjects' likely initial hypotheses, and thus subjects would start out with a hypothesis that was too narrow, making false-negative but not

Table 13.1 / Rule-Discovery Problems and Typical Initial Hypotheses

Example Given	Typical first guesses	Correct generating rule		
		Broader	Overlapping	Narrower
Numbers				
[2,4,6]	Evens; consecutive evens; increasing by 2	Ascending numbers	Single-digit numbers	Consecutive evens that end in 2, 4, 6
[2,5,8]	Increasing by 3	Constant difference: B-A = C-B	Even, odd, even	Even number, add 3, add 3 again
[10,20,30]	Multiples of 10; consecutive multiples of 10	Even numbers	Two-digit numbers	Consecutive multiples of 10 that end in a multiple of 30
Cities				
[Rabat, Luanda, Cape Town]	African cities	Cities on the same continent	Cities on an ocean	African capitals on the Atlantic
[Santiago, Rio de Janeiro, Buenos Aires]	Latin American cities; South American cities	New World cities	Cities south of the equator	Latin American cities south of the equator
[Osaka, Honolulu, Wellington]	Cities on the Pacific; cities on islands	Cities on an ocean	Cities from north to south	Ocean ports on Pacific islands

Source: Klayman and Ha (1989).

false-positive errors. Another set of rules was designed to overlap the most likely initial hypotheses, so that subjects would start out with a rule that made some errors of both types. A third set of rules was designed so that subjects' initial guesses would be too broad and thus would be prone to false-positive but not false-negative errors.

We found that, regardless of the problem they received, subjects conducted twice as many positive tests as negative tests, and they generally moved in the direction of narrower hypotheses. At the end of eighteen tests, about half the subjects had found the correct rule. Of the remainder, 65 percent ended with overly narrow rules—rules that selected only a subset of the class of triples that worked. Even subjects who started out with broad hypotheses often ended up too narrow. For example, one subject got the [Osaka, Honolulu, Wellington] example, with the "ports on Pacific islands" rule. He thought at first that the rule was "island cities" but he kept getting falsifications. He eventually narrowed his rule to "port cities of Japan, New Zealand, and Hawaii." That rule seemed to work, and he never discovered that he had overrestricted himself.

Resistance to change in ethical dilemmas may sometimes stem from an inability to recognize an overly narrow hypothesis—that is, to form the belief that what is sufficient is also necessary. For example, an engineering team may have developed a production method that works reliably and efficiently. They have learned from past mistakes until what they do almost never produces an unwanted result. Now, suppose that they discover that the production process has undesirable health or safety effects. The engineers know very little about alternative production methods, or even which features of their successful production methods are critical. Very little has been learned about the range of feasible changes. Throw in some risk aversion and fear of the unknown, and the result will be resistance to change.

Or consider the personnel department faced for the first time with serious attention to affirmative action rules. They may have a well-honed idea of the type of person they like to hire. Affirmative action essentially requires them to hire people they would not normally hire. That is something with which they have little experience, so they have little information about where they might find good employees outside the traditional pool.

People's positive hypothesis-testing tendencies are reinforced by the environment. There are good, practical reasons for doing things this way; doing otherwise can be costly. For example, if there is any validity to your personnel judgments, then hiring people you don't think will perform well can produce a lot of extra problems. In many cases, the job of the manager may require simply finding a way that works well. Who cares if there are six other good ways of doing things that you don't know about? If the people you hire usually work well, then who cares if you reject some applicants who would have been just as good? Furthermore, false-positive errors are much more visible and painful than false negatives in many cases. Everyone knows soon enough about the turkey you gave that important job to, but how often do you find out about the potential top-notch employee you didn't hire? This imbalance in feedback and consequences applies to ideas as well as actions. Chances are that no one will ever know about the good idea you chose not to mention, but what happens to you if you expound an idea that others think is stupid or unacceptable?

Perception of Uniqueness

Another aspect of thinking that promotes a narrow view of what's feasible is a tendency to see oneself, one's group, and one's situation as unique, and usually superior (see chapter 8; see also Suls and Wan 1987; Taylor and Brown 1988). This bias diminishes an important potential source of information about false negatives, namely information about what has worked in other times and places. Looking for what has worked elsewhere may reveal some ways of doing things that you thought would not work but do. Perhaps other organizations have switched to "greener" technologies, or have improved worker safety, or have implemented plans to increase work force diversity. Such evidence that the old way may not be the only way can provide suggestions for alternative courses of action. This sort of information gathering can offset much of the hypothesis-narrowing effect of positive hypothosis testing (Klayman and Ha 1989). But if people have an exaggerated view of the extent to which their situation is unique, they may discount such evidence: "That wouldn't work here." The resulting lack of viable-looking alternatives reinforces commitment to the status quo.[1]

Here, again, the environment may amplify cognitive difficulties. Inter-organizational secrecy, for example, limits one's ability to learn from competitors' actions, because competitors are not very eager to let you know what works for them. Competition between individuals and groups within the same organization can have the same limiting effect.

Biased Interpretations

Another important cognitive element in resistance to change is the potential for bias in the interpretation of evidence. A common standard for unbiased and open-minded use of data is the method of the objective scientist. The scientific ethic dictates that theories are theories and data are data, and the two must be clearly distinguished and treated differently. Data must be given the upper hand; when theory and data conflict, the theory must fall. Yet this is an untenable doctrine. In a world of vague and ambiguous information, we must ask whether the hypothesis supports the data as well as vice versa. As Charles Lord, Lee Ross, and Mark Lepper (1979) commented in their study of polarization of beliefs, if a new method for measuring the speed of light comes up with a value different from the generally accepted one, it is reasonable to dismiss the data as invalid and to hold on to the old hypothesis (see also Koehler 1993; Thagard 1989).

It follows, then, that people who differ in their theories will—even should—also differ in their interpretation of the evidence. The ambiguity of this process enhances the potential for abuse. How much is the "right" amount to discount data that run counter to your beliefs and to credit data that fit your beliefs? Take, for example, the continuing furor over cold fusion (see, for example, Storms 1994). Early reports indicated that certain reactions produced heat in excess of that expected from known chemical reactions, along with certain unexpected by-products. The hypothesis was put forth that nuclear fusion had been induced at near room temperatures and was generally dismissed by the established scientific community. Does this denigration of the cold-fusion hypothesis represent reasonable skepticism when dubious evidence contradicts solid theory, or is it intellectual imperialism by the scientific establishment? This debate over cold fusion has itself generated significant excess heat.

Phenomena related to cognitive dissonance (see Eagly and Chaiken 1993) can be seen as part of this general process of balancing data and hypotheses. People have fairly strong beliefs about who they are. When our self-theories seem to conflict with some action we've taken, we are inclined to revise our interpretation of our actions and our circumstances and to leave our beliefs alone. A similar connection can be made to the processes of rationalization and self-serving interpretations that are implicated in many ethical difficulties, as George Loewenstein describes in chapter 11. People start with the basic hypothesis that they are decent human beings, that their actions are reasonable and appropriate, and that the organizations to which they belong also behave appropriately. When evidence begins to conflict with such theories, the evidence is subject to revision. Whistle-blowers may have ulterior motives, apparent hazards may have other causes, estimates for the cost of changing production techniques may be based on questionable assumptions, and so on.

Consideration of Alternatives

The last cognitive factor I will discuss is closely tied to many different problems of human reasoning, including the previous three. That is the difficulty people have in giving full consideration to alternative hypotheses. If people found it easier to generate and think about alternatives, many of the problems they have with reasoning would be reduced. Take positive testing, for example. When people have alternative hypotheses in mind, they tend to look for evidence that is expected under each of them and therefore to search more broadly (Tweney and others 1980; Klayman 1995). Some of the things expected under hypothesis 1 are not expected under hypothesis 2 and vice versa, so one ends up performing both positive and negative tests of both hypotheses. Furthermore, when people have specific alternatives in mind, they tend to look for contrasting cases, in which the hypotheses make different predictions (Klayman and Ha 1989). That is, of course, a very effective hypothesis-testing approach, as John Platt (1964) pointed out.

Consider again the rule-discovery study (Klayman and Ha 1989). Subjects were asked not only to test triples of cities or numbers but to indicate the hypotheses they were considering while trying to figure out the rule. We counted the number of trials on which subjects indicated they were considering a specific alternative hypothesis in addition to their current best guess. We found that subjects who successfully solved their puzzles thought of alternatives roughly three times as often as did unsuccessful subjects. When they thought of alternatives, subjects almost always conducted a test that could distinguish the two hypotheses. Such tests can be much more useful than random try-something-you-think-won't-work (negative) tests, because they simultaneously provide evidence for or against another plausible rule.

Part of people's difficulty with generating hypotheses stems from a failure to generate a sufficiently large and varied set of them. Charles Gettys and his colleagues (1987), for example, asked student subjects to generate alternative ideas for solving real-world problems such as how to reduce parking problems at their university. He found that each individual generated only a small subset of the major plausible alternative hypotheses that were collected across all subjects. Many creativity enhancement techniques recognize this limitation and use group processes to help generate a larger set of alternatives (see Adams 1986). As common wisdom and research in the "group-think" tradition (Janis 1972) suggest, however, groups don't always facilitate the generation of good alternatives. Organizations in trouble are probably among the least hospitable group environments for encouraging alternative hypotheses, because of the defensive atmosphere that develops as John Darley and Robert Cialdini describe in chapters 1 and 2, respectively.

Even if some good alternatives are generated, however, they may not receive full consideration. People often have difficulty reframing and reinterpreting evidence in the different light cast by an alternative view of the world. A study that Jackie Gnepp and I did (Gnepp and Klayman 1992) provides an example. We presented college students and children of different ages with scenarios describing various emotion-provoking situations and asked them what they thought the protagonist's reaction to the situation was. (The protagonists were described as being of the same age and gender as the subject, and scenarios were adapted to be age appropriate.) Some of the situations were unequivocal—that is, nearly everyone has a similar emotional reaction to that situation. For instance, almost everyone is upset at losing a race he or she hoped to win and happy at getting a new bicycle. Other scenarios were equivocal; pretesting showed that there was considerable disagreement among people in how they would react in those situations. For example, some people would enjoy having an egg-salad sandwich for lunch, others would find that aversive. Some would be pleased to be asked to recite their poem in front of the class, others would be very uncomfortable.

As one might expect, older subjects were better able to distinguish these two types of situations. Improvement leveled off at about eleven years of age, however, at well below perfect. For unequivocal situations, almost all subjects said that only a single emotion was plausible. But both sixth graders and college students also said that about the equivocal situations about one-third of the time. In an earlier study (Gnepp, McKee, and Domanic 1987) subjects were asked a more general question about similar situations, without reference to any specific person. They were asked to distinguish those situations in which nearly everyone felt the same way from those in which some people felt positively and some negatively. When asked about people in general, rather than a specific character, discrimination was close to perfect by the end of the grade-school years. So, the difficulty in the Gnepp and Klayman study stems from limitations in thinking about alternatives for the specific case at hand, rather than a lack of social knowledge. When we prompted subjects in several different ways to think of alternative hypotheses about the protagonists' reactions, the older subjects complied, but they also judged those alternatives to be of low probability.

Interestingly, the older subjects showed much less difficulty recognizing alternatives when they thought that the same person might feel one way on one occasion and a different way on another (for example, if the protagonist likes singing in front of people on some occasions but not others). Nor did they find it difficult to acknowledge uncertainty when the situation itself was ambiguous (for example, they know if the protagonist was approached by a dog but didn't know if it was a small friendly dog or a large threatening one). It seems that people have a hard time coordinating the knowledge that there is a single right answer or best course of action with the fact that there are multiple possibilities for what that single best option is. The knowledge of one good answer inhibits consideration of other good answers, analogous to the phenomenon of hindsight bias (Fischholf 1975), in which knowledge of the outcome of an event makes it harder to see how the event could possibly have turned out differently.

People's limited facility in generating good, plausible alternatives and giving them full consideration robs them of an important tool for facilitating revision of beliefs. In many situations, people are used to the idea that the current way of doing things is good and find it difficult to consider simultaneously that alternative courses of action might also be good or even be better.

WHAT'S SPECIAL ABOUT ETHICAL PROBLEMS?

Given the body of evidence concerning processes that promote the cognitive status quo, I think there are good reasons to believe that people get themselves into—and fail to get themselves out of—unethical situations in part because of some basic processes of human hypothesis development. There is nothing intrinsically ethics related about these processes, but I think there are several characteristics of ethically troubling situations that make them particularly susceptible to the sorts of problems outlined here.

First, the tendency to maintain the status quo favors the unethical behavior. This of course has been the focal feature in my discussion so far. Certainly, people sometimes engage in actions that produce harm knowing full well from the outset what they are getting into. Even then, I doubt there are many perpetrators of harm who don't engage in some facilitating rationalizations about why their actions are really justifiable in the light of compelling need, earlier injustice, the victims' misbehavior, or whatever. More interesting and more troubling are the cases in which basically well-intentioned people stray into or are trapped in unethical behavior. In such situations, as I have argued, ethical problems develop when people fail to change their beliefs and their behavior, instead staying with, defending, and justifying the status quo. Recent research suggests that people have a status quo bias that seems to be even more general and multiply determined than I've portrayed it here (see, for example, Klayman 1995; Samuelson and Zeckhauser 1988). Thus, having the status quo line up with unethical behavior is bad news.

Changing unethical situations is also difficult because it involves challenging basic prior beliefs. Problems of resistance to change are greatest, naturally enough, when people hold strong prior beliefs. In ethically problematic situations, people bring with them several fundamental beliefs that they are likely to hold very strongly. These include such basic hypotheses as "I am a decent human being who behaves responsibly," "Ours is a decent group/organization that behaves responsibly," and "The people in charge are competent" or, if not competent, at least not evil.

Hypotheses like these are firmly entrenched first because they are held with high confidence, and second because of the asymmetry between the costs of falsely rejecting or falsely accepting them. I most certainly do not want to reject the hypothesis that I am a decent human being if there is any possibility that it is true, and the consequences of facing rejection of the other such hypotheses are similarly serious.

Moreover, most ethically problematic situations entail a great deal of ambiguity. What is ethical or unethical is not completely clear; responsibilities are not clearly delineated; and observations and communications are open to a variety of interpretations. Within an organization, there are usually multiple perspectives on the situation that fail to jibe completely. Christopher Hsee (1995) has noted the "elasticity" in ethical tradeoffs. Much of the information available to decision makers is only approximate. Estimates of dangers, costs, profitability, time required, and so on are not exact. There is thus considerable latitude in deciding what to believe. The more ambiguity and elasticity there is in the information one has, the more room there is for weak data to yield to strong hypotheses.

Finally, a lack of good feedback is often a problem for people trying to test and revise their hypotheses, and ethically troubling situations are especially bad on that dimension. Inside the organization, it is often very difficult or very dangerous to raise questions about dubious practices. Additional feedback may arrive from outside the organization, once word of problems gets out. But for those in the organization, feedback from the outside can't really be trusted; outside critics don't know the situation as well as insiders do, they are prone to hindsight bias, and they often have ulterior motives. A need for public justification can further bias the available information within the organization. The justification process requires a deliberate search for facts and arguments that support the legitimacy of the organization's position. People are unlikely to devote as much effort to searching for reasons to believe they are in the wrong. Thus, even if managers recognize that their public relations efforts are deliberately one-sided, the balance of thought and attention—and thus the apparent balance of arguments—is shifted toward legitimation.

In sum, ethical problems are subject to the same cognitive difficulties that foster resistance to change in other contexts. Ethically troubling situations, however, often have characteristics that tend to make them especially susceptible to such difficulties. Furthermore, affective and motivational forces in such situations are likely to be especially strong, and such forces can interact with cognitive processes in ways that make straight thinking all the more difficult.

IMPLICATIONS OF A COGNITIVE PERSPECTIVE ON ETHICAL PROBLEMS

If, as I propose, cognitive problems are a fundamental part of what gets people into ethical trouble, then changing how people think about ethical problems may be an effective means of helping tham avoid and escape such trouble. Positive hypothesis testing, a false sense of uniqueness, biased interpretation of evidence, and limited consideration of alternatives all can contribute to exaggerated beliefs about the impossibility of changing one's course of action. Cognitive antidotes can be administered in the form of institutionalized procedures that encourage the continual development of alternative courses of action, with ethical standing as an explicit criterion. These might include spending more time and money investigating successful practices in other organizations and establishing procedures that encourage people to propose and investigate alternatives that deviate from current beliefs about what is best. The risk of maladaptive perseverance is great in many ethically troubling situations because the status quo favors maintaining cur-

rent questionable behaviors, basic beliefs about oneself and one's organization are challenged, and evaluative feedback is skimpy and biased. These
conditions can be improved by actions such as establishing recognized bail-
out procedures, so that terminating or modifying a project is viewed as more
of an ordinary event, and by increasing the involvement of outside parties
(for example, customer and community representatives) in evaluating operations throughout the span of a project.

The implications of a cognitive perspective on ethics are intriguing, but we
are obviously far from having a complete understanding of how cognitive
processes contribute to unethical behavior and how to intervene effectively.
Most research on hypothesis development has been conducted with intellectual tasks of no particular emotional significance to the subjects (except for the
challenge of performing well), without much involvement of personal, social,
and cultural values. Moreover, most research looks at individual problem
solvers working alone or at small, self-contained groups working on a particular problem. In contrast, ethical problems involve norms, values, and high
personal stakes, individual and group thinking, public and private argument,
and the flow of information and ideas within an established, hierarchical
organizational structure. Thus, there is still much to be learned about how
cognitive, motivational, social, and cultural forces interact in promoting or
undermining ethical behavior. Along with a number of other contributors to
this volume, I believe that examining underlying cognitive processes can help
to clarify how people get into and remain in unethical situations and how
they can be helped to stay out or get out of them. Basic cognitive processes
provide the mechanisms by which social and motivational forces translate
into behavior—sor misbehavior, as the case may be.

ENDNOTE

1. It must be noted, however, that people do not always tend to see themselves as
   exceptional; in fact, under some circumstances they may underestimate the extent
   to which they differ from others. The question of when one or the other bias (or
   neither) prevails is still unsettled (see Dawes 1990; Suls and Wan 1987).

Chapter 14

Environmental Degradation: Exploring the Rift Between Environmentally Benign Attitudes and Environmentally Destructive Behaviors

Max H. Bazerman, Kimberly A. Wade-Benzoni, and Francisco J. Benzoni

Many of the ethical issues confronting individual and organizational decision makers are directly linked to the natural environment. These issues include decisions about the use of scarce resources, creating dysfunctional by-products, exposing workers to risky substances, and marketing profitable but potentially harmful products. Past decisions have already degraded many of the earth's ecological systems. We live under the threat of global warming; a significant percentage of the protective ozone layer has already been destroyed; growth and ravenous consumption have resulted in worldwide pollution, rapid resource depletion, and massive species extinctions. This degradation, destruction, and wastefulness speak powerfully to the need to consider the implications of our actions with respect to future generations, whose quality of life is contingent upon current decisions and actions of individuals and organizations.

It is widely assumed that environmental problems result from a disjunction between individual and collective interests, as described by Garrett Hardin (1968) in his famous essay on the tragedy of the commons. Although this tension between individual and collective interests is certainly part of the story, it overlooks another, possibly more ubiquitous factor. In many cases individual and collective interests are more closely aligned than the tragedy

This paper was jointly supported by the Dispute Resolution Research Center and the Kellogg Environmental Research Center at Northwestern University. The authors wish to thank Baruch Fischhoff, George Loewenstein, Dave Messick, Larry Susskind, Ann Tenbrunsel, Leigh Thompson, and Kathleen Valley, whose unusually thorough, critical, and helpful comments provided excellent guidance in creating the final version of this paper.

of the commons implies. Many people care about the environment and their impact on it.[1] We argue that, in general, people agree that the world should be left to future generations in as good condition as it was inherited. Yet both individual and collective behavior end up being at variance with this concern.

Despite widespread concern over the integrity of the natural environment, a steady deterioration of the earth's physical condition and quality of life for the human majority is revealed by any objective tracking of planetary vital signs (Gladwin 1993). The general attitude reflects deep concern for the natural environment, yet human behavior is destructive to this environment. This gap between attitude and behavior inspires the central question of this chapter: Why are our behaviors often inconsistent with our attitudes?

We posit that the attitude/behavior gap emerges from the tension within individuals between what they *want* to do and what they think they *should* do. When asked to articulate their values and beliefs, people typically communicate an attitude consistent with what is considered to be normatively appropriate. In other words, their attitude reflects what they think they should do. This attitude is most likely sincere in that people would like to behave in accordance with their stated beliefs. In situations where they actually must make decisions and act, however, there are a variety of factors that influence people's behavior in a manner that is not always congruent with their attitudes. Their behavior reflects not only what they want to do but what social pressure may subtly influence them to do, what is convenient at that time, and/or what may be intuitively appealing. We will also argue that a pivotal determinant of whether behavior will be in accordance with what individuals want to do or think they should do is the degree of ambiguity about the implications of a given behavior. The more ambiguity involved in a decision, the more leeway is given to people to do what they want. Thus, the degree of ambiguity may determine the size of the attitude/behavior gap.

The attitude/behavior gap observed in individuals is not unconnected to the discrepancy in implicit and explicit cultural values of their societies. Explicit cultural ideals help individuals to define what they think they should do, which in turn forms their attitudes. For example, in the United States, valuing the natural beauty and health of the country is an explicit ideal exemplified in the song "America the Beautiful." The opening lyrics— "Oh, beautiful for spacious skies, for amber waves of grain, for purple mountains' majesty above the fruited plain"—convey the pride that Americans take in the natural beauty of their country and characterize the value that American culture places on the health and vitality of the natural environment. More implicit cultural values, however, influence people to act in ways that degrade the natural environment. The culture is organized around an economy that relies on constant growth for its survival and thus encourages continual consumption, since possession of material goods contributes to the construction of social identity and measurement of success. The incongruity between the explicit and implicit values of the culture sends a mixed message, and as a result people may develop attitudes based on the explicit values and behave according to the implicit ones.

We will discuss a number of causes of this discrepancy between individual concern for and destruction of the environment. The chapter is organized around four central phenomena that may help explain the attitude/behavior gap that surfaces from the want/should tension: (1) inappropriate time discounting, (2) self-serving biases, (3) preference reversals, and (4) problem censoring.

CONSUMPTION, DISCOUNTING, AND VALUING THE FUTURE

We assume that most people would agree that the earth should not be treated, in Herman Daly's words, "as if it were a business in liquidation" (cited in Gore 1993, 191). In fact, most of us would argue that the earth ought not be degraded in the aggregate. Implicit in these values is a concern for future generations. People generally believe that we ought to pass on to future inhabitants the resources and systems of the natural environment in as good a state as when we inherited them.

Our ongoing decisions, however, are inconsistent with the above argument. We are not pursuing policies of restraint and sustainability but rather are consuming environmental resources and generating pollution at an ever-increasing rate. Apparently the way we *want* to live collides with the way we *should* live in order to bring our behavior into accord with our attitude.

Consumption is one of the three interrelated human phenomena to which virtually all global environmental degradation can be traced; the other two are population growth and pollution (Reitze 1989; Plater, Abrams, and Goldfarb 1992). In the industrialized nations, consumption is almost certainly the most important driver of environmental degradation. Where the population is growing in these countries, the problem is, of course, compounded. For instance, in 1994 approximately ninety million people were born. Of these, eighty-five million were born in the developing nations and five million in the industrialized nations. Yet because of the high consumption in the industrialized West, the impact of the five million new citizens of the industrialized nations put as much strain on the environment as the eighty-five million new citizens of the much poorer developing countries (Rolston 1994).

The myopic patterns of consumption seen in the industrialized nations reveal the degree to which people discount the future costs of their consumption. These patterns may work against an individual's own self-interest, or they may be myopic only from an intergenerational, global perspective.

Empirical studies provide strong evidence of the discounting of the future effects of consumption (Loewenstein and Thaler 1989; Gately 1980; Ruderman, Levine, and McMahan 1986). For example, most homeowners do not have enough insulation in their attics and walls and do not buy more expensive, energy-efficient appliances even when they would recoup the extra costs in less than a year. We can also see the dysfunctional use of discounting in large organizations. One of the finest universities in the United States has begun an extensive effort to improve its infrastructure. Because of a limited budget, many decisions have been made not to use products that in the long term would be the most cost efficient. Present benefits (lower costs) were secured at the expense of future costs (greater energy consumption). Interestingly, the construction process involved forgoing returns that the investment group of the university would have been delighted to receive. In an environmental context, such discounting results in environmental degradation, as these myopic decisions result in wasteful use of resources.

Myopic patterns of consumption may have many underlying causes. We suggest that one of the deepest and most pervasive sources of individual consumption patterns in the United States is the very structure of our culture. Simply by participating in this culture, people find a high consumption profile to some extent necessary. They no longer live where they work, so commuting and often car ownership become necessary. They no longer grow their own food, so they must buy it in stores, where it is often imported from distant lands. The food they buy presupposes owning a refrigerator. Their jobs presuppose owning a telephone and sometimes a computer. These jobs often require business clothing. The list, of course, goes on. These apparent necessities cause people to discount the future (at least in the long-term, global, environmental sense) as they consume to meet present needs.

But this baseline of necessities does not seem adequate to explain the ever-increasing levels of consumption in the United States. Russell Belk (1984) suggests that in industrial nations individuals increasingly seek personal identity through material possessions. These societies tend to be highly individualistic, with weak group identity. Individuals often have specialized roles and greater anonymity than in more traditional societies. These factors, coupled with the affluence of large numbers of people, result in the increased use of possessions to help individuals define a sense of self. This shift in values—from seeking meaning and security in community to seeking meaning and security in material possessions—has been underwritten by an industrial economy that requires growth for health (see, for example, Daly and Cobb 1994). This need for growth, in turn, encourages producers to reinforce the definition of self through possessions. Advertisements and mass media are particularly powerful and effective instruments in supporting and reinforcing this self-definition through materialism (Belk 1985). In order to be effective, marketing strategies highlight, inflate, and create wants; they encourage people to define themselves in terms of these wants.

It is possible that as people continue to define themselves at least partially in terms of possessions, they develop new baselines of necessities around which society becomes organized. For example, the automobile, once a status symbol and means of self-definition, in time became a necessity, and society became organized around it.

At the individual level, the rate at which people discount the future and their impatience to consume are strongly impacted by the way in which they internally represent their choices. Thus, discounting is subject to framing effects (Loewenstein 1988). Two psychological mechanisms, which seem to reflect as well as to affect the underlying cultural phenomena, strongly influence consumption patterns and, hence, the discounting of the future. These mechanisms are the preference for an increasing consumption profile and the impatience for consumption that results from imagining a potential item of consumption as already possessed. They may be driven largely by the underlying cultural paradigm in which the self is defined at least partly on the basis of material possessions. While perhaps encouraged by myopic framing, these mechanisms introduce further framing considerations.

Robert Frank (1989) argues that frame of reference, or context, is pivotal in matters of human satisfaction. To know what is attainable, people notice what others in their local environment have attained and what they themselves have attained in the past. They feel pleasure more strongly when their condition is improving than when it is simply good on an absolute scale. People experience enjoyment and satisfaction not primarily from the maximization of utility functions (of which consumption levels are the principal determinants) but by doing well relative to local norms. They receive pleasure, then, by consuming more than others in comparable situations and by consuming more than they did in the past. The two critical dimensions of the frame of reference are comparison with others and comparison with the past. Since people are loss averse, they prefer a pattern of increasing consumption over time. While we agree with Frank's analysis, we argue that the individual who strives to stand out through consumption is not simply seeking enjoyment, satisfaction or pleasure, but much more basic needs, identity and self-definition. Environmentally, this bias toward increasing consumption is devastating. It indicates that one of the most powerful drivers of the environmental crisis (that is, consumption) will prove extremely difficult to control.[2]

In addition to the bias toward an increasing consumption profile, a second mechanism, embodied in the idea of possession, tends to increase impatience for consumption (Loewenstein 1988). Several studies indicate that anticipated consumption may cause subjects to shift their reference point to accommodate the idea of possession. That is, ownership of the item becomes the new reference point. This shift in reference point causes immediate deprivation and, consequently, impatience and impulsiveness. Andrew Tomarken and Daniel Kirschenbaum (1984), for instance, found that when subjects expected to eat a meal high in calories in the near future, their determination broke and they began to eat immediately. Audrey Ruderman (1986) reported similar results for dieters. We suggest that, in our society, advertising and popular culture create an atmosphere that encourages following our wants by forming a frame of reference that includes the idea of possession. The result is impatience and desire for possession. The impatience, coupled with the preference for increasing consumption profiles, may bias individuals toward escalating consumption at an ever-increasing pace.

The recognition of the finitude of natural resources; the greater understanding of the intricacy, interdependency, and frailty of the natural world; and the sense of obligation toward generations to come are presenting new challenges. In order to match actions to values, people can begin to base their decisions on a frame of reference that includes consideration for future inhabitants of the earth and the integrity of the natural world. Perhaps the most effective way to expand the frame of reference and close the gap between attitude and behavior is through commitment to careful use of and respect for the natural world. Such a commitment can result in less discounting of the future (Ainslie and Haslam 1992). Without this commitment, the ambiguity of individual, serial decisions permits people enough leeway to follow their wants. This commitment, however, always presents the alternative of making the optimal environmental decision, including the option of nonconsumption. With such a commitment, a consumption decision is never simply an isolated act but is always compared against the standard of the environmentally optimal decision. Furthermore, the commitment itself may help to form self-identity independent of consumption. The bias toward an increasing consumption profile might be replaced with a commitment toward increasingly environmentally benign behavior.

SELF-SERVING BIASES

Perceptions and expectations are often biased in a self-serving manner (Babcock and others 1994; Loewenstein and others 1993; Diekmann and others 1995). People interpret information in a way that enables them to feel better about themselves. Some theorists argue that these biases have a useful, adaptive function, while others contend that they are an artifact of cognitive processes and serve little motivational or adaptive purpose (Loewenstein and others 1993). Although the cause of the biases is debated, their existence is rarely disputed, and most agree that self-serving biases are an intrinsic part of human nature (Diekmann and others 1995). In particular, self-enhancement and interpretations of fairness are two ways in which self-serving bias tends to cause people's behavior to accord more fully with what they want to do rather than what they think they should do, resulting in a discrepancy between attitude and behavior.

Two Sides of Self-enhancement

The self-enhancement bias pertains to inaccurate, overly positive perceptions of the self. Two means by which individuals achieve self-enhancement are *protection of self-image,* which entails avoiding any evidence that may depress a self-evaluation, and *embellishment of self-image*, which involves creating or exaggerating evidence that may inflate a self-evaluation. Both processes lead to self-evaluations that are more positive than would be judged by an objective standard.

PROTECTION OF SELF-IMAGE.   Self-serving biases play a role in the assignment of blame for environmental problems. These biases lead people to focus on the aspects of a problem that allow them to avoid blame and point to others as its primary cause, thus enabling them to protect a self-image of being no threat to the environment. Many sources contribute to, and can be blamed for, unhealthy conditions in the natural environment. For example, the United States blames the Third World for burning the rain forests and for overpopulation. The Third World blames the West for pollution caused by industrialization and excessive consumption. In these instances, each party perceives its own negative contributions to environmental problems as less important than the other party's.

Social perspective influences the interpretation of a given situation in a self-serving manner; people who view the same problem from different social perspectives are likely to reach different conclusions about who is to blame. Consider the problem of acid rain. The use of tall smokestacks to reduce local air pollution contributes to the regional problem of acid rain; the higher the pollution is emitted, the farther it travels from its source (Gore 1993). When people in northeast Canada are affected by acid rain, they claim that it is caused by the industrialization of the northeastern and midwestern United States. To the Canadians, the causal connections are clear: The United States is to blame. The United States's response is to claim that there is no clear causal connection, as acid rain may be caused by the local burning of coal.

Thus, when different arguments can be made to support competing theories as to how a given environmental problem came about, people focus on the explanation that does not involve themselves as a cause. They feel that their actions should be environmentally benign, but when they have the leeway to blame others they feel free to continue doing what they want. They can maintain the attitude that they care about the state of the natural environment while their behavior degrades it, and their self-image is protected.

EMBELLISHMENT OF SELF-IMAGE.   People tend to perceive themselves as better than others on a variety of desirable attributes (Brown 1986; Goethals 1986; Messick and others 1985; Messick and Sentis 1979); as a result they have unrealistically positive self-evaluations across a wide range of social contexts (Brown 1986). There are limits to self-enhancement, however. Studies suggest that the extent to which people can maintain unrealistically positive beliefs about themselves may be constrained to some degree by the objectivity and credibility of those beliefs, and their potential for disconfirmation

(Allison, Messick, and Goethals 1989; Schlenker, Weigold, and Hallan 1990). For example, it is easier to maintain the view that one is more honest or fair than others than that one is a more witty conversationalist or more skillful at a particular activity such as racquetball or chess.

Self-enhancement biases may lead people to think that in comparison to others their behaviors and attitudes are environmentally sensitive and that they are doing their fair share of sacrificing and working toward the resolution of environmental problems, even though their self-assessments may, in reality, be inflated. The degree to which the bias distorts the self-assessment may depend on how much ambiguity surrounds the self-assessment. Specifically, people may maintain unrealistically positive beliefs about their environmental sensitivity when their self-evaluation is difficult to disconfirm but assess themselves more realistically when they are constrained by the objectivity of the evaluation. For example, assessments of more general beliefs such as one's awareness of, concern for, understanding of, and interest in environmental issues and problems are difficult to confirm or disconfirm. In contrast, beliefs about how well one does in specific activities such as recycling, donating money to environmental organizations, and using energy-saving light bulbs can be checked against objective measures. If people define their environmental sensitivity in terms of general (not easily confirmable) behaviors instead of specific (objectively measurable) behaviors, their self-evaluations are likely to be inflated.

Recent research by Wade-Benzoni and Bazerman (1996) provides some empirical evidence for the above argument. Subjects were asked to rate themselves relative to others on a variety of environmentally relevant activities, including both general items, such as awareness and understanding of environmental issues and problems, and specific items, such as recycling and taking public transportation. The general items were used as a measure of conceptual or abstract environmental sensitivity, and the specific items were used as a measure of concrete environmental sensitivity. Subjects were also asked to assess the importance of each of the activities for which they had provided a self-rating.

Results indicated evidence of the bias in self-ratings on general but not specific activities. In addition, a strong correlation existed between how subjects rated themselves on an item and their judgments of the importance of an item. The difference in ratings between general and specific behaviors indicated that there is more room for the self-enhancement bias when the rating on the behavior is difficult to confirm or disconfirm. When it is difficult to test the rating against some real measure of behavior, there is some ambiguity about how well one is doing in reality. Once again, this ambiguity enables people to do what they want to do instead of what they should do. In this way, the self-enhancement bias contributes to the attitude/behavior gap by enabling people to maintain the belief that their behavior, which they assessed as environmentally sensitive, is in fact consistent with their attitude that environmental sensitivity is important. In this case, the gap exists, at least in part, because the behavior in reality does not measure up to the inflated self-perceptions.

One explanation for the relationship between self-ratings and assessment of the importance of the behaviors is that the self-serving bias enables subjects to believe that they are doing well relative to others on important activities (and that the ones they are not doing well on are not important).[3] These biases may cause people to believe that their positive contributions to environmental issues are more important than the contributions of others. For example, a person who puts a lot of effort into recycling but refuses to take public transportation may justify this decision by taking the position that recycling is the most important aspect of addressing the environmental crisis. Again, the attitude/behavior gap results, in this case because there is ambiguity as to which behaviors are the most important in reality. Since people have the liberty to judge that what they already do (perhaps what conveniently fits into their lives) is more important than behaviors that may represent inconvenient lifestyle changes, they are able to do what they want to do instead of what they should do in order to be truly consistent with an environmentally benign attitude.

FRAMING OF SELF-EVALUATIONS. In the study just described (Wade-Benzoni and Bazerman 1996), it was also found that the strength of a person's bias depended on how issues were framed. In one condition, items were framed in a positive manner; subjects rated themselves on how "good" they were relative to others. In the other condition, items were framed in a negative manner; subjects rated themselves on how "not bad" they were relative to others. For example, in the positive-frame condition, subjects rated themselves relative to others on "awareness of environmental issues," while in the negative-frame condition, subjects rated themselves on "lack of awareness of environmental issues." Self-ratings on most items were higher in the negative-frame condition than in the positive-frame condition, indicating a greater propensity to deny harm to the environment than to claim good. This framing effect suggests that protection of self-image may be a stronger component of self-enhancement than embellishment of self-image in self-evaluations of environmental sensitivity. Individuals may frame their decisions in a manner that allows them to believe that their behavior is not incompatible with the attitude that one should not contribute to environmental degradation (at least not more than others do on average), when in reality their behavior is inconsistent with that attitude. In addition, people are less motivated to modify their behavior if they believe that they are not the source of the problem because blame can be placed elsewhere.

In sum, the self-enhancement bias may impede the ability to address environmental problems optimally insofar as it causes people to underestimate the amount of environmental damage they cause and overestimate the amount of environmental benefit they contribute. The aggregate effect of this assessment is that people may not be as environmentally sensitive as they would be if they had a more realistic understanding of the impact of their behavior.

Our discussion so far has supported the view that the self-enhancement bias can have negative social consequences (Tyler and Hastie 1991; Kramer, Newton, and Pommerenke 1993). Others contend, however, that such biases contribute to psychological well-being by protecting an individual's positive sense of self and the motivation to persist at difficult tasks (Taylor and Brown 1988). Seen in this light, self-enhancement biases may help people to persist at behaviors that are environmentally friendly in the face of the reality that their individual contributions make almost no difference in the big picture. If many individuals afflicted by the self-enhancement bias were to follow this course, the collective result would be significant positive contributions to the quality of the natural environment. In our judgment, however, the self-enhancement bias is more likely to lead to negative rather than to positive environmental consequences.

Interpretations of Fairness

There is considerable evidence of a self-serving bias in judgments of fairness (Messick and Sentis 1983; Babcock and others 1994). When people are personally involved in a situation, judgments of fairness are likely to be biased in a manner that benefits themselves (Walster, Walster, and Berscheid 1978). Different people's perceptions of identical information differ dramatically depending on their own role in the situation. Individuals first determine their preference for a certain outcome on the basis of self-interest and then justify this preference on the basis of fairness by manipulating the importance of attributes affecting what is fair (Messick and Sentis 1979, 1983).

The self-serving bias in judgments of fairness is relevant in the conservation of resources. In a resource dilemma, collective noncooperation leads to a serious threat of depletion of future resources. The resource dilemma refers to a situation in which a group shares a common resource (for example, fish, water, forests, or energy) from which the individual members can harvest. If individual members maximize their own consumption from the common source, the resource is likely to become exhausted. Scarcity is at the heart of the dilemma, as it turns the choice into a mixed-motive situation in which individuals are motivated by both individual and group concerns. The group interest requires moderate harvest, but personal interests may induce the individual members to harvest excessively. A characteristic of virtually all real-world dilemmas is asymmetry. In asymmetric dilemma situations, where parties contribute to the cause of the problem and depend on the outcome by different amounts, the self-serving bias is likely to show up, because there are multiple ways to decide on a fair distribution of the resource.

When people must choose how much of a common resource to consume for themselves, an easily evoked normative rule is the *equal division* rule, which prescribes that whatever is being allocated should be divided equally among participants (Allison and Messick 1990). In symmetric dilemmas, it is easy to use a fairness norm of equality for the distribution of burdens and benefits; since all parties occupy identical positions, it is fair for everyone to share the burdens and benefits equally. In contrast, asymmetry in interests and outcomes creates ambiguity concerning what should be considered a "fair" solution. In addition, real life resource dilemmas create ambiguity about how the resource will behave in the future—how fast it will be able to replenish itself and how each party will be affected. When faced with so much ambiguity, people's judgments are biased in a manner that favors themselves (Thompson and Loewenstein 1992).

The bias works to make people believe that it is honestly fair for them to have more of the resource than an independent advisor would judge. The collective result is resource depletion that does not necessarily result from greed but from biased perceptions of fairness. Ambiguity enables individuals to make self-serving interpretations of the situation and to judge as fair distributions of resources that favor themselves. Thus, the problem lies not in the desire to be unfair but in the inability to interpret information in an unbiased manner (Messick and Sentis 1983; Diekmann and others 1995). Findings in a recent study (Wade-Benzoni, Tenbrunsel, and Bazerman 1995) are consistent with the above argument. It was found that self-serving interpretations of fairness existed in an asymmetric resource dilemma. In the same study, it was also found that harvesting of the resource was positively related to the strength of the bias.

Thus, the pervasive real-world resource dilemma represents a critical area where ambiguity enables individuals to justify behavior characterizing what they want to do (take a larger share of a limited resource) instead of what they should do (practice self-restraint in the use of the resource). Self-serving biases allow individuals the illusion of consistency between attitude and behavior, ironically presenting a barrier to closing the real gap between the attitude of concern for the environment and behavior that contradicts this concern.

ENVIRONMENTAL PREFERENCE REVERSALS AND THE FRAMING OF DECISIONS

Economics may be distinguished from the other social sciences by the basic theoretical assumption that people have stable, well-defined preferences and make rational choices consistent with these preferences. In contrast, contemporary research in behavioral decision theory suggests that people often lack encoded, well-defined preferences. Rather, such preferences are constructed when prompted by a decision task (Payne, Bettman, and Johnson 1992). One result of this construction process is inconsistency in preference and the reversal of preferences (Tversky and Kahneman 1991). This inconsistency is evidence of irrationality and, we will argue, causes harm to the environment. In addition, we will argue that the framing of decisions is critical in determining whether people follow what they want to do or what they think that they should do.

In a novel set of experiments involving the trade-off between obtaining better commodities for one's own use and public goods improvements in the environment, Julie Irwin and her colleagues (1993) demonstrated the importance of the elicitation mechanism. They created a set of matched pairs of commodities and public goods (for example, adding a printer stand to your computer printer versus a specified improvement in air quality). One group of subjects was asked which they would choose. The other group of subjects was asked the maximum amount they would pay for each of these improvements (a standard willingness-to-pay measure frequently used to assess the value of environmental improvements and losses). For subjects choosing between the two improvements, 81 percent of the subjects preferred the air quality improvement over the printer improvement. In contrast, in assessing the same two options, 76 percent of the subjects stated that they were willing to pay a higher amount for the printer improvement than for the improvement in air quality. The shift in preference was quite consistent across a number of pairs of commodity versus environment decisions. The authors concluded that "choice invokes arguments and there are many powerful, even noble, arguments in favor of one's placing high personal value on improved environmental quality" (p. 8). This result is also consistent with findings in earlier research (Brown 1984; Magat, Viscusi, and Huber 1988).

In a style very similar to the study by Irwin and her colleagues, Daniel Kahneman and Ilana Ritov (1994) posed a variety of item pairs that pitted the existence of animal species against human health or safety. Again, one group of subjects provided their willingness to pay for each item in the pair, while another group of subjects selected between the two. Across seven paired items, a significant preference reversal was found. People valued the animal/environmental item more in the willingness-to-pay measure but selected the human health or safety item more in choice. Kahneman and Ritov concluded, "If choice is viewed as the more fundamental operation, these results imply that the willingness to pay question systematically overestimates the value of existence [environmental/animal] goods" (p. 27). It should be noted, however, that Kahneman and Ritov's conclusion of overestimation of the value of existence goods is valid only within their comparison with human health and safety. On the basis of the data from Irwin and her colleagues, we argue that the willingness-to-pay question systematically *under*estimates the value of existence (maintaining environmental and animal life) goods in comparison with most ways in which humans spend their money.

Kahneman and Ritov (1994) explain the reversals found in both studies in terms of the *prominence effect* (Tversky, Sattath, and Slovic 1988; Tversky, Slovic, and Kahneman 1990). The prominence effect proposes that, in general, the most important (prominent) attributes of options have greater weight in choice than in pricing. The definition of the prominent attribute has remained an ill-specified issue, however. While we agree with Kahneman and Ritov that choice should be viewed as the more fundamental operation, we see a different theoretical mechanism explaining the pattern of preference described. Our explanation, consistent with that of Loewenstein, Blount, and Bazerman (in press), derives from the tension that exists in many comparisons between what people want to do and what they think that they should do. We argue that without having a second option as a vivid alternative, people lean toward what they want to do. When choosing between two or more alternatives, however, people tend to select the most justifiable option—what they think they should do. Thus, people want the commodity over the environmental public good but believe that they should select the environmental public good over the commodity. Similarly, the animal issue is more vivid and creates a greater desire to contribute to a solution than does an abstract human health and safety issue, yet people believe that humans should be valued over animals. We believe that this want/should distinction cuts across a variety of nonenvironmental preference reversals beyond those described here (Bazerman, Loewenstein, and White 1992; Bazerman and others 1994; Hsee 1994b).

The conflict between what people believe they should do and what they want to do has implications for the earlier discussion of intergenerational equity. When asked explicitly about intergenerational environmental issues, people place themselves in a frame of reference that extends to and includes future generations. Within this frame of reference, a concern for environmental integrity and beliefs about fairness to future generations come to the fore. Therefore, people concur with the assessment that they should do more to preserve environmental integrity. When making actual decisions that affect the environment, however, people focus on what they want now—an ever-increasing pattern of consumption. Unfortunately, life often presents one option at a time and thus fosters a bias toward consumption over the good of the environment.

We would also predict environmental preference reversals based on the vividness of information. Tversky and Kahneman (1974) argue that vivid information is overly weighted in decision making. We would predict this effect to be stronger when people are evaluating single options than when they are making choices between multiple options. This effect is illustrated in donation requests by environmental organizations. The vast majority of environmentalists value biodiversity over the lives of a small number of animals, but biodiversity lacks the vividness that is needed to raise money. One problem facing environmentalists is the fact that the public values more vivid symbols of the environment. A term exists to describe what will raise money: "charismatic mega-fauna." The fact that these charming animals depend on diversity to survive is lost on the public.

The wide variety of preference reversals that are relevant to environmental decision making suggests that many of our behaviors are inconsistent with our underlying attitudes. We believe that these preference reversals provide useful guidance in highlighting areas in which individuals might change their behavior if they were more aware of the inconsistencies between their behaviors and their attitudes.

PROBLEM CENSORING

Vice-President Albert Gore, in *Earth in the Balance* (1993), his comprehensive account of the precarious state of the earth's ecology, posed a series of troubling questions:

> Why haven't we launched a massive effort to save our environment? To come at the question another way: Why do some images startle us into immediate action and focus our attention on ways to respond effectively? And why do other images, although sometimes equally dramatic, produce instead a kind of paralysis, focusing our attention not on ways to respond but rather on some convenient, less painful distraction? (p. 27)

In suggesting at least a partial answer to this puzzle, he has described what social psychologists call *problem censoring*:

> I suspect that many of those who say it is probably all right to run these risks—to make no change in our current pattern—are really saying that they simply do not want to think about the disruption that would accompany any serious effort to confront the problem. Our vulnerability to this form of procrastination is heightened where strategic threats to the environment are concerned because they seem so big as to defy our imagination. (p. 38)

Problem censoring consists of altering the definition of a given dilemma to make it more emotionally comfortable, manageable, or calculable. In addition to the biased assessment of various attributes and probabilities, environmental decision making suffers from a major problem in the complete exclusion of certain issues from consideration.

On the surface, problem censoring seems similar to the availability effect in the literature on behavioral decision theory. According to this theory, people assess the frequency, probability, and likely causes of an event by the degree to which instances or occurrences of that event are readily "available" in memory (Tuersky and Kahneman 1973) . Availability, however, is a cognitive bias, and we believe problem censoring is rooted primarily in motivation. That is, problem censoring is a tool that allows us to do what we want to do at the expense of what we should do. In addition, availability focuses on the (incorrect) weighting of information, while problem censoring focuses on the complete denial of parts of the problem.

Problem censoring results in procrastination on environmental issues that require action. It occurs in three primary forms: (1) hiding from the evidence, (2) explicitly excluding data from action implications because of low probability, and (3) excluding data that are not easily quantified.

The first of these censoring processes, hiding from the evidence, can be seen at the individual, organizational, and national levels. Hiding from the evidence refers to structuring decisions in such a way that information that would emphasize the *should* over the *want* is hidden from consideration. One of the authors of this chapter (Bazerman) can offer an example at the individual level. One of the things that motivated him to focus his attention on environmental issues was the discrepancy between his beliefs and his actions. He had been concerned with animal rights for years but continued to be a carnivore. In the summer of 1993, he noticed that he hadn't had any meat for a month and decided that he was a vegetarian. He made another interesting observation: During the year prior to becoming a vegetarian, he never ate any visible chunk of meat, only what he calls in retrospect "disguised meat." That is, he ate meat only in hard-to-identify forms, such as in Indian or Thai curries and in Szechuan dishes, where the meat is less recognizable. He believes that eating disguised meat was his means of hiding from the evidence on an issue that he had been thinking about for years.

Organizations that harm the environment often hide from evidence when footprints of data cannot be found. Cigarette manufacturers long denied evidence on the causal link between cigarette smoking and cancer and currently deny the link between secondhand smoke and cancer. They do not claim that the probability of being affected is lower than the evidence suggests or that the contribution to disease is weaker; rather, they assert that there is *no* causal connection. We believe that many people in this industry are deluded into actually believing that no causal connection exists. How can this be so? The motivation to hide from the evidence can be strong, particularly when no simple, concrete, conflicting data are available. Recently, a court allowed a class action suit against the cigarette industry to be filed on behalf of smokers. This was a major setback to the industry, because it is far harder to deny the link between smoking and cancer in the aggregate than it is to deny that smoking caused a particular case of cancer.

In another example, as we implied earlier in this paper, the United States has long hidden from the evidence that industry in the Northeast is the likely source of acid rain in Canada. Again, in the absence of a clear, direct link between a specific cause and a specific effect, the culprit in the unfriendly environmental behavior can follow every possible alley to deny its role in creating the environmental harm.

The second censoring process—explicitly excluding data on the basis of low probabilities—is a common coping mechanism of people who are constantly exposed to a high level of environmental danger. Smokers often have a cognitive awareness of the link between cigarette smoking and cancer; for this reason, many of them do not want their children to smoke. They assume, however, that because of the small probability of the bad event, it will not happen to them (see the discussion of self-serving biases earlier in the chapter). Thus, smokers are not cognitively changing the probability of hazard; rather, they are excluding the risk from their thought processes on a day-to-day basis. They are overlooking the risk (Weinstein 1984; Freudenburg and Pastor 1992). The tendency to ignore risks or to assume personal exception has been noted in people engaged in teenage promiscuity (Loewenstein and Furstenberg 1991), parachute jumping (Epstein and Fenz 1967), coal mining (Fitzpatrick 1980), and offshore oil drilling (Heimer 1988). These people are not simply biased in their risk assessment; rather, they seem to have developed a personal strategy of excluding these risks from day-to-day consideration.

The final censoring process—excluding data that do not fit the equation—is a problem that proliferates in the field of economics. At the organizational level, economists admit that externalities exist from the production process up. Since externalities are hard to measure, however, they end up being excluded from many organizational decisions, at least until the threat of regulations and penalties exists. Even then, the cost/benefit analysis often focuses on the costs of regulatory compliance, not the cost of the externalities to the earth. Some would argue that private sector companies are simply doing their job by engaging in profit-maximizing behavior within the existing laws (Friedman 1957). Thomas Gladwin at an informal presentation in the summer of 1994 assigned an M.B.A. class the exercise of determining the full cost to society of a McDonald's cheeseburger. The median answer was $200. Even if this result is high, it highlights the problems created for the environment when organizations focus only on the costs that they have to pay. The law encourages companies to exclude costs that will be borne by other parties.

A parallel set of issues concerning how nations account for their total economic achievement is currently being discussed. The main measure is gross domestic product, which excludes any loss of nature as a stock with future value. That is, the existing value of resources has been excluded because it did not fit the equation. Gladwin and his colleagues (1994) argue that national accounting systems that make it easy to ignore the depletion of a huge portion of our assets make "easy to understand the laissez-faire championing of unlimited and undifferentiated growth, market consumption, and debt in modern management education and practice" (p. 38). Many environmentalists see the inclusion of natural resource depletion into national accounting systems as crucial for sustainable development (Cairncross 1993).

We see a pattern emerging in which much information is excluded or ignored and many problems are censored. All too often this censoring process is harmful to the environment. We posit that a more complete assessment of the problems that confront individuals, organizations, and nations would be beneficial to the environment.

CONCLUSIONS

The central contribution of this chapter has been the identification of inconsistencies between attitudes and behaviors that have a net harmful effect on the environment. One suggestion offered is that if people and organizations changed their behaviors to be more consistent with their attitudes, they would act in more environmentally friendly ways. Changing human decision processes is difficult (Fischhoff 1982), however, and the motivation for change does not yet exist for many people.

Because of the difficulty in bringing about voluntary change in individuals and organizations, we see a role for national and international change to encourage more environmentally friendly behaviors. The free market beliefs that have caught on in much of the world—and that we believe have created great benefits—also cause environmental harm because of a failure to consider externalities. Some policy makers suffer from the cognitive illusion of the self-correcting properties of a free market. Yet ample evidence suggests that individually rational action does not lead to collectively rational solutions (Dawes 1988; Messick and Brewer 1983). Realization of the need for government intervention is not new, as the following passage from John Stuart Mill testifies:

> Is there not the Earth itself, its forest and waters, above and below the surface? . . . These are the inheritance of the human race. . . . What rights, and under what conditions, a person shall be allowed to exercise over any portion of this common inheritance cannot be left undecided. No function of government is less optional than the regulation of these things, or more completely involved in the idea of a civilized society. (cited in Cairncross 1993, p. 6)

Nor is it limited to the political left; Nicholas Ridley was the British environmental secretary under Margaret Thatcher:

> Pollution, like fraud, is something you impose on others against their will so that you can perhaps gain financial advantage. It is an ill for which the operation of the free market provides no automatic cure. Like the prevention of violence and fraud, pollution control is essentially an activity which the State, as protector of the public interest against particular interests, has to regulate and police. (cited in Cairncross 1993)

Thus, government must play a role in solving the problems of the common good by responding to an economic system that encourages environmental defection and by helping to improve the rationality of individuals and organizations that are causing harm to the environment. For example, it might use tax incentives or legislation to create opportunities promoting effective cooperative management planning in the environmental arena.

There is a growing chorus of voices calling for government intervention to help curb environmentally destructive behavior. Many people have come to realize that individual self-control will not ultimately save the natural environment (in part because of the environmentally unfriendly biases described in this chapter). It is unlikely, however, that strong government action will be taken on behalf of the environment in the near future. While most people truly want to preserve the environment, it is considerably less clear that they are willing to sacrifice for it. Preserving the environment would likely mean curtailment of consumption and restrictions on freedoms. For example, a gasoline tax of $1.00 per gallon would go a long way toward promoting efficiency in gasoline consumption and reducing resource waste and noxious emissions, but people simply will not support this kind of legislation because of the necessary short-term sacrifice. As time goes on and the environmental crisis deepens, the call for true change in the way we interact with the natural environment may result in debiasing the public and strengthening the will of politicians to enact truly meaningful environmental legislation. We can only hope that the change will not come too late to preserve future options.

ENDNOTES

1. We frequently hear of the ever-increasing interest in environmental issues. A *New York Times*/CBS News poll conducted from 1981 to the present reflects this trend. In 1981, 40 percent of the respondents agreed with the following statement: "Protecting the environment is so important that requirements and standards cannot be too high, and continuing environmental improvements must be made regardless of the cost." By 1989, the percentage of respondents in agreement had jumped to 80 percent. This increase did not come mainly from the fraction who were undecided in 1981 but rather from the fraction who had actually disagreed (V. K. Smith 1989). Given the general nature of the polling question, the widespread accord reflects a general attitude rather than an unbounded willingness to pay for continuing environmental improvements. Nevertheless, this general attitude does reflect strong concern for protecting the natural environment.

2. One of the ways in which people might ensure an increasing consumption profile is to accept a job that has an increasing wage profile. George Loewenstein and Nachum Sicherman (1991) found that people preferred a job with an increasing wage profile even when such a job was economically disadvantageous. They surveyed 100 adults, asking them to choose a hypothetical job from among seven offered. The jobs were all for six years, and all paid the same total, undiscounted

wages. For five of the jobs, the wages increased yearly; for another, the wages decreased yearly; and for the last one they remained flat. Virtually every economic indicator favored the job with the declining wage profile. For example, it would allow greater interest to accumulate on wages earned, and if the job were left before the end of six years this option would provide the greatest total payment. Despite the incentives, only 12 percent of the subjects chose the declining wage profile, and only another 12 percent chose the flat wage profile. Even after subjects were presented with economic arguments favoring the declining wage profile and psychological arguments favoring the increasing wage profile, very few switched from the increasing wage profiles. Interestingly, then, the bias toward increasing consumption profiles may actually result in negative time discounting in certain circumstances.

3. Another explanation for the relationship is that people try to do well on the activities that they consider more important. We cannot determine from the research conducted to date which of these alternative explanations may be responsible for this relationship.

Chapter 15

The "Public" Versus the "Experts": Perceived Versus Actual Disagreements About Risks

Baruch Fischhoff

Citizens in modern societies live in a world of risks to their health, safety, and environment. Often these risks can be attributed to the activities of businesses in those societies. These attributions can, in turn, pose significant financial risks to these businesses. They may be fined or sued for their past actions; their future plans may be delayed or denied; their reputations may be stained, undermining their ability to raise capital or recruit skilled workers. Firms define themselves, in part, by how they manage their risks and their relations with the public concerned about those risks. Acquitting themselves requires understanding both the risks and the public. Unfortunately, there are often significant conceptual barriers to that understanding. They are the topic of this chapter.

Over fifteen years ago, a public opinion survey (Harris 1980) reported the following three results:

1. Among four "leadership groups" (top corporate executives, investors/lenders, congressional representatives, and federal regulators), 94–98 percent of respondents within each group agreed with the following statement: "Even in areas in which the actual level of risk may have decreased in the past twenty years, our society is significantly more aware of risk."

2. Between 87 percent and 91 percent of those in each of the four leadership groups felt that "the mood of the country regarding risk" will have a substantial or moderate impact "on investment decisions—that is, the allocation of capital in our society in the decade ahead."

This is an edited and updated version of a paper (Fischhoff, Slovic, and Lichtenstein 1983) delivered at the first meeting of the Society for Risk Analysis, revealingly mislabeled "The Analysis of Actual vs. Perceived Risk."

(The remainder believed that it would have a minimal impact, believed it would have no impact at all, or were not sure.)

3. The four groups were divided, however, on the appropriateness of this concern about risk. A majority of the top corporate executives and a plurality of lenders believed that "American society is overly sensitive to risk," whereas a large majority of congressional representatives and federal regulators believed that "we are becoming more aware of risk and taking realistic precautions." A sample of the public endorsed the latter statement over the former by 78 percent to 15 percent.

In the ensuing period, relatively little has changed in this basic picture. Democrats in the 103rd Congress and Republicans in the 104th have introduced major legislation designed to break the logjam on risk. Title III of H.R. 9, the legislative realization of the Republican Contract with America is labeled "The Risk Communication Act of 1995." Like some of its predecessors, this piece of legislation calls for routinely comparing the risks of a technology that might be regulated with other, everyday risks—in order to help the public put things in perspective. In general, people agree that risk decisions will have a major role in shaping our society's future and that those decisions will be shaped by public perceptions of risk. There is, however, much disagreement about the appropriateness of those perceptions. Some believe the public to be wise; others do not. These contrary beliefs imply rather different roles for public involvement in risk management. As a result, the way in which this disagreement is resolved will affect not only the fate of particular technologies but also the fate of our society and its social organization.

The views about risk perceptions given by the respondents to the Harris poll, like those offered by other commentators on the contemporary scene, are at best based on intense but unsystematic observation. At worst they represent attempts to bias the political process through the promulgation of self-serving beliefs. Such an attempt might, for example, involve the claim that people are so poorly informed (and uneducable) that they require paternalistic institutions to defend them or that they would be better off surrendering some of their political rights to technical experts. Or, at the other extreme, it might involve the claim that people are so well informed (and offered such freedom of choice) that they can fend for themselves in the marketplace and need no governmental protection. Thus, these behavioral claims are often intended to prejudice the outcomes of ethical debates regarding the allocation of rights and responsibilities in society. They attempt to influence arguments about who *should* make decisions about risk by making claims about who *can* make those decisions, in the sense of having the requisite competence.

Like speculations about chemical reactions, speculations about human behavior need to be disciplined by fact (Mills 1965). To that end, various investigators have been studying how and how well people think about risks. Although the results of that research are not definitive, they clearly indicate that a careful diagnosis is needed whenever "the public" and "the experts" appear to disagree. It is seldom adequate to attribute all such discrepancies to public misperceptions. From a factual perspective, that assumption is often wrong. From a societal perspective, it is generally corrosive, in that it encourages disrespect between the parties involved. When the research does not permit a confident diagnosis, the reasonable and respectful assumption is that there is some method in anyone's apparent madness. This chapter suggests some ways to find that method. Specifically, it offers six reasons why disagreements between the public and the experts need not be interpreted as clashes between actual and perceived risks.[1]

REASON 1: THE DISTINCTION BETWEEN "ACTUAL" AND "PERCEIVED" RISKS IS MISCONCEIVED

Although there are actual risks, nobody knows what they are. All that anyone does know about risks can be classified as perceptions. Even those assertions that are called "actual risks" (or "facts" or "objective information") inevitably contain some element of judgment on the part of the scientists who produce them. The element is most minimal when judgment is needed only to assess the competence of a particular study conducted within an established paradigm. It grows as one needs to integrate results from diverse studies or to extrapolate results from one domain into another (for example, from animal studies to human effects). Judgment is everything when no credible data are available yet a policy decision requires some assessment of a fact (Funtowicz and Ravetz 1990; Morgan and Henrion 1990; National Research Council 1994).

The expert opinions that constitute the scientific literature are typically considered to be objective in two senses, neither of which can ever be achieved absolutely and neither of which is the exclusive province of technical experts. One meaning of objectivity is reproducibility; one expert should be able to repeat another's study, review another's protocol, reanalyze another's data, or recap another's literature summary and reach the same conclusions. Clearly, as the role of judgment increases in any of these operations, the results become increasingly subjective. Typically, one would expect reproducibility to decrease (and subjectivity to increase) to the extent that a problem attracts scientists with diverse training or to the extent that the field entrusted with a problem has yet to reach a consensus on basic issues of methodology.

The second meaning of objectivity is immunity to the influence of value considerations. Scientists' interpretations of data should not be biased by their political views or pecuniary interests. Most applied sciences have developed great sensitivity to such problems and are able to invoke some penalties for detected violations, such as falsified data. There is, however, little possibility of regulating the ways in which values influence other acts, such as in scientists' choices of topics to study (and ignore). Some of these choices might be socially approved, in the sense that the values are widely shared; for example, few people fault scientists who decide to study cancer, even though that means not studying other important problems. Other choices might be more problematic—for example, not studying an issue because one's employer does not wish to have troublesome data created. Similarly, prescriptions for ensuring informed consent routinely focus on what information is delivered, rather than what is produced (Gibson 1985; Merz and others 1993). Although a commitment to separating issues of fact from issues of value is a fundamental aspect of intellectual hygiene, a complete separation is never possible (Bazelon 1979; Fischhoff and others 1981; National Research Council 1996).

At times, this separation is not even desired—when, for example, experts are asked for (or volunteer) their views on how risks should be managed. Because they mix questions of fact and value, such views might be better called *the opinions of experts* rather than *expert opinions*, a term that should be reserved for expressions of substantive expertise. Often the reasons for eliciting such opinions are obscure. It would seem as though members of the public are the experts when it comes to striking the appropriate trade-offs between costs, risks, and benefits. That expertise is best tapped by surveys, hearings, and political campaigns (Dryzek 1990; Hammond and Adelman 1976; Mazur 1981).

Of course, there is no all-purpose public any more than there are all-purpose experts. The ideal expert on a matter of fact has studied that particular issue and is capable of rendering a properly qualified opinion in a form useful to decision makers. Using the same criteria for selecting value experts might lead one to philosophers, politicians, psychologists, sociologists, clergy, intervenors, pundits, shareholders, or bystanders, depending upon how these criteria were interpreted (Schnaiburg 1980; Slovic and Dixon 1992; Thompson 1980). Thus, whenever someone says "expert" or "public," one must ask, "In what sense?" "Expert" is used here in the restrictive sense, while "public" and "laypeople" refer to everyone else, including scientists in their private lives.

REASON 2: LAYPEOPLE AND EXPERTS ARE TALKING DIFFERENT LANGUAGES

Explicit risk analyses are a fairly new addition to the repertoire of intellectual enterprises. As a result, the risk experts are only beginning to reach consensus on terminology and methodology. They disagree among themselves and communicate inconsistently with the public (Crouch and Wilson 1981).

Experimental studies (Rohrmann 1994; Slovic, Fischhoff, and Lichtenstein 1979, 1980) have found that when expert risk assessors are asked to assess the "risk" of a technology on a undefined scale, they tend to respond with numbers that approximate the number of recorded or estimated fatalities in a typical year. When asked to estimate "average year fatalities," laypeople produce fairly similar numbers. When asked to assess "risk," however, laypeople produce quite different responses. These estimates seem to be an amalgam of their judgments of average-year fatalities, along with their appraisal of other features, such as a technology's catastrophic potential or how equitably its risks are distributed. Their judgments of catastrophic potential match those of the experts in some cases but differ in others, such as nuclear power.

On semantic grounds, terms can mean whatever a population group wants them to mean, as long as that usage is consistent and does not obscure important substantive differences. On policy grounds, the choice of a definition is a political question regarding what a society should be concerned about. When dealing with risk, we may attach special importance to potential catastrophic losses of life, or we may convert such losses to expected annual fatalities (that is, by multiplying the potential loss by its annual probability of occurrence) and add them to the routine toll. The choice involves a value question, as would a decision to weight those routine losses equally rather than giving added weight to losses among the young, for example, or among the nonbeneficiaries from a technology (Fischhoff, Watson, and Hope 1984).

Analogous ethical issues lurk in the definition of other social science terms, such as *benefit, employed, room,* and *ethnicity* (Fischhoff and Cox 1985; Turner and Martin 1984). A common claim in risk discussions is that different standards of stringency should apply in controlling voluntarily and involuntarily incurred risks (see, for example, Lowrance 1976; Starr 1969). Hence, for example, skiing could (or should) legitimately be a more hazardous enterprise than living below a major dam. There is general agreement among experts and laypeople about the voluntariness of skiing and using foods that contain preservatives. There seems to be considerable disagreement within both expert and lay groups, however, regarding the voluntariness of the use of technologies such as prescription antibiotics, commercial aviation, hand guns, and home appliances (Fischhoff and others 1978; Slovic, Fischhoff, and Lichtenstein 1980). These disagreements may reflect differences in the reference groups considered; for example, the use of commercial aviation may be voluntary for vacationers but involuntary for many business people and professionals. Or they may reflect broader social issues and even the meaning of "voluntary." For example, every ride one takes in a car may be taken voluntarily and could in principle be forgone (that is, one could use an alternative mode of transportation or not travel at all), but in a modern industrial society, these alternatives may be somewhat fictitious. Indeed, in some social and professional sets, the decision to ski may have an involuntary aspect. Even if one makes a clearly volitional decision, some of the risks that one assumes voluntarily may be indirectly and involuntarily imposed on one's family or on the society that must pick up the pieces (for example, by paying for hospitalization due to skiing accidents).

Such definitional problems are not restricted to subjective terms such as *voluntary*. Even a technical term such as *exposure* may be consensually defined for some hazards (for example, medical X rays), but not for others (for example, handguns). In such cases, the disagreements within expert and lay groups may be as large as those between them (Crouch and Wilson 1981). For debate to proceed, one needs some generally accepted definition for each important term—or at least a good translating dictionary. For debate to be useful, one needs an explicit analysis of whether each concept, so defined, makes a sensible basis for policy. Ideas such as the importance of voluntariness or catastrophic potential, when they have been repeated often enough, tend to assume a life of their own (Slovic, Lichtenstein, and Fischhoff 1984). The desirability of setting a double standard on the basis of voluntariness or catastrophic potential, however they are defined, should not be taken for granted. Technical experts could work up their data using alternative definitions of key terms and let readers decide which definitions are most pertinent. Failure to do so means obscuring the nature of expertise and imposing the values implicit in the chosen definitions (National Research Council 1996).

REASON 3: LAYPEOPLE AND EXPERTS ARE SOLVING DIFFERENT PROBLEMS

Many debates turn on whether the risk associated with a particular configuration of a technology is acceptable. Research (Slovic, Fischhoff, and Lichtenstein 1985) has found substantial disagreements not only between people belonging to different population groups but also within groups when the question is posed in different ways. Although these disagreements may be interpreted as reflecting conflicting social values or confused individual values, closer examination suggests that the acceptable-risk question itself may be poorly formulated.

To be precise, one does not accept risks. One accepts options that entail some level of risk among their consequences. When benefits or other (non-risk) costs are weighed in the decision-making process, the most acceptable option need not be the one with the least risk. Indeed, one might choose (or accept) the option with the highest risk if it has enough compensating benefits. The attractiveness of an option depends upon its full set of relevant positive and negative consequences (Fischhoff and others 1981).

In this light, the term *acceptable risk* is ill-defined; it does not specify the options and consequences to be considered. Once all options and consequences are specified, *acceptable risk* might be used to denote the risk associated with the most acceptable alternative. When that designation is used, people may fail to remember how context dependent it is. That is, they may disagree about the acceptability of risks not only because they disagree on how to evaluate the consequences (that is, they have different values) but also because they disagree about what consequences and options are to be considered.

A number of well-known policy debates might be attributed, at least in part, to differing conceptions of the set of possible options. For example, the risks (or possible risks) of saccharin may look unacceptable when compared with the risks of (the option of) life without sweeteners. They may, however, seem more palatable when the only alternative option is another sweetener that appears to be more costly and more risky. Nuclear power may seem acceptable when compared with alternative sources of generating electricity (with their risks and costs) but not so acceptable when aggressive conservation is added to the option set. Nuclear-industry experts seem to prefer the narrower problem definition, perhaps because it casts a favorable light on their energy source, perhaps because it focuses on solutions within their domain of expertise. Citizens involved in energy debates may feel themselves less narrowly bound; they may also be more comfortable with solutions like conservation or regulation, which they feel better able to understand (Bickerstaffe and Pearce 1980).

People who agree about the facts and share common values may still disagree about the acceptability of risks because they have different notions about which of those values are relevant to a particular decision. All parties may think that equity is a good thing in general, without also agreeing that energy policy is the proper arena for resolving inequities. For example, one may be troubled both by the new inequities caused by a technology and by the old ones endemic to a society yet feel that they are best handled separately (for example, through the courts or with income policies).

Thus, when laypeople and experts disagree about the acceptability of a risk, they may be addressing different problems, with different alternatives or relevant consequences. If each group has a full understanding of the implications of the problem definition it favors, the choice between definitions is a political question. When the public's definition is adopted in whole or in part, then this aspect of public perceptions has implicitly been accommodated in the decision-making process (Stallen 1980). A more explicit form of recognition for public concerns might be to require compensating benefits for every individual exposed to the risk (Fischhoff 1994).

REASON 4: DEBATES OVER SUBSTANCE MAY DISGUISE BATTLES OVER FORM—AND VICE VERSA

In most political arenas, the conclusion of one battle often helps set the initial conditions for its successors. Insofar as risk management decisions are shaping the economic and political future of a country, they are too important to be left to risk managers (Leiss and Chociolko 1994; Nelkin 1994; Wynne 1980). When people from outside the risk community enter into risk battles, they may try to master the technical details, or they may concentrate on the risk-management process itself. The latter strategy may exploit their political expertise and keep them from being outclassed (or misled) on technical issues (M. Fischhoff 1993). As a result, their concern about how large a risk is may emerge as carping about how it is studied. They may be quick to criticize any risk assessment that does not have such features as eagerly sought peer review, ready acknowledgment of uncertainty, or easily accessible documentation. Although these features are consonant with good research, scientists may resent having laypeople tell them how to conduct their business even more than they resent having novices tell them how large particular risks really are.

Lay critics may be even more irritating when they focus on how scientists' agendas are set, questioning scientists' ethics and not just their competence. As veteran protagonists in risk-management struggles know, without scientific information it may be hard to arouse concern about an issue, to allay inappropriate fears, or to achieve the certainty needed to produce action. In general, however, information is created only if someone has a professional, political, or economic use for it. Thus, we may know something only if someone with resources decides that it is worth knowing. G. B. Doern (1978) argued that lack of interest in the fate of workers was responsible for the dearth of research on the risks of uranium mining; Jerzy Neyman (1979) wondered whether the special concern over radiation hazards had restricted the study of chemical carcinogens; Barry Commoner (1979) accused oil interests of preventing the research that could establish solar power as a viable energy option. In some situations, knowledge is so specialized that all relevant experts may be in the employ of a technology's promoters, leaving no one competent to discover troublesome facts (Gamble 1978). Whether because of fads or finances, failure to study particular topics can thwart particular parties and may lead them to impugn the scientific process.

At the other extreme, debates about political processes may underlie disputes that are ostensibly about scientific facts. As I have argued, the definition of an acceptable-risk problem circumscribes the set of facts, consequences, and options that are considered. This agenda setting is often so powerful that a decision has effectively been made once the definition is set (Fischhoff and Cox 1985). Indeed, the official definition of a problem may preclude reasonable discussion. Consider, for example, a person who opposes increased energy consumption but is asked to decide only which energy source to adopt. That person may have little choice but to fight dirty, criticize unconstructively, engage in radical skepticism, and ridicule opponents adhering to the narrower definition. This apparently irrational behavior can be attributed to the rational pursuit of officially unreasonable objectives (Furby and others 1988).

Another source of deliberately unreasonable behavior arises when participants in technology debates are in it for the fight. Analytical approaches to risk management make the strong ethical assumption that our society is sufficiently cohesive and has enough common goals that its problems can be resolved by reason and without struggle. "Getting on with business" is an orientation that will please those in power but not the disenfranchised. To those who do not believe that society is in a fine-tuning stage, a bureaucratic procedure (such as cost/benefit analysis) that fails to mobilize public consciousness and involvement has little to recommend it. Their strategy may involve a calculated attack on what they interpret as narrowly defined rationality.

A variant on this theme occurs when participants will accept any process as long as it does not lead to a decision. Delay, per se, may be the goal of those hoping to preserve some status quo. These may include environmentalists who do not want a project to begin or industrialists who do not want to be regulated. An effective way of thwarting practical decisions is to insist on the highest standards of scientific rigor.

REASON 5: LAYPEOPLE AND EXPERTS DISAGREE ABOUT WHAT IS FEASIBLE

Laypeople are often berated for worrying about the wrong risks (see, for example, Burke 1988; Wildavsky 1992). Yet priorities that are casually dismissed may seem more reasonable with a more careful diagnosis. For example, Rene Zentner (1979) criticized the public because its rate of concern about cancer (as measured by newspaper coverage) was increasing faster than the cancer rate. This pattern would be quite defensible, however, if people believed that too little concern had been given to cancer in the past (if, for example, concern for acute hazards like traffic safety and infectious disease had allowed cancer to creep up on us). It would also be defensible if people realized that some forms of cancer were among the few major causes of death with rising rates. Indeed, the typical pattern might be for problems to grow gradually until they are suddenly detected by science and society, at which point attention picks up appreciably.

Systematic observation and questioning are, of course, needed to tell whether these speculations are accurate and the pattern does reflect reasonable behavior. False positives in assessing people's degree of rationality can be as deleterious as false negatives. Erroneously assuming that people understand an issue may deny them a needed education; erroneously assuming that they do not understand may deny them a needed hearing. Pending systematic studies, estimates of these error rates are likely to be determined largely by the rationalist or emotionalist cast of one's view of human nature (Fischhoff 1988; Jungermann 1983).

In lieu of data about specific cases, perhaps the most reasonable general assumption is that people's investment in problems is determined by their feelings of personal efficacy. That is, they do not get involved unless they feel that they can make a difference, personally or collectively. In this light, their decision-making process is dominated by a concern that is known to dominate other psychological processes: perceived feelings of control (Bandura 1977; Seligman 1975). As a result, people will deliberately ignore major problems if they see no possibility of effective action. They might reject the charge of having "misplaced priorities" when they neglect a hazard that poses a large risk if

1. the hazard is needed and has no substitutes;
2. the hazard is needed and has only riskier substitutes;
3. no feasible scientific study can yield a sufficiently clear signal to legitimate action;
4. the hazard is distributed naturally, hence cannot be controlled;
5. no one else is worried about the risk in question, so no one will heed messages of danger or be relieved by evidence of safety; or
6. no one is empowered to act on the basis of evidence about risk.

Thus, the problems that actively concern people need not be those whose resolution they feel should rank highest in society's priorities. For example, one may acknowledge that the expected deaths from automobile accidents over the next century are far greater than those expected from nuclear power yet still focus on fighting nuclear power, believing "here, I can make a difference. This industry is on the ropes now. It's important to move in for the kill before it becomes as indispensable to American society as automobile transportation."

Where the priorities of experts and laypeople differ, the difference may reflect not disagreements about the sizes of risks but disagreements about what can be done. At times, the technical knowledge or can-do attitude of experts may lead them to see a broader range of feasible actions. At other times, laypeople may feel that they can exercise the political clout needed to make something happen, while experts feel constrained to stay within their formal job descriptions. In still other cases, both groups may be silent about very large problems because they see no options. That might be the most charitable explanation of the relative silence (in 1981) of scientists and citizens regarding the threat of nuclear war.

REASON 6: LAYPEOPLE AND EXPERTS SEE THE FACTS DIFFERENTLY

There are, of course, situations in which disputes between laypeople and experts cannot be traced to disagreements about objectivity, terminology, problem definitions, political process, or perceived feasibility. Having eliminated those possibilities, one may assume that the two groups really do see the facts differently. In those cases, it may be useful to distinguish situations where laypeople have no source of information other than the experts and situations in which they do. The reasonableness of disagreements and the attendant policy implications look quite different in each case.

How might laypeople with no source of information other than the experts come to see the facts differently? One way is for the experts' message to fail to get through intact. The experts may not care about disseminating their knowledge or be hesitant to do so because of its tentative nature. Or a biased portion of the experts' information may get out, selected by vested interests eager to create a particular impression. The message may also be garbled, either in transmission, perhaps with the help of ignorant or sensationalist journalists, or upon reception, by recipients lacking the technical basis for understanding it (Friedman 1981; Hanley 1980; Nelkin 1977; Wynne 1994).[2]

Moreover, the scientific process itself might produce confusion. For example, it might seem sensible to assume that the amount of scientific attention paid to a risk is a good measure of its importance. Such an assumption would be false. Scientists can be drawn to minor problems by research contracts, public limelight, stimulating blue-ribbon panels, and juicy controversies. In that light (and in hindsight), science may have done a disservice to public understanding by the excessive attention it paid to saccharin. The disputatious nature of science can create further confusion. It may be all too easy for observers to feel that "if the experts can't agree, my guess may be as good as theirs" (Handler 1980). Or they may feel justified in picking the expert of their choice, perhaps on spurious grounds such as assertiveness, eloquence, or political views. Typically, the distribution of lay opinions overlaps at least a portion of the distribution of expert opinions. Laypeople may also be baffled by the veil of qualifications that scientists often cast over their work. All too often, audiences may be swayed more by two-fisted debaters eager to make definitive statements than by two-handed scientists saying "on the one hand x, but on the other hand y," in an effort to achieve balance.

In each of these cases, the misunderstanding is excusable, in the sense that it need not reflect poorly on the intelligence of the public nor on its ability to govern itself. Nevertheless, it would seem hard to justify using lay perceptions of risk instead of (or in addition to) expert perceptions. A more reasonable strategy would be education—as distinguished from propaganda—that attempts to bring the public along by treating recipients respectfully and aims to help them reach decisions in their own best interests, rather than pushing them toward some predetermined end.

For laypeople to know more than the experts, they would need some independent source of knowledge. What might that be? One possibility is having a better overview on scientific debates than do the active participants.

Laypeople may see the full range of expert opinions and hesitations, immune to the temptations and pressures to overstatement that actual debaters might feel. Laypeople may be less convinced than practicing scientists by the paradigmatic assumptions—about the nature of the world and the validity of methodologies—that every discipline adopts in order to go about its business. Laypeople may have observed how often yesterday's confident scientific beliefs are confidently rejected today (Frankel 1974; Henrion and Fischhoff 1986; Shlyakhter and others 1994).

Finally, there are situations in which members of the public, as a result of their life experiences, are privy to information that has escaped the experts (Brokensha, Warren, and Werner 1980). For example, the MacKenzie Valley Pipeline (or Berger) Inquiry discovered that natives of the Far North knew things about the risks created by ice-pack movement and sea-bed scouring that were unknown to the pipeline's planners (Gamble 1978). Postaccident analyses often reveal that the operators of machines were aware of problems that the designers of those machines had missed (Reason 1990; Sheridan 1980). Moreover, scientists may shy away from studying behavioral or psychological effects (for example, dizziness or tension) that are hard to measure yet still are quite apparent to the people who suffer from them. In such cases, lay perceptions of risk should influence the experts' risk estimates.

CONCLUSIONS

There are many reasons for laypeople and experts to disagree. These include misunderstanding, miscommunication, and misinformation. Discerning the causes of a particular disagreement requires a combination of careful thought, to clarify the nature of the debate and the possibility of agreement, given the disputants' differing frames of reference, and careful research, to clarify just what the various parties know and believe. Once the situation has been clarified, the underlying problem can be diagnosed as calling for scientific, educational, semantic, or political solutions.

The most difficult situations are those where participants cannot agree on the problem definition and where education, despite a diligent effort, has failed. In the former case, if the definition is not resolved, then people will continue to talk past one another. If it is resolved by administrative fiat rather than agreement, some parties may feel officially disenfranchised, having had their issues set aside. In the latter case, policy makers must either go against their own better judgment by using public (mis)perceptions of risk or go against the public by using untrusted expert estimates. As a result, their policies may seem overly cautious (as requiring use of motorcycle helmets seems to some people) or insufficiently cautious (as advocacy of nuclear power seems to some people). When fears are ignored, the result can be stress or psychosomatic effects, whose impacts can be as real as their source is illusory

(Wandersman and Hallman 1993). When strong public opinions are ignored, the result can be hostility, mistrust, and alienation. Because a society does more than just manage risks, policy makers must consider whether the social benefits of optimizing the allocation of resources in one decision outweigh the social costs of overriding a concerned public. A pessimistic view on "going with the public" might argue that "it only encourages the forces of irrationality." An optimistic view might argue that risk questions are going to be with us for a long time. For a society to deal with them wisely, it must learn about their subtleties, including how appearances can be deceiving. One way of learning is by trial and error. Often, the experts will be able to say, "We told you so. It would have been better to listen to us." In other cases, they may be surprised. Learning is possible as long as some basic respect remains between teacher and pupil. That respect may be one of a society's greatest assets.

POSTSCRIPT

In the fifteen years since this essay was originally written, the volume of risk communications and related research has grown enormously. The principles that it offers, however, still seem as valid. Regrettably, conflicts are still exacerbated by inaccurate diagnoses of the reasons for disagreements between experts and laypeople. Indeed, it often seems as though organizations go through the same painful learning process when they discover that they are held responsible for a problematic risk (Fischhoff 1995). They begin by brushing aside concerns that disagree with their risk estimates, but over time, they may be pressured into increasing openness and recognition of the need for compromise.

One significant (and positive) development has been the emergence of more cooperative arrangements for communication between experts and laypeople. The most common of these may be the citizens' advisory councils that have been convened for purposes such as monitoring activities at chemical plants or guiding the clean-up at military bases or defense nuclear sites. In the last few years, the Environmental Protection Agency (1990, 1993) has promoted a large number of state and local risk-ranking exercises, in which diverse groups attempt to identify the most important risks for their community. These efforts vary widely in their character and outcome. Their success will shape not only the future of technologies and the individuals affected by the risks and benefits that they create but also the nature of our corporate management and democratic processes. They offer an opportunity for citizens to show their sophistication and for organizations to show their openness. All those involved will be different for the experience.

The psychological research has played a hard-to-assess part in this process (Fischhoff 1990). By helping to decipher the nature of the disputes, it may have contributed to a society with fewer but better conflicts. By emphasizing the need to ground claims about human behavior in systematic research, it may have facilitated a more honest and ethical public debate.

ENDNOTES

1. Fuller expositions of the research upon which this summary is based may be found in sources such as Fischhoff, Bostrom, and Quadrel 1993; Fischhoff, Slovic, and Lichtenstein 1982; National Research Council 1989; Royal Society 1992; Slovic 1987; Slovic, Fischhoff, and Lichtenstein 1979, 1980; and Warner and Slater 1981.

2. For example, Lord Rothschild (1978) has noted that the BBC does not like to trouble its listeners with the confidence intervals surrounding technical estimates.

Chapter 16

Incremental Validity, Expertise, and Ethics

Robyn M. Dawes

Ethical principles and mandates imply capacity. If, for example, I feel ethically bound to fulfill a promise, the act of making the promise implies the capacity of fulfilling it. (I admit at the outset that assessment of capacity cannot be absolute; there is always the element of greater or lesser uncertainty in any such assessment.) If, for example, as a nonviolent protester I believe I should love—or learn to love—the person assaulting or beating me, I must believe that such love is possible (as did Martin Luther King, Jr.). If, in contrast, I believe that such love is impossible or extremely improbable, I may believe in an ethical mandate to remain nonviolent despite my own anger and hate. (That is the same principle, phrased in terms of negation of the consequence; "cannot" implies the absence of a should.)

Ought I present myself as expert in something? Ought I affect someone else's decision making and receive recognition and remuneration for my services? Should I have as an expert a greater impact on society than I would have were I not recognized as an expert? If my answer is yes, then what capacity is implied? Surely, I cannot (or rather should not) maintain that I am an expert but that no particular capacity is implied by the status—none that in principle anyway can be supported or refuted on an empirical basis. What then is the capacity implied?

The thesis of this paper is that the implied capacity is that of *incremental validity*. That is, in order to present myself as an ethically justified expert, I should be able to add knowledge, advice, or skill not otherwise available to the person enlisting my services (or enlisting the services of a similar "expert"). If I cannot add in this manner, I should not present myself as an expert.

INCREMENTAL VALIDITY

Incremental validity is best known as a technical concept familiar to statisticians and well-trained psychologists. I believe that this concept can be interpreted quite broadly while retaining this technical meaning. To explain that meaning, let me elaborate it in the context of regression equations.

Suppose that an optimal weighting of a set of predictor variables $(1 \ldots k)$ has a certain correlation with a criterion variable of interest. A new $(k + 1)$st variable has incremental validity if and only if a new optimal weighting of the previous k predictor variables plus the $(k + 1)$st results in a higher correlation with the criterion variable than does the optimal weighting of the other k variables alone. That is, the new variable has incremental validity if prediction improves when it is added to the old variables.[1]

Now, what does incremental validity *not* mean in the context of a regression equation? It doesn't mean that the new variable is simply correlated in and of itself with the criteria of interest. That can happen when the new variable is sufficiently redundant (correlated) with the previous ones that adding it has no impact. Nor does it simply mean that the new variable has some positive weight in the regression equation involving all $k + 1$ variables. What it means is that the new variable literally *adds* to the accuracy of predicting the criterion.

One way in which a variable can be assured of yielding incremental validity is that it be both valid and *conditionally independent* of the other variables (that is, that its correlation with the criterion is unchanged after partialling out the prediction from the other variables). While such a combination of validity and conditional independence is a sufficient condition for incremental validity, however, it is not necessary. What is necessary is that *some* variance the variable shares with the criterion be conditionally independent of the variance the other variables share with it—that is, that although its correlation with the criterion may be reduced when the other variables are partialled out, its partial correlation, hence b-weight, remains positive.[2]

When, therefore, I assert that the capacity implied by an ethical claim to expertise is incremental validity, I mean that something is predicted better when we include the expert's opinion than when we ignore it or that a more favorable outcome is obtained when we make use of the expertise than when we don't. The expert must "increment" the desired outcome.

Whether we are concerned with favorable outcomes or simply an understanding of what is happening, the test of knowledge is predictability:

> Predictability is not synonymous with knowledge—a horribly complex, ad hoc system that could predict would not involve as much knowledge as a theoretically simpler one that didn't predict quite so well. Nor is predictability the only criterion we use to assess whether we have knowledge. Such an esthetic notion as "beauty in one's equations" may be a criterion. . . . But a crucial test of understanding is the ability or lack of ability to predict. (Dawes 1994, 76–77)

Of course, it is not possible that in every single instance a better prediction or more favorable outcome will result from including rather than ignoring the expert. At least, it is not possible in a probabilistic world (which ours is, at least from the vantage point of our ability to predict and control it). What must happen is that to be ethically justified an expertise must increment a desirable result (for example, better predictability or control) *in general*. That qualification is no different from the one found in assessing the incremental validity of a predictive variable in a regression equation. Certainly, some outcomes here or there might be better predicted by ignoring an incrementally valid predictor. But the fact that it is incrementally valid means that prediction is improved over the entire set of instances examined (and after correcting for chance, in the hypothetical population sampled). Such general incremental validity implies *expected* incremental validity in the individual case. It is simply not true that "statistics do not apply to the individual." As Jacques Bernouilli (1654–1705) demonstrated many centuries ago, there is an intimate relationship between the single case and the aggregate; even those who reject statistical reasoning might do well to ask smokers with lung cancer or alcoholics with cirrhosis of the liver whether they believe that statistics apply to them. Specifically, the statistical *expectation* for a single case is equivalent to the expected long-term frequency. In the context of expertise, this equivalence implies that evidence of overall incremental validity means that we should expect it in the individual case (*ceteris paribus*, of course, but any factors that make the individual case unique can be specified and a new analysis incorporating them can be conducted to assess incremental validity).

In summary, to have incremental validity, expertise must supply not just valuable information or advice but generally valid information or advice that is not available from other sources. The client must not have "known that" already, must not have decided to "do that" independently of the expert's input. While this requirement for incremental validity may appear to be trivial, it often conflicts with people's tendency to accept expertise *to the degree to which the experts agree with them* in those areas in which they believe they have intuitive knowledge already. Most people seeking expertise in fields such as medicine, engineering, or law believe that they do not have such knowledge and hence will not be prone to evaluate expertise in terms of prior belief. In fields such as psychology, however, many (or even most) people believe they have intuitive expertise already, and I suspect that many areas of business may be such fields.

AN EXAMPLE

I will illustrate both the principle and the tendency with an example from psychology. In his presidential address to the American Psychological Association (Matarazzo 1990), a noted forensic psychologist defended expert testimony in court (after correctly covering many issues concerning the reliability and validity of such testimony). He reviewed the literature concerning the superiority of statistical to clinical prediction but then stated that his own predictions involve constructing "psychological portraits" of people in order to assess them and predict their behavior; thus this research literature was not relevant to what he did. He proclaimed that while there were no empirical studies justifying the accuracy of such portraits, he was sure that were any such studies to be done in the future, their results would be positive. His justification of these portraits involved agreement between "expert" psychologists and legal authorities. These examples of agreement, however, involve no incremental validity—and hence no justification of alleged "expertise" in a court setting—because people claiming no expertise at all would undoubtedly agree as well.

That is, he established such agreement about this type of assessment by citing two extreme cases (presumably ones with which he had been involved). One was of a twenty-two-year-old woman who had scored at the 98th percentile on aptitude tests and was elected to Phi Beta Kappa in college but subsequently tested in the mentally defective range (3rd percentile) following an automobile accident. The other case was of a man whose tested mental abilities were totally unchanged after exposure to neotoxins in his workplace. "When such assessment is done well, it is patently obvious to all involved (judges, juries, and attorneys for *both* plaintiff and defense) that what such a psychologist–expert witness concluded was valid (true) within the reasonable degree of certainty required in such litigation" (p. 1015). Yes, it is "patently obvious," and therefore a "psychologist–expert witness" is unnecessary (except for providing employment to a psychologist–expert witness). Judges and juries are perfectly capable of understanding both the implications of a difference between the 98th and the 3rd percentile on standardized tests of intelligence and the implications of no change. Psychologist–expert witnesses who provide expert testimony in such cases fail the implicit empirical mandate that to testify ethically they must provide incremental validity.

I have heard friends argue that such witnesses are necessary for courts to rule that someone obviously psychotic or addicted to drugs or alcohol is indeed psychotic or addicted. Once again, judges and juries are perfectly capable of deciding when someone is obviously out of touch with reality or addicted, and it is they, not the professional expert, who have been chosen by our legal system to make such a determination. An additional problem is that in those cases where such a decision cannot be made with clarity, psychological experts perform at their worst. Ignoring the overwhelming finding that the best predictor of future behavior is past behavior—even though it is a far from perfect predictor—the experts are far too apt to reason that "while on the surface it appears that . . . I can tell . . ." Reasoning in this manner is the only way in which they *could* provide incremental validity, and such reasoning is at best dubious.

How is incremental validity demonstrated? By demonstrating it. That may appear to be a tautological conclusion, except that so many socially defined experts make claims to incremental validity in the absence of evidence. We don't need to search back copies of Little Abner (for "J. Colossal McGenius") to find them. For example, in responding to a recent (devastating) critique of Freudian psychology by Frederick Crews (1993), Robert R. Holt—a well-known and highly respected clinical psychologist—challenged Crews's objection that free association is inherently incapable of yielding knowledge about psychic determinants from dreams and symptoms. Holt asserted that "the alleged inherent incapacity has not been demonstrated" and that Crews "has not proved that any particular set of free associations are useless as a basis for given type of inference" (1994, 66). Presumably, then, some people really do have expertise in interpreting free associations about dreams and hence can provide people with greater knowledge about themselves as a result of the interpretation than they would have without the interpretation. But look at the logic. Crews has failed to demonstrate an "inherent *in*capacity" and thus to "prove" the use*less*ness of something. Otherwise, Crews should accept Freudian expertise.

No. It is up to the person claiming an ethical right to expert status to prove that there *is* capacity, to prove that something is use*ful*. That does not mean demonstrating capacity or usefulness in every particular instance; in fact, it is not even necessary to demonstrate capacity for the particular individual expert. Rather, it is necessary to demonstrate capacity for people with similar training, employing similar techniques, with similar experience, and so on. If an ethically defensible claim to expertise implies empirical capacity, then such capacity must be demonstrated *somewhere*, and in a context that permits a reasonable inference to the person making the claim to expertise. (Again, I am not insisting on an airtight case for such capacity, just a reasonable statistical inference that it is there, subject even to the fuzzy reasoning involved in deciding what constitutes similar training, technique, and experience.) Otherwise, we must accept the claim that many ravens are purple, because no matter how many ravens we sample, we could not conclude that there aren't some purple ones out there. In fact, in my own work (Dawes, Faust, and Meehl 1989) indicating the superiority of statistical as opposed to clinical prediction of important human outcomes (for example, rearrest, recommitment to a mental hospital, success or failure at a career, or even longevity), I have been accused of sampling the wrong ravens. There simply *must* be truly sensitive clinicians out there who, "understanding the particulars of an individual case" (without reference to actuarial predictions based on "similar" cases), can do better than regression equations at predicting outcomes, but my colleagues and I have consistently sampled the wrong ones; at the extreme, "Anyone who was truly competent would have refused to be in your study" (see Dawes 1994, 91).

How do we demonstrate "general" incremental validity, as opposed to demonstrating that a particular individual's advice, opinion, or information possesses incremental validity in a particular situation? The most common way is to ask the purported expert to provide the evidence. That request will lead, most usually, to a recital of credentials and experience, intended to imply that experience in the expert's field translates into validity. I suggest that this "inside view" is one of the worst ways to evaluate whether expertise exists, bogus experts themselves often being "the last to know" (like an aging NFL quarterback), along with gullible people at least some of whom have had good fortune and ascribed it to some form of "expert help," such as from astrology. Instead, an "outside view" based on experimentation and statistics is desirable. Thus, for example, the AMA, the FDA, and drug companies all conduct double-blind randomized trials of new drugs, treatments, and procedures; NFL teams evaluate their quarterbacks in large part by their statistics, not by their self-proclaimed skills. Occasionally, the evaluation is very fuzzy, as when we conclude by comparing our lives with those of our great-grandparents that modern medicine has all but eradicated the fatal possibilities of most common infections (particularly in childhood) and has contributed to longevity. Our belief that modern medicine has brought about these changes in turn leads us to ascribe expertise to its practitioners in general, and hence to particular medical doctors—just as we conclude that a particular imperfect vaccine will reduce the probability that our particular child will contract the disease against which it provides partial protection—even though (1) the conclusion is based on comparing aggregate outcomes for those who received the vaccine versus those who received a placebo; (2) it is not possible to tell exactly which people in the experimental group were helped by the vaccine and which people in the control group who contracted the disease would have gotten sick even if they had received the vaccine; and (3) our child was not in either group. This inference from an aggregate or group of others to a particular instance or person not included among them is, as pointed out earlier, quite common in many areas—for example, in concluding that it is safer to fly from Chicago to Pittsburgh than to drive with an inebriated friend.

In psychological, as opposed to physical or external contexts, however, generalizing from the group to the individual sometimes "rankles"—as in being told one is likely to vote Republican given one's income and neighborhood (an inference from aggregate to particular), as opposed to the inference from people planning to vote Republican or Democratic to statistical statements about their incomes and neighborhoods. It is ironic that logically the inference from aggregate to particular is generally stronger than the reverse (Nisbett and Ross 1980; Dawes 1989). It is also ironic that experts in some fields, such as psychology, reinforce the intuition that inferences from the aggregate to the particular are inappropriate ("I evaluate each person in terms of his or her individuality"), thereby negating their claim to expertise.

I make no claims to knowledge of the prevalence of purported expertise without demonstrated incremental validity in the business world. I have had some hunches about it, but these are invariably affected by availability biases, given the media preference for reporting disasters that do not represent actual frequency, and are undoubtedly reinforced by my own stereo-types. I do, however, have a background in psychology. In addition to serving for five years as head of a psychology department with an accredited clinical program, I have served as a state president of the American Psychological Association and as a member of its National Ethics Committee.[3] I am, frankly, appalled by the social acceptance of expertise in psychology in the absence of any demonstration of incremental validity. Yes, psychotherapy works, but study after study has demonstrated that paraprofessional therapists with minimal training achieve the desired outcomes for their clients (again, on a statistical basis) every bit as well as do licensed clinical psychologists or psychiatrists (Christensen and Jacobson 1994; Stubbs and Bozarth 1994; Faust, in press). What appears to be important is realistic empathy (see Dawes 1994).

The general conclusion about irrelevance of training and experience does not imply that every type of *therapy* has been shown to be effective in alleviating every condition, certainly not equally effective. In fact, the number of therapies that have been demonstrated to be effective using wait-list randomized experimental versus control group studies is quite small (Chambliss 1993). Moreover, there are very few studies comparing different types of therapy addressed to the same condition.

And then, clinical psychologists and psychiatrists start appearing in court settings[4]: Some are called to testify whether a child was really sexually abused who in the first three interviews had denied anything happened and later recounted ritualized satanic abuse with sharp utensils that left no scars, in settings involving elephants, giraffes, and cannibalized infants. Others are called to testify whether a so-called recovered repressed memory (recovered following hypnotic or sodium amytal sessions but not during such sessions) is or is not historically accurate. These experts widely ignore all the research evidence that memory is reconstructive, that confidence is not a good cue to accuracy, and that techniques such as hypnosis and sodium amytal enhance recall only at the expense of enhancing false positive recall. Such "experts" in fact provide what might be termed *decremental* validity in the court system (or, at best, "noise"). "There was really no good evidence. It was the therapist's notes that convinced me she was guilty."[5] (For a catalog of such horrors, see Dawes 1994).

Thus, at least in the field of mental health—I strongly suspect in business consulting as well[6]—there are claims of expertise without any demonstration of incremental validity. Worse yet, in my view, are assertions that an unsubstantiated claim of expertise in itself serves a useful social function, as well as a very useful egoistic function for the person making it. A number of rationales have been presented to me personally for this claim, even some that include admission that there might be no incremental validity at all, not just that it has not been demonstrated. I would like to share these rationales.

BOGUS JUSTIFICATIONS WHEN INCREMENTAL
VALIDITY IS ABSENT

The first is that "it's good for people to believe in experts," whether or not these experts can provide anything of "true" value. In effect, the belief itself becomes the value. Stated differently, belief in one type of incremental validity provides another type, even though the first type might be nonexistent. Even clinical psychologists I respect have stated to me on occasion that they believe that they should "exaggerate" the degree to which they truly understand mental illness and the particulars of their clients' distress, "because trust in me is part of the therapeutic process, and if they really knew how much in the dark I was, they might lose that trust—hence the value of therapy." The problem with this claim is that the second type of incremental validity—whatever is to be gained by such trust in the therapist—might equally well be achieved by means other than (to put it bluntly) lying. The ethical failing here is that these other means have not been generally investigated, in part perhaps because the profession has grown on the basis of the socially assumed incremental validity that has not been demonstrated. So, in effect, the therapist feels trapped in the social perception that she or he has some sort of remarkable powers that don't exist and believes that to deny these powers would, in fact, hurt the client—or at least retard the therapeutic process. But don't we all have an ethical mandate not to allow ourselves to get trapped in a lie? The philosopher R. M. Hare (1963, 1973), for example, argues that while it is true that people face ethical dilemmas on occasion, they also have an ethical mandate to anticipate when such dilemmas may arise and to behave in a way that minimizes the likelihood of facing them. Can we not, similarly, anticipate that by behaving in certain ways we can enhance the probability that one type of success might be predicated on a fallacious belief in another type of success, and avoid such behavior?

The other problem is that while enhancing false belief—or belief in that which is not demonstrated—may be valuable in a particular therapeutic session, such belief can hardly be valuable outside the context of therapy. Before clients have entered psychotherapy, the most important people in their lives have been their spouses, lovers, children, close friends, and colleagues, as Terry Campbell (1994) points out. Moreover, these will be the most important people in the client's life after psychotherapy is completed. To encourage false beliefs that may be valuable in the therapeutic hour but—like all false beliefs—potentially harmful when interacting with these significant others outside it is, as Campbell argues, hardly a valuable service to the client. In fact, Campbell argues that a common ethical failing on the part of the psychotherapist is to allow herself or himself to become the most important person in the client's life, when in reality other people are more important before, after, and even during psychotherapy. Such unethical behavior, Campbell claims, is enhanced by the tendency of psychotherapists to make negative evaluations of the other important people in their clients' lives (over 90 percent negative in published case history accounts of psychotherapy; see Campbell 1992).

Now consider business consultants who are enhancing an unrealistic—or at least undocumented—belief in their own special expertise, as opposed to the expertise of business colleagues or even close friends or spouses. Surely, the same principles that Campbell enumerates apply. Before and after consultation, the business person must deal with others in the absence of the "special expertise" of the consultant. Business people must develop their own abilities to deal with problems. Business people should not be encouraged to think in a derogatory way of those with whom they interact. Any claim lacking incremental validity based on the idea that the claim itself is valuable can have these negative side effects. Surely, whatever value is obtained by the belief in the expert itself must be balanced against these negatives. While I have no proof, the presumption that the negatives generally outweigh the positives in the absence of incremental validity is plausible.

Another justification given for believing in undemonstrated incremental validity is that the person seeking expert advice often does so only to provide a rationalization for a decision that must be made in the absence of good reasons, or for a decision made already. Such a rationalization is particularly attractive when there is a plausible prospect of a negative outcome or disaster. Thus, "We did everything possible for Great Aunt Louise, but she died anyway" (as everyone does eventually). Or, "The expert we hired insisted that it was necessary to downsize this corporation in order to remain competitive." Or, "We really didn't take a gamble in entering this new field, because the expert recommended that we do so." Yes, it is certainly true that people often want rationalizations for behavior that cannot be justified, or for accepting the inevitable. But are such rationalizations without incremental validity really desirable? They're certainly desirable from the perspective of an egoistic expert, because they tend to become more compelling the more the expert is paid. Thus, we did not just do everything possible for Great Aunt Louise, we demonstrated that we did everything possible by hiring the most expensive surgeon in the state of Pennsylvania. Is it desirable, however, to encourage people to shirk responsibility for their own decisions? To refuse to admit that they are gambling when in fact they are gambling? To deny ignorance when in fact they are ignorant? Such activities are the "value" that can be supplied by expertise with an implicit claim to an incremental validity that has not been documented. The experts help people deny responsibility for their own behavior.

The final claim that people make is that just by being human experts provide the uniquely personal—and therefore satisfying—quality to whatever interaction the client has involving them. "Would you really," they ask, "want to make a decision on the basis of a statistical analysis rather than on the basis of advice from an expert who has a personal involvement with you and a concern with the outcome?" That was basically the rationale for medicine prior to the turn of this century. Doctors might not have helped much, but at least they were there. Moreover, a good bedside manner may have a placebo effect, at least for mild conditions. The answer to that rationale is that clients are real people who deserve the best help possible, especially when they are making a sacrifice (for example, forking over money). Bedside manners can be obtained elsewhere—from spouses, lovers, good friends, and ministers and priests for those religiously inclined. Experts are not the only humans in the world.

In sum, an ethical claim to expertise involves the implication that the expert will increment judgment or decision. Moreover, the expert must increment what it is the client believes the expert can increment, not simply enhance whatever other good things might follow from belief in the expertise of the purported expert—while ignoring, of course, the bad things that might follow. And how is incremental validity demonstrated? By responding to the challenge "Show me."

For example, one might study the outcomes of children in custody cases. In many locations in this country, a judge cannot rule in a disputed custody case unless both parents have been evaluated by licensed psychologists. Sometimes, as Matarazzo (1990) points out, these evaluations lead to reinforcing beliefs already held by the judge and other legal and child protection people; sometimes the evaluations influence these views; and sometimes the evaluations result in a (bitter and lucrative) battle of the experts. Many of the people involved no doubt believe that these evaluations are valuable. But are they valuable? One way to find out would be to conduct simple experiments in several locations in which some randomly chosen disputing parents were required to be evaluated by psychologists and others weren't and later to evaluate the well-being of the children. (No one in the control group would be losing a constitutional right to be evaluated by a psychologist.) If the results favored psychologists' evaluation, they would not imply with certainty that the evaluations of a particular psychologist of particular parents were necessarily valuable. But the implication that such psychological evaluation helps in general would be supported, and, as I pointed out earlier, one can infer from the general to the particular as part of good statistical reasoning (first inductively from the sample to the class and then deductively from the class to a particular member of it). If, on the other hand, the results were negative, the practice should be stopped. Moreover, any distress that judges might feel at having to give up the comfort supplied by allegedly—but not actually—expert advice could easily be balanced by the comfort of knowing that irrelevant noise had been eliminated from the judicial process.

ENDNOTES

1. The worst that can happen is that a new variable is given zero weight in the new optimal linear combination and the rest are given the same weight they were given previously, resulting in exactly the same correlation. We expect at least *some* improvement, therefore, purely on the basis of chance variation in sampling. There are many standard ways of "correcting" the resulting correlation to account for "capitalizing on chance" by the addition of a new variable; the most common is nothing but a standard "correction for chance" found in multiple-choice testing.

2. I am not considering the perverse possibility that the added predictor has incremental validity as a "suppressor variable"—one that is negatively related to the criterion but so much more negatively related to the other variables that it receives positive weight in the final linear combination. Certainly one would not wish the input of an expert to constitute such a variable.

3. When I served on it, the primary concern of the committee was sex (not necessarily harassment, just sex): between therapist (who was assumed to have unlimited power) and client, therapist and former client, professor and graduate student, professor and former graduate student, supervisor and intern, and so on. While actual and potential exploitation was involved in such sexual relationships, the status of the profession was as well. In fact, my impression was that the only behaviors that were proscribed with much vigor were those that were of potential harm both to clients and to the status of the profession. Asinine court testimony, for example, no matter how harmful to those involved who complained about it, was considered unethical only if the expert psychologist testifying had some sort of dual relationship with a lawyer that might jeopardize objectivity.

4. In 1990, of 44,901 clinical psychologists and psychiatrists surveyed, 15,509 testified in court at least once, according to a communication from Janet Cole of the American Psychological Association's office, February 22, 1991.

5. This statement was made by two jurors who found the second defendant in the 1991 Little Rascals Day Care Center sex abuse trial guilty, a verdict that led to a sentence of life in prison. The interviews in which the jurors made the statement were shown on public television, in an evening program aired on WQED in Pittsburgh, Penn., July 22, 1993.

6. As I have argued elsewhere (Dawes 1994), the roles and approaches of psychotherapists and business consultants are similar in many respects. Both tend to experience concern for the outcomes of their clients; both—if functioning well—analyze their clients' problems with a set of constructs that are not otherwise available to their clients, or at least that have not been employed spontaneously by their clients. Neither is (or should be) committed to the sunk costs their clients might incur at the expense of change.

Chapter 17

Ethical Dilemmas in Risk Communication

Helmut Jungermann

Industrial and political development in modern societies has produced, as a side effect, the task of *risk communication*. We are faced increasingly with technologies, projects, products, and activities that are associated with new, potentially severe, and long-range risks; correspondingly, many people are increasingly sensitive to such risks and demand to be informed about risks and to participate in risk decisions. As a result, communication about risks to health and environment has become a political necessity as well as a moral obligation. Such communication might influence decisions people make, either for themselves or for others. For example, physicians must inform their patients about the risks of a treatment, and patients must then give their informed consent. A chemical company must inform the public about the risks of its production processes, and the authorities and the area residents then decide about emergency and regulatory measures. Scientists must inform representatives of the public and the public itself about the risks of genetic engineering before laws concerning the approval and control of laboratories are proposed and adopted.

Agents and agencies undertaking risk communication face many problems (see Covello, von Winterfeldt, and Slovic 1986; Fischhoff 1987). In the present context, risk communication can be conceptualized simply as a process in which an agent—the source of information—transmits a message through a channel to some recipient. In the process then, there can be *source* problems, such as disagreements among scientific experts or lack of trust and credibility; *message* problems, such as the quantity and complexity of risk analyses or large uncertainties in risk estimates; *channel* problems, such as selective and biased media reporting or distortions in interpreting technical risk information; and *receiver* problems, such as inaccurate perceptions of levels of risk or difficulties in understanding probabilistic information.

Clearly risk communication has ethical aspects, at least when some authority or expert informs people who are potentially exposed to risks about which they have little knowledge. Whether people are informed and how they are informed involve ethical considerations. Dictates such as "I should be open and honest," "I should be fair," and "I should not harm another person" often come into conflict with "I should maximize shareholders' wealth." Whenever there are potential conflicts where a choice is to be made about the if and how of risk communication, ethical aspects are relevant.

The explicit goal of risk communication is to give people the information they need to judge for themselves the risks posed to health and the environment (Morgan and others 1992). One can, however, easily imagine other implicit motives, such as serving the commercial interests of a company selling risky products or getting the public's acceptance for some new technology. The explicit and the implicit goals of the agent or agency informing about risks need not—but can—conflict, and the resolution of the conflict may involve a kind of risk communication that violates ethical principles. For example, facts may be misrepresented or concealed to achieve a self-serving goal, such as the success of one's company. It is important to identify such conflicts, often characterized as conflicts between egoistic and altruistic motives, and to control how they are solved. But although an effective control may pose practical problems, the way a conflict should be solved in order not to violate ethical principles is simple; altruism should dominate egoism, and overt declaration of motives is better than covert pursuing of motives. In principle, the solution of such conflicts is straightforward. There is an option that violates an ethical principle (for example, honesty), and there is another that does not; the identification of the ethically correct choice is easy, but ensuring that this choice is made may require willpower and/or laws and rules.

These conflicts, however—conflicts in which the ethical solutions are clear—I will not deal with here. Rather, I will take a look at problems for which solutions are more difficult to identify and to evaluate; these are ethical dilemmas in which it is not obvious which communication modes and strategies conform to our ethical standards—that is, respect the values and interests of the people to whom the communication is directed and who are affected cognitively, emotionally, and behaviorally. As I will illustrate, this situation can arise for a physician who informs a patient about the risks of some surgical treatment, for a company that has to inform potential consumers about the risks of a new drug, for scientists who have to inform laypeople about nuclear power, and for a government agency that has to inform a community's citizens about the risks of constructing a new hazardous facility. Such problems will be examined from a *decision theoretic* perspective. The communicator faces a dilemma if there is an opportunity or necessity to choose between options of informing people about risks. These message options may have different consequences, for the recipient as well as for the sender of the message. Whichever option is chosen, ethical principles will be affected such that one or another principle will be violated or will appear to be violated.

I will look at three classes of psychologically interesting problems, all concerning verbal statements about risks. The first class includes dilemmas in choosing *whether to provide or withhold information*. The other two classes of dilemmas arise if the choice is made in favor of informing; the second class includes dilemmas in choosing *what information to present*, and the third class includes dilemmas in choosing *how to present information*. From a decision-theoretic perspective, I will take a look at some real-world ethical dilemmas in different domains, at an individual and institutional level of responsibility, with one single recipient and with a heterogeneous group of recipients of the information. Findings from the area of judgment and decision making may help us better to understand these dilemmas. I do not have solutions to offer. Perhaps it is the philosophers' task to propose solutions, but psychologists may be able to help philosophers, who then may be able to help practitioners of risk communication.

WHETHER OR NOT TO PROVIDE INFORMATION

Ethical problems may arise when the communicator has a choice concerning whether to provide or withhold information about a potential risk. More specifically, the communicator may honestly believe that withholding information will lead to a better outcome for the recipient's situation than providing the information would, but the affected person expects the information to be provided. That is, my focus here is on situations in which people want the best for others and do not want to violate any ethical principle.

For example, should a physician inform a patient about a bad prognosis—that cancer will spread fast, may soon affect the patient's mental capacities, and will cause increasing physical pain—even if there is evidence that the patient may become suicidal? Or should a physician inform a patient about the possible bad outcomes of a treatment if she has reason to believe that the patient will then refuse the treatment, which she herself considers absolutely necessary to save the patient's life? If the physician informs the patient about the risks, she might feel that she violates the principle to do the best for every patient—that is, to optimize the outcome. But if she does not inform the patient, she violates the principle to respect the patient's right to know and his autonomy to make his own choice, and perhaps her personal principle to be open and honest and not paternalistic.

As another example, consider a problem currently discussed in a number of countries. New, tasty, wonderfully big red tomatoes now on the market have been altered through genetic engineering. Should such tomatoes be marked "genetically altered"? Or perhaps marked with some label like the yellow label for radioactive substances and materials? The idea of marking genetically altered tomatoes is especially problematic because few experts maintain that eating genetically altered tomatoes poses a risk for health.

Some people know that the manner of production does not matter but would prefer to know about genetic alteration to maximize their enjoyment. Others believe that it matters and want to know. Unfortunately, we cannot discriminate between these groups. In any case, the information about the manner of production seems to be important to many people.

This is a common dilemma in risk communication. Difficult decisions sometimes have to be made in emergency situations (for example, an approaching forest fire or storm or chemical cloud), when the agency responsible for the management of the situation has to choose between immediately informing the public or withholding specific information in order to avoid panic reactions that might result in blocking exit roads. Or, a company might want to inform the public about the very low possibility of a major accident but knows that its message will be misunderstood: The simple fact that the company itself publishes such information will be perceived as the admission of a major problem, and the very low probability of, say, 0.0001 will be interpreted to have a higher (but vague) value than it has. If the company does not inform the public, it is not open; if it does publish the information, it may cause unjustified worries. A similar problem in medical practice is how to deal with the uncertainty of medical knowledge. For instance, should patients be informed about the high uncertainty associated with a proposed treatment, or even about the possibility of malpractice, which may increase with complexity of a procedure? Providing information in these cases reduces ambiguity but at the same time may also *increase* ambiguity. How can the goal be achieved of warning a patient sufficiently without alarming the patient unnecessarily?

In all these cases, it is reasonable to expect that simply hearing of the possibility that something has gone wrong, is going wrong, or may go wrong, would have consequences for the recipients of the information that they themselves would not want. People may have ambivalent feelings and thoughts—they may want to be informed *as well as* protected from information. On the interaction level, people might prefer one choice (to be provided information), but on the outcome level they might prefer a different choice (to have information withheld). Which choice should the communicator make? Which choice is ethically better?

The dilemma for the communicator is that whatever choice is made, it can be questioned from an ethical point of view. Take the tomato example. There are two options, no label and label. If a company chooses the concept of risk according to the standard definition of risk—some potential negative outcome—then it will not label its tomatoes as genetically altered. This is a legitimate choice, and the company manager has reason to believe that it is in the best interest of those people who will eat the tomatoes, because these tomatoes do no harm (or the Food and Drug Administration would not have approved putting the product on the market) and have a longer shelf life because they ripen more slowly. Of course, this information strategy is also in the manager's personal interest if he believes that more people will buy his tomatoes if they do not bear a label "genetically altered." But the choice not to label the tomatoes also withholds information that many consumers feel is important, and therefore the choice may be ethically questionable. But if the manager chooses to label the tomatoes, this choice will lead to lower sales and thus harm not only his business but also people who would be better off if they bought these tomatoes. Therefore, this choice is also ethically questionable. Whatever the manager does, he will potentially violate an ethical principle, either on the direct outcome level or on the interaction level. Should communicators base their choices on people's preferences in order to choose what is ethically correct? Or on their own? What should communicators do when they face a "tomato" dilemma?

Given the assumptions about the quality of the tomatoes and the effect of labeling, people should prefer—from a strictly consequentialist perspective—that the tomatoes *not* be marked as genetically altered, because this withholding the information optimizes the consequences for recipients. But one can assume that many people take a nonconsequentialist perspective and will therefore prefer that the tomatoes be marked, even when doing so implies worse consequences for the recipients' health and wallet. To explore the extent to which people prefer to be informed, Karen Fischer and I undertook an informal study.

We presented students not a tomato but a potato problem. The story was that a research institute had run a long and thorough study about the quality and potential risks of genetically altered potatoes. The result of the study was said to be that these potatoes posed absolutely no risks to health; they were actually better for the consumers' health, because they contained significantly more nutrients and vitamins than conventionally grown potatoes. The director of the institute had to decide whether the genetically altered potatoes should be labeled as such, even if then very few people would buy them. The dilemma was explicitly explained to the subjects. A large majority of our subjects said the director should mark the potatoes as genetically altered, apparently giving priority to the right or need to know over the actual health consequences of this information; only very few subjects gave priority to these consequences.

It was possible, however, that these evaluations reflected not the subjects' ethical concerns regarding information versus outcomes but strong doubts about the safety of genetic engineering. Therefore, we presented other subjects a story about a patient who is admitted to a hospital in critical condition. The only chance to save his life is an immediate operation. This operation is seldom performed and in rare cases causes irreversible defects. Furthermore, the possibility of malpractice cannot be excluded. The surgeon knows that the operation is the only chance for the patient. But she has also good reason to assume that the patient would not give his consent if she were to inform him about these possible, though small, risks. What should the surgeon do?

Not inform the patient about the risks of the operation in order to save the patient's life? Or inform the patient about the risks, even if it is to be expected that the patient will then refuse the operation and die? The proportion of subjects voting to inform the patient was not quite as high as the proportion to inform the consumer in the potato story, but still a two-thirds majority favored informing the patient, even though doing so might lead to his death. Only one-third thought that the information should be withheld, and we might speculate that they based their recommendation on the consequence for the patient's life.

This finding supports the assumption that people prefer—at least in foresight—that communicators facing such dilemmas ignore the bad consequences on the direct outcome level and choose to inform the persons affected by the decision. Whether they would stick to that position in hindsight—for instance, when the patient has died—is another question.

How can such dilemmas be solved? For some of the situations discussed, solutions have emerged on a political level. For instance, in the United States the legal specifications of the right to know have basically solved the dilemma of informing or not informing a patient; the patient is entitled to the information. This solution implies that bad consequences in an individual case—a "local minimum"—are accepted (for example, a patient refused a medical treatment after being informed and died). The principle of *always* informing patients is given absolute priority, because it is believed to guarantee a "global maximum." In terms of ethics, rule consequentialism is given priority over act consequentialism. That is, consequences for the individual patient are ignored in favor of consequences in the long run for all patients because their right to know is respected. But is there a point where it becomes ethically questionable to inform persons who do not want to be informed or those who will suffer from the information in the name of the principle to inform? It is usually agreed that there is also a "right not to know," but how can a physician find out whether the patient truly wants information or not? whether the patient prefers to trust to the physician's competence rather than being informed about survival probabilities? General rules for ethically correct behavior sometimes do not help the practitioner very much.

WHAT INFORMATION TO PRESENT

Ethical problems may also arise when the communicator has a choice of what information to present. More specifically, which concept of risk should be chosen, and which scope of the risk in question should be chosen? Again, I will discuss the situation of people who have the best intentions concerning the consequences for the recipient of the information as well as the ethical quality of their own behavior.

For example, the proponents of new technologies tend to use a very narrow technical conception of risk, such as the probability of a loss times amount of loss, whereas the opponents use a broad conception of risk, such as the catastrophic potential and/or qualitative aspects like potential social and political changes. We have reason to assume that the first group—often from industry, science, and government—is aware that their conception makes the technology in question look good, and that the second group—often from environmental protection groups—is aware that their conception makes the technology in question look bad. It is often difficult or even impossible to say whether the choice of a conception is based primarily on one's own motives to achieve a personal goal or primarily on one's factual conviction of what a risk is or how a risk should be conceptualized. But we do not want somebody for whom the end justifies all means, nor do we want an opportunist (that is, somebody who acts contrary to his or her factual convictions and works with whatever conception placates the public), nor do we want somebody who imposes a conception on others without sensitivity for their opinions and concerns. In both cases, we are likely to call the behavior irresponsible, either because the communicator is not honest or because the communicator does not respect the recipient.

As another example, consider genetic counseling. Counselors have to inform potential parents about the risk of having a genetically handicapped child. The information provided often includes both quantitative information about the probability of the handicap and qualitative information about the nature and severity of potential consequences. The counselor may inform expectant parents about these consequences with various scenarios from case studies describing the personal mental and social stress or may even ask the clients to generate scenarios themselves. Or the counselor may give some generalized information in more technical terms, such as the types of problems to be expected, the life expectancy of the child, and the costs associated with medical treatments. We may choose to present both kinds of information, of course. But we know that scenario information has a stronger effect on risk judgments than statistical information; for example, research has shown that people adjust their risk estimates more on the basis of scenario information about the risk (how the event happened) than on the basis of frequency information (how often the event happened) (Hendrickx, Vlek, and Oppewal 1989). Thus, we can anticipate that scenario information will overwhelm statistical information if both types of information are presented. If scenario information in genetic counseling predictably increases the clients' aversive feelings toward having a child, is it ethically correct to present such information? Or if scenario information decreases the perceived risk of some activity (for example, driving a car) because people can now more easily imagine ways of controlling the risky situation, should one provide this kind of information?

Clearly these are dilemmas for risk communicators. Every choice about the kind of information provided can be questioned from an ethical point of view. Should communicators present risk information straightforwardly according to the conception in which they believe (for example, provide sound statistical data only), or should they present risk information according to the demands of the recipients (for example, provide only emotionally assuring concrete information)? People react differently to the description of particular cases than to the presentation of statistical information. Whatever information is chosen, it may be correct but have different effects. What should a communicator do? Is each choice of risk communication equally ethically acceptable?

There are other variants of such dilemmas. One type was briefly mentioned earlier but will be elaborated here. We know that the intuitive conception of risk differs from the technical and economic conception in many ways (see chapter 15; see also Slovic 1987; Jungermann and Slovic 1993). Which one should be used in the communication about risks between experts and laypeople? When an agency or company informs the public about the risks of some new technology, should it include information about the catastrophic potential of this technology, even if the probability is extremely low? We know from many studies that people are more concerned with the catastrophic potential of a technology—that is, the number of fatalities at one point in time—than with the expected number of fatalities over some period of time. As a result, one technology might be rejected because of its catastrophic potential although the expected number of fatalities is low (for example, nuclear power), whereas another technology with a high expected number of fatalities but no catastrophic potential (for example, automobiles) might be accepted. Both components—the catastrophic potential and the expected number of fatalities—are legitimate aspects for risk evaluation, but prioritizing one of them may de-emphasize the other. In the case of a technology that would actually save lives, if an agency or company emphasizes information about catastrophic potential, knowing that the effect of this information will be increased opposition, the firm might be said to violate the principle to save as many lives as possible. If it does not include this information in order to optimize the long-range outcomes, it might be accused of violating the principle to respect the autonomy of citizens.

As a real-world example, the so-called Seveso Directive of the European Union requires that hazardous facilities inform the public about materials, processes, and products, and also about the possibilities of accidents and their specific and immediate consequences. For example, they must be told if toxic steam is released into the air. They are not asked, however, to include in their notices the size or type of potential catastrophe—say, the potential poisoning of thousands of people and animals as a result of the release. Yet, this information would play a major role in lay people's perception of risks associated with hazardous facilities.

It is obvious that there is no "right" definition of risk and that it is a socially construed concept. Therefore, what components are taken into account and how they are weighted are not questions that can be decided scientifically or technically. Instead, the risk construct emerges and changes in the course of social and political debates. And many if not all positions on the risk issue will be represented in the political arena. But each individual agent has to make his or her own choice. In our democratic political system, we do not prohibit or request specific conceptions. But does this mean that it does not matter which conception a particular communicator chooses? If it does matter, what is our criterion for choice—the social consensus about the construct only, or the consequences of taking the consensus as our choice criterion? We certainly want agents to consider carefully the consequences of their messages.

Another type of dilemma is related to our knowledge that people's decisions are often influenced by the temporal distance of the consequences (see Loewenstein and Elster 1992). Consequences expected to occur later in time are generally regarded as being less important. This phenomenon may strongly affect risk judgments and decisions about long-term (for example, environmental) risks. Should communicators choose to present primarily information according to the recipients' time preferences (for example, more information about short-term consequences than about long-term consequences), knowing that long-term risks will then receive less attention than they should, according to the communicators' beliefs? Or should they choose to present information that works against the recipients' intuitive time discounting, emphasizing long-term risks? Is any choice ethically more correct than the other? Here again we face the problem of whether to solve the dilemma by taking as the choice criterion the public's revealed and often expressed perspective or one's own beliefs about the effects of an information strategy upon the assumed welfare of the public.

There are variations of this kind of dilemma. Should the communicators emphasize information about the immediate, geographically local, personal consequences—as may be preferred by the audience—or about the far-reaching, geographically and socially global consequences? As long as we feel that the communicators have good intentions, we may not mind ignoring the public's perspectives and favor some kind of paternalism. But what if we do not share the communicators' intentions? Then it is easy for us to see their information strategies as some kind of propaganda. But does it make any ethical difference whether we share the intentions of the communicators?

The common denominator of all these examples is that there are substantially different kinds of information about risks, each having its specific effect upon the recipient of the message. There is no way to choose the information in a neutral way, disregarding the effects and hoping that they will balance out. And whatever choice is made, one may question its ethical quality.

Either an ethical principle is violated on the interaction level because the communicator uses different criteria for the choice of information than the recipients demand, or an ethical principle is violated on the outcome level because the communicator knowingly chooses information that the recipients demand but that will potentially result in bad physical, social, or economic consequences.

How can such dilemmas be solved? In the case of risk components, the consensus that risk is a social construct may suggest the solution for risk communicators. Baruch Fischhoff and his colleagues (Fischhoff, Watson, and Hope 1984) have proposed a multidimensional risk definition that could be taken as an index compatible with the public's as well as with the experts' understanding of risk. Even if the use of a socially agreed upon risk definition may lead to undesirable outcomes in the long run, the communicators then cannot be blamed for their choice. The individual situation in which a physician informs or does not inform a patient excludes the solution of offering multiple perspectives, however; it is an all-or-nothing situation. At an institutional level, one may demand from agencies or companies that they themselves inform from multiple perspectives, which may increase their credibility, or one may allow them to choose the information they feel is important and rely on the presentation of other perspectives from other institutions and organizations. On a societal level, the presentation of multiple perspectives can even be organized, as, for instance, it was in societal debates about nuclear energy in the 1970s and 1980s in the Netherlands and Austria.

As a principle, providing more rather than less information is probably the best guideline. This strategy might not always lead to the best consequences in a particular case, but if it could be predicted to have undesirable consequences, the question of whether and how the principle should be modified could be addressed. In any case, a strategy of telling all is at least less prone to misuse than a strategy of withholding or selecting information. The application of norm-based rules, similar to the rule that more information is better than less, has been discussed and justified from a consequentialist perspective even for situations in which the rule appears to lead to undesirable consequences (see, for example, Hare 1981; Baron 1994). A justification from a consequentialist position can refer to empirical observations such as consequences for a majority of people, consequences in the long run, or higher-order consequences (for example, trust and credibility), even if pertinent data might be difficult to obtain, and thus different opinions can in principle be resolved. If the available data are inconsistent with an outcome-optimizing goal, a justification is more difficult and will have to refer to basic norms (for example, fairness and honesty), which may be considered as valid independent of their specific consequences in a particular case. Most of the time, of course, there are no clear-cut data, or no data at all on the issue.

HOW TO PRESENT INFORMATION

Finally, ethical problems may arise when the communicator has a choice of how to present information about risk. Each mode of presentation is correct, but the choice of any mode is also questionable because of its effects. For example, should a company frame the results of a risk-assessment study in terms of potential harm or in terms of potential benefit? Assume that these are complementary outcomes but that a presentation in terms of potential harm will increase rejection of the risky product and a presentation in terms of benefit will increase its acceptance. And further assuming that managers know or could know the potential effects of the message, which communication decision can be called unethical? If the managers choose the option in terms of benefit, they may act according to their beliefs concerning the quality of the product and subjectively optimize the outcome for the consumer, but they may also have a self-serving bias and give their personal or organizational interests priority over the interests of the consumers. If the managers choose the option in terms of harm, they may act against their beliefs and may not optimize the effects for the consumer.

There are many situations in which risk communicators face this kind of decision dilemma. In one study (Levin, Schnittjer, and Thee 1988), one group of subjects was given a scenario in which a new medical technique had been developed to treat a particular kind of cancer; this technique was said to have a 50 percent success rate. Another group received the same scenario, but this time the technique was said to have a 50 percent failure rate. Subjects in the first group rated the effectiveness of the technique significantly higher than subjects in the second group. If asked to take the perspective of a doctor at a hospital, subjects in the success group were more willing to recommend the technique to a patient than subjects in the failure group, and the success group also was more ready to encourage a family member to undergo treatment with the new technique.

The issue here is not people's judgments and recommendations concerning the medical treatment but what people think and feel about how a patient should be informed about the new medical technique. Assuming that the effects of the two modes of presentation are known, which framing of the information would people choose? Which presentation of the risks of the new technique is ethically preferable? Are the communicators' motives relevant for a choice, and for people's evaluation of their choice? It is easy to see that there is no simple solution.

Real-world risk communication messages provide many examples of this type of framing dilemma. For example, medical information brochures almost always provide information in terms of survival, not in terms of mortality. Even articles in the *New England Journal of Medicine* usually report data from studies on the efficacy of drugs or treatments in terms of survival. Another example comes from the debate about nuclear power; when the

German Nuclear Safety Commission published a new study about the effects of a number of measures upon the safety of nuclear plants, the nuclear industry issued a statement that the risk of a major accident now had been reduced by 70 percent, whereas the antinuclear movement issued a statement that 30 percent of the original risk remained.

In these and similar cases, it seems plausible that the effects of the mode of presentation are the same as the effects observed in the experiment by Levin and others (1988). If the risks are expressed in terms of success, survival, or gains, they are more likely to be accepted than if they are expressed in terms of failure, mortality, or losses. In addition, we have good reason to assume that the designers of such messages are aware of the effects and make a conscious, intentional choice of a frame, one in which the effects match their personal or organizational interests. But do such intentions make their choices ethically questionable? Should we expect them to choose a frame whose effects are contrary to their own interests?

The situation puts communicators in a dilemma, because whatever frame of the message is chosen, they will perceive themselves as potentially violating an ethical principle. Take the nuclear risk or safety example. If a company chooses a frame that will *decrease* the perceived risk, then this effect is in its own interest; the firm may be actually ignoring the consequences for others and just pursuing a self-serving strategy, which is ethically questionable. But if the company chooses a frame that will *increase* perceived risk, because it fears that people will not believe in its good intentions, then it acts against its commercial interests. Moreover, it acts against the assumed interests of the recipients, if the company thinks that people will then be more worried and less willing to support this environmentally efficient energy source. But then this choice is also ethically problematic. Even if the director of the company flips a coin, he will push the recipient by the message into a certain direction. He will act in some sense paternalistically, whether he wants to or not. Furthermore, choosing by coin flipping will be considered by many as irresponsible because such behavior gives the impression that the decision maker is cynical and does not care about the consequences.

From the observer's point of view, the intention of the communicator is probably crucial for an ethical evaluation. If the communicator chooses a message in the interest of the recipient (that is, in terms of outcomes), normally we would consider the choice as a responsible one; otherwise we would not. If, however, we have reason to assume that the choice of the frame also serves the goal of the communicator, the evaluation might become difficult for many observers. In the example of nuclear safety or risk, it is actually impossible to say whether a decrease or an increase of the perceived risk of nuclear power is in the true interest of the recipients. Both communicators will claim that the effect of their message is in the interest of the recipient. The problem is that in both cases the effect also matches the interest of the communicator, and we cannot disentangle the interests of the recipients from those of the communicators.

If observers evaluate a choice from a pure consequentialist point of view, they should prefer the "reduction of risk" message irrespective of whether the communicator profits from the effects or not. I assume, however, that observers do not ignore the motives of the communicator and that nonconsequentialist considerations enter in. In that case they would prefer the message that is best for recipients, given that there are no personal interests involved, over the same message when such interests *are* involved. In extreme cases, they might even prefer a message with a potentially bad outcome for recipients—in our case the "remaining risk" message (if the effects do not match the communicator's interest)—over a message with a better outcome for recipients—in our case the "reduction of risk" message (if this message's effects match the communicator's interest). The perceived motive of an actor may deflect the attention from the action's consequences. And the communicator knows this, of course. Should communicators base their choices on people's preferences in order to be ethically correct or on their own?

Fischer and I examined how students evaluated choices of frames in problems similar to the one described above. For instance, one scenario stated that an environmental protection group was active in support of the construction of a new energy-producing facility that was particularly benign environmentally and was financially acceptable. But the environmentalists needed the approval of the town council. The technical data said that this type of facility works safely, but that in rare cases (about 1 percent) incidents had been observed in which toxic substances had been released into the atmosphere. The environmentalists could inform the town council in two ways. They could say that the facility runs to 99 percent without incidents, or they could say that the facility has a frequency of incidents of 1 percent. The environmentalists knew that people are more ready to approve the construction of a hazardous facility if the information is in terms of safety (that is, 99 percent without incidents) than when it is in terms of danger (1 percent incidents). The environmentalists themselves would not profit personally from the construction of the facility. Other subjects received the same scenario, except that this time it was not an environmental protection group but a commercial company that wanted to build the facility and to which the contract was financially very important. Our assumption was that environmentalists are perceived as primarily altruistic actors and company managers as primarily egoistic actors. Subjects were asked which of the two presentations they considered substantially more correct, or if they considered both presentations equally correct. Surprisingly, averaged over the two conditions (the environmentalists and the commercial company) only 67 percent considered both presentations equally correct. After subjects had given their judgments of the correctness of each mode of presentation, the dilemma facing the two groups of the communicators was explained to them, and they were asked which mode of presentation each group should choose in this conflict. If people focus on consequences, we should find in both groups a majority either for the safety version or for the danger version; they should favor the choice of one or the other mode of presentation without regard to the source of the information. But that was not the case. Of the group with the environmentalists as agents, a majority said they should choose the safety version; of the group with the company as agent, a majority said the company should choose the danger version. The difference was not very large but still in line with the speculation that people might tend to ignore the actual consequences of some action (in this case, the good effects of the new facility) if they are suspicious of the motives of the actor.

My illustration of the problem is one situation in which there is a choice between modes of presentation that are known to have different effects on the recipient of the information. Briefly, I will point out a few other similar situations.

First, risk communicators also often have a choice about how to present uncertainties. M. Granger Morgan and Lester Lave (1990, 357) give the following example: Governmental institutions might tell the public, "Stop behavior X or you will double your chances of cancer," or they might say, "Stop behavior X or you will increase your chances of getting cancer from 0.0000001 to 0.0000002." Both presentations are correct, but they establish different frames of reference and therefore have predictably different effects on the recipient of the information. I found a real example of this type in a press release by the German Federal Health Agency that said that the frequency of impairments of the inner ear among adolescents had doubled during the 1980s, probably because of the exposure to Walkman radios and loud disco music. But no information was given about the absolute frequency of such impairments. It seems impossible to present such information in a neutral way. There is extensive research on risk comparisons demonstrating strong effects of the chosen comparison on people's risk assessments. Which is the right framing?

Second, there is almost always a choice of how much detail to present. For example, if a chemical company informs citizens about the risks of its production processes using the fault tree method, it may do so by describing a few major categories of human error and system failures that might cause an accident, or it might describe in fine detail the specific kinds of errors and failures in all the possible causal chains leading to their occurrence. Of course, the company will not choose the latter information policy, for obvious reasons. Research on the judgment of probabilities in fault trees (for example, Fischhoff, Slovic, and Lichtenstein 1978; van Schie and van der Pligt 1990) and on the judgment of weights in value trees (for example, Weber, Eisenführ, and von Winterfeldt 1988) has shown which effects to expect, depending on the kind and degree of splitting the information. Is there anything ethically wrong with the choice of one or the other presentation? An answer would have implications—to mention just one real-world example—for the presentation of value trees, as they were developed for structuring Germany's energy objectives (Keeney, Renn, and von Winterfeldt 1987). About ten years ago, Ralph Keeney, Ortwin Renn, and Detlof von Winterfeldt developed a tree of criteria to evaluate energy systems from interviews with leading representatives in Germany. These trees of evaluative criteria were then used in twenty citizen groups all over Germany for the discussion of alternative energy policies. The discussion included the weighting of the criteria and the evaluation of the options given these criteria; preferences for the options were calculated with an additive model in which the evaluations based on the criteria are multiplied with the weights and then added. If weighting depends on the elaboration of the criteria, then the resulting preferences do not reflect the "true" preferences but also the effect of the representation of the criteria.

Third, there is often a choice of how vividly to present the information. For example, whereas the cigarette industry, forced by the law, puts a simple sentence on a package saying that the surgeon general has declared smoking hazardous to the health, antismoking groups show color pictures of healthy and diseased lungs. We do not need research to know the differences in the effects the communicators want to elicit. (More difficult to evaluate is the almost cynical risk communication of a British cigarette company that sells a brand called Death, in a black package.) Varying degrees of vividness, specificity, detail, and concreteness also distinguish the way scenarios of events are written. Numerous studies have shown that vivid, specific, detailed, and concrete scenarios have a stronger impact on people's risk judgments than more pallid, general, and abstract scenarios.

In each of these examples there are formally different though factually equivalent ways to present information; "equivalent" means here that, from a normative perspective, transformations of the message from one form into the other should not change the recipients' preferences, because the factual information remains the same. To borrow a concept from linguistics, there is one deep structure (the "real" outcome or uncertainty), for which there are many admissible surface structures (modes of presentation); there is no one neutral transformation, and many surface structures represent the deep structure equally correctly. The difference in the mode of presentation is important if there is reason to assume or even to know that the modes have different effects on recipients. Whether these effects are beneficial or not cannot be decided on substantive grounds but depends to a high degree on the beliefs of the communicator, whose interests may be matched better by the effects of one frame than by another. Communicators are aware of this fact, and they face a dilemma in choosing a frame, because observers might question whether the frame was chosen for egoistic or altruistic reasons. Whereas the communicators' perspective is determined by the consequences of the messages for themselves and for the recipients, observers may shift from a consequentialist to a nonconsequentialist perspective if they perceive personal goals of the communicators to be the only or major reason for the choice. As in the example of the genetically engineered tomatoes, they may prefer a frame that does not support the interests of the communicators, even if this preference implies that the consequences are worse for the people affected than if a different frame were chosen. People do not like it if others pursue self-serving goals when risks to health or environment are at stake, even if the selfish action is in the interest of those affected. This attitude may dominate our consequentialist judgment. Such a finding would not be surprising, because people show such behavior in social dilemmas as well—they prefer a distribution of a common good that prevents a member from receiving an "unfair" high proportion of the good, even if then each member gets less than would have been available with the "unfair" distribution.

How can dilemmas of the type described in this chapter be solved? Can they be solved? If communicators want to exploit the effect of a mode of presentation like framing or splitting, they may do it for selfish and/or altruistic reasons. A typical example is choosing how to present information about the risks of smoking. Assuming that the communicators' intentions are good (that is, to do best for the people affected), they must justify their choice to themselves and possibly to others. They must be able to justify their motives and paternalism by demonstrating that another choice would have been detrimental to the people affected. This justification is easy if there is some societal consensus on the issue, as there is on smoking; it is less easy if a social minority is claiming to know what is best for the people, as in the case of biotechnological products. If motives and paternalism are made explicit, there is, of course, a danger that the effect intended by the risk message will be attenuated or even reversed.

What can communicators do if they do not want to exploit the effects of a mode of presentation—that is, if they want to give their most balanced and unbiased message, so that recipients can form their own independent judgment? One possibility has already been mentioned: explaining explicitly the motives and intentions for the chosen presentation, a strategy that may, of course, weaken the effect of the message. The other possibility is to offer multiple perspectives, when possible using multiple measures of risks (such as annual fatality rates, individual fatality probability, and reduction of life expectancy) to allow the audience to compare results and select the measures most relevant to them (Covello, von Winterfeldt, and Slovic 1986). At first glance, this solution is not paternalistic and gives the recipient full autonomy. But offering multiple perspectives has some intricacies (see also Morgan and Lave 1990). First, in some cases the effect of giving two perspectives may equal the effect of giving only one of them. If some risk information is presented in rather abstract and pallid terms *as well as* in concrete and vivid terms, and if we know the effect of vivid, dramatic presentations, then this latter effect may predictably dominate the effect of the abstract presentation. Second, even if such dominance is not to be expected, it is difficult to say what the result of offering multiple perspectives should be. Take the example of 50 percent survival versus 50 percent mortality. Will people make cognitively independent risk judgments for each mode of presentation? Will they then average their risk judgments somehow? Will each recipient pick cognitively only one presentation, the one that matches best his or her a priori perspective or attitude? Or will people form some hybrid representation and experience *cognitive flips*—oscillate the two perspectives? Offering multiple perspectives is an easy solution only as long as we do not know the specific effects and/or if we want to avoid paternalism at all costs. On a societal level (for example, when the communicators are industrial or political stakeholders), multiple perspectives may be the best solution; on a personal level, however, as in the physician/patient relationship, a more individualized communication strategy might be required.

CONCLUSIONS

I have described three types of ethical dilemmas that may arise in risk communication even when the people involved have only the best of intentions. The first kind occurs when the communicator faces a choice to provide or to withhold information. A typical example is the dilemma of a physician in deciding whether or not to inform a patient about a bad prognosis. Both actions, informing and not informing, have ethically problematic implications. The second kind of dilemma occurs when the communicator has a choice of what information to present. Different conceptions of risk may be legitimate and substantially correct but may have different effects on the recipients. An example is the labeling of a product with a warning referring to the manner of its production but irrelevant for its risk assessment. Again, any choice may be questioned for ethical reasons, either because the communicator is behaving paternalistically toward the recipient by not giving the wanted information or, on the contrary, gives in to the information demand at the cost of the well-being of the recipient. The third kind occurs when the communicator has a choice concerning how to present some information about a risk. All modes of presentation may be correct but again may have different effects on the recipient. For example, risk may be presented in terms of mortality or in terms of survival rates. Each choice may be questioned from an ethical point of view; the communicator may be either pursuing primarily personal interests or acting against the interests of the recipient to avoid any impression of pursuing personal interest.

The dilemmas are interesting for theoretical as well as practical reasons. At a theoretical level, they stimulate research questions, such as whether we can solve such dilemmas by offering multiple perspectives and, if so, how ambiguous nonvisual presentations are cognitively represented and whether there are cognitive flips analogous to the flips we experience with ambiguous visual figures. In the context of the present discussion about the basic premises of decision theory, they may be taken as examples with which to examine the validity or usefulness of a strict consequentialism. They are of practical relevance because they make us aware of the difficulties in communicating risks even when there is no conflict between egoistic and altruistic motives, the conflict most often discussed. Having good intentions does not spare communicators from the need to consider the effects of their messages. As Morgan and Lave (1990) pointed out, "Ethical [risk communication] is not just a matter of good intentions and a thoughtful analysis of motivations. Risk messages must be understood by recipients, and their impacts and effectiveness must be understood by the communicators" (p. 358). Clearly, more research on such effects is needed, and the practitioners of risk communication need to pay attention to the results. One could argue that one has only to study which mode of presentation or which conception of risk a communicator chooses in order to know, first, the communicator's intentions and, second, the effects of the message. But that would be too simple. The effects should be scientifically proved so that one can confront communicators with them and they cannot claim to have had no prior knowledge. The ethical problems of risk communication could be made more explicit and, if desired, strategies for balancing the effects could be developed. One criterion for a balanced message might be whether the message passes a kind of Turing test: The message is "perfect" if the recipient cannot tell whether the message comes from a proponent or an opponent of the risky activity or system in question. The better and more realistic solution, however, might be for communicators to state explicitly their beliefs and intentions and leave it to the recipients to agree or to disagree.

Chapter 18

The Ethics of Not Spending Money on Safety

Willem A. Wagenaar

Safety is like oil; there is a sufficient supply, but getting the last drops of it involves bigger and bigger marginal costs. With a limited budget, complete safety is unattainable. Hence all companies face the decision about how much to spend on safety and consequently about how much safety will be bought. Having made that decision, they are in the awkward position of knowing that a little more safety could be obtained in principle but will not be obtained in practice. What, then, is a company to tell the widow whose husband died in a preventable accident—"We are very sorry, but our profit was more important than your husband's life"? "Your husband's death is fully within the planned accident rate"? "The decision that your husband was going to run this risk was taken unanimously by the board of directors in London"? The ethical position of spending a limited budget on safety looks very unattractive when presented in this way, but in practice it is unavoidable. Moreover, against the background of a general theory of accident causation, the ethical problems may look a little less bleak.

THE PROBLEM WITH SLOGANS

My own experience with safety problems was acquired mainly in the oil production industry, where I noticed an attempt to ease this awkward position by means of two slogans. The first is, "Nothing is more important than safety." Thus, an unsafe operation will never be condoned because a deadline must be met, because production has to go on, or because costs must be cut. Every supervisor knows that after an accident, he or she cannot use the excuse that a known risk was accepted because one of the other goals was more important. The second slogan is, "Every accident is preventable." The implication is that the company strives for the target of zero accidents.

Analysis of the two slogans reveals that they simply deny the ethical dilemma. Even if nothing is *more* important than safety, operational achievements are still *equally* important, and since they provide the means to finance safety they cannot be held less important than safety. Take a drilling supervisor who is responsible for drilling holes in a jungle area. It is known that drilling operations in difficult country have a nonzero accident rate, not only because of the possibility of blowouts but also because of silly accidents, like the monkey man falling from a height of twenty meters, drillers getting their fingers squeezed in the open machinery, or the cook cutting his thumb with a kitchen knife. If the safety of these people is more important than drilling and accidents are certain to happen, is the company in essence asking the drilling supervisor to stop all operations and go home? Certainly not. But when an accident happens, will the supervisor be allowed to argue that he knew about the risks but decided that the operations had to go on? The dilemma is still there, despite the equal-importance rule. Similarly, the thesis that all accidents are preventable can be correct only when it is assumed that there are no budget limitations. The thesis that "all accidents are preventable on a limited budget" is definitely untrue. In hindsight, of course, every accident *looks* as if it could have been avoided, because every accident seems to have a preventable cause. But hindsight analysis does not reveal how many possible causes underly the total set of accidents and how costly the elimination of all these causes would be.

The example of the drilling supervisor reveals another aspect of the problem, that is, the level at which the relevant decisions are made. The drilling supervisor is not in the position to decide whether or not there will be any drilling. He is given a task, a large collection of equipment and supplies, and a crew. The situation is probably very much like previous drilling operations, which were approved by the same company. If there is no indication that this new operation is *extra* risky, there is no basis for stopping the drilling operation. Only higher up in the organization, where this specific operation is planned—or even higher, where drilling is defined as a core task of the company—does the power exist to decide whether or not the normal risks of drilling operations are compatible with the company's safety goals. At these higher levels, some officials must be in the schizophrenic position of proclaiming the equal-importance doctrine and planning a drilling operation in which it must be expected that one or more people will die. The *practical* problem of safety is at the lower end of the organization, where people run the risks and commit the errors that constitute the direct causes of accidents; the *ethical* problem is entirely at the higher end of the organization, where people decide what will be done and how it will be done.

THE GENERAL ACCIDENT CAUSATION MODEL

A more formal analysis of the locus of the safety problem is provided by the General Accident Causation Model that my colleagues and I have proposed (Wagenaar, Hudson, and Reason 1990). A summary of the model is presented

Figure 18.1 / The General Accident Causation Model

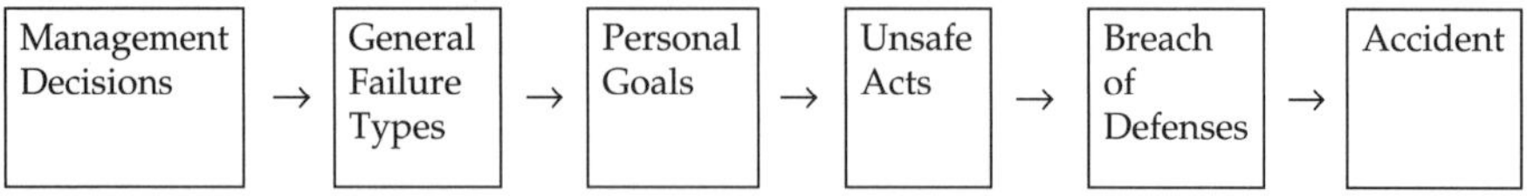

| Management Decisions | → | General Failure Types | → | Personal Goals | → | Unsafe Acts | → | Breach of Defenses | → | Accident |

in figure 18.1. Preceding the accident there is an unsafe act that is not compensated by one of the system's defense mechanisms. Sometimes such a defense mechanism is simply absent (for example, protective trousers for chain saw users are not available). Sometimes the defenses are made unoperative (the protective cover has been removed from a grinding machine). Unsafe acts, in this model, are called unsafe because they allow accidents to happen, not because they are recognized as unsafe *at the time*; in fact, most such unsafe acts have been committed many times previously without accident and therefore are not experienced as unsafe. A simple example is speeding in an automobile. The dominant property of unsafe acts is not their lack of safety but their usefulness. It is useful to speed, because it saves time. Unsafe acts are often violations of rules, but they help to attain one's goals; these goals are often created by the company itself, by means of structural deficits that we call *General Failure Types*. A complete list of areas in which General Failure Types occur is presented in table 18.1. (For a fuller discussion, see Wagenaar, Hudson, and Reason 1990; Wagenaar and others 1995.)

APPLYING THE MODEL: THE MONKEY MEN

In a drilling operation, a person called the monkey man works on a small platform, about twenty meters above the drilling rig. The floor of this monkey box is an open grid, because it is designed to hold the pipes that are lowered into the hole or lifted from the hole. The monkey man is so called because he jumps back and forth across the grid. The work of a monkey man is inherently unsafe, because of the design of the rig and the way in which pipes are handled. It is possible to design a rig without a monkey man, but

Table 18.1 / The Areas in Which General Failure Types Occur

Design	Incompatible goals
Hardware	Communication
Procedures	Organization
Error-enforcing conditions	Maintenance management
Housekeeping	Defenses
Training	

such a rig would be more expensive and would leave the problem that old rigs are phased out only gradually. In the General Accident Causation Model, then, the decision to drill holes is made at the management level; a General Failure Type is seen in the design of the monkey box; the monkey man develops a personal pride in doing the job efficiently and therefore makes somewhat larger jumps than is advisable; he breaches the defenses against falling by refusing to wear the safety belt, because it hinders his movement; finally, the monkey man falls, and from a height of twenty meters he is almost certain to be killed.

The analysis by means of the General Accident Causation Model is useful, because it reveals that the critical point is in the General Failure Type—the design of the monkey box. The decision to drill holes is not likely to be changed by a company with a mission to find and produce oil. Jumping across the monkey box is not likely to change, once the box is constructed in this manner. But who decides that there will be a monkey box, that the monkey box will be of this particular type, and that the life of the monkey man will be protected by a procedural rule about a safety belt? Who decides that the design is to remain unchanged, even after a number of fatalities?

Top management may be unaware of the specific problems of monkey men. If they are aware of the jumping and its dangers, they may believe that strengthening procedural controls will help. They will issue a slogan saying that drilling is not more important than safety and that therefore there is no reason to jump around without a safety belt. That action denies the perfectly normal personal goal of working quickly and making as large jumps as possible. It denies the empirical fact that monkey men *do* jump, no matter what you tell them. It is perfectly possible that the construction of monkey boxes has never been a subject of concrete discussions followed by a decision. The monkey box design stems from a time in which safety was not a big issue. When safety became important, the traditional tool of rules was tried first. Procedural rules are cheap, provided that one does not control whether they are followed and does not punish when they are violated. Control is expensive, because it is effective only when it is continuous or at least frequent and therefore is a never-ending cost. Punishment is also expensive, because it disrupts working relations and may, in the end, lead to the removal of valuable staff. Many companies are full of badly imposed procedural rules that are meant to compensate for design problems but do not in fact do so effectively. Boards of management that solve design problems through the introduction of procedures are not acting unethically, unless they are aware of the simple fact that rules cannot compensate for bad design. Hence, from the perspective of the management board, the jumping monkey men do not pose an ethical problem. The managers see only mischief or stupidity, which they attributed to the psychological make-up of the monkey men.

From the monkey man's perspective, the only ethical problem is related to the fact that he is violating a rule. But violating rules is perfectly normal in such operations. Some rules are incomprehensible; some are impossible to follow; some are wrong or even dangerous to follow; some are clumsy, failing to prescribe the obvious and most easy way to go about things. Rules about jumping in the monkey box conflict with the practice to which a monkey man is used. If all other monkey men violate these rules, can he be condemned for mimicking the behavior of the others?

ADDRESSING THE FAILURE: TYPES AND TOKENS

The analysis shows that the ethical problem arises only if it is recognized that the design of the monkey box is an instance of a design error. The error reveals that something is amiss in the design procedure, so that continuing to produce wrong designs is unethical. It is highly unlikely, however, that the design problem is limited to the monkey box. There are probably many aspects of the rig and the drilling operation that could be designed to yield a safer operation. In our analyses of accidents we have discovered four reasons for inadequate designs, listed in table 18.2.

Establishing that the monkey box is a bad design is only a start, and improving the monkey box does not in itself solve the problem, for the design of the monkey box is no more than a token of a larger problem *type*, to which management should address itself (see Wagenaar and Reason 1990). The type of problem in this cas, could be that management is not providing the designers feedback on accident rates or explicit instructions to base design practices upon accident rates. It could also be that the introduction of a newly designed rig is judged to be too expensive. Clearly the ethical dilemma is localized precisely in the stage in which management decides what to do when a structural cause of a General Failure Type is discovered. If it is the lack of feedback from user to designer, the ethical dilemma seems to be slight. Any organization that has designers and users should ensure proper feedback; that is not an ethical dilemma but a matter of good business practice. Even if conveying feedback costs money, it is expected to yield far more and therefore to be profitable.

Table 18.2 / Reasons for Inadequate Design

1. Lack of standardization
2. Insufficient knowledge of human needs and limitations
3. No adequate user/designer communication before, during, or after the design phase
4. Time or financial constraints

If on the other hand financial constraints prohibit the design of better rigs, we seem to be back where we started, with the impossibility of buying complete safety on a limited budget. But the analysis has changed the situation significantly. When management was trying to address the problem of accidents by means of instructions to the staff, they were not conscious of an ethical dilemma. Now it is realized that there is a design problem and furthermore that the problem is caused by financial constraints. Hence management will now be aware that a conscious decision must be made about how much should be spent on the design of drilling rigs, taking into account the relevant information about accident rates. Thus our analysis has the power to reduce the problem either to one of good business practice or to an explicit decision problem. In the latter case the ethical dilemma has not disappeared, but its explicit structure has made it manageable. I will pursue this line of thinking later in the chapter but first I will present a second example, just to make the sort of analysis that I propose perfectly clear.

A CASE OF H₂S POISONING

Mr. A is a well-known chemist who came to the Netherlands from abroad. It is Friday afternoon, and he wants to finish an experiment for an important client. In order to do this, he needs a certain piece of equipment. Because there is a shortage of maintenance personnel, the equipment has not been properly maintained and cannot be used. He could use another piece of equipment, but it has a defective connector; nobody had reported the fact, so it was not repaired. He looks around the laboratory for a connector, goes to the storage room, but finds no spare connector. Mr. A is an ambitious man and does not want to wait till after the weekend. He becomes irritated and tries to find another solution. He discovers that another instrument has the connector he needs on it. Mr. A decides that he will remove the connector from this equipment and use it. He has attended a course on connectors, but since he does not understand Dutch, he did not learn the elementary skills for this job. Nobody checked whether he had acquired the essential knowledge. Colleagues have never explained to him how connectors are replaced, because there are no scheduled work discussions. Relevant procedure instructions are available only in Dutch. English instructions are available in the library, but Mr. A does not know that. This particular connector turns clockwise instead of counterclockwise. Mr. A does not know that, but he should notice it from the difficulty of turning it. Unfortunately the proper wrench is missing, so he uses a heavy-duty wrench instead. With this wrench he does not feel the difficulty, and the connector breaks loose. The system is still in open connection with the H₂S supply, and Mr. A is overcome by the poisonous gas.

Table 18.3 / Indicators of Training Problems

1. Employees do not know how to do their jobs.
2. On-the-job training period exceeds normal length.
3. Excessive supervision is needed.
4. Excessive number of people are needed to do the job.
5. Job execution is not meeting expected quality (with respect to time, end product, waste).

This accident scenario is full of indicators of General Failure Types. I will concentrate on indicators signaling that something is wrong with training. Table 18.3 lists the indicators for training problems.

These indicators are to be taken as diagnostic symptoms, not as signals of training problems alone. For instance, quality problems may also indicate the presence of error-enforcing conditions, such as fatigue or heat. In the case of Mr. A, there are at least two symptoms related to training problems: He does not know how to do the job, and he learned too little from on-the-job training. Hence we may suspect that this laboratory suffers from a General Failure Type in the area of training. As in a medical diagnosis, this suspicion can be confirmed by determining whether any causes of training problems are present. The causes of training problems are listed in table 18.4.

Obviously several of these structural deficits are present in Mr. A's organization. There was no assessment of the level of training that Mr. A (or anybody else) reached in the course. Mr. A should not have been selected for the course, because he does not understand the language in which it was taught. His prior education was not checked. These causes are definitely not limited to Mr. A or this particular course; they are affecting the effectiveness of the whole training program in this company, which means that a good deal of money is wasted.

The normal reaction to an accident like Mr. A's would be to punish or even fire him, if he survives the poisoning. But this reaction is based on the belief that the source of the problem is within Mr. A and that the company cannot use the accident for its own improvement. I, on the other hand, would argue that there is nothing wrong with Mr. A, apart from the fact that he is

Table 18.4 / Reasons for Training Problems

1. Trainee obtains insufficient experience after the training.
2. Trainee's prior education not compatible with training program.
3. Ineffective or no selection of trainees.
4. No structured planning of training program.
5. No assessment of training results.
6. Low training standards.

ambitious and somewhat cantankerous. He felt seriously offended when he was sent to a course on connectors, which as a scientist he judged far below his level. So he sat through the course without mentioning that he did not understand the language. But ambition and obstinacy are qualities that most scientists have, almost by definition. There is no guarantee that hiring another scientist will improve the situation one bit. Rather, the problem is how one can operate a safe laboratory full of smart-alecks. The answer is that General Failure Types need to be found and removed, and Mr. A's accident is an excellent opportunity.

The proper selection of trainees and the assessment of their skills after the training will cost a little money but will prove to be a good investment. Hence the removal of this General Failure Type is a matter of good business practice. It is also a matter of ethics, because blaming the person instead of the organization, apart from being ineffective, is not fair. It is unfair to Mr. A and also unfair to others who, in the future, will cause accidents for the same reasons.

ETHICS AND GOOD BUSINESS PRACTICE

The case of redesigning the monkey box made explicit the decision problem of trading safety for money. One may wonder whether keeping a structural deficit in the organization to save money will have an effect on safety alone or whether it will not, for instance, affect product quality or environmental pollution. Consider that the handling of pipes on a conventional rig is so time and labor intensive that it will be limited to the minimum. The tendency to lift the pipes during the drilling operation—for measurement or inspection, for instance—will be minimal. The result might be that, in the end, more holes have to be abandoned, or that blowouts are a little more probable, or that the wells are slightly less productive. One can build a good case for the argument that the monkey box problem relates not only to the safety of the monkey man but also to the quality of the entire operation. A study by the British Government (UK Health and Safety Executive 1993) revealed that, on average, investments in safety lead to increased efficiency or to a cost reduction that more than pays back the initial investment. This fact is often obscured because budgets are kept separate; the profit is not in the area where the investment was made. A simple example: The expenditure of buying seat belts leads to a huge reduction of the costs of treating victims of automobile accidents. The individual car buyer notices the expenditure, not the corresponding cost reduction for insurance companies or society at large. Another factor that obscures the profits of investment in safety is the short time horizon chosen for accounting. The full effect cannot be expected to be seen in the year in which the expenditure is made.

It is my belief that the ethical dilemma of trading safety for money is often the product of keeping budgets separate and of limiting comparison of effects to short time horizons. Within the scope of the entire company, and measured over a reasonably long time horizon, spending money on safety will usually be profitable, as long as the money is spent wisely. Wisdom can be guaranteed by basing investments upon an analysis of General Failure Types that threaten the safety of a company's operations. Money should not be spent on issues that do not constitute the real causes of a company's accidents. For instance, the production of multicolored posters in three sizes and ten languages, telling monkey men not to make dangerous jumps across the monkey box, is a waste of money, because lack of knowledge is not the cause of the problem. Spending money without a proper analysis is like administering a medication without first making a diagnosis.

A proper analysis of safety problems usually leads to affordable and even profitable safety measures. Not taking these measures leads to a violation of ethical principles. On the other hand, no ethical principle may force a company to take safety measures beyond what follows from a systematic analysis, which will determine a level of investment that has an attainable optimum. That is the reason why I believe there is no real dilemma. Once the optimal level of investment in safety has been reached, the widow who lost her husband in an industrial accident can be told, "We are very sorry for you, but we spent as much money on safety as could be spent wisely." "We did our very best to avoid this accident." "The entire management considers the occurrence of such accidents fully unacceptable." This still does not help the widow, but it is a great deal less cynical.

OBSTACLES TO AN ETHICAL BALANCE

In practice, of course, the situation is not as rosy as I have described. One reason is that short time horizons and separate budgeting, which force people to balance money against safety in a quite unethical manner, are the rule rather than the exception. Managers are evaluated over short time spans and within their own parts of the operation, whereas the profits of investment in safety may pop up in entirely different areas.

A worse problem, however, is that society at large tends to create unfavorable conditions that prevent the development of optimal safety strategies. Take as an example the grounding of the *Exxon Valdez* on the coast of Alaska. Exxon was held responsible and ordered to pay several billion dollars toward the cost of the clean-up. The size of the fine prevents the tanker operation from becoming safer. Future accidents must be avoided at any price, and a strategy for safety improvement can never provide the necessary guarantees. Therefore there is a tendency within the large oil companies to declare tanker transport as not belonging to the core business of the company and leaving it to other, smaller companies. These smaller companies are less safe, but they are also less wealthy, so that they do not run the risk of being fined billions. The net effect is a decrease in safety, which is the opposite of what was intended by the imposition of the fines. The proper analysis that should follow the *Exxon Valdez* accident is not made, and the improvements it would show to be needed do not happen.

Another example of conditions unfavorable to safety is the nationalization of the work force. Oil companies tend to be large internationals, sending their own staff into every country that has oil supplies. From the point of safety this practice is beneficial, because in this way expertise is brought in and transmitted most effectively. The "expats" (for expatriots), as the foreign staff are called, are supplemented by a staff of local people, usually unskilled or marginally skilled hands, and a slowly increasing number of more highly trained technicians and officials. In quite a few countries there is now a tendency to limit the number of expats and force oil companies to hire substantial numbers of locals, even when not enough properly educated staff are available. There are several ways in which the resulting problem can be met. One is to slow down operations and wait till the employees have reached the proper training levels. That is of course not a very attractive option and often is not even permitted by the local government. A second reaction is to stop operations and leave the country. That is an even less attractive alternative and will mean only that less responsible companies come in and pick up the business. A third possibility, since the quota of local employees is expressed in proportions, is to hire enormous numbers of locals, in order to keep enough expats to run the operation. That may work, but it will definitely not promote safety. The crux of the matter is that such governments are not interested in safety and the lives of employees in the first place. Consequently the companies are not allowed to develop appropriate safety strategies.

These two examples illustrate that ethical problems with respect to safety can be aggravated by the societies in which companies operate, even to a level where the company cannot handle them any more. Such societies get the type of ethics that they impose and the accident rate that they deserve. I predict that the United States will experience a host of tanker accidents, because of the ban on the companies that are large enough to afford a sound safety strategy. Ethics in business must be affordable, and it *is* affordable when a company is large enough to apply wide horizons both in time and across many operations.

Commentary

The Business Ethics of Risk, Reasoning, and Decision Making

Patricia H. Werhane

T
he chapters in this section have focused on the psychological, social, and ethical aspects of risk, risk analysis, and our perception and communication of risks, harms, and benefits. A number of themes are evident in these different approaches. Some of the themes exemplify the distinction between the empirical and the normative; others focus on the notion of cognitive frames, or what I shall call *conceptual schemes*; and all raise questions of the role of the affective imagination, or what I shall call *moral imagination*, in business ethics and in moral decision making. These themes give us insights into the richness of these papers and illustrate how the methods of social scientists and those of philosophers both diverge and intersect with respect to ethical issues in business.

Social scientists sometimes accuse philosophers, particularly philosophers who address the problems of business ethics, of being nonempirical; that is, we do not engage in empirical research, we have a blatant disregard for data and facts, and we are preoccupied with the normative, not the descriptive. Furthermore, they say, we virtually ignore causal connections or influences from culture and from social exchanges, the social, political, and natural environment in which things occur and people engage in activities. Instead we concentrate on the individual as an autonomous decision maker in isolation from—and apparently causally unaffected by—situation, history, and social relationships. As a result, our normative focus is primarily on individual moral dilemmas and less on organizational or systemic issues.

Moreover, according to this view, philosophers engaging in normative analysis tend to appeal to the perspective of a disinterested or ideal spectator; they take a Rawlsian view from behind a veil of ignorance (Rawls 1971) or what Thomas Nagel once called a "view from nowhere" (Nagel 1989), where the emphasis is on individuals making autonomous, usually rational, moral judgments from an idealized ivory tower or from a purely impartial or objective perspective. As a result, philosophers tend to focus on rationality as the ideal if not the common mode of human motivation and behavior, ignoring the role and influence of the affective side of human nature.

These accusations, while exaggerated, are partly true. Because they are partly true, looking at them in more detail will help to sort out a philosophical approach, in contrast to a social science approach, to the themes of the papers in this section and, it is hoped, give the reader some other perspectives on the important issues raised in these chapters.

Philosophers and social scientists commonly distinguish between empirical, descriptive, or factual analysis and a normative or prescriptive analysis. This distinction, while not clear-cut, is nevertheless useful in clarifying the differences between a social science and a philosophical approach to business ethics (Goodpaster 1984; Donaldson 1994; Werhane 1994; Weaver and Trevino 1994). By and large, philosophical approaches in ethics are nonempirical. Philosophers do not study how people behave, how people react to risk, how self-interested behavior affects choices or collective welfare, or even how people think about the environment. Philosophers depend little on prediction or explanation, nor do they focus on causal factors of behavior, for at least one reason. While philosophers disagree about the nature, scope, and extent of human freedom, most would conclude that human action is not predetermined, and the notion of human freedom is not a trivial concept. Most philosophers assume that while human behavior is in a causal nexus, a causal explanation is not enough, by itself, to account for human action. Human beings are capable of making choices from alternatives that reformulate the causal nexus—that is, that create change.

In business ethics there is one respect with which philosophers do engage in descriptive analysis. Philosophers use cases—real cases involving actual business situations—and in fact one cannot teach or think about applied ethics without focusing on specific cases, issues, and dilemmas. But rather than do empirical research they usually steal explanations about human nature from social scientist friends.

The normative aspect of business ethics focuses not merely on individuals but more generally on what individuals, corporations, other institutions, and even political economies ought to do—what standards or principles come to bear on these persons and institutions in their decision making, what codes or laws should or should not be in place, and what values are or should be operative. I shall say more about the normative aspect of business ethics later in the chapter.

The normative/descriptive distinction is helpful in clarifying a number of points in the chapters in this section. Jonathan Baron, in chapter 10, "Do No Harm," points out correctly that most ethical theories conclude that doing or causing harm is wrong, all things considered. At the same time, there is an asymmetry of moral judgments. We are almost always held responsible for harms we cause, but we are not always held accountable to the same degree for harms we fail to prevent. Thinking about this distinction between acts and omissions, one often finds a difference in intention that accounts for the difference in commitment to the negative injunction. That is, almost everyone is morally committed not to harm others deliberately but not everyone is so absolutely committed to do good. But even when the intentions are the same, Baron points out, omissions usually come out ahead of positive rules; that is, while we are agreed that harming others is wrong, there is less agreement on how one should act to prevent harm or to produce good.

I would argue that the reason might not be merely that one perceives omissions differently from acts but that when one links acts and omissions to harm and good the distinction becomes more clear-cut. Baron argues rightly that a harm may be justified if it produces a greater good, and many philosophers would agree. But the difficult question is, What is the "greater good"? Baron uses the example of a physician who overrides the desires of a patient in treating the patient's condition. Some philosophers would object to that act because, they would contend, autonomy is the greater good, more important than even the health of the patient, assuming that the person is a sane, conscious adult (Beauchamp and Childress 1994). And this is a difficulty. Beginning with the pre-Socratics, a multitude of theories of the good have been proposed. But as Michael Walzer (1994) recently pointed out, while we can usually agree about what constitutes a harm (for example, murder or rape), any empirical study of what is held to be the good would be subject to challenge by other empirical studies of the same phenomenon. Given that we can seldom agree on what the good is, it may turn out that although one is never justified in creating or causing a net quantity of harm, one is not always obligated in the same way to produce good. In philosophical language, this is the claim that we always have perfect duties not to harm others deliberately because it is always a wrong but we have only imperfect duties to come to another's assistance, because it is not always perfectly good to do so (A. Smith [1759]1976). Thus the fact of the acts/omissions distinction is grounded in more normative claims.

The normative/descriptive distinction is important in clarifying why human beings can act according to their ideals, or agree to be coerced by regulation into doing so, but actually do not always do so. Max Bazerman, Kimberly Wade-Benzoni, and Francisco Benzoni observe in chapter 14 that although individuals and organizations appear to care deeply about the environment, their behavior belies these attitudes. This disjunction between what people think they should do (individually and/or collectively) and how they in fact behave is explained, in part, by the fact that their normative ideals are just that—ideals that they espouse, norms by which they judge themselves and others.

The distinction between how we act and what we hold as norms also accounts for the fact that we do not evaluate each other's behavior or that of our institutions on the basis of how individuals or organizations have behaved in the past or historical or cultural modes of behavior. This point is important in understanding George Loewenstein's analysis. Loewenstein argues in chapter 11 that unethical business behavior—and, indeed, unethical behavior in general—is caused by our overriding interest in ourselves. Moreover, most of us are parochial in our vision. We tend to be disproportionately influenced by short-term costs and benefits; we are less likely to harm identifiable persons than people who are merely statistical others, despite the injustice of such actions. In general, we are egoists, not altruists; short-term, not long-term, reward seekers; and uncaring about others whom we do not know or cannot identify.

This bleak picture of human behavior echoes only partly what Adam Smith noticed two centuries ago. Smith argued that each of us is motivated by both selfish and social passions; unlike Loewenstein, he saw human beings as egoists and altruists in equal measure. But most of us are small-minded, Smith continued. We do not have a clear picture of global events or of human beings as a species, and we act accordingly, caring most about those we know or are related to, focusing on short-term rather than long-term rewards for ourselves, our families, and our friends (A. Smith [1759] 1976; Werhane 1989).

Smith made an important distinction, however, that is not evident in Loewenstein's chapter. He argued that how we behave is different from how we think we ought to act. Principles of prudence, benevolence, and justice set the norms for how we ought to act when we act in our self-interest (the norm of prudence), when we interact with others (benevolence), and when we deal with strangers or statistical subjects (justice). These norms, Smith thought, could be enacted and enforced by moral rules. So despite our small-mindedness and parochialism—and even, among some of us, selfishness—we need not and do not always behave inhumanely, nor do we admire or approve of greed, unkindness, or injustice. Indeed, some of us engage in supererogatory behavior, acting beyond any ordinary expectations. While Loewenstein has adequately accounted for the fact of unethical behavior, he neglects another fact. Human beings do not always behave predictably or selfishly, even when it is to their benefit to do so; indeed, we can and do behave prudently, benevolently, and even not unjustly.

The normative/descriptive distinction is also helpful in explaining why, as Baruch Fischhoff notices, most of us contend that in theory there are no risks that qualify as "acceptable," while in fact most of us take a number of risks every day and expect others to do so as well. What we do and how we behave are not in agreement, much of the time, with the ways in which we evaluate behavior and the norms we use for those evaluations. While this discrepancy is due, in part, to the fact that everyone has different perceptions of risk (a point to which I shall return later in this chapter), it is also due in no little part to the descriptive/normative dichotomy. Indeed, it is tempting to argue that human beings may be the only species that is able to propose behavioral standards while not always—indeed, sometimes seldom—acting in accordance with those standards, despite the fact that most standards are viable and achievable, albeit with some sacrifice of short-term comfort or rewards. The same is clearly true in the case of the environmental ideals of sustainable development we set for the globe while failing to practice the ideals in our daily lives.

While the descriptive/normative distinction is important in sorting out different methodological approaches to issues in ethics, nevertheless it is clear that the descriptive and normative overlap. Normative ethics requires some content (that is, facts, cases, data), and empirical studies employ a methodology that includes a set of assumptions and a theoretical framework that are, in part, normative. That set of assumptions and that framework set the parameters for the study in question and function as a control for the kinds of outcomes produced. For example, as Robyn Dawes points out in his penetrating critique of so-called expert witnesses, our perception and acceptance of what counts as an "expert" affect the way we value the expertise. The result is that we often accept advice from "experts" that simply affirms what we know already; it does not add value to what we know. Only by changing our definition of what it means to be an "expert" and assumptions about *expert advice* can we also change what we expect from these professionals.

How does the descriptive/normative distinction affect what one does in business ethics? To understand that, one must appeal to a third distinction, that of metaethics. Using this third approach philosophers find it important to analyze the nature of institutions such as the modern corporation and to distinguish individual from organizational or collective moral decision making. One important philosophical question is whether one can make sense out of collective moral agency, a question also raised by social scientists in their longstanding debate about methodological individualism. That debate goes too far afield from the present context for discussion here, but what is important both for social scientists and for philosophers is that one can sort out and distinguish individual, organizational, and collective descriptions and normative judgments. A simple matrix (next page) illustrates these distinctions (Goodpaster 1983). Collective judgments about the environment or about the extent of risk are often different from individual judgments, and indeed, that fact should not be surprising, particularly when one is referring to the collective judgments of regulators or governments. Where the discussion becomes interesting is the area of organizational judgments—for example, actions by corporations sometimes are in their own collective self-interest, at other times may reflect merely the interests of its managers, and at still other times appear to take the general welfare into account.

Stakeholder theory is particularly helpful for metaethical analysis. A stakeholder approach sorts out descriptively who in a particular context is affected and how, and, normatively, what responsibilities each party has to

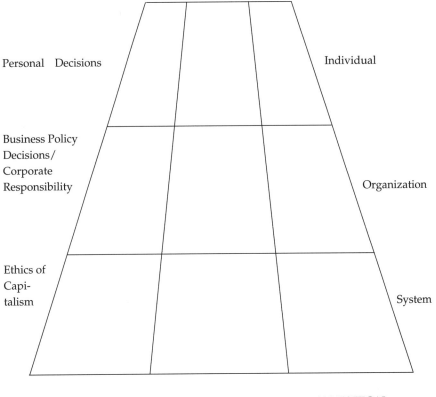

Personal   Decisions

Individual

Business Policy
Decisions/
Corporate
Responsibility

Organization

Ethics of
Capi-
talism

System

DESCRIPTIVE   NORMATIVE   ANALYTICAL
(METAETHICAL)

the other. Stakeholders are any persons, social groups, collectives, institutions, political/economic systems, or even the ecosystem that affects, participates in, or is affected by a particular situation, dilemma, or action (Freeman and Gilbert 1988). The sorting out of these subjects and thus the subject matter for business ethics helps to delineate a variety of approaches to ethical issues. Individual and collective judgments on risk, for example, differ from each other in important respects. Loewenstein points out that when one is faced with real, specific individuals, one is less likely to harm them or treat them unjustly than if one is faced with a nonidentifiable collective group of people. Stakeholder theory can be very effective in bringing to attention individuals affected by a particular decision if one thinks of each stakeholder concretely as an individual, a particular individual or organization, not as a statistical other. Wagenaar's analysis of the failure of rules to enforce safety is an example of how it is that we identify more closely with the particular than the general. Similarly, when one particularizes the oil rig worker, for example, the steps one takes to reduce his risks are quite different from those one would take thinking of oil rig workers as part of a collective group of employees.

Obviously, all three approaches—the descriptive, the normative, and the metaethical, or analytic—overlap. What is important is that neither philosophers nor social scientists work at only one kind of approach and a good deal of the time social scientists and philosophers engage in metaethical analysis. Philosophers as metaethicists are often accused of being pre-Darwinian, attempting to appeal to impartial decisions that are without context, ahistorical, "views from nowhere." Yet this characterization is only partly true. From a philosopher's point of view, in business ethics one begins with a case, a particular situation or set of situations. But one does more than merely focus on a particular case or set of empirical data. Given a set of facts, one then steps back from the case, analyzes it using stakeholder theory, sorts out individual from collective decision makers, and appeals to normative frameworks for moral reasoning and moral standards in an attempt to reach some resolutions of the dilemmas a particular case presents. In stepping back, the philosopher, like the social psychologist, is not functioning at the normative level alone but also engaging in analysis as well. One asks questions such as, What is the best decision or solution that produces the least harm or most benefits? One appeals to good reasons and commonly accepted moral rules. One asks whether or not this decision or solution is the best, all things considered; whether it is generalizable to other similar situations; and, ideally, whether it would contribute positively to our moral life. This is not merely a view from nowhere or from behind a veil of ignorance; it is a view from somewhere, a somewhere that other people and other organizations can understand, albeit disengaged from the particular situation so that one can extract more general moral evaluations that set precedents and have wide application.

Such techniques are not lost on the social scientists. For example, William Wagenaar examines a series of cases in which setting out rules for safety precautions has little effect on people. Those cases become models for Wagenaar's more general conclusions concerning the role of rules and how one must deal with issues of safety. Similarly, Robyn Dawes's case of what he calls the "decremental" validity of alleged evidence for child sexual abuse, given by so-called experts, illustrates his more general conclusions about the role of expert witnesses.

Nevertheless, even a metaethical "disengaged view from somewhere" may fail to take into account a phenomenon most social scientists have dealt with for some time, the fact that human beings experience the world through conceptual frames. This is what Ann McGill calls *causal frames* and what Joshua Klayman calls *cognitive processes*; I shall refer to them as *conceptual schemes*. Moreover, some philosophers neglect the affective side of human conduct in the context of ethics, what I shall call moral imagination.

Beginning with Immanuel Kant, philosophers and psychologists have argued that each of us perceives and experiences through a schema or series of conceptual schemes that determine how we select, organize, filter, and focus our perceptions. Indeed, as one contemporary philosopher succinctly states, "Our conceptual scheme mediates even our most basic perceptual experiences" (Railton 1986, 172). There is no one model for these schemes; that is, they are not all formal concepts that structure our experience, as Kant thought. Rather, these conceptual schemes also take the form of images, assumptions, stories or myths, and theories. They frame our perceptions and guide the ways in which we recognize, react to, and conceptually organize the world. Each of us has, or is capable of having, a number of overlapping conceptual schemes that may function differently in different contexts and that can be manipulated and changed by us or by our social environment. "Conceptual schemes ... are ways of organizing experience; they are systems of categories that give form to the data of sensation; they are points of view from which individuals, cultures, or [historical] periods survey the passing scene" (Davidson 1974, 5). Indeed, following Kant, most philosophers today claim that one cannot experience the world except through some conceptual scheme or frame. Schemes are socially learned and altered through language, religion, culture, and educational upbringing. Moreover, such schemes are not merely cognitive, although the focus in many chapters of this part is on cognitive framing; we also color our experiences with our emotions, interests, and focus (Kant [1785]1959; Senge 1990, chapter 10).

The role of conceptual schemes, at least in the form of causal or cognitive frames, is a theme that runs through a number of chapters in this section. Some cognitive frames are in the form of causal schemes that delineate causal relationships in certain ways. Ann McGill discusses the ways in which the kind of causal background one selects for explanation affects that explanation. Moreover, people often search for a causal explanation that fits with their perceptions, with their attitudes or biases, or with what they would like to have been the cause. Causal explanations are sometimes selected to exempt individuals or institutions from blame. For example, Mercedes-Benz recently denied responsibility for the poor performance of one of its top-of-the-line automobiles, blaming the performance on the drivers of this model. It turned out that the engineering of the model in question was indeed responsible, but the initial manipulation of this causal frame at first deflected attention from Mercedes-Benz for liability (Carley 1995).

Joshua Klayman notes that most human beings are resistant to change, in particular to initiating change in the middle of a project. This resistance, I suggest, is due to a reluctance to change one's cognitive processing scheme; indeed, it may in part be due to the fact that it is difficult to recognize what scheme is at work. This resistance to change skews our hypothesis testing so that we often frame phenomena to exclude certain kinds of data. Thus, we often resist recognizing and taking responsibility for harms we create. This tendency has had disastrous outcomes for a number of companies, as John Darley illustrates in his chapter in part 1; for example, Goodrich's failure to recognize a problem led to unethical behavior. Max Bazerman and his colleagues also write about what they call "framing effects" that create cognitive biases. These framing effects are also often self-enhancing. One can get trapped in such a frame or cognitive scheme that prevents one from being aware of one's own environmentally destructive behavior or skews judgments of fairness about distributions of scarce resources. Let me give another illustration.

During the Pinto era, Dennis Gioia, now a professor of organizational behavior at Pennsylvania State University, was an employee at Ford, in charge of recalls of defective automobiles. Gioia's job was to orchestrate their recall program; he identified problems that might require a recall and organized the recalls themselves. Gioia had always thought of himself as an extremely moral and socially responsible person. Yet he relates how, while functioning as recall coordinator, he was aware of a number of Pintos that had burst into flames on impact, but he failed to recommend the Pinto's recall. He was convinced through his own reasoning and by other seemingly thoughtful managers not to recall those cars, because, it was argued, the evidence was not conclusive that the Pinto was defective; many subcompact autos had similar dreadful accidents; and the Pinto was a popular, best-selling auto. Gioia even drove a Pinto and sold one to his sister. Gioia has written, "In the context of the times my actions were *legal* . . . they were in accord with accepted professional standards and codes of conduct [at Ford]" (Gioia 1992, 384; Werhane 1996).

Looking back on this scenario Gioia (1992) concluded:

> My own schematized (scripted) knowledge influenced me to perceive recall issues in terms of the prevailing decision environment and to unconsciously overlook key features of the Pinto case, mainly because they did not fit an existing script. Although the outcomes of the case carry retrospectively obvious ethical overtones, the schemas driving my perceptions and actions precluded consideration of the issues in ethical terms because the scripts did not include ethical dimensions. (p. 385)

Thus the risk to drivers of Pintos because of the gas tank location was simply not recognized.

In analyzing risk, Baruch Fischhoff argues that all risks are "perceived." That is, one cannot and does not deal with risk or risk assessment except through some cognitive frame or other. Even risk experts infect their analyses with judgments that are not purely objective. If the way one frames the notion of risk affects one's perceptions of risk, then, as Helmut Jungermann points out, how one communicates information on risk can have a significant effect on public perception and opinion. The communicator therefore has enormous responsibility for the mode of communication. Part of this responsibility is to find out how various segments of the public frame their experiences and how they will interpret what is presented.

The discussion of cognitive frames, conceptual schemes, and cognitive biases points to two conclusions. First, not all conceptual schemes are cognitive. The biases with which we frame experiences are often triggered by interests, desires, emotions, and feelings. Second, all that we experience is known through some scheme or frame. The ideal may be pure objectivity, but such an ideal is unobtainable, as Werner Heisenberg taught us some eighty years ago (Heisenberg 1958). If the very act of observing affects the observed, then any approach to a subject affects the subject. In this case, we are presented with a dilemma. How can one ever know in what frame one is operating, and how is one able to evaluate whether or not an allegedly parochial or biased frame is biased? How does one develop the ability to get out of a particular scheme, when should one do so, and on what basis?

The answers to these questions are difficult. Two suggestions present themselves as possibilities. First, as Donald Davidson (1974) carefully argued in questioning the possibility of this form of conceptual relativism, "Different points of view [different conceptual schemes] make sense, but only if there is a common coordinate system on which to plot them; yet the existence of a common system belies the claim of dramatic incomparability" (p. 5). What is meant by a "common coordinate system" would be the subject of a different paper. Ludwig Wittgenstein, Richard Rorty, and Hilary Putnam, for example, all argue, in different ways, that the common system is language (Rorty 1993). In their view, the fact that we communicate, that we understand each other, that we sometimes understand the notion of a conceptual scheme or cognitive frame, and that we are sometimes even able to change the conceptual scheme at work can be accounted for only by postulating a common coordinate system that is the basis for language and communication.

An appeal to what Amartya Sen calls "positional objectivity" helps to clarify this point. According to Sen (1993), "What we can observe depends on our position vis-à-vis the objects of observation. . . . Positionally dependent observations, beliefs, and actions are central to our knowledge and practical reason" (p. 126).

Position dependency defines the way in which the object appears "from a delineated somewhere." This "delineated somewhere," however, is positionally objective. That is, any person in that position will make similar observations, according to Sen. The parameters of positionality are not merely spatial but could involve a shared schema. For example, Gioia and his cohorts at Ford all had access to the same data about the Pinto, and from their schema they all viewed that data similarly. Gioia's decision not to recall the Pinto could be defended as a positionally objective belief based on the ways in which managers at Ford processed information on automobile crashes.

A positionally objective point of view could be mistaken, however, if it did not take into account all available information, and in most cases one need not accept a positionally objective view. Because of the variety of schema with which one can shape a position, almost any position has alternatives, and almost every position has its critics. According to Sen, we often engage in "trans-positional" assessments or what Sen also calls a "constructed 'view from nowhere.' " A trans-positional view from nowhere is a constructed critique of a particular conceptual scheme, and no positionally objective view is merely relative nor immune from challenge. This sort of assessment involves comparing various positionally objective points of view to see if one can make coherent sense of them and develop some general theories about what is being observed. These trans-positional assessments are *constructed* views from nowhere, because they too depend on the conceptual scheme of the assessors. From a trans-positional point of view, conceptual schemes themselves can be questioned on the basis of their coherence and/or their explanatory scope. Although that challenge could be conducted only from another conceptual scheme, that assessment could take into account a variety of points of view. Revisions of the scheme in question might produce another conceptual scheme that more adequately or more comprehensively explained or took into account a range of phenomena or incidents (Sen 1993).

At this point I shall engage in speculation. I suspect that merely engaging in a Rawlsian or Senian rational approach is not enough, by itself, to help us disengage ourselves from a particular scheme. It is not enough because the notion of rationality one employs is often part of the conceptual scheme in which one is embedded. Even Rawls admits now that his approach to principles of justice is a Western post-Hellenistic approach deeply embedded in rights theory and a Western conception of justice (Rawls 1993). Simply taking an allegedly impartial perspective is not always enough, in itself, to avoid problems such as the Pinto example, since from a Ford-biased rational scheme the Pinto accidents were an expected part of manufacturing small automobiles. Thus moral reasoning, by itself, is not enough to assure that many disasters in business can be avoided.

What I want to suggest, then, is that in addition to moral reasoning there is an affective focus of business ethics, a focus on the ability to develop awareness of, evaluate, and change one's conceptual scheme. This ability, I shall argue, is what I call the development of moral imagination.

Moral imagination is not a new term. It was introduced into philosophical thinking in the moral psychology of Adam Smith. In *A Theory of Moral Sentiments*, Smith argued that sympathy is a general principle of "fellow-understanding" each of us has that enables us to understand the passions and interests of another, even if we feel resentment or even abhorrence toward those passions or toward that person. Imagination is important in this scheme, because it is through imagination that one is able to recreate mentally the feelings, passions, and even the point of view of another. In this imaginative sympathetic process one does not literally feel the passion of another, but one is able to understand what another is experiencing from that person's perspective and therefore to understand what another is feeling, even when one is revolted by that feeling. I might, then, understand how someone like a mass murderer feels, although I could not approve of his feelings and passions. Imagination is also useful in self-evaluation, allowing one to look at oneself from the point of view of another.

Smith, like his teacher David Hume, broke with a rationalist tradition by linking moral judgment to moral sentiment. According to Smith, sympathy and imagination are necessary for moral judgment, since one must first understand what another feels or engage in imaginative self-evaluation in order to experience a sentiment of approval or disapproval, a sentiment that is the basis for judgment. Sympathy with imagination allows us to disengage ourselves and evaluate ourselves and others dispassionately or impartially. These impartial judgments form the basis of moral rules, those rules that impartial people would agree that society should adopt as measures of human behavior (Smith [1759]1976).

Smith's work is limited by his faculty psychology and his assumption that all of us deal with the world in the same way—through the conceptual scheme of a Scottish gentleman. On his assumption one can more easily project and sympathize with another person or make self-evaluations and actually be correct a good deal of the time. But Smith's analysis is prescient, because it forms the basis for much of the contemporary discussion of moral imagination as the ability to empathize, to understand another point of view or one's own more clearly, and be creative in ethical decision making.

Using Smith's analysis as a base, we can ask, What, in contemporary terms, is moral imagination? Imagination is "moral" when it is evaluative of individual and collective human behavior. It includes "the ability to imaginatively discern various possibilities for acting within a given situation and to envision the potential help and harm that are likely to result from a given action" (Johnson 1993, 202).

Moral imagination consists, first, in being aware of one's situation, including both the "script" or conceptual scheme functioning in that situation and possible moral conflicts or dilemmas that might arise in that situation. Moral imagination also entails some ability to revamp one's conceptual scheme to take into account new possibilities within the scope of one's situation, including the ability to envision and actualize possibilities that are not context dependent. Moral imagination also includes the ability to evaluate. The phenomenon of moral imagination explains the fact that one can get at a distance from a particular operative conceptual scheme and make evaluative judgments, not merely about actions but also about the ways in which people and organizations structure their experiences and decisions. Without moral imagination one could not engage in the level of analysis apparent in the chapters in this section.

That people can be imaginative is difficult to prove; that there is often a paucity of moral imagination in important decision contexts is evident. What is missing, for example, in the "expert witness" examples Robyn Dawes describes is moral imagination. As Dennis Gioia did when he was at Ford, these expert witnesses often think they *are* experts, that they are doing the right thing. And it is a temptation, a philosophical temptation, to argue that these experts lack the virtue of telling their patients and clients the truth. But the problem here is more complicated. They lack, I suspect, not moral principles but moral imagination, the ability to see themselves from another point of view, and therefore they fail to expose their own conceptual schemes and the principles they allegedly espouse to self-scrutiny. Thus it is moral parochialism that may account for their weaknesses as experts.

There is one more important element in moral imagination, the ability to embed one's moral principles in practice. Most decision makers have a set of values and, if asked, would argue that they care deeply about issues concerning the environment and future generations. But some of us fail to integrate these values or apply them in the context of the organization or the political economy. We lack the imagination to see ourselves as value-laden in our roles in an organization or in interacting with the ecosystem. We are unable to integrate personal value systems in our work because the conceptual scheme we adopt does not allow us to do so. What Bazerman, Wade-Benzoni, and Benzoni call "problem censoring" is due, in part, to this disjunction between what one values (one's normative inclinations) and how one acts. Problem censoring, which biases our environmental practice, can be mitigated only when one becomes cognizant of the conceptual scheme or frame one is using so that new initiatives such as those demanded by ecologists become feasible alternatives to be considered in practice.

The role of imagination is important in Jungermann's work as well. To be successful a marketer must create and communicate an image that is attractive enough to manipulate or reshape one's conceptual framework or that demonstrates the connection between what one values (for example, safety) with how one behaves. Great marketers do that. In communicating risk it is even more important to communicate such an image. But as manipulators of cognitive frames, communicators have a great moral responsibility, particularly when they are dealing with risk.

Moral imagination alone, however, cannot replace moral reasoning, for if imagination is the sole arbitrator, one sometimes engages in fantasy. An example of such fantasy can be seen in Bazerman, Wade-Benzoni, and Benzoni's account of the problem censoring performed by cigarette manufacturers who ignore the well-grounded data of causal explanations of lung cancer. There the imagination is allowed to disregard what is obvious from almost any cognitive frame.

Applied ethics, and in particular business ethics, should be in the form of a dialogue between moral imagination and the ideal of rational decision making. In engaging in that dialogue and in attempting to achieve what Heisenberg told us some time ago is unachievable, we develop a series of disengaged views from somewhere, where part of that view is self-reflective. In this process one tests both one's assumptions and one's judgments in particular contexts against moral principles and traditions, practices, narratives, and presuppositions in which an individual or an organization is embedded. This process takes into account context; it attempts to unearth cognitive frames and biases and to engage moral reasoning and particularize the norms most of us claim to espouse. Such a process uses both moral imagination and a "disengaged view from somewhere" to arrive at partial solutions. The process is never complete; pure objectivity is impossible, and infallibility of judgment is not part of its goal. Indeed, moral judgments are, at best, partial solutions, solutions that serve as the starting place for new series of decisions.

Thus philosophers engage in moral evaluation, just as the authors of the chapters in this section engage in analysis of risk, causation, self-interest, and communication. This evaluation is a dialogue on the level of analysis. It is on this level, too, that philosophers and social scientists can learn a great deal from each other. The distinction between the normative and the descriptive should be clarifying for all those working in this field, since both philosophers and social scientists sometimes confuse or conflate them. Empirical work on ethical issues, and more importantly empirical work on how conceptual schemes or cognitive frames are manipulated, is invaluable to thinking about how managers behave and how they might think more clearly about their behavior. The normative bent of philosophical analysis depends on well-grounded empirical data. Much more work, too, needs to be done on the notion of moral imagination and its relation to moral reasoning. Some of this work could consist of empirical studies of whether and how, in fact, people are and are not imaginative, and whether becoming more imaginative is teachable. Social scientists and philosophers learn from interchanges with each other; we become more self-reflective and self-critical, and eventually all disciplines make progress in the slow, value-driven dialogue that makes intellectual life worthwhile.

Summary

The Psychology of Business Ethics

Russell Hardin

The central problem of ethics is the problem of motivation. Indeed, one of the oldest characterizations of ethics is that it is about the conflict between self-interest and other concerns, such as the interests of others or doing the right thing in some sense. Morality is supposed to help us make the trade-off between our own interests and other concerns. To a large extent, that means that ethics is a subject for psychology as much as for philosophy, and this was evidently the view of one of the greatest moral theorists, David Hume, in whose massive *Treatise* ([1739–40] 1978) the third book on ethics follows that on psychology, which focuses especially on the passions. It is therefore apt that psychologists and philosophers have joined in a conference on behavioral research and business ethics. It will be even more apt if we hereafter contribute extensively to this joint debate, which reached its apogee in the work of one lonely Scottish-Enlightenment philosopher.

In discussions of ethics in business from a psychological perspective, there are several tendencies that mirror tendencies in the modern history of moral debate, some of which are about matters that are almost guaranteed to confuse. I will address three such issues: the problems of facts and values, altruism, and intuitions. I will then turn to an institutional theory of moral behavior—that is to say, a theory of moral behavior in institutional and organizational settings. This theory should be especially congenial to social scientists, and indeed several of the psychologists represented in this book discuss elements of it or parallel to it (for example, Darley, chapter 1; McGill, chapter 12; Wagenaar, chapter 18).

To moral theorists in general, the stance of social scientists would count as remarkably uniformly consequentialist. That is, social scientists (perhaps psychologists and economists more than most) are especially inclined to count as moral that which produces good consequences. Moreover, they are even relatively utilitarian, in that they suppose good consequences are primarily (or even exclusively) related to human welfare. When my account requires specific moral assumptions in order to carry through a particular argument, I will resort to utilitarian principles. It is important to note, however, that the central drive of the account is to fit behavior to organizations and their plausible goals, not specifically to a utilitarian's goals. The overall argument here should therefore be of interest to most moral theorists, including those most ardently opposed to utilitarianism. The rough structure of the argument is that, whatever our moral principle is, we want our organizations to achieve it. If they are to do so, they will have to be properly designed for the purpose, because organizations have effects beyond what the individuals in them intend. A moral theory that is exclusively about individuals and is irrelevant to organizations is irrelevant to business—as well as to most of contemporary life. A moral theory that does not work for institutions cannot work for people.

FACTS AND VALUES

Social science is generally concerned with explanation of what is. Moral philosophy is generally concerned with normative evaluations, with right and wrong or with bad and good. According to a dictum of Hume, one cannot infer an *ought* from an *is* (Hume [1739–40]1978). That is to say, nothing moral follows from the mere facts of any matter. I cannot look at your act of killing your father and judge your parricide, merely from the observed facts, to be morally wrong. If I reach such a judgment, it is because I apply the normative principle that killing one's father is wrong or some other principle from which this conclusion follows, at least for the circumstances of your case. Every substantive normative judgment is, at least in part, an inference from a normative principle.

Then why is it worthwhile to bring social science and philosophy together on such issues? Philosophers bring one set of ideas, and they typically push for systematic treatment; social scientists bring other ideas, and they push for realism and relevance—and, often, common sense. Together, there is likely to be heightened discovery on both sides from the findings and arguments of the other side, as the philosophical commentators (Thomas Donaldson and Patricia Werhane) have noted. Moreover, the moral theory that is forced into engagement with realism and relevance is likely to be much better theory; social science is important for the fundamental arguments of moral theory. And the social science theory or explanation that is forced to be normatively systematic is likely to be a far better prescriptive and policy-relevant theory.

Consider an example of the effects of focusing on real problems for constitutional theory. Arguably the best body of constitutional thought to have come from a brief period is the debates over the U.S. Constitution that took place during its writing and adoption, 1787–1788. This debate was driven by the real and urgent need to find a better system of government, and the debate was carried on by practical men, not theorists. The central figure was

James Madison, especially in the larger part of *The Federalist*, although there were also valuable contributions from dozens of others. John Jay and Alexander Hamilton did some of their best writing for *The Federalist*, although their writing and ideas were inferior to Madison's. Madison was a statesman, but not a philosopher or legal theorist. John Adams, Thomas Jefferson, and perhaps James Wilson were major intellects in their own right, but while Wilson was a leading figure at the constitutional convention and in the politics of ratification in Pennsylvania, Adams and Jefferson were more nearly peripheral; indeed, Jefferson was out of the country and contributed relatively little to the constitutional debates. Though not a major intellect, Madison was very accomplished, very commonsensical, and remarkably open—and he had an unusually good instinctive strategic sense. These men achieved what they did largely because they were forced to work by the facts of the matter.

ALTRUISM

Much of the debate in social/psychological motivation is about the prevalence of altruism. Some psychologists and many economists provide clever arguments to show that apparently altruistic actions are really self-interested. Sociobiologists attempt to construct models for how altruism could be genetically selected. Real-world examples and experimental data are elicited to demonstrate the validity of the varied claims. Much of the discussion, however, is confusing in that it often runs together altruism that occurs at very different levels of interaction. Three levels are especially of interest: (1) individual-to-individual interactions over odd events, (2) frequent or large-scale interactions between individuals and other actors; and (3) systematic interactions that are often handled by institutions or by policy. These levels can be motivationally independent; an individual might be altruistic at one of the levels but not at another. They can also be causally distinct; the altruism that would work for problems at one level would not work for problems at another level. There is therefore not a single, simple altruism motivation.[1]

Most of the discussion of altruism in philosophy and in sociobiology is focused on individual-to-individual problems. The traditional philosophers' example is the altruism of stepping into a pond to rescue someone—typically a small child—foundering there, at the mere cost of muddy or shrunken clothing that might ruin one's day. Such cases fit Hume's characterization of natural duty: We know that our own action produces enough good to justify our taking it (Hume [1739–40] 1978). Many one-on-one actions that might once have been called altruistic are now seen to be at least congruent with self-interest. For example, I behave generously toward you because I know you well and will benefit from continuing to know you well. If you were a complete stranger in a one-time encounter, I might be far less generous. As

Hume noted, it is typically self-interested to keep one's promises; similarly it is congruent with self-interest to behave generously toward many people. A striking fact of general altruism, however, is that the weight of individual-to-individual problems in odd circumstances is relatively small in the balance of all problems. The problems with which individuals—or at least those who live in contemporary cities—most often have to contend are on the second level of interactions. And, arguably, the problems that have the greatest weight for accomplishing genuine good in the world are on the third level, institutional and policy problems.

Much of the discussion of altruism in institutional settings such as business seems to focus on problems on the second level and to treat them as matters for individuals to resolve. In my position in my organization, I can do good for a large number of people only at some cost to myself. For example, as an independent auditor of corporate practices, I can act as an individual to report management misbehavior. But if I do, I might not be rehired by the corporation the next time it is due for an audit, nor will I be fully trusted by other firms that might hire me. This is a standard example that seems likely to be a very commonplace problem. Insofar as it is commonplace, we should seek institutional devices to give incentives for generally good behavior. At one time, the norms of professionalism were thought adequate to control such conflicts of interest. Those norms were also thought to be the only available device. In many professional contexts the past norms are still pushed, but there are also institutional devices to change the self-interest calculation. In many contexts, self-interest may be the more reliable device for trumping self-interest.

Many of the people—both at professional meetings and in ordinary life—with whom I have discussed the middle category of frequent one-on-one interactions seem to be unsure how to deal with it. Some are unsure that, for example, giving to a street beggar improves the beggar's life. Hence, they are not sure that charity really is altruistic. Others are apparently unsure primarily because they think the larger problem is to improve many lives, which might be better if the system of street begging were not as remunerative as it is. Some of these people seem to feel that they often suffer from a moral variant of the logic of collective action. A gift to the beggar of the moment would make life better for that beggar but would make life for the whole class of potential beggars worse by giving them perverse incentives (R. Hardin 1990). Those incentives have led to the rise of what is perhaps a large class of very accomplished professional beggars who have mastered deceptive techniques. This moral variant of the logic of collective action is a peculiar but increasingly important social dilemma of a kind that should interest social psychologists in the social-justice perspective (Kramer and Messick, chapter 3).

As I have noted earlier, the three categories of altruism are motivationally independent. It was said of Bertrand Russell that he loved humanity but did not much care for individual humans. Someone with such views might happily vote for altruistic policies but balk at face-to-face altruism. Hume, to the contrary, said that he felt far greater sympathy for one individual's suffering that he could see than for the vastly greater suffering of the millions destroyed in an earthquake in China. He also thought that state-managed distributive justice would be pernicious in its effects (R. Hardin 1988). Someone with his views might vote against redistributive policies but act altruistically toward an individual in distress. In the case of the intermediate category of frequent individual interaction with a particular class of demands for altruism, people might react roughly as they would to the other class to which they might tend to assimilate it, either the strictly occasional one-on-one encounter or the systematic interaction. Or, given the difficulty of understanding it causally, they might simply be unsure how to treat it.

The categories are also causally distinct. The chief reason many people support some variant of President Clinton's health-care reform is that they altruistically wish to have health care provided to the substantial fraction of Americans who have no coverage. Presumably, almost no one would suppose that individual-to-individual altruism could handle this problem. One's altruistic impulse here could be successfully put to work only through an institutional arrangement. John Darley (chapter 1) says, aptly, that harm-doing is a team sport; so too must altruism be if it is to be effective at all in many contexts.

Given the causal structures of various demands for altruism, it follows that one or another level of altruism will be more or less necessary if the relevant good is to be done. Without individual-to-individual altruism, individuals in idiosyncratic dire distress in acute moments will not be helped in time. Without enough altruism toward systematic problems to create institutions and establish government policies, various welfare goals cannot be met. These two categories of altruism are often necessary if their respective goods are to be achieved. That people are prepared to act altruistically in one arena, however, need not imply that they will act altruistically in the other arena. Mean-spirited citizens might be wonderful face-to-face, and wonderful citizens might be mean-spirited face-to-face.

Economists are sometimes thought to believe that there is no significant incidence of altruism. Moreover, they are thought to hold that if there were much altruism, it would be harmful; self-interest would produce better results on the whole than altruism would. This second claim is not as silly as it superficially seems to many critics. If most people most of the time were not being partial to their own and their families' interests, these would be badly served and we would all be worse off. Hence, altruism must motivate at most a fraction of our actions. But the skepticism about economists seems to go further than this, to the idea that they *really oppose* altruism. Indeed, they are thought to rely heavily on the market economists' bible, Adam Smith's *Wealth of Nations* ([1776] 1976), although Ayn Rand (1971) comes closer to holding the harsh view that self-interest should be the only motivator.

When Smith wrote in support of market organization of economic life and therefore in support of self-interest, he was opposing religious and group-based values that he thought burdened and even wrecked society. For example, towns and guilds excluded many laborers and severely restricted markets in order to protect their own from competition and to protect their local way of life. For Smith, self-interest spoke for egalitarianism and against especially favored interests. He was not fighting altruism, and his brilliantly quotable line about interests as motivating production is a claim for the possibility that interest can make things work well and beneficially. This was once a startling claim, because interest was formerly known as avarice, the greatest of all evils and the opposite of charity, the greatest of all virtues. In virtue theory, interest had been evil, while in Smith's view it was enormously beneficial to the larger society. Smith's claims for the beneficial superiority of interest still apply today to many values, such as the group-based values of racism and sexism and other in-group biases (Brewer, chapter 8; Rothbard, chapter 7; Tyler and Belliveau, chapter 9). Letting individual interest dominate these values would be widely beneficial, as it was also in Smith's time and has been ever since.

Then where must the Smith of *The Wealth of Nations* have stood on altruism? First, he cannot have opposed altruism of our first category, individual-to-individual, which is not related to his argument for the market economy. Second, he had the beginnings of an understanding of the logic of collective action, and he might have suffered our own ambivalence over altruism in the second category, individual action in the face of frequent demand. Or, given his views of the poor laws, one might suppose he would have opposed such altruism as not efficacious in at least some instances; this, of course, is a contingent matter of social science, not merely a matter of principle. Finally, whether he had an interpretable view of the third category of systematic altruism beyond the cases in which it would not be efficacious may be unclear. But he certainly favored public expenditures for broad public benefit and even for some relatively narrow benefits. These policies can, of course, be seen to serve mutual advantage rather than to be redistributive. Hence, we cannot unambiguously conclude where Smith stood on what is today the most important category of altruism.

There was, of course, an earlier Smith, of *A Theory of Moral Sentiments*. That Smith strongly argued for "universal benevolence," or altruism (A. Smith [1759]1976, 235). Possibly his views had changed in the nearly twenty years between these two works, so that by the time of *The Wealth of Nations* he held the views often attributed to economists. It seems implausible that he made a complete switch, although it seems likely that he made at least a partial switch. The later Smith was motivated to argue, as Bernard Mandeville ([1714]1924) had done earlier, that self-interest is a profoundly good motivation in the sense that it produces the best results we can expect. The struggle against botched values and their destructive intrusions may have been more important to the later Smith than the concern with character and morality had been to the earlier Smith. Even more important than this, however, was the clearer understanding he seemed to have of the real weight of economic progress in making lives better. If I were to argue that their own altruism is what, say, Bangladeshis need, I would rightly earn Smith's dismissal and ridicule. Bangladeshis primarily need action from their own self-interest, without which they will remain in dreadful poverty. As the third category of problems for altruism swamps the other categories in our society, so Smith had evidently come to hold that the value of economic motivations swamped the value of normative motivations in his society. His view is arguably still true even in the most advanced societies.

When we study other motivations, moreover, we may find that, when they seem to be typically effective, they are often congruent with self-interest. This means that actions are overdetermined by supposedly contrary motivations. The hard task in analyzing motivations is to avoid simplistic claims of direct effects and to see how complex the relationships may be. When we do so, we may find that acting normatively well is simultaneously acting in our interests. This is what Hume ([1739–40]1978) showed in his account of promise keeping, with his implicit argument from the incentive structure of an iterated prisoner's dilemma. In parallel, we might find that actual instances of what we first think of as altruistic actions are actions of sensible generosity toward friends and associates, with whom we are in iterated prisoner's dilemma interactions. The altruistic act that is strictly against one's interest is substantially rarer, although surely common (Frank, chapter 4).

INTUITIONS

In moral debates, intuitions often play large roles.[2] There are at least three kinds of intuitions that are of interest in moral theory: (1) factual intuitions, (2) formal intuitions, and (3) substantive moral intuitions. Factual intuitions include both direct and indirect or inferential intuitions. For example, I may have the direct intuition that the world is flat. And I may have the inferential intuition that if x is true then y is true, but I know x is true, therefore I intuit that y must be true. Aristotle is justifiably notorious for having faulty factual intuitions about trivially checked matters, such as his belief that heavier objects fall faster than lighter objects. For a distressingly long period of time, leaders of the Roman Catholic Church suffered the inferential intuition that if Aristotle said it, it is true.

Consider a couple of factual intuitions. At the conference at which the papers in this book were presented, Robert Bies asked for a show of hands on who would rather live in a world in which everything about everybody was known to everybody and who would rather live in a world in which nothing about anybody was known to anyone else. Many people had an instant intuition in favor of one or the other. Unfortunately, those two worlds would be so radically unlike the world we know that we probably cannot begin to think through the implications, even if we had weeks to work them out. Instant intuitions can be of no value in such a matter. This conclusion suggests that credible intuitions are often or perhaps even typically grounded in experience that makes them seem to be learned.

To cite a second example, I arrived at that conference immediately after being abroad for more than three weeks. Most of the people I knew at the conference I had previously seen more in Europe than in the United States. Since Evanston was not home for me, it seemed rather like a continuation of my prior sojourn in Europe, and throughout the conference I kept having the odd intuition that I was abroad. Or perhaps for me, after more than a decade at the University of Chicago, Evanston was something of a foreign country. In any case, whatever its origin, when the intuition intruded I was able to think through what I knew about where I was and realize that the intuition was wrong. Discovering that it was wrong once, however, did not block it from coming again. Each time it came, I had to rethink what I knew—for example, that after landing at O'Hare, I had got to Evanston in a taxi whose driver was from Chicago's South Side.

Formal intuitions are necessary in any field of inquiry. Mathematicians, logicians, linguists, scientists, musical creators, and many others have formal intuitions that underlie their arguments. Before the rise of communitarian moral and political theory, virtually every moral theorist had the formal intuition that ethical principles are universal in their scope; if they apply to anyone, then they apply to everyone. Utilitarians further have the intuition that welfare is the general good of humanity (or of all sentient beings). Other theorists, such as John Rawls, have the intuition that fairness is what is generally right for humanity. Or they intuit that autonomy, agreement, human rights, or whatever is the basic principle of morality. For all these principles, there is no further argument. These are ground principles that are like the rules of arithmetic in that they must first be accepted before we can go further in our deductions.

The problem of formal intuitions did not arise in the discussions of the conference on business ethics. Perhaps the lack of comment was evidence that such intuitions are not a contested or difficult issue. They are, however, a difficult issue in philosophical treatments of morality. This issue arises as the central question of modern moral theory, perhaps of all moral theory. That question is, Why be moral? If we simply stipulate the ground principles of our theory as, say, Kantian or utilitarian, we then leave ourselves open to this question. To answer it, we would have to say why some ground principles must be accepted by a sensible person. Answers in recent centuries have included evolutionary arguments, religious claims, and intuition pure and simple—as well as, of course, occasional arguments that beg the question. None of these is adequate in the sense of convincing most participants in the discussion.

At one time, logicians and mathematicians may have implicitly assumed that all their ground-level intuitions were valid and consistent. Now logicians and mathematicians are willing to stipulate radically different axioms from which quite different theoretical conclusions follow. Unfortunately, moral theorists have always been in the position of contemporary logicians and mathematicians. One theorist starts from axioms that another theorist dislikes, but neither theorist can give a compelling reason for accepting one or another set of fundamental principles.

The unique problem of moral theory, however, as compared with theories of other matters, is that moral theorists often have substantive moral intuitions—for example, to lie or break a promise is wrong, or failure to cooperate with others who are cooperating in some joint venture is wrong, or doing harm even to accomplish good is wrong. As Jonathan Baron says, they do psychology with an n of 1, since it is only their own intuitions that interest them. Such intuitions are the curse of modern moral theory. At earlier moments in philosophical history, it was supposed that we could trust such intuitions, because they must have been implanted by god. For many people today that is not a credible argument. In any case it cannot fit the facts of our intuitions, unless god is playing vicious tricks on us, because we too often radically disagree about what is intuitively true. To whitewash this dispiriting fact, intuitionists in moral theory often talk about the "common" morality, as though there were agreement when there is not. Ridiculously many people—philosophers and others—think they have firm, correct intuitions about substantive moral matters. Furthermore, they solipsistically think that their having these intuitions *makes them right*, or proves the intuitions are right, or at least gives them standing in moral debate and moral theory.

To some extent, substantive moral intuitions might seem similar to factual intuitions. But consider the odd factual intuition that I was in a foreign country in Evanston. I could demonstrate to myself that the intuition was in fact false. Suppose I have the intuition that it is always wrong to tell a lie, and I now face the dreadful problem put to Kant. An assassin appears at my door and asks whether you, his intended victim, are in my home. Alas, you are. To protect you, I can lie. Or to protect my moral purity, I can answer truthfully and then do my best to try to prevent your murder—but consequences may not matter much to me. Kant said that morality requires truth even in this grim instance.[3] Any utilitarian would likely say it requires saving you, if possible—if necessary, by lying.[4] Suppose I am a utilitarian (I have the formal intuition that welfare is the human good), but I seem to suffer from Kant's odd intuition. I can readily see that these two intuitions conflict, but I have no way to show that one of them is inherently wrong. There are no facts of the matter to help settle the issue. I could correct my false factual intuition about being abroad in less than a minute (except when I had it upon awakening—then it took longer). I cannot settle my substantive moral intuition except at the level of pretheory. I simply reject the authority of such intuitions and accept the authority of my formal utilitarian intuition.

Some moral theorists have made the opposite choice and assert the authority of their ragbag of substantive moral intuitions over formal intuitions. The misfortunes of this move are, again, that these theorists do not agree with each other about which intuitions are morally correct and which morally wrong and that there is no way to ensure that the intuitions escape contradiction. Intuitionist ethics is therefore typically casuist and sophistic, requiring many words to rationalize away apparent contradictions. And it is largely impenetrable for systematic moral theorists, such as Kantians and utilitarians, who can never count on reaching the correct answers, either because they do not happen to have the intuitions or because when they do seem to have the intuitions, they too readily associate these with bits of their upbringing in a church, community, or family. If their intuitions are learned (perhaps by indoctrination), there is no compelling reason to hold them in principle to be valid. They are nothing more than a particular group's social conventions.[5] In some cases they are vicious and depraved.

It takes very little thought about substantive moral intuitions to begin to wonder how they come into our heads. But moral philosophers have spent most of their effort on analyzing and identifying the intuitions we supposedly have and very little on how we come to have them. Social psychologists may have special talents and methods for learning how we acquire them and, especially important, why they carry their sometime conviction. (People have knowingly died for holding to their intuitions.) Political psychologists have tended to suppose that certain values get inculcated early and then stay relatively fixed thereafter. That would be a dispiriting conclusion, precluding any hope of moral behavior, because, according to the literature of political psychology, among the values that get fixed are values of racism, sexism, and vicious variants of partiality of other kinds, such as familial, communal, and ethnic. Perhaps because children are often taught principles of behavior that would be beneficial for the larger family, however, the inculcated values may also tend to include values of cooperativeness, face-to-face honesty, and even modest generosity.

These two bundles of partly contradictory values may complicate the moral lives of most of us. For example, Gunnar Myrdal (1944) worried that the white children of the American South were taught contradictory values of equality and racial superiority that must eventually come into severe political and perhaps even psychological conflict. Myrdal was clearly not concerned that moral theory was inherently contradictory. Rather, he was noting that our moral education can be inconsistent. What we would like to know, in trying to respond to claims of substantive moral intuition, is how they work psychologically and socially. It is conceivable that if we understood them better we would find them more credible or, alternatively, less credible. In this odd problem, such facts could help us to determine what moral force to give to such intuitions, because, as Kant said, *ought* implies *can*. If people cannot be having justifiable moral intuitions about specific substantive matters, then they cannot be morally bound by the claims of such intuitions.

INSTITUTIONAL MORALITY

So far, the discussion here has largely been about morality at the level of the individual, although, as I have noted, the bulk of our concern today may well be the morality of institutional and organizational actions, as in the third category of problems of altruism. This is surely the bulk of the problem of ethics in business. In an earlier age, the conditions of the market and the technology of the times made simple self-interest in mutually beneficial market transactions a sufficient condition for generally good and moral outcomes. Today, it can still be true that self-interest suffices only if organizations that dominate production and exchange can similarly control their participants with nothing more than self-interest to generate results that are profitable or otherwise desirable to the organizations—but even then, only if there are no deleterious external effects of organizational behaviors. In general, there typically are major external effects, such as pollution, skewed information and deception, social dislocation, discrimination, and so forth. And there are often opportunities for individuals to gain at the expense of the organizations for which they work and at the expense of the clients or customers of those organizations. We therefore face at least four possible devices for controlling individual behavior: (1) traditional Smithian self-interest, (2) individual moral principles, (3) legally backed enforcement, and (4) organizationally induced self-interest.

Self-interest

Traditional Smithian self-interest probably still successfully governs an enormous percentage of relevant behaviors, although we may have grown so accustomed to its working that we take little note of it. It is most obviously ineffective when individual incentives for gain conflict with organizational gain, as in various professional conflicts of interest. For example, consider recent accounts of the questionable practices of some mutual fund managers who invest to benefit themselves, their relatives, and their associates while risking their clients' funds (for example, *New York Times*, August 7, 1994). But it is also often ineffective when organizational interests conflict with broader social concerns.

Individual Morality

Much of the writing on organizations—and especially on business, and especially popular writing—focuses on inculcating relevant moral principles. It is probably for social psychologists to say whether such an effort can be expected to succeed, but it seems the least likely of the four devices to work. Even if we could inculcate various values, it is not obvious that doing so could resolve the problems organizations face. The crude theory that an aggregation of individual behaviors can produce organizational results will typically fail, for at least two general reasons.

First, it is a fallacy of composition to suppose that a cluster of people individually aiming at some organizational goal, such as reaching a particular moral outcome, will collectively achieve that goal. Rather, each may have to act in ways that are superficially unrelated to the organization's goals. (It is a fallacy of composition to suppose without argument that the characteristics of a group are the same as those of its members. For example, although the members of a group may be rational, it does not follow that the group will be rational in the same sense.) Second, for many purposes we wish to control individuals' behavior for stochastic, not directly individual, reasons. For example, it seems clear that we have far greater success in reducing road accidents by arresting those who test as drunk than by merely punishing those who are in fact personally responsible for accidents. On some moral theories, obtaining the result of reducing fatalities to innocent others is good reason to commend punishing a driver who drives drunk whether or not that person has actually caused harm.

A very important special case of attempting to inculcate moral principles to override the incentive of self-interest is the effort to get certain professionals to act according to a code of ethics. For example, accountants, auditors, and other agents of corporations may typically be in positions in which their interests and the interests of the corporation or of its owners or managers are in conflict. There is an enormous literature on such professionals, and the issue is too big to address here. It is plausible that this is the biggest unresolved area of conflict between individual interest and role requirements in all of public life. One way to resolve the conflict, at least in certain cases, is to change, say, the audit function to a form that would be much more a matter of public record and would make it easier to hold individuals liable for wrongdoing.

Incidentally, to suppose that good individual actions can simply be aggregated to produce good collective organizational results is to suppose that there is nothing distinctive about business, or professional, or government ethics, that they are all wholly the same in content as ordinary personal ethics. In that case, there would be little point in holding a conference on behavioral research and business ethics. All this might be a correct view, but one should probably suppose the contrary—that the structure of roles for various purposes entails distinctive principles for action in those roles.

Legal Enforcement

Legal sanctions have, of course, been a major device since ancient times, and they can be used in many business contexts, as in governmentally imposed conflict-of-interest standards for the securities industry. For three reasons, however, law is apt to be a clumsy device for organizational ethics in general. First, it is too expensive and cumbersome to bring into play for minor matters, which are common and collectively important. If organizations are to be efficient, therefore, they must find ways to handle most of their own moral problems. Second, law will typically lag the state of the art. For example, many of the most familiar problems of organizational behavior that have caused harms externally were problems that taught us what the law should be. Wrongs come first, and then law follows. Third, and arguably most important, law runs up against the problem of complex causation within organizations. Let us consider this problem in more detail.

The usual causal model for determining responsibility in the law works reasonably well for criminal law. That model is spelled out by H. L. A. Hart and A. M. Honoré (1959); a similar, far more accessible account is presented by Ann McGill in chapter 12. In these accounts, *the* cause, for the purposes of assigning responsibility, is what seems anomalous in the series of actions and conditions that lead to a perverse result, such as a death or an organizational wrong. The model takes for granted that many actions and conditions likely contribute to any result of interest and that therefore we do not literally want a full causal account; we want only a somehow relevantly focused account. This model of causation will not work for moral theory, for the trivial reason that there is no moral agency analogous to the legal system to enforce it (R. Hardin 1988). Hence, in moral applications it lacks a value—decisive finality—that strongly commends it to legal use: In the law it tends to get definitive results despite the fact that its application is highly conventionalized. This is important in the law because we want order and finality in order to make our plans and investments. We want the legal system to settle things and let us move on. (Even better, of course, would be to have things settled in our favor.) The law tells us in advance what will determine culpability and thereby gives us incentive to act well in our own longer-run interest. A moral analog without a credible, stable enforcer cannot do this.

Despite its specifically legal peculiarities, the model of legal responsibility is a good starting point for a model of organizational responsibility. It sidesteps the problem of the fallacy of composition that undercuts simplistic causal accounts of such responsibility; if we are to get anywhere, we must get past this problem. Hence, we turn from the fallacious composition to a full causal model of our organization. Unfortunately, a full causal account of a significant organization's actions would require massive understanding far beyond what is possible for any individual agent. But if this is true, then the agent can hardly be held accountable for fitting all actions precisely to the organization's goals. Instead, the agent must fit actions to standard routines and even rules, which have been designed with the hope that they fit the desired result. It is this design that constitutes the fourth of the devices for controlling individual behavior in an organization.

Organizationally Induced Self-interest

This last device, organizational design, has been the least well studied of the four. Its rise in importance has paralleled the rise of relatively specific legal sanctions in the era of the modern corporation. Organizational design for achieving the central purposes of organizations is, of course, an old art that goes back several millennia in military, agricultural, navigational, and other activities. But the additional concern of achieving moral outcomes more or less by the way is a more recent concern. Typically, all organizational design takes the form of building in incentives for proper behavior. Hence, there need be little or no direct oversight or sanctioning. Rather, each agent of the organization simply faces a schedule of incentives that make the agent's self-interest and the organization's purpose congruent. Each individual agent acts as a Smithian producer for the market would.

In essence, morality must be designed into institutions and organizations (R. Hardin 1996). This is essentially what Willem Wagenaar in chapter 18 recommends for safety in the workplace. His example of the monkey man, who leaps about dangerously on an elevated platform, is, in an odd sense, structurally equivalent to some immoral behavior that is standard practice in the organization. Both are also structurally equivalent to organizational design to achieve any purpose, such as to produce its goods or services.

A well-designed organization might leave no room for anything other than specific individual responsibility for bad outcomes; then we could use McGill's causal account to establish culpability. Few organizations of substantial complexity and scale are likely to be so well designed, however. Investigations into bad behavior and bad outcomes should therefore focus sharply on organizational design. For example, while it is true that, in the moment when it really counts, it is the monkey man's own personal misstep that leads to his fall and likely death, it is also true that his risk of doing so was designed into the drilling procedure. Worker safety could be greatly enhanced by designing a new procedure that did not entail putting anyone at such risk. So too, a person's immorality on the job might be a risk to which the person is exposed by the organization's poor design for motivating action. True, a monkey man who is more agile and has quicker reactions might face less risk than another, and a saint might be less at risk of immorality on the job than a person of average fallibility. But in both cases, the organization would commonly be better served by finding procedures that did not call for exceptional people rather than trying to find exceptional people.

Note an implication of the argument from design. Suppose that our organization is to produce x and that this is a morally good purpose (according to our moral theory). If we design the organization to produce x in a particular way, with various roles and expectations for behavior in them, then it follows that in each of our roles it is moral for us to do what the role specifies. Might there ever be an exception to this conclusion? Yes. Suppose our background moral theory is utilitarianism and I can assess that, by violating some specification of what I should do in my role, I could cause a much better general result for the organization.[6] That is to say, it is much better in the organization's own terms. My organization might hold it correct for me to act in such a way and might even make that a part of my role. The organization would then be right to chastise me should I fail to act in this way, to go beyond my narrow role specification.

Indeed, even the law might be invoked in favor of going beyond narrowly defined roles. In tort law, the so-called reasonable-person rule is sometimes invoked. If a reasonable person would have taken some step to prevent a potential harm, then I should have done so.[7] And if I did not, then I am tortiously liable (or my adversary is less liable than he or she might otherwise have been). That is to say, the court can decide, ex post facto, what would have been good or right behavior and hold someone accountable to this previously unstated criterion. In criminal law in the United States, laws cannot be applied ex post facto to actions taken before the laws were passed. My actions in a corporation similarly cannot be held criminally liable if there was no law already in effect to proscribe such action. But I and my corporation can be held financially liable for tort actions under the reasonable-person doctrine.

We might even go further and suppose that a corporation could be held liable under an analogous reasonable-corporation rule. It might then be up to the corporation to decide whether to hold me to account for being unreasonable in actions in my role in the corporation. The corporation's own reasonable-person rule would stipulate that role holders should act with at least some discretion to disobey their role's rules (Kadish and Kadish 1973). Some organizations might strongly discourage and punish such discretion; others might encourage it. Virtually all might expect more discretion to be exercised in some roles than in others. As though to parallel the law of torts, organizations can and do punish people for failing to do what is "reasonable" even to the point of disobeying their normal rules if necessary to be reasonable. Hence, they implicitly judge from a standard of the reasonable agent.

It is striking that the combination of a reasonable-corporation rule in the tort law and a reasonable-agent rule within the corporation would be roughly adequate to produce morally good action that is congruent with both agents' self-interest and morality. Since it is the opposition of these two that is widely thought to drive most immoral behavior, corporations could achieve moral outcomes over a broad range. The central difficulty in organizational morality, therefore, is perhaps not the possible immorality toward others, as in actions with grossly harmful external effects, but the violation of organizational interests. Organizations typically must want to prevent such harmful actions but they fail to (Darley, chapter 1; Wagenaar, chapter 18). Exxon will have lost more from the *Exxon Valdez* oil spill than it will have made in oil transport overall, and the company has therefore sold off its tankers to eliminate the risk of future disastrous losses (Wagenaar, chapter 18). There might have been an incentive problem for Exxon in that case, but if so it was the failure of incorporating the new incentive into old routines for individual employees as tort responsibility for oil spills was expanded. Increasingly, the reasonable corporation will come around to being reasonable about redesign of processes and procedures to match them better with incentives.

We are left with the problem of immorality within organizations. It is at least conceivable that, while our moral theory would typically commend productivity or profit as an organization's principal goal, it would also require fairness and other values in dealing with employees. And if both these principles are to apply, it is conceivable that on occasion they will conflict. Then we might expect to see profit override fairness. At this point, one might think we could resort to a variant rule of reasonableness about the trade-off between these two concerns. Unfortunately, if our theory does not give us a trade-off function, reasonableness will not either. In the reasonable-corporation and reasonable-agent rules, the standard of reasonableness is tested against actual results. In balancing two normative principles, there is no fact of the matter against which to test reasonableness. Anyone who invokes reasonableness in such a context (many moral philosophers do) is essentially resorting to substantive moral intuitions.

Such trade-off problems might be resolved in the law, which might stipulate how corporations are to handle such matters as fairness and discrimination. Lesser problems may not be suited to legal resolution and might give moral critics of organizations a great deal of difficulty. In such cases, we might readily expect organizations to limit their concern with these issues and to concentrate on what is legally regulated and on productivity. It will be hard for moral critics to say that this is a wrong policy.

In general, it seems likely that those matters that are regulated by legal mandates and restrictions and those that are regulated by the threat of tort actions together constitute the bulk of what matters morally in corporate behavior. Hence, it is clear that moral action of and within corporations can be made largely congruent with self-interest. If so, then Smith's reliance on self-interest is still adequate for most of what matters in business today.

It is also clear that this conclusion would not follow if there were nothing equivalent to a strong tort regime to make it the interest of corporations not to harm others far beyond the benefits they bring them. One might suppose that during the Second World War Johns-Manville acted as badly as it did in exposing workers to harm from asbestos in large part because its officers did not foresee the disastrous tort settlement that eventually bankrupted the firm. (Tobacco company executives today may have the same vision of their likely limited responsibility.) That is to say, they did not face an adequate incentive of self-interest to act well. In this, they differed from the Exxon executives and perhaps from the executives in the oil-drilling company with the badly designed monkey man role and, indeed, from executives in most corporations in legally advanced nations today.

There remain at least two major problems. First, today's executives might face no cost from tomorrow's tort action and might therefore severely discount it in deciding what is in their personal interest, as Johns-Manville executives may have done. Second, a corporation might organize with very little capital to be seized in a tort action while making great profits until being bankrupted by such tort action, as the small operators who have taken over Exxon's oil tankers perhaps do. Limited liability reduces the incentive of self-interest. Regulation might be necessary for such cases, although regulation is apt to be a clumsy device and it is likely to lag the problem even longer than tort action would.

INTEREST IN MORALITY

In sum, note again that the role account is essentially institutionalist and functional. It is not essentially utilitarian. We could work up a functional account of business ethics if we could first stipulate a general principle for which particular actions or classes of actions might be functionally relevant. For example, a Rawlsian might stipulate as the background normative principle some principle of fairness. Or a utilitarian would stipulate some principle of welfare. There might be other background principles, but these two may be the only systematic and coherent ones that cover most of what might be of interest. Such supposed general principles as rights and virtues seem to require grounding in manifold intuitions and are not systematic.

There are two conspicuous issues that the functional account of roles does not appear to address. First, perhaps it is true, as is sometimes supposed in the literature on professionalism, that many professionals inherently must be normatively driven, at least in part because they cannot be monitored. wEven for such people, however, organizations and the law can be designed to bring moral action more nearly into congruence with self-interest to keep George Loewenstein's balance of self and others (chapter 11) from tipping too heavily toward self.

Second, for some values, such as certain environmental values (as Bazerman and his colleagues describe in chapter 14), there may be no one whose interests are adversely affected who could be expected to enter a tort claim. Hence, these values plausibly cannot be secured with the combination of the reasonable corporation and its reasonable agents that are given incentive to make their actions congruent with the relevant values and their own interests. The environmental lawyer Christopher Stone (1972) has proposed that we give trees legal standing, so that any lawyer could defend a tree against assault and gain the lawyer's fee in a successful suit. In such a legal regime, the reasonable corporation would have to take environmental values into account. Hence, environmental values would be brought into congruence with corporations' and their agents' interests. There are difficulties in this resolution, however. How is a court to decide the monetary value of a tree's suffering in order to assign a lawyer's fee? And should, for example, whales, the snail darter, the Grand Canyon, and rain forests have standing? And how do we handle the interests of future generations whose particular members would come into existence only because of long-past actions? Can those people reasonably hold someone responsible for harming them when they would not even have existed but for the ostensibly harmful action?

When the functional account of roles and the morality of their occupants can bring agents' actions into congruence with the relevant values and the agents' own interests, the chief problem organizations then face is bringing agents' actions into congruence with the organizations' interests by inducing the agents not to make rational blunders that lead them astray. The problems surveyed by Jonathan Baron (chapter 10), John Darley (chapter 1), Robyn Dawes (chapter 16), Helmut Jungermann (chapter 17), Josh Klayman (chapter 13), Willem Wagenaar (chapter 18), and others then should dominate our concern. Such problems may be especially important when they are compounded by the dynamics of changing technology and the rigidity of past practice, as Darley and others suggest. As a first cut, it is plausible that there is far more failure of rationality than of morality in organizations and that much of what seems to be immorality is rather irrationality. What organizations typically need is not so much to alter their agents' values but to be, as Patricia Werhane (commentary, part 2) suggests, more creative in thinking through and resolving problems they face and, as Robert Cialdini (chapter 2) suggests, inclined to make their control systems simple and clear enough for workers who are neither moral nor rational specialists.

Finally, in the discussion of the fact/value distinction there is often a somewhat contrary issue flirting in the wings. Kant supposed that *ought* implies *can*. That is to say, if you cannot possibly do action *x*, then it is not the case that you ought to do it. But this means that the fact/value distinction is slightly violated. The fact of the matter—that you cannot do *x*—immediately tells us something about the morality of the matter—that it cannot be supposed that you ought to do *x*. This is, incidentally, one point at which social science matters fundamentally for the content of moral theory. Being able to do something is at least a necessary condition for being morally obligated or duty-bound to do it. Virtually all moral theorists think this principle is true, although their views of the constraints that qualify for saying you cannot do

x may vary enormously. If we accept the principle, there is an odd implication for us. People who are better able to reason through the moral arguments for what it is right to do are bound to a higher standard than are those less able to reason them through. For example, if you are relevantly smarter, better educated, or more knowledgeable about our problems than I am, you can plausibly know to act better. But, by Kant's principle, if you can act better, then you should.

This conclusion might have an important structural implication for organizations. They can achieve better results if they have specialists to think about their problems, plan their results, and design solutions. At the same time, because they then can do better, they can reasonably be held to higher standards. What I do in a corporation that is struggling to survive and that has no resources to plan and second-guess its actions may be less constrained morally than what you do in a very self-aware, highly organized corporation. Courts might hold, however, that there is a correct standard for a reasonable corporation and might hold any corporation to that standard. Giving corporations incentive to be reasonable according to dynamically changing standards may be the best to be expected for the morality of business.

ENDNOTES

1. There may be other differences as well. For example, one might be provoked to altruism by the opportunity to relieve suffering, somehow defined, but not by the opportunity to make someone simply better off. More generally, one's altruism might be constrained by one's sense of justice.

2. For further discussion, see R. Hardin 1988, especially pp. 22–29, 178–191.

3. Incredibly, Kant argued that violating the formal principle against lying "is much worse than to commit an injustice to any individual" ([1797]1909, 365; see also R. Hardin 1989b, 78–79). If he would not permit lying for such a grave matter as saving someone's life, he presumably also would reject it when it had mere functional value, as in negotiation.

4. A sometime response to such problems is to argue from what must be only contingent facts that it is unlikely that one would have to violate a particular moral rule, such as, in this instance, not to lie. This is a pointless response to rationalize a rule that cannot be universally consistent with the relevant other general principle, which in this case is welfare. All that must be true is that some utilitarian in some such case might genuinely and honestly conclude that lying would most likely produce the best result.

5. Despite his statement of the fact/value distinction (perhaps, alas, as an afterthought), Hume ([1739–40]1978, 569) thought this a compelling argument in defense of the rightness of these intuitions.

6. I will carry through the argument from utilitarian assumptions. But every moral theory must be fitted to a similarly institutional structure if it is to be relevant to organizational behavior.

7. The reasonable-person rule began life as the reasonable-man rule, and it is severely criticized by many scholars for having enforced middle-class white male reasonableness on those other than middle-class white males. But the way such a rule has been used need not determine how it will be used hereafter. For an engaging discussion, see Calabresi 1985, especially chapter 2.

Aaker, D. A. 1991. *Managing Brand Equity*. New York: Free Press.

Abelson, R., and A. Levi. 1985. "Decision Making and Decision Theory." In *Handbook of Social Psychology*, Vol. 2, ed. G. Lindzey and E. Aronson. New York: Random House.

Abelson, R. P., D. Kinder, M. Peters, and S. T. Fiske. 1982. "Affective and Semantic Components in Political Person Perception." *Journal of Personality and Social Psychology* 42: 619–30.

Adams, J. L. 1986. *Conceptual Blockbusting: A Guide to Better Ideas*, 3rd ed. Reading, Mass.: Addison-Wesley.

Ainslie, G., and N. Haslam. 1992. "Self-control." In *Choice Over Time*, ed. G. Loewenstein and J. Elster. New York: Russell Sage Foundation.

Akerlof, G. 1970. "The Market for Lemons," *Quarterly Journal of Economics* 84: 488–500.

Allison, S. T., and E. Midgley. 1994. "The Quest for 'Similar Instances' and 'Simultaneous Possibilities': Metaphors in Social Dilemma Research." Unpublished manuscript, University of Richmond.

Allison, S. T., and D. M. Messick. 1990. "Social Decision Heuristics in the Use of Shared Resources." *Journal of Behavioral Decision Making* 3: 195–204.

Allison, S. T., D. M. Messick, and G. R. Goethals. 1989. "On Being Better But Not Smarter Than Others: The Muhammad Ali Effect." *Social Cognition* 7: 275–96.

Allport, G. W. 1954a. "The Historical Background of Modern Social Psychology." In *Handbook of Social Psychology*, vol. 1, ed. G. Lindley. Reading, Mass.: Addison-Wesley.

Allport, G. 1954b. *The Nature of Prejudice*. Cambridge, Mass.: Addison-Wesley.

Altman, I. 1975. *The Environment and Social Behavior*. Monterey, Calif.: Brooks/Cole.

American Institute of Certified Public Accountants. 1988. "Reports on Audited Financial Statements." Statement on Auditing Standards No. 58. New York: AICPA.

Anderson, E. 1993. *Value in Ethics and Economics*. Cambridge: Harvard University Press.

Anderson, N. H. 1981. *Foundations of Information Integration Theory*. New York: Academic Press.

Arendt, H. 1963. *Eichmann in Jerusalem: A Report on the Banality of Evil*. New York: Viking.

Arrow, K. J. 1951. *Social Choice and Individual Values*. New Haven, Conn.: Yale University Press.

Asch, D., J. Baron, J. C. Hershey, H. Kunreuther, J. Meszaros, I. Ritov, and M. Spranca. In press. "Determinants of Resistance to Pertussis Vaccination." *Medical Decision Making*.

Asch, S. 1952. *Social Psychology*. Englewood Cliffs, N.J.: Prentice-Hall.

Asch, S. E. 1946. "Forming Impressions of Personality." *Journal of Abnormal and Social Psychology* 41: 1230–40.

Asch, S. E. 1951. "Effects of Group Pressure Upon the Modification and Distortion of Judgments." In *Groups, Leadership, and Men*, ed. H. Guetzkow. Pittsburgh: Carnegie Press.

Ashford, S. J. 1989. "Self-assessment in Organizations: A Literature Review and Integrative Model." In *Research in Organizational Behavior*, Vol. 11, ed. L. L. Cummings and B. M. Staw. Greenwich, Conn.: JAI Press.

Babcock, L., G. Loewenstein, S. Issacharoff, and C. Camerer. 1995. "Biased Judgments of Fairness in Bargaining." *American Economic Review*. 85: 1337–43.

Bandura, A. 1977. *Social Learning Theory*. Englewood Cliffs, N.J.: Prentice Hall.

Barnett, R. C., N. L. Marshall, S. W. Raudenbush, and R. T. Brennan. 1993. "Gender and the Relationship Between Job Experiences and Psychological Distress." *Journal of Personality and Social Psychology* 64: 794–806.

Baron, J. 1992. "The Effect of Normative Beliefs on Anticipated Emotions." *Journal of Personality and Social Psychology* 63: 320–30.

Baron, J. 1993. *Morality and Rational Choice*. Dordrecht: Kluwer.

Baron, J. 1994. "Nonconsequentialist Decisions (With Commentary and Reply)." *Behavioral and Brain Sciences* 17: 1–42.

Baron, J. 1995. "Blind Justice: Fairness to Groups and the Do-No-Harm Principle." *Journal of Behavioral Decision Making* 8: 71–83.

Baron, J., and I. Ritov. 1993. "Intuitions About Penalties and Compensation in the Context of Tort Law." *Journal of Risk and Uncertainty* 7: 17–33.

Baron, J., and I. Ritov. 1994. "Reference Points and Omission Bias." *Organizational Behavior and Human Decision Processes* 59: 475–98.

Baron, J., and J. G. Miller. 1994. "Differences Between Indian and U.S. College Students in Judged Obligation to Help Others in Need." Unpublished manuscript, University of Pennsylvania.

Baron, J., and J. Jurney. 1993. "Norms Against Voting for Coerced Reform." *Journal of Personality and Social Psychology* 6: 347–55.

Barry, B., and R. Hardin. 1982. *Rational Man and Irrational Society*? Beverly Hills: Sage.

Batson, C. D., J. G. Batson, J. K. Slingsby, K. L. Harrell, H. M. Peekna, and R. M. Todd. 1991. "Empathic Joy and the Empathy-Altruism Hypothesis." *Journal of Personality and Social Psychology* 61: 413–26.

Bazelon, D. L. 1979. "Risk and Responsibility." *Science* 205: 277–80.

Bazerman, M. H. 1994. *Judgment in Managerial Decision Making*. New York: Wiley.

Bazerman, M. H., G. F. Loewenstein, and S. B. White. 1992. "Psychological Determinants of Utility in Competitive Contexts: The Impact of Elicitation Procedure." *Administrative Science Quarterly* 57: 220–40.

Bazerman, M. H., M. A. Schroth, P. P. Shah, K. A. Diekmann, and A. E. Tenbrunsel. 1994. "The Inconsistent Role of Social Comparison and Procedural Justice in Reactions to Hypothetical Job Descriptions: Implications for Job Acceptance Decisions." *Organizational Behavior and Human Decision Processes* 60: 326–52.

Beaney, W. M. 1966. "The Right to Privacy and American Law." *Law and Contemporary Problems* 31: 253–71.

Beauchamp, T. L., and J. F. Childress. 1994. *Principles of Biomedical Ethics*. New York: Oxford University Press.

Belk, R. 1984. "Cultural and Historical Differences in Concepts of Self and Their Effects on Attitudes Toward Having and Giving." *Advances in Consumer Research* 11: 753–60.

Belk, R. 1985. "Materialism: Trait Aspects of Living in the Material World." *Journal of Consumer Research* 12: 265–79.

Belk, R., and J. Painter. 1983. "Effects of Causal Attributions on Pollution and Litter Control Attitudes." In *Non-profit Marketing: Conceptual and Empirical Research*, ed. F. K. Shuptrine and Peter Reingen. Tempe, Ariz.: Bureau of Business and Economics Research.

Belk, R., J. Painter, and R. Semenik. 1981. "Preferred Solutions to the Energy Crisis as a Function of Causal Attributions." *Journal of Consumer Research* 8 (December): 306–31.

Bell, N. E., and P. E. Tetlock. 1989. "The Intuitive Politician and the Assignment of Blame in Organizations." In *Impression Management in the Organization*, ed. R. A. Giacalone and P. Rosenfeld. Hillsdale, N.J.: Lawrence Erlbaum.

Belliveau, M. A. 1995. "Understanding Employee Reactions to Affirmative Action Implementation: Identity versus Interest Effects on Procedural Fairness Judgments." Ph.D. diss., University of California, Berkeley.

Berry, S. H., and D. E. Kanouse. 1987. "Physician Response to a Mailed Survey: An Experiment in Timing of Payment." *Public Opinion Quarterly* 51: 102–14.

Bhide, A., and H. H. Stevenson. 1990. "Why Be Honest If Honesty Doesn't Pay?" *Harvard Business Review* (Sept.–Oct.): 317–26.

Bickerstaffe, J., and D. Pearce. 1980. "Can There Be a Consensus on Nuclear Power?" *Social Studies of Science* 10: 309–44.

Biernat, M., and M. Manis. 1994. "Shifting Standards and Stereotype-based Judgments." *Journal of Personality and Social Psychology* 66: 5–20.

Biernat, M., M. Manis, and T. E. Nelson. 1991. "Stereotypes and Standards of Judgment." *Journal of Personality and Social Psychology* 60: 485–99.

Bies, R. J. 1987. "The Predicament of Injustice: The Management of Moral Outrage." In *Research in Organizational Behavior*, Vol. 9, ed. L. L. Cummings and B. Staw. Greenwich, Conn.: JAI Press.

Bies, R. J. 1993. "Privacy and Procedural Justice." *Social Justice Research* 6: 69–86.

Bies, R. J., and J. S. Moag. 1986. "Interactional Justice: Communication Criteria of Fairness." In *Research on Negotiation in Organizations*, ed. R. J. Lewicki, B. H. Sheppard, and M. H. Bazerman. Greenwich, Conn.: JAI Press.

Bies, R. J., and S. B. Sitkin. 1993. "Law Without Justice: The Dilemmas of Formalization and Fairness in the Legalistic Organization." *Employee Responsibilities and Rights Journal* 6: 271–75.

Bies, R. J., and T. M. Tripp. 1993. "Employee-Initiated Defamation Lawsuits: Organizational Responses and Dilemmas." *Employee Responsibilities and Rights Journal* 6: 313–24.

Bies, R. J., and T. M. Tripp. 1995. "The Use and Abuse of Power: Justice as Social Control." In *Organizational Politics, Justice, and Support: Managing Social Climate at Work*, ed. R. Cropanzano and M. Kacmar. New York: Quorum Press.

Bies, R. J., and T. M. Tripp. In press. "Beyond Distrust: 'Getting Even' and the Need for Revenge." In *Trust and Organizations*, ed. R. M. Kramer and T. Tyler. Thousand Oaks, Calif.: Sage.

Bies, R. J., T. M. Tripp, and M. A. Neale. 1993. "Procedural Fairness and Profit Seeking: The Perceived Legitimacy of Market Exploitation." *Journal of Behavioral Decision Making* 6: 243–56.

Bies, R. J., and T. Tyler. 1993. "The "Litigation Mentality" in Organizations: A Test of Alternative Psychological Explanations." *Organization Science* 4: 352–66.

Blackburn, J. D., E. I. Klayman, and R. O. Nathan. 1993. "Invasion of Privacy: Refocusing the Tort in Private Sector Employment." *DePaul Business Law Journal* 6: 41–75.

Blanchard, F. A., T. Lilly, and L. A. Vaughn. 1991. "Reducing the Expression of Racial Prejudice." *Psychological Science* 2: 101.

Blanz, M., A. Mummendey, and S. Otten. 1994. "Evaluating Positive versus Negative Outcome Allocations Between Groups: The Role of Prescriptive and Statistical Norms." Unpublished manuscript, Westfälische Wilhelms University, Münster, Germany.

Blass, T. 1991. "Understanding Behavior in the Milgram Obedience Experiment." *Journal of Personality and Social Psychology* 60: 398–413.

Bloustein, E. J. 1964. "Privacy as an Aspect of Human Dignity: An Answer to Dean Prosser." *New York University Law Review* 39: 962–1007.

Boles, T. L. and D. M. Messick. 1995. "A Reverse Outcome Bias: The Influence of Multiple Reference Points on the Evaluation of Outcomes and Decisions." *Organizational Behavior and Human Decision Processes* 61: 262–75.

Bolton, G. E., E. Katok, and R. Zwick. In press. "Dictator Game Giving: Rules of Fairness Versus Acts of Kindness." *International Journal of Game Theory.*

Bonacich, P., and S. Schneider. 1992. "Communication Networks and Collective Action." In *A Social Psychological Approach to Social Dilemmas*, ed. W. G. Liebrand, D. M. Messick, and H. A. M. Wilke. Oxford: Pergamon Press.

Boulton, D. 1978. *The Grease Machine.* New York: Harper & Row.

Bowers, D. K. 1993. "Privacy at a Price." *Marketing Research: A Magazine of Management & Applications* 5(4): 40–41.

Braithwaite, R. B. 1955. *Theory of Games as a Tool for the Moral Philosopher.* Cambridge: Cambridge University Press.

Brandt, R. B. 1961. *Value and Obligation.* New York: Harcourt, Brace & World.

Brehmer, B. 1980. "In One Word: Not from Experience." *Acta Psychologica* 45: 223–41.

Brewer, M. B. 1979. "In-group Bias in the Minimal Intergroup Situation: A Cognitive-Motivational Analysis." *Psychological Bulletin* 56: 307–24.

Brewer, M. B. 1991. "The Social Self: On Being the Same and Different at the Same Time." *Personality and Social Psychology Bulletin* 17:475–82.

Brinthaupt, T. M., R. L. Moreland, and J. M. Levine. 1991. "Sources of Optimism Among Prospective Group Members." *Personality and Social Psychology Bulletin* 17: 36–43.

Brockner, J. 1988. *Self-Esteem at Work: Research, Theory, and Practice.* Lexington, Mass.: Lexington Books.

Brockner, J. 1992. "The Escalation of Commitment Toward a Failing Course of Action: Toward Theoretical Progress." *Academy of Management Review* 17: 39–61.

Brockner, J., and J. Z. Rubin. 1985. *Entrapment in Escalating Conflicts.* New York: Springer-Verlag.

Brokensha, D. W., D. M. Warren, and O. Werner. 1980. *Indigenous Knowledge: Systems and Development*. Lanham, Md.: University Press of America.

Brown, J. D. 1984. "Effects of Induced Mood on Causal Attributions for Success and Failure." *Motivation and Emotion* 8: 343–53.

Brown, J. D. 1986. "Evaluations of Self and Others: Self-enhancement Biases in Social Judgment." *Social Cognition* 4: 353–76.

Brown, J. D. 1990. "Evaluating One's Abilities: Shortcuts and Stumbling Blocks on the Road to Self-knowledge." *Journal of Experimental Social Psychology* 26: 149–67.

Brown, R. 1986. *Social Psychology*. New York: Free Press.

Burke, E. J. 1988. "How Citizens Think About Risks to Health." *Risk Analysis* 8: 309–14.

Burke, M. J., C. C. Borucki, and A. E. Hurley. 1992. "Reconceptualizing Psychological Climate in a Retail Service Environment." *Journal of Applied Psychology* 77: 717–29.

Bylinski, G. 1991. "How Companies Spy on Employees." *Fortune* 124 (November): 131–40.

Cacioppo, J., and G. Berntson. 1994. "Relationship Between Attitudes and Evaluative Space: A Critical Review, with Emphasis on the Separability of Positive and Negative Substrates." *Psychological Bulletin* 115: 401–23.

Cairncross, F. 1993. *Costing the Earth*. Boston: Harvard Business School Press.

Calabresi, G. 1970. *The Costs of Accidents: A Legal and Economic Analysis*. New Haven: Yale University Press.

Calabresi, G. 1985. *Ideals, Beliefs, Attitudes, and the Law: Private Law Perspectives on a Public Law Problem*. Syracuse, N.Y.: Syracuse University Press.

Campbell, T. W. 1992. "Therapeutic Relationships and Iatrogenic Outcomes: The Blame-and-Change Maneuver in Psychotherapy." *Psychotherapy* 29: 474–80.

Campbell, T. W. 1994. *Beware the Talking Cure: Psychotherapy May Be Hazardous to Your Mental Health*. Boca Raton, Fla.: Upton Books.

Cappel, J. J. 1993. "Closing the E-Mail Privacy Gap." *Journal of Systems Management* 44(12): 6–11.

Carey, J. T. 1987. "Benton Harlow: Distributor of Unsafe Drugs." In *Corporate Violence*, ed. S. L. Hills. Totowa, N.J.: Rowman & Littlefield.

Carley, W. L. 1995. "Whole Lotta Shakin' Has Some Owners Rattled at Mercedes." *Wall Street Journal*, June 7, 1995, A1, 14.

Carr, A. 1968. "Is Business Bluffing Ethical?" In *Ethical Issues in Business*, 4th ed., ed. Thomas Donaldson and Patricia Werhane. Englewood Cliffs, N.J.: Prentice-Hall.

Carroll, A. B. 1989. *Business and Society: Ethics and Stakeholder Management*. Cincinnati: SouthWestern Publishing Company.

Carsten, J. M., and P. E. Spector. 1987. "Unemployment, Job Satisfaction, and Employee Turnover." *Journal of Applied Psychology* 72: 374–81.

Cartwright, D. 1959. *Studies in Social Power*. Ann Arbor, Mich.: Research Center for Group Dynamics, Institute for Social Research.

Cascio, W. F. 1991. *Costing Human Resources*. 3rd ed. Boston: PWS-Kent.

Caudill, H. M. 1987. "Manslaughter in a Coal Mine." In *Corporate Violence*, ed. S. L. Hills. Totowa, N.J.: Rowman & Littlefield.

Cha, J. H., and K. D. Nam. 1985. "A Test of Kelley's Cube Theory of Attribution: A Cross-cultural Replication of McArthur's Study." *Korean Social Science Journal* 12: 151–80.

Chaiken, S., A. Liberman, and A. H. Eagly. 1989. "Heuristic and Systematic Information Processing Within and Beyond the Persuasion Context." In *Unintended
Thought*, ed. J. S. Uleman and J. A. Bargh. New York: Guilford Press.

Chaiken, S., and C. Stangor. 1987. "Attitudes and Attitude Change." *Annual Review of
Psychology* 38: 575–630.

Chalykoff, J., and T. A. Kochan. 1989. "Computer-aided Monitoring: Its Influence on
Employee Satisfaction and Turnover." *Personnel Psychology* 40: 807–34.

Chambless, D. L. 1993. "Task Force on Promotion and Discrimination of Safe and
Effective Psychological Procedures." Report of Division 12 (clinical) Board, American Psychological Association.

Chatman, J. A. 1991. "Matching People and Organizations." *Administrative Science
Quarterly* 36: 459–84.

Christensen, A., and M. S. Jacobson. 1994. "Who (or What) Can Do Psychotherapy:
The Status and Challenge of Nonprofessional Therapies." *Psychological Science*
5: 8–14.

Christensen-Szalanski, J. J. 1984. "Discount Functions and the Measurement of
Patients' Values: Women's Decisions During Childbirth." *Medical Decision Making*
4: 47–58.

Cialdini, R. B. 1993. *Influence: Science and Practice*. 3rd ed. New York: HarperCollins.

Cialdini, R. B., J. T. Cacioppo, R. Basset, and J. A. Miller. 1978. "The Low-Ball Technique for Producing Compliance: Commitment then Cost." *Journal of Personality
and Social Psychology* 36: 463–76.

Cialdini, R. B., M. Schaller, D. Houlihan, K. Arps, J. Fultz, and A. Beaman. 1987.
"Empathy-Based Helping: Is It Selflessly or Selfishly Motivated." *Journal of Personality and Social Psychology* 52: 749–58.

Cialdini, R. B., R. R. Reno, and C. A. Kallgren. 1990. "A Focus Theory of Normative
Conduct: Recycling the Concept of Norms to Reduce Littering in Public Places."
Journal of Personality and Social Psychology 58: 1015–26.

Clark, N. K., and D. R. Rutter. 1985. "Social Categorization, Visual Cues, and Social
Judgment." *European Journal of Social Psychology* 15: 105–19.

Clarke, M. 1990. *Business Crime: Its Nature and Control*. New York: St. Martin's Press.

Clinard, M. B., and P. C. Yeager. 1980. *Corporate Crime*. New York: Free Press.

Clore, G. L. 1992. "Cognitive Phenomenology: Feelings and the Construction of Judgment." In *The Construction of Social Judgments*, ed. L. L. Martin and A. Tesser. Hillsdale, N.J.: Lawrence Erlbaum.

Cohen, M., and N. Davis. 1981. *Medication Errors: Causes and Prevention*. Philadelphia:
G. F. Stickley.

Cohen, S., D. A. J. Tyrrell, and A. P. Smith. 1991. "Psychological Stress and Susceptibility to the Common Cold." *New England Journal of Medicine* 325: 606–12.

Colman, A. 1982. *Game Theory and Experimental Games*. Oxford: Pergamon Press.

Commoner, B. 1979. *The Politics of Energy*. New York: Knopf.

Cooper, J., and R. T. Croyle. 1984. "Attitudes and Attitude Change." *Annual Review of
Psychology* 35: 395–426.

Cousins, S. 1989. "Culture and Selfhood in Japan and the U.S." *Journal of Personality
and Social Psychology* 56: 124–31.

Covello, V. T., D. von Winterfeldt, and P. Slovic. 1986. "Risk Communication:
A Review of the Literature." *Risk Abstracts* 3: 171–82.

Coy, P. 1992. "Big Brother, Pinned to Your Chest." *Business Week*, August 17, 1992, 38.

Crews, F. 1993. "The Unknown Freud." *The New York Review of Books*, November 18, 1993, 55–65.

Croall, H. 1992. *White Collar Crime: Criminal Justice and Criminology*. Philadelphia: Open University Press.

Crosby, F. 1982. *Relative Deprivation and Working Women*. New York: Oxford University Press.

Crossen, B. R. 1993. "Managing Employee Unethical Behavior Without Invading Privacy." *Journal of Business and Psychology* 8: 227–43.

Crouch, E. A. C., and R. Wilson. 1981. *Risk Analysis*. Cambridge, Mass.: Ballinger.

Culnan, M. J., H. J. Smith, and R. J. Bies. 1994. "Law, Privacy, and Organizations: The Corporate Obsession to Know v. the Individual Right Not to Be Known." In *The Legalistic Organization*, ed. S. B. Sitkin and R. J. Bies. Thousand Oaks, Calif.: Sage.

Cupchick, G. C., and H. Leventhal. 1974. "Consistency Between Evaluative Behavior and the Evaluation of Humorous Stimuli." *Journal of Personality and Social Psychology* 30: 429–42.

Dalal, A. K., R. Sharma, and S. Bisht. 1983. "Causal Attributions of Ex-criminal Tribal and Urban Children in India." *Journal of Social Psychology* 119: 163–71.

Daly, H. E., and J. B. Cobb. 1994. *For the Common Good*. Boston: Beacon Press.

Darley, J. 1992. "Social Organization for the Production of Evil." *Psychological Inquiry* 3: 199–218.

Darley, J., and B. Latane. 1968. "Bystander Intervention in Emergencies: Diffusion of Responsibility." *Journal of Personality and Social Psychology* 8: 377–83.

Darley, J. M., and P. H. Gross. 1983. "A Hypothesis-Confirming Bias in Labeling Effects." *Journal of Personality and Social Psychology* 44: 20–33.

Davidson, D. 1974. "On the Very Idea of a Conceptual Scheme." *Proceedings of the American Philosophical Association* 48.

Dawes, R. M. 1980. "Social Dilemmas." *Annual Review of Psychology* 31: 169–93.

Dawes, R. M. 1988. *Rational Choice in an Uncertain World*. New York: Harcourt Brace Jovanovich.

Dawes, R. M. 1989. "Statistical Criteria for Establishing a Truly False Consensus Effect." *Journal of Experimental Social Psychology* 25: 1–17.

Dawes, R. M. 1990. "The Potential Nonfalsity of the False Consensus Effect." In *Insights in Decision Making: A Tribute to Hillel J. Einhorn*, ed. R. M. Hogarth. Chicago: University of Chicago Press.

Dawes, R. M. 1994. *House of Cards: Psychology and Psychotherapy Built on Myth*. New York: The Free Press.

Dawes, R. M., D. Faust, and P. E. Meehl. 1989. "Clinical Versus Actuarial Judgment." *Science* 243: 1668–74.

Dawes, R. M., D. Singer, and F. Lemons. 1972. "An Experimental Analysis of the Contrast Effect and Its Implications for Intergroup Communication and the Indirect Assessment of Attitude." *Journal of Personality and Social Psychology* 21(3): 281–95.

Dawkins, R. 1976. *The Selfish Gene*. New York: Oxford University Press.

Day, G. S. 1991. *Learning About Markets*. Marketing Science Institute Report No. 91-117.

Dépret, E. F., and S. T. Fiske. 1993. "Social Cognition and Power. Some Cognitive Consequences of Social Structure as a Source of Control Deprivation." In *Control Motivation and Social Cognition*, ed. G. Weary, F. Gleicher, and K. Marsh. New York: Springer-Verlag.

Deci, E. L., and R. M. Ryan. 1987. "The Support of Autonomy and the Control of Behavior." *Journal of Personality and Social Psychology* 53: 1024–37.

Deci, E. L., J. P. Connell, and R. M. Ryan. 1989. "Self-Determination in a Work Organization." *Journal of Applied Psychology* 74: 580–90.

Deutsch, M. 1985. *Distributive Justice: A Social Psychological Perspective.* New Haven: Yale University Press.

Deutsch, M. 1990. "Psychological Roots of Moral Exclusion." *Journal of Social Issues* 46: 21–25.

Devine, P. G. 1989a. "Overattribution Effect: The Role of Confidence and Attributional Complexity." *Social Psychology Quarterly* 52: 149–58.

Devine, P. G. 1989b. "Stereotypes and Prejudice: Their Automatic and Controlled Components." *Journal of Personality and Social Psychology* 56: 5–18.

Devine, P. G., and M. J. Monteith. 1993. "The Role of Discrepancy-Associated Affect in Prejudice Reduction." In *Affect, Cognition, and Stereotyping: Interactive Processes in Group Perception*, ed. D. M. Mackie and D. L. Hamilton. San Diego, Calif.: Academic Press.

Dewe, P. 1993. "Measuring Primary Appraisal." *Journal of Social Behavior and Personality* 8: 673–85.

Diekmann, K. A., S. Samuels, L. Ross, and M. H. Bazerman. 1995. "Asymmetric Interpretations of Fairness and Justification in Evaluation and Allocation Decisions." Working paper, Northwestern University.

Djerassi, C. 1989. "The Bitter Pill." *Science* 245: 356–61.

Dockson, R. R. 1993. *Justice in the Balance: Report of the Commission of the California Court.* San Francisco: Supreme Court of California.

Doern, G. B. 1978. "Science and Technology in the Nuclear Regulatory Process: The Case of Canadian Uranium Miners." *Canadian Public Administration* 21: 51–82.

Dollard, J., L. Doob, N. Miller, O. H. Mowrer, and R. R. Sears. 1939. *Frustration and Aggression.* New Haven, Conn.: Yale University Press.

Donaldson, T. 1982. *Corporations and Morality.* Englewood Cliffs, N.J.: Prentice-Hall.

Donaldson, T. 1989. *The Ethics of International Business*, Oxford: Oxford University Press.

Donaldson, T. 1994. "Where Integration Fails: The Logic of Prescription and Description in Business Ethics." *Business Ethics Quarterly* 4: 157–70.

Donaldson, T., and L. Preston. 1995. "The Stakeholder Theory of the Corporation: Concepts, Evidence, Implications." *Academy of Management Review* (January): 65–91.

Donaldson, T., and T. Dunfee. 1995. "Integrative Social Contracts Theory: A Communitarian Conception of Economic Ethics." *Economics and Philosophy*: 85–112.

Donaldson, T., and T. W. Dunfee. 1994. "Towards a Unified Conception of Business Ethics: Integrative Social Contracts Theory." *Academy of Management Review* 19: 252–84.

Dorsey, D. 1994. *The Force.* New York: Random House.

Dowie, M. 1987. "Pinto Madness." In *Corporate Violence*, ed. S. L. Hills. Totowa, N.J.: Rowman & Littlefield.

Drachman, D., A. deCarufel, and C. A. Insko. 1978. "The Extra Credit Effect in Interpersonal Attraction." *Journal of Experimental Social Psychology* 14: 458–67.

Driscoll, R., K. E. Davis, and M. E. Lipetz. 1972. "Parental Interference and Romantic Love: The Romeo and Juliet Effect." *Journal of Personality and Social Psychology* 24: 1–10.

Dryzek, J. S. 1990. *Discursive Democracy: Politics, Policy, and Political Science*. New York: Cambridge University Press.

Eagly, A. H., and M. E. Kite. 1987. "Are Stereotypes of Nationalities Applied to Both Men and Women?" *Journal of Personality and Social Psychology* 53: 457–62.

Eagly, A. H., and S. Chaiken. 1993. *The Psychology of Attitudes*. Fort Worth, Tex.: Harcourt Brace Jovanovich.

Eberhardt, J., and S. T. Fiske. 1995. "Motivating People to Change—Or at least to Treat You Right." In *Foundations of Stereotypes and Stereotyping*, ed. N. M. Macrae, M. Hewstone, and C. Stangor. New York: Guilford Press.

Einhorn, H. J., and R. M. Hogarth. 1986. "Judging Probable Cause." *Psychological Bulletin* 99: 3–19.

Elliott, R. K., and J. J. Willingham. 1980. *Management Fraud: Detection and Deterrence*. New York: Petrocelli.

Elsbach, K., and R. Kramer. 1994. "Cognitive Strategies for Managing Organizational Identity." Unpublished manuscript, Stanford University.

Environmental Protection Agency. 1990. *Reducing Risk: Setting Priorities and Strategies*. Washington, D.C.: Author.

Environmental Protection Agency. 1993. *A Guidebook to Comparing Risks and Setting Environmental Priorities*. Washington, D.C.: Author.

Epstein, S., and W. D. Fenz. 1967. "The Detection of Areas of Emotional Stress through Variations in Perceptual Threshold and Physiological Arousal." *Journal of Experimental Research in Personality* 2: 191–99.

Erber, R., and S. T. Fiske. 1984. "Outcome Dependency and Attention to Inconsistent Information." *Journal of Personality and Social Psychology* 47: 709–26.

Faulkner, P. 1987. "Exposing Risks of Nuclear Disaster" [Confessions of a Whistle Blower]. In *Corporate Violence*, ed. S. L. Hills. Totowa, N.J.: Rowman & Littlefield.

Faust, D. In press. "Use Then Prove or Prove Then Use? Some Thoughts on the Ethics of Mental Health Professionals' Courtroom Involvement." *Ethics and Human Behavior*.

Festinger, L. 1957. *A Theory of Cognitive Dissonance*. Stanford: Stanford University Press.

Fincham, F. D., and J. M. Jaspars. 1980. "Attribution of Responsibility: From Man the Scientist to Man as Lawyer." In *Advances in Experimental Social Psychology*, Vol. 13, ed. L. Berkowitz. New York: Academic Press.

Fischhoff, B. 1975. "Hindsight = Foresight: The Effect of Outcome Knowledge on Judgment Under Uncertainty." *Journal of Experimental Psychology: Human Perception and Performance*, 1: 288–99.

Fischhoff, B. 1982. "Latitudes and Platitudes: How Much Credit Do People Deserve?" In *New Directions in Decision Making*, ed. G. Ungson and D. Braunstein. New York: Kent.

Fischhoff, B. 1987. "Treating the Public with Risk Communications: A Public Health Perspective." *Science, Technology, and Human Values* 12: 3–19.

Fischhoff, B. 1988. "Judgment and Decision Making." In *The Psychology of Human Thought*, ed. R. J. Sternberg and E. E. Smith. New York: Cambridge University Press.

Fischhoff, B. 1990. "Psychology and Public Policy: Tool or Tool Maker?" *American Psychologist* 45: 57–63.

Fischhoff, B. 1994. "Acceptable Risk: A Conceptual Proposal." *Risk: Health, Safety & Environment* 1: 1–28.

Fischhoff, B. 1995. "Risk Perception and Communication Unplugged: Twenty Years of Process." *Risk Analysis* 15: 137–46.

Fischhoff, B., A. Bostrom, and M. J. Quadrel. 1993. "Risk Perception and Communication." *Annual Review of Public Health* 14: 183–203.

Fischhoff, B., and L. A. Cox, Jr. 1985. "Conceptual Framework for Regulatory Benefit Assessment." In *Benefits Assessment: The State of the Art*, ed. J. D. Bentkover, V. T. Covello, and J. Mumpower. Dordrecht, The Netherlands: D. Reidel.

Fischhoff, B., P. Slovic, and S. Lichtenstein. 1978. "Fault Trees: Sensitivity of Assessed Failure Probabilities to Problem Representation." *Journal of Experimental Psychology: Human Perception and Performance* 4: 330–44.

Fischhoff, B., P. Slovic, and S. Lichtenstein. 1982. "Lay Foibles and Expert Fables in Judgments About Risk." *American Statistician* 36: 240–55.

Fischhoff, B., P. Slovic, and S. Lichtenstein. 1983. "The "Public" vs. the "Experts": Perceived vs. Actual Disagreement About the Risks of Nuclear Power." In *Analysis of Actual vs. Perceived Risks*, ed. V. Covello, G. Flamm, J. Rodericks and R. Tardiff. New York: Plenum.

Fischhoff, B., P. Slovic, S. Lichtenstein, S. Read, and B. Combs. 1978. "How Safe is Safe Enough? A Psychometric Study of Attitudes Towards Technological Risks and Benefits." *Policy Sciences* 8: 127–52.

Fischhoff, B., S. Lichtenstein, P. Slovic, S. Derby, and R. Keeney. 1981. *Acceptable Risk.* New York: Cambridge University Press.

Fischhoff, B., S. Watson, and C. Hope. 1984. "Defining Risk." *Policy Sciences* 17: 123–39.

Fischhoff, M. 1993. *Ordinary Housewives: Women Activists in the Grass-Roots Toxics Movement.* Unpublished honors thesis, Harvard University.

Fiske, S. T. 1992. "Thinking Is for Doing: Portraits of Social Cognition from Daguerrotype to Laserphoto." *Journal of Personality and Social Psychology* 63: 877–89.

Fiske, S. T. 1993a. "Controlling Other People: The Impact of Power on Stereotyping." *American Psychologist* 48: 621–28.

Fiske, S. T. 1993b. "Social Cognition and Social Perception." *Annual Review of Psychology* 44: 155–94.

Fiske, S. T., and P. Glick. 1995. "Ambivalence and Stereotypes Cause Sexual Harassment: A Theory with Implications for Organizational Change." *Journal of Social Issues* 51: 97–115.

Fiske, S. T., and S. E. Taylor. 1991. *Social Cognition*, 2nd ed. New York: McGraw-Hill.

Fiske, S. T., and S. L. Neuberg. 1990. "A Continuum of Impression Formation, from Category-Based to Individuating Processes: Influences of Information and Motivation on Attention and Interpretation." In *Advances in Experimental Social Psychology*, Vol. 23, ed. M. P. Zanna. New York: Academic Press.

Fiske, S. T., S. A. Goodwin, L. D. Rosen, and A. M. Rosenthal. 1995. "Romantic Outcome Dependency and the (In)accuracy of Impression Formation: A Case of Clouded Judgment." Unpublished manuscript, University of Massachusetts at Amherst.

Fiske, S. T., S. L. Neuberg, A. E. Beattie, and S. J. Milberg. 1987. "Category-Based and Attribute-Based Reactions to Others: Some Informational Conditions of Stereotyping and Individuating Processes." *Journal of Experimental Social Psychology* 23: 399–427.

Fitzpatrick, J. S. 1980. "Adapting to Danger: A Participant Observation Study of an Underground Mine." *Sociology of Work and Occupations* 7: 131–80.

Fletcher, J. S. O., and C. Ward. 1988. "Attribution Theory and Processes: A Cross-cultural Perspective." In *The Cross-cultural Challenge to Social Psychology*, ed. M. H. Bond. Newbury Park, Calif.: Sage.

Folger, R., and R. J. Bies. 1989. "Managerial Responsibilities and Procedural Justice." *Employee Responsibilities and Rights Journal* 2: 79–90.

Folkes, V. S. 1984. "Consumer Reactions to Product Failure: An Attributional Approach." *Journal of Consumer Research* 13: 398–409.

Folkes, V. S. 1988. "Recent Attribution Research in Consumer Behavior: A Review and New Directions." *Journal of Consumer Research* 14: 548–65.

Frank, N. 1987. "Murder in the Workplace." In *Corporate Violence*, ed. S. L. Hills. Totowa, N.J.: Rowman & Littlefield.

Frank, R. H. 1993. "What Price the Moral High Ground?" Unpublished manuscript, Cornell University.

Frank, R. H. 1988. "Passions Within Reason: The Strategic Role of the Emotions." New York: Norton.

Frank, R. H., T. Gilovich, and D. Regan. 1993. "The Evolution of One-Shot Cooperation," *Ethology and Sociobiology* 14 (July): 247–56.

Frank, Robert. 1989. "Frames of Reference and the Quality of Life." *The American Economic Review* 79 (May): 80–85.

Frankel, C. 1974. "The Rights of Nature." In *When Values Conflict*, ed. T. Schelling, J. Voss, and L. Tribe. Cambridge, Mass.: Ballinger.

Freedman, J. L., and S. C. Fraser. 1966. "Compliance Without Pressure: The Foot-in-the-Door Technique." *Journal of Personality and Social Psychology* 4: 195–203.

Freeman, R. E., and D. R. Gilbert. 1988. *Corporate Strategy and the Search for Ethics.* Englewood Cliffs, N.J.: Prentice-Hall.

Freeman, R. E. 1984. *Strategic Management: A Stakeholder Approach.* Boston: Pitman Press.

French, J. R. P., and B. Raven. 1959. "The Bases of Social Power." In *Studies in Social Power*, ed. D. Cartwright. Ann Arbor, Mich: Research Center for Group Dynamics, Institute for Social Research.

Frenzen, J. R., and H. L. Davis. 1990. "Purchasing Behavior in Embedded Markets." *Journal of Consumer Research* 17: 1–12.

Freudenburg, W. R., and S. K. Pastor. 1992. "Public Responses to Technological Risks: Toward a Sociological Perspective." *Sociological Quarterly* 33(3): 389–402.

Friedman, L. M. 1990. *The Republic of Choice: Law, Authority, and Culture.* Cambridge: Harvard University Press.

Friedman, M. 1957. *A Theory of Consumption Function.* Princeton: Princeton University Press.

Friedman, M. 1970. "The Social Responsibility of Business Is to Increase Its Profits." *New York Times Magazine* 33 (September 13): 122–26.

Friedman, S. M. 1981. "Blueprint for Breakdown: Three Mile Island and the Media Before the Accident." *Journal of Communication* 31: 116–29.

Funtowicz, S. O., and J. R. Ravetz. 1990. *Uncertainty and Quality in Science for Policy.* Boston: Kluwer Academic Press.

Furby, L., P. Slovic, B. Fischhoff, and R. Gregory. 1988. "Public Perceptions of Electric Power Transmission Lines." *Journal of Environmental Psychology* 8: 19–43.

Fusilier, M. R., and W. D. Hoyer. 1980. "Variables Affecting Perceptions of Invasion of Privacy in a Personnel Selection Situation." *Journal of Applied Psychology* 65: 623–26.

Gaertner, S. L., and J. F. Dovidio. 1977. "The Subtlety of White Racism, Arousal, and Helping Behavior." *Journal of Personality and Social Psychology* 35: 691–707.

Gaertner, S. L., and J. F. Dovidio. 1986. "The Aversive Form of Racism." In *Prejudice, Discrimination, and Racism*, ed. J. Dovidio and S. Gaertner. Orlando, Fla.: Academic Press.

Gaertner, S. L., and J. P. McLaughlin. 1983. "Racial Stereotypes: Associations and Ascriptions of Positive and Negative Characteristics." *Social Psychology Quarterly* 46: 23–30.

Gaertner, S. L., J. Mann, J. Dovidio, A. Murrell, and M. Pomare. 1990. "How Does Cooperation Reduce Intergroup Bias?" *Journal of Personality and Social Psychology* 59: 692–704.

Gamble, D. J. 1978. "The Berger Inquiry: An Impact Assessment Process." *Science* 199: 946–51.

Garland, E. 1994. "Entering the Virtual Office." *Marketing Computers* 14(2): 6–7.

Gately, D. 1980. "Individual Discount Rates and the Purchase and Utilization of Energy-using Durables." *Bell Journal of Economics* 11: 373–74.

Gautier, D. 1986. *Morals by Agreement*. New York: Oxford University Press.

Gentile, M. C. 1994. *Differences That Work: Organizational Excellence Through Diversity*. Cambridge, Mass.: Harvard University Press.

George, A. 1980. *Presidential Decision Making and Foreign Policy*. Boulder, Col.: Westview.

George, W. H., S. J. Gournic, and M. P. McAfee. 1988. "Perceptions of Postdrinking Female Sexuality." *Journal of Applied Social Psychology* 18: 1295–1317.

Gettys, C. F., R. M. Pliske, C. Manning, and J. T. Casey. 1987. "An Evaluation of Human Act Generation Performance." *Organizational Behavior and Human Performance* 39: 23–51.

Gibbons, A. 1992. "Researchers Fret over Neglect of 600 Million Patients." *Science* 256: 1135.

Gibson, M., ed. 1985. *To Breathe Freely: Risk, Consent, and Air*. Totowa, N.J.: Rowman & Allanheld.

Gilbert, D. T. 1989. "Thinking Lightly About Others: Automatic Components of the Social Inference Process." In *Unintended Thought*, ed. J. S. Uleman and J. A. Bargh. New York: Guilford Press.

Gilbert, D. T., B. W. Pelham, and D. S. Krull. 1988. "On Cognitive-Busyness: When Person Perceivers Meet Persons Perceived." *Journal of Personality and Social Psychology* 54: 733–40.

Gilligan, C. 1982. *In a Different Voice*. Cambridge: Harvard University Press.

Gilovich, T. 1991. *How We Know What Isn't So: The Fallibility of Human Reason in Everyday Life*. New York: Free Press.

Gioia, D. 1992. "Pinto Fires and Personal Ethics: A Script Analysis of Missed Opportunities." *Journal of Business Ethics* 11: 379–89.

Gladwin, T. N. 1993. "The Global Environmental Crisis and Management Education." *Total Quality Environmental Management* 3(1): 109–14.

Gladwin, T. N., T. K. Freeman, and J. J. Kennelly. 1994. "Ending our Denial and Destruction of Nature: Toward Biophysically Sustainable Management Theory." Working paper, New York University.

Glazer, M. P., and P. M. Glazer. 1989. *The Whistleblowers*. New York: Basic Books.

Gnepp, J., and J. Klayman. 1992. "Recognition of Uncertainty in Emotional Inferences: Reasoning About Emotionally Equivocal Situations." *Developmental Psychology* 28: 145–58.

Gnepp, J., E. McKee, and J. A. Domanic. 1987. "Children's Use of Situational Information to Infer Emotion: Understanding Emotionally Equivocal Situations." *Developmental Psychology* 23: 114–23.

Goethals, G. R. 1986. "Fabrication and Ignoring Social Reality: Self-serving Estimates of Consensus." In *Relative Deprivation in Social Comparison: The Ontario Symposium*, Vol. 4, ed. J. Olsen, C. P. Herman, and M. Zanna. Hillsdale, N. J.: Lawrence Erlbaum.

Goethals, G. R., D. M. Messick, and S. T. Allison. 1990. The Uniqueness Bias: Studies of Constructive Social Comparison. In *Social Comparison: Contemporary Theory and Research*, ed. J. Suls and T. A. Wills. Hillsdale, N. J.: Lawrence Erlbaum.

Goffman, E. 1959. *The Presentation of Self in Everyday Life*. Garden City, N.Y.: Doubleday.

Goffman, E. 1974. *Frame Analysis*. Boston: Northeastern University Press.

Goldberg, L. R., J. R. Grenier, R. M. Guion, L. B. Sechrest, and H. Wing. 1991. *Questionnaires Used in the Prediction of Trustworthiness in Pre-employment Decisions*. Washington, D.C.: American Psychological Association.

Goleman, D. 1985. *Vital Lies, Simple Truths: The Psychology of Self-deception*. New York: Simon and Schuster.

Goodpaster, K. 1983. "The Concept of Corporate Responsibility." In *Just Business*, ed. T. Regan. New York: Random House.

Goodwin, S. A., and S. T. Fiske. 1995. "Power and Motivated Impression Formation: How Powerholders Stereotype by Default and by Design." Unpublished manuscript, University of Massachusetts at Amherst.

Goodwin, S. A., S. T. Fiske, and V. Y. Yzerbyt. 1995. *Social Judgment in Power Relations: A Judgment Monitoring Perspective*. Poster session presented at the annual meeting of the American Psychological Association, Washington, D.C. (August).

Goodwin, S. A., V. Y. Yzerbyt, and S. T. Fiske. 1994. "Hierarchical Power Relationships and Impression Formation." Unpublished raw data, University of Massachusetts at Amherst.

Gore, A. 1993. *Earth in the Balance*. New York: Penguin Books.

Gottfredson, D., L. Wilkins, and P. Hoffman. 1978. *Guidelines for Parole and Sentencing*. Lexington, Mass.: Lexington Books.

Gouldner, A. W. 1960. "The Norm of Reciprocity: A Preliminary Statement." *American Sociological Review* 25: 161–78.

Greenberg, J. 1990. "Employee Theft as a Reaction to Underpayment Inequity: The Hidden Cost of Pay Cuts." *Journal of Applied Psychology* 75: 561–68.

Greenberg, M. S., and S. P. Shapiro. 1971. "Indebtedness: An Adverse Effect of Asking For and Receiving Help." *Sociometry* 34: 290–301.

Greenwald, A. G. 1980. "The Totalitarian Ego: Fabrication and Revision of Personal History." *American Psychologist* 35: 603–18.

Güth, W., R. Schmittberger, and B. Schwarze. 1982. "An Experimental Analysis of Ultimatum Bargaining." *Journal of Economic Behavior and Organization* 3: 367–88.

Guarasci, R. 1987. "Death by Cotton Dust." In *Corporate Violence*, ed. S. L. Hills. Totowa, N.J.: Rowman & Littlefield.

Haidt, J., and J. Baron. 1995. "Social Roles and the Moral Judgment of Acts and Omissions." *European Journal of Social Psychology.*

Hall, E. T. 1966. *The Hidden Dimension.* Garden City, N.Y.: Doubleday.

Hall, J. A. 1987. "On Explaining Gender Differences: The Case of Non-verbal Communication." In *Review of Personality and Social Psychology,* Vol. 7, ed. P. Shaver and C. Hendrick. Beverly Hills, Calif.: Sage.

Halpern, S. 1992. "Big Boss is Watching You." *Details* 16: 18–23.

Hamilton, D. L., and S. J. Sherman. 1989. "Illusory Correlations: Implications for Stereotype Theory and Research." In *Stereotypes and prejudice: Changing conceptions,* ed. D. Bar-Tal, C. F. Graumann, A. W. Kruglanski, and W. Stroebe. New York: Springer-Verlag.

Hamilton, V. L. 1980. "Intuitive Psychologist or Intuitive Lawyer? Alternative Models of the Attribution Process." *Journal of Personality and Social Psychology* 39: 767–72.

Hammond, K. R., and L. Adelman. 1976. "Science, Values, and Human Judgment." *Science* 194: 389–96.

Handler, P. 1980. "Public Doubts About Science." *Science* 208: 1093.

Hanley, J. 1980. "The Silence of Scientists." *Chemical and Engineering News* 58(12): 5.

Hanson, K. 1991. "We Must Find Our Business Heroes." *Executive Excellence* 8: 5–6.

Hardin, G. 1968. "The Tragedy of the Commons." *Science* 162: 1243–48.

Hardin, G. 1988. "Living on a Lifeboat." In *Managing the Commons,* ed. G. Hardin and J. Baden. San Francisco: W. H. Freeman.

Hardin, G., and J. Baden. 1988. *Managing the Commons.* San Francisco: W. H. Freeman.

Hardin, R. 1988. *Morality Within the Limits of Reason.* Chicago: University of Chicago Press.

Hardin, R. 1989a. "Autonomy, Identity, and Welfare." In *The Inner Citadel: Essays on Individual Autonomy,* ed. John Christman. New York: Oxford University Press.

Hardin, R. 1989b. "Ethics and Stochastic Processes." *Social Philosophy and Policy* 7 (Autumn): 69–80.

Hardin, R. 1990. "Incentives and Beneficence." *Social Justice Research* 4 (June): 87–104.

Hardin, R. 1991. "To Rule in No Matters, To Obey in All: Democracy and Autonomy," *Contemporary Philosophy* 13 (12, November–December): 1–7.

Hardin, R. 1996. "Institutional Morality." In *The Theory of Institutional Design,* ed. Robert E. Goodin. Cambridge: Cambridge University Press.

Hare, R. M. 1963. *Freedom and Reason.* Oxford: Clarendon Press.

Hare, R. M. 1973. *Applications of Moral Philosophy.* Berkeley, Calif.: University of California Press.

Hare, R. M. 1981. *Moral Thinking: Its Levels, Method and Point.* Oxford: Oxford University Press.

Harris, L. 1980. "Risk in a Complex Society." Public opinion survey conducted for Marsh and McLennan Companies, Inc., New York.

Harris, L. 1991. *Harris-Equifax Consumer Privacy Survey 1991.* Atlanta: Equifax.

Harris, L., and A. F. Westin. 1979. *The Dimensions of Privacy: A National Opinion Research Survey of Attitudes Toward Privacy.* Stevens Point, Wis.: Sentry Insurance Company.

Harris, M. J., R. Milch, E. M. Corbitt, D. W. Hoover, and M. Brady. 1992. "Self-fulfilling Effects of Stigmatizing Information on Children's Social Interactions." *Journal of Personality and Social Psychology* 63: 41–50.

Hart, H. L. A., and A. M. Honoré. 1959. *Causation in the Law.* Oxford: Oxford University Press.

Hastie, R. 1984. "Causes and Effects of Causal Attribution." *Journal of Personality and Social Psychology* 46: 44–56.

Heath, C. 1995. "Escalation and De-escalation of Commitment in Response to Sunk Costs: The Role of Budgeting in Mental Accounting." *Organizational Behavior and Human Decision Processes* 62: 38–54.

Heimer, C. A. 1988. "Social Structure, Psychology, and the Estimation of Risk." *Annual Review of Sociology* 14: 491–519.

Heisenberg, W. 1958. *Physics and Philosophy*. New York: Harper.

Hendrickx, L., C. Vlek, and H. Oppewal. 1989. "Relative Importance of Scenario Information and Frequency Information in the Judgment of Risk." *Acta Psychologia* 72: 41–63.

Henrion, M., and B. Fischhoff. 1986. "Assessing Uncertainty in Physical Constants." *American Journal of Physics* 54: 791–98.

Hesslow, G. 1983. "Explaining Differences and Weighting Causes." *Theoria* 49: 87–111.

Hewstone, M. 1990. "The 'Ultimate Attribution Error'? A Review of the Literature on Intergroup Causal Attribution." *European Journal of Social Psychology* 20: 311–35.

Hewstone, M., C. N. Macrae, R. Griffiths, A. B. Milne, and R. Brown. In press. "Cognitive Models of Stereotype Change: Measurement, Development and Consequences of Subtyping." *Journal of Experimental Social Psychology*.

Hewstone, M., F. Fincham, and J. Jaspars. 1981. "Social Categorization and Similarity in Intergroup Behaviour: A Replication with 'Penalties.' " *European Journal of Social Psychology* 11: 101–07.

Higgins, E. T. 1987. "Self-discrepancy: A Theory Relating Self and Affect." *Psychological Review* 94: 319–40.

Higgins, E. T. 1989. "Knowledge Accessability and Activation: Subjectivity and Suffering from Unconscious Sources." In *Unintended Thought*, ed. J. S. Uleman and J. A. Bargh. New York: Guilford Press.

Higgins, E. T., and C. Stangor. 1988. 'A Change of Standard' Perspective on the Relations Among Context, Judgment, and Memory." *Journal of Personality and Social Psychology* 54: 181–92.

Higgins, E. T., and J. A. Bargh. 1987. "Social Cognition and Social Perception." *Annual Review of Psychology* 38: 369–425.

Hilton, D. J. 1990. "Conversational Processes in Causal Explanation." *Psychological Bulletin* 107: 65–81.

Hilton, D. J., and B. R. Slugoski. 1986. "Knowledge-based Causal Attribution: The Abnormal Conditions Focus Model." *Psychological Review* 93: 75–88.

Hiramatsu, T. 1993. "Protecting Telecommunications in Japan." *Communications of the ACM* 36(8): 74–77.

Hoerr, J., K. M. Hafner, G. DeGeorge, A. R. Field, and L. Zinn. 1988. "Privacy." *Business Week*, March 28, 1988, 61–68.

Hoffman, E., K. McCabe, K. Shachat, and V. Smith. In press. "Preferences, Property Rights and Anonymity in Bargaining Games." *Games and Economic Behavior*.

Hoffman, P., and B. Stone-Meierhofer. 1977. Application of Guidelines to Sentencing. *Law & Psychology Review* 3: 53–60.

Hofstede, S. 1980. *Culture's Consequences: International Differences in Work-Related Values*. Beverly Hills, Calif.: Sage.

Hollinger, R. C., and J. P. Clark. 1983. *Theft by Employees*. Lexington, Mass.: Lexington Books.

Holt, R. R. 1994. "Unknown Freud: Yet Another Exchange." Letter to the editor, *The New York Review of Books*, April 21, 66.

Hornstein, H. A., E. Fisch, and M. Holmes. 1968. "Influence of a Model's Feeling About his Behavior and his Relevance as a Comparison Other on Observers' Helping Behavior." *Journal of Personality and Social Psychology* 10: 222–26.

Howard, D. J. 1990. "The Influence of Verbal Responses to Common Greetings on Compliance Behavior: The Foot-in-the-Mouth Effect." *Journal of Applied Social Psychology* 20: 1185–96.

Hsee, C. 1994a. "The Elasticity Effect: Uncertainty-Allowed Choice Shift Toward a Tempting but Task-Irrelevant Direction." Working paper, Graduate School of Business, University of Chicago.

Hsee, C. K. 1994b. "Elastic Justification: Affective Influences on Monetary Decision Making." Working paper, University of Chicago.

Hsee, C. K. 1995. "Elastic Justification: How Tempting but Task Irrelevant Factors Influence Decisions." *Organizational Behavior and Human Decision Processes* 62: 330–37.

Huber, P. W. 1988. *Liability: The Legal Revolution and Its Consequences*. New York: Basic Books.

Hui, C. H., and H. C. Triandis. 1986. "Individualism and Collectivism: A Study of Cross-Cultural Researchers." *Journal of Cross-Cultural Psychology* 17: 225–48.

Hume, D. [1739–40] 1978. *A Treatise of Human Nature*, ed. L. A. Selby-Bigge and P. H. Nidditch. Oxford: Oxford University Press.

Iaffaldano, M. T., and P. M. Muchinsky. 1985. "Job Satisfaction and Job Performance: A Meta-analysis." *Psychological Bulletin* 97: 251–73.

Irwin, J. R., P. Slovic, S. Lichtenstein, and G. H. McClelland. 1993. "Preference Reversals and the Measurement of Environmental Values." *Journal of Risk and Uncertainty* 6(1): 5–18.

Jacobs, D. 1994. "The Perils of Policing Employees." *Small Business Reports* 19(2): 22–26.

Jahoda, G. 1982. *Psychology and Anthropology: A Psychological Perspective*. London: Academic Press.

Janis, I. 1972. *Victims of Groupthink: A Study of Foreign-Policy Decisions and Fiascos*. New York: Houghton-Mifflin.

Jarvis, W. B. G., and R. E. Petty. In press. "The Need to Evaluate." *Journal of Personality and Social Psychology*.

Jenni, K., and G. Loewenstein. 1994. "Explaining the Identifiable Victim Effect." Working paper, Carnegie Mellon University.

Johnson, M. 1993. *Moral Imagination*. Chicago: University of Chicago Press.

Johnston, L., and M. Hewstone. 1992. "Cognitive Models of Stereotype Change: Subtyping and the Perceived Typicality of Disconfirming Group Members. *Journal of Experimental Social Psychology* 28: 360–86.

Jones, E. E., and K. E. Davis. 1965. "From Acts to Dispositions: The Attribution Process in Person Perception." In *Advances in Experimental Social Psychology*, Vol. 2., ed. L. Berkowitz. New York: Academic Press.

Jost, J. T., and M. R. Banaji. 1994. "The Role of Stereotyping in System Justification and the Production of False Consciousness." *British Journal of Social Psychology* 33: 1–27.

Joule, R. V. 1987. "Tobacco Deprivation: The Foot-in-the-Door Technique Versus the Low-Ball Technique." *European Journal of Social Psychology* 17: 361–65.

Jourard, S. M. 1966. "Some Psychological Aspects of Privacy." *Law and Contemporary Problems* 31: 307–18.

Judd, C. M., and B. Park. 1993. Definition and assessment of accuracy in social stereotypes. *Psychological Review* 100: 109–28.

Judd, C. M., C. S. Ryan, and B. Park. 1991. "Accuracy in the judgment of in-group and out-group variability." *Journal of Personality and Social Psychology* 61: 366–79.

Jungermann, H. 1983. "The Two Camps on Rationality." In *Decision Making under Uncertainty*, ed. R. W. Scholz. Amsterdam: Elsevier.

Jungermann, H., and P. Slovic. 1993. "Characteristics of Individual Risk Perception." In *Risk Is a Construct*, ed. B. Rück. Munich: Knesebeck.

Jussim, L. 1991. "Social Perception and Social Reality: A Reflection-Construction Model." *Psychological Review* 98: 54–73.

Kadish, M. R., and S. H. Kadish. 1973. *Discretion to Disobey: A Study of Lawful Departures from Legal Rules*. Stanford: Stanford University Press.

Kahn, W. A. 1990. "Toward an Agenda for Business Ethics Research." *Academy of Management Review* 15: 311–28.

Kahneman, A., and A. Tversky. 1979. "Prospect Theory: An Analysis of Decision Under Risk." *Econometrica* 47: 263–91.

Kahneman, D., and A. Tversky. 1982. "The Simulation Heuristic." In *Judgment Under Uncertainty: Heuristics and Biases*, ed. D. Kahneman, P. Slovic, and A. Tversky. New York: Cambridge University Press.

Kahneman, D., and A. Tversky. 1984. "Choices, Values, and Frames." *American Psychologist* 39: 341–50.

Kahneman, D., and D. T. Miller. 1986. "Norm Theory: Comparing Reality to its Alternatives." *Psychological Review* 93: 136–53.

Kahneman, D., and I. Ritov. 1994. "Determinants of Stated Willingness to Pay for Public Goods: A Study in the Headline Method." *Journal of Risk and Uncertainty* 9: 5–38.

Kahneman, D., J. Knetsch, and R. Thaler. 1986. "Perceptions of Unfairness: Constraints on Wealth Seeking," *American Economic Review* 76: 728–41.

Kant, I. [1797]1909. "On a Supposed Right to Tell Lies from Benevolent Motives." In *Kant's* Critique of Practical Reason *and Other Works on the Theory of Ethics*, 6th ed., ed. T. K. Abbott. London: Longman.

Kant, I. [1785]1959. *Foundations of the Metaphysics of Morals*, trans. L. W. Beck. New York: Liberal Arts Press.

Karnow, S. 1983. *Vietnam: A History*. New York, Viking.

Katz, I., and R. G. Haas. 1988. "Racial Ambivalence and American Value Conflict: Correlational and Priming Studies of Dual Cognitive Structures." *Journal of Personality and Social Psychology* 55: 893–905.

Keeney, R. L. 1993. *Value-Focused Thinking: A Path to Creative Decisionmaking*. Cambridge: Harvard University Press.

Keeney, R. L., O. Renn, and D. von Winterfeldt. 1987. "Structuring West Germany's Energy Objectives." *Energy Policy* 15: 352–62.

Kelley, H. H. 1967. "Attribution Theory in Social Psychology." In *Nebraska Symposium on Motivation*, ed. D. Levine. Omaha: University of Nebraska Press.

Kelman, H. C., and V. C. Hamilton. 1989. *Crimes of Obedience: Towards a Social Psychology of Authority and Responsibility*. New Haven: Yale University Press.

Khanna, T., R. Gulati, and N. Nohria. 1995. "The Dynamics of Learning Alliances: Competition, Cooperation, and Relative Scope." Harvard Business School Weekly Paper No. 95-055. Cambridge, Mass.: Harvard Business School.

Klayman, J. 1995. "Varieties of Confirmation Bias." In *Decision Making from the Perspective of Cognitive Psychology*, ed. J. R. Busemeyer, R. Hastie, and D. L. Medin. New York: Academic Press.

Klayman, J., and Y.-W. Ha. 1987. "Confirmation, Disconfirmation, and Information in Hypothesis Testing." *Psychological Review* 94: 211–28.

Klayman, J., and Y.-W. Ha. 1989. "Hypothesis Testing in Rule Discovery: Strategy, Structure and Content." *Journal of Experimental Psychology: Learning, Memory, and Cognition* 15: 596–604.

Klein, B., and K. Leffler. 1981. "The Role of Market Forces in Assuring Contractual Performance." *Journal of Political Economy* 89: 615–41.

Kluegel, J. R., and E. R. Smith. 1986. "Beliefs About Inequality." New York: Aldine de Gruyter.

Koehler, J. J. 1993. "The Influence of Prior Beliefs on Scientific Judgments of Evidence Quality." *Organizational Behavior and Human Decision Processes* 56: 28–55.

Komin, S. 1991. *Psychology of the Thai People: Values and Behavioral Patterns*. Bangkok: National Institute of Development Administration.

Komorita, S. S., and C. D. Parks. 1994. *Social Dilemmas*. Madison, Wis.: Brown & Benchmark.

Kramer, R. C. 1922. "The Space Shuttle *Challenger* Explosion: A Case Study of State-Corporate Crime." In *White-Collar Crime*, ed. K. Schlegel and D. Weisburd. Boston: Northeastern University Press.

Kramer, R. M. 1989. "Windows of Vulnerability or Cognitive Illusions? Cognitive Processes and the Nuclear Arms Race." *Journal of Experimental Social Psychology* 25: 79–100.

Kramer, R. M. 1991. "Intergroup Relations and Organizational Dilemmas: The Role of Categorization Processes." In *Research in Organizational Behavior*, Vol. 13, ed. L. L. Cummings and B. M. Staw. Greenwich, Conn.: JAI Press.

Kramer, R. M., D. Meyerson, and G. Davis. 1990. "How Much is Enough? Psychological Components of 'Guns Versus Butter' Decisions in a Security Dilemma." *Journal of Personality and Social Psychology* 58: 984–93.

Kramer, R. M., E. Newton, and P. Pommerenke. 1993. "Self-enhancement Biases and Negotiator Judgment: Effects of Self-esteem and Mood." *Organizational Behavior and Human Decision Processes* 56: 110–33.

Kruglanski, A. W. 1970. "Attributing Trustworthiness in Worker-Supervisor Relations." *Journal of Experimental Social Psychology* 6: 214–32.

Kruglanski, A. W. 1989. *Lay Epistemics* and *Human Knowledge: Cognitive and Motivational Bases*. New York: Plenum Press.

Kunda, Z. 1990. "The Case for Motivated Reasoning." *Psychological Bulletin* 108: 480–98.

Kunda, Z., and K. C. Oleson. 1994. "Maintaining Stereotypes in the Face of Disconfirmation: Constructing Grounds for Subtyping Deviants." Unpublished manuscript.

Kunen, J. S. 1994. *Reckless Disregard*. New York: Simon and Schuster.

Labich, K. 1992 "The New Crisis in Business Ethics." *Fortune*. April 20, 1992. 167–76.

Ladd, J. 1970. "Morality and the Ideal of Rationality in Corporate Organizations." In *Ethical Issues in Business*, 2nd ed., ed. T. Donaldson and P. Werhane. Englewood Cliffs, N.J.: Prentice-Hall.

LaFrance, M. 1985. "Postural Mirroring and Intergroup Relations." *Personality and Social Psychology Bulletin* 11: 207–17.

Langer, E. J. 1975. "The Illusion of Control." *Journal of Personality and Social Psychology* 32: 311–28.

Lea, J. A., H. J. Smith, and T. R. Tyler. 1994. "Predicting Support for Compensatory Public Policies." Unpublished manuscript, University of California, Berkeley.

Leiss, W., and C. Chociolko. 1994. *Risk and Responsibility*. Kingston and Montreal: Queens and McGill University Press.

Lerner, M. J., and D. T. Miller. 1978. "Just World Research and the Attribution Process: Looking Back and Ahead." *Psychological Bulletin* 85: 1030–51.

LeRoy, M. H. 1990. "Drug Testing in the Public Sector: Union Member Attitudes." *Journal of Collective Negotiations in the Public Sector* 19: 165–73.

Levin, I. P., S. K. Schnittjer, and S. L. Thee. 1988. "Information Framing Effects in Social and Personal Decisions." *Journal of Experimental Social Psychology* 24: 520–29.

Lewin, K., and P. Grabbe. 1945. "Conduct, Knowledge, and Acceptance of New Values." *Journal of Social Issues* 53–64.

Lewis, M. 1989. *Liar's Poker*. New York: Norton.

Lewis, S. B. 1990. *Ideals as prototypes: The role of representational complexity*. Doctoral diss., University of Oregon, Eugene.

Leyens, J.-Ph. 1983. *Sommes-nous tous des psychologues? Approche psychosociale des théories implicites de personalité*. Brussels: Mardaga.

Leyens, J.-Ph., and Yzerbyt, V. Y. 1992. "The Ingroup Overexclusion Effect: Impact of Valence and Confirmation on Stereotypical Information Search." *European Journal of Social Psychology* 22: 549–70.

Leyens, J.-Ph., V. Y. Yzerbyt, and G. Schadron. 1992. "Stereotypes and Social Judgeability." In *European Review of Social Psychology*, Vol. 3, ed. W. Stroebe and M. Hewstone. Chichester, Eng.: Wiley.

Leyens, J.-Ph., V. Y. Yzerbyt, and G. Schadron. 1994. *Stereotypes and Social Cognition*. London: Sage.

Leyens, J.-Ph., V. Y. Yzerbyt, O. Corneille, D. Vilain, and G. Gonçalves. 1995. "The Role of Naive Theories in the Emergence of the Overattribution Bias." Unpublished manuscript, Université Catholique de Louvain, Belgium.

Lifton, R. J. 1986. *The Nazi Doctors: Medical Killing and the Psychology of Genocide*. New York: Basic Books.

Lind, E. A., T. R. Tyler, and Y. J. Huo. 1994. "Situational and Cultural Variation in the Antecedents of Procedural Justice Judgments in Personal Disputes." Unpublished manuscript, University of California, Berkeley.

Lind, E. A., Y. U. Huo, and T. R. Tyler. 1994. ". . . And Justice for All: Ethnicity, Gender, and Preferences for Dispute Resolution Procedures." *Law and Human Behavior* 18: 269–90.

Lippmann, W. [1922]1961. *Public Opinion*. New York: MacMillan.

Lipset, S. M., and W. Schneider. 1983. *The Confidence Gap: Business, Labor, and Government in the Public Mind*. New York: Free Press.

Locke, K. S., and L. M. Horowitz. 1990. "Satisfaction in Interpersonal Interactions as a Function of Similarity in Level of Dysphoria." *Journal of Personality and Social Psychology* 58: 823–31.

Loewenstein, G. 1988. "Frames of Mind in Intertemporal Choice." *Management Science* 34: 200–14.

Loewenstein, G., and D. Adler. 1995. "A Bias in the Prediction of Tastes." *Economic Journal* 105: 929–37.

Loewenstein, G., and F. Furstenberg. 1991. "Is Teenage Sexual Behavior Rational?" *Journal of Applied Psychology* 21 (12): 957–86.

Loewenstein, G., and J. Elster. 1992. *Choice Over Time*. New York: Russell Sage Foundation.

Loewenstein, G., and N. Sicherman. 1991. "Do Workers Prefer Increasing Wage Profiles?" *Journal of Labor Economics* 9 (1): 67–84.

Loewenstein, G., and R. Thaler. 1989. "Anomalies: Intertemporal Choice." *Journal of Economic Perspectives* 3: 181–93.

Loewenstein, G., L. Thompson, and M. H. Bazerman. 1989. "Social Utility and Decision Making in Interpersonal Contexts." *Journal of Personality and Social Psychology* 57: 426–41.

Loewenstein, G., S. Blount, and M. H. Bazerman. In press. "The Inconsistent Evaluation of Comparative Payoffs in Labor Supply and Bargaining." *Journal of Economic Behavior and Organizations*.

Loewenstein, G., S. Issacharoff, C. Camerer, and L. Babcock. 1993. "Self-Serving Assessments of Fairness and Pretrial Bargaining." *Journal of Legal Studies* 22: 135–59.

Lord, C., L. Ross, and M. C. Lepper. 1979. "Biased Assimilation and Attitude Polarization: The Effects of Prior Theories on Subsequently Considered Evidence." *Journal of Personality and Social Psychology* 37: 2098–2109.

Lord, M. W. 1987. "A Plea for Corporate Conscience." In *Corporate Violence*, ed. S. L. Hills. Totowa, N.J.: Rowman & Littlefield.

Lorenz, E. 1988. "Neither Friends Nor Strangers: Informal Networks of Subcontracting in French Industry." In *Trust: The Making and Breaking of Cooperative Relations*, ed. Diego Gambetta. New York: Basil Blackwell.

Lowrance, W. 1976. *Of Acceptable Risk*. San Francisco: Kaufmann.

Lutane, B., K. Williams, and S. Harkins. 1979. "Social Loafing." *Psychology Today* 13: 104–10.

Lynn, M. 1991. "Scarcity Effects on Value: A Quantitative Review of the Commodity Theory Literature." *Psychology and Marketing* 8: 43–57.

MacDonald, E. M., and T. Tritch. 1993. "Nosy IRS Employees May Be Peeking at Your Returns for Kicks." *Money* 22(10): 16–17.

Mackie, J. L. 1974. *The Cement of the Universe: A Study of Causation*. Oxford: Clarendon Press.

Mackie, J. L. 1978. "The Law of the Jungle: Moral Alternatives and Principles of Evolution." *Philosophy* 53: 455–64.

Mackie, D. M., and L. T. Worth. 1989. "Cognitive Deficits and the Mediation of Positive Affect in Persuasion." *Journal of Personality and Social Psychology* 57: 27–40.

Macrae, C. N., A. B. Milne, and G. V. Bodenhausen. 1994. "Stereotypes as Energy-Saving Devices: A Peek Inside the Cognitive Toolbox." *Journal of Personality and Social Psychology* 66: 37–47.

Magat, W. A., W. K. Viscusi, and J. Huber. 1988. "Paired Comparison and Contingent Valuation Approaches to Morbidity Risk Valuation." *Journal of Environmental Economics & Management* 15 (4): 395–411.

Mandeville, B. [1714]1924. *The Fable of the Bees*, ed. F. B. Kaye. Oxford: Oxford University Press; reprint, Indianapolis: Liberty Press, 1988.

March, J. G. 1994. *A Primer on Decision Making*. New York: Free Press.

Markus, H. R., and S. Kitayama. 1991. "Culture and the Self: Implications for Cognition, Emotion, and Motivation." *Psychological Review* 98: 224–53.

Masters, M. F., G. R. Ferris, and S. L. Ratcliff. 1988. "Practices and Attitudes of Substance Abuse Testing." *Personnel Administrator* 33: 72–78.

Matarazzo, J. 1990. "Psychological Assessment Versus Psychological Testing: Validation from Binet to the School Clinic." *American Psychologist* 45: 999–1017.

Mauro, R. 1994. *An Evaluation of the Drug Courier Profile and Its Use in Drug Interdiction searches*. Report, Institute of Cognitive and Decision Sciences, University of Oregon and at Eugene.

Mauro, R., and M. Kubovy. 1992. "Caricature and Face Recognition." *Memory and Cognition* 20: 433–40.

Mazis, M. B. 1975. "Antipollution Measures and Psychological Reactance Theory." *Journal of Personality and Social Psychology* 31: 654–66.

Mazur, A. 1981. *The Dynamics of Technical Controversy*. Washington, D.C.: Communications Press.

McClelland, D. C. 1975. *Power: The Inner Experience*. New York: Irvington.

McGill, A. L. 1989. "Context Effects in Judgments of Causation." *Journal of Personality and Social Psychology* 57: 189–200.

McGill, A. L. 1990a. "Conjunctive Explanations: The Effect of Comparison of the Target Episode to a Contrasting Background Instance." *Social Cognition* 8: 362–82.

McGill, A. L. 1990b. "Predicting Consumers' Reactions to Product Failure: Do Responsibility Judgments Follow from Consumers' Causal Explanations." *Marketing Letters* 2: 1, 59–70.

McGill, A. L. 1991. "The Influence of the Causal Background on the Selection of Causal Explanations." *British Journal of Social Psychology* 30: 79–87.

McGill, A. L. 1993. "Selection of a Causal Background: Role of Expectation Versus Feature Mutability." *Journal of Personality and Social Psychology* 64: 701–07.

McGill, A. L. In press. "American and Thai Managers' Explanations for Poor Company Performance: Role of Perspective and Culture in Causal Selection." *Organizational Behavior and Human Decision Processes*.

Meadows, D. H., D. L. Meadows, and J. Randers. 1992. *Beyond the Limits*. Post Mills, Vt.: Chelsea Green.

Merz, J. F., B. Fischhoff, D. J. Mazur, and P. S. Fischbeck. 1993. "A Decision-Analytic Approach to Developing Standards of Disclosure for Medical Informed Consent." *Journal of Products and Toxics Liabilities* 15: 191–215.

Messick, D. M. 1994, March 1. "Mortgage-Bias Complexities." *Chicago Tribune*.

Messick, D. M. 1994. "Social Categories and Business Ethics." Ruffin Lecture in Business Ethics, University of Virginia.

Messick, D., and M. Brewer. 1983. "Solving Social Dilemmas: A Review." In *Review of Personality and Social Psychology* 4, ed. L. Wheeler & P. Shaver. Newbury Park, CA: Sage.

Messick, D. M., and K. P. Sentis. 1979. "Fairness and Preference." *Journal of Experimental Social Psychology* 15: 418–34.

Messick, D. M., and K. P. Sentis. 1983. "Fairness, Preference and Fairness Biases." In *Equity Theory: Psychological and Sociological Perspectives*, ed. D. M. Messick and K. S. Cook. New York: Praeger.

Messick, D. M., and M. H. Bazerman. 1996. "Ethical Leadership and the Psychology of Decision Making." *Sloan Management Review* 37: 9–22.

Messick, D. M., S. Bloom, J. P. Boldizer, and C. D. Samuelson. 1985. "Why We Are Fairer Than Others." *Journal of Experimental Social Psychology* 21: 480–500.

Miceli, M. P., and J. P. Near. 1992. *Blowing the Whistle*. New York: Lexington Books.

Milgram, S. 1965. "Some Conditions of Obedience and Disobedience to Authority." *Human Relations* 18: 57–76.

Milgram, S. 1974. *Obedience to Authority: An Experimental View*. New York: Harper & Row.

Milgram, S., L. Bickman, and O. Berkowitz. 1969. "Note on the Drawing Power of Crowds of Different Size." *Journal of Personality and Social Psychology* 31: 79–82.

Mill, J. S. [1872]1973. "System of Logic." In *Collected Works of John Stuart Mill*, Vols. 7 and 8, ed. J. M. Robson. Toronto: University of Toronto Press.

Miller, D. T., and S. Gunasegaram. 1990. "Temporal Order and the Perceived Mutability of Events: Implications for Blame Assignment." *Journal of Personality and Social Psychology* 61: 5–12.

Miller, D. T., B. Taylor, and M. Buck. 1991. "Gender Gaps: Who Needs To Be Explained?" *Journal of Personality and Social Psychology* 61: 5–12.

Miller, J. B. 1976. *Toward a New Psychology of Women*. Boston: Beacon Press.

Miller, J. G. 1984. "Culture and the Development of Everyday Social Explanations." *Journal of Personality and Social Psychology* 46: 961–78.

Miller, J. G., D. M. Bersoff, and R. L. Harwood. 1990. "Perceptions of Social Responsibilities in India and in the United States: Moral Imperatives or Personal Decisions?" *Journal of Personality and Social Psychology* 58: 33–47.

Mills, C. W. 1965. *The Sociological Imagination*. New York: Oxford University Press.

Milsram, S. 1974. *Obedience to Authority*. New York: Harper & Row.

Mintz, M. 1985. *At Any Cost: Corporate Greed, Women, and the Dalkon Shield*. New York: Pantheon Books.

Morgan, M. G., and L. Lave. 1991. "Ethical Considerations in Risk Communication Practice and Research." *Risk Analysis* 10: 355–58.

Morgan, M. G., and M. Henrion. 1990. *Uncertainty: A Guide to Dealing with Uncertainty in Quantitative Risk and Policy Analysis*. New York: Cambridge University Press.

Morgan, M. G., B. Fischhoff, A. Bostrom, L. Lave, and C. J. Altman. 1992. "Communicating Risk to the Public." *Environment, Science, and Technology* 26: 2048–56.

Mummendey, A., B. Simon, C. Dietze, M. Grunert, G. Haeger, S. Kessler, S. Letigen, and S. Schaferhoff. 1992. "Categorization Is Not Enough: Intergroup Discrimination in Negative Outcome Allocation." *Journal of Experimental Social Psychology* 28: 125–44.

Myers, D. G. and H. Lamm. 1976. "The Group Polarization Phenomenon." *Psychological Bulletin* 83: 602–27.

Myrdal, G. 1944. *An American Dilemma: The Negro Problem and American Democracy*. New York: Harper.

Nacoste, R. 1990. "Sources of Stigma: Analyzing the Psychology of Affirmative Action." *Law and Policy* 12: 175–95.

Nagel, T. 1989. *A View From Nowhere*. New York: Oxford University Press.

National Research Council. 1989. *Improving Risk Communication*. Washington, D.C.: Author.

National Research Council. 1994. *Judgment in Risk Assessment*. Washington, D.C. Author.

National Research Council. 1996. *Understanding Risk: Informing Decisions in a Democratic Society*. Washington, D.C.: National Research Council.

Neisser, U. 1976. *Cognition and Reality*. San Francisco: W. H. Freeman.

Nelkin, D. 1977. "Technological Decisions and Democracy." Beverly Hills, Calif.: Sage.

Nelkin, D. 1994. "Science Controversies." In *Handbook of Science and Technology Studies*, ed. S. Jasanoff, G. E. Markle, J. C. Petersen, and T. Pinch. Thousand Oaks, Calif.: Sage.

Neuberg, S. L. 1989. "The Goal of Forming Accurate Impressions During Social Interactions: Attenuating the Impact of Negative Expectancies." *Journal of Personality and Social Psychology* 56: 374–86.

Neuberg, S. L., and J. T. Newsome. 1993. "Personal Need for Structure: Individual Differences in the Desire for Simple Structure." *Journal of Personality and Social Psychology* 65: 113–31.

Neuberg, S. L., and S. T. Fiske. 1987. "Motivational Influences on Impression Formation: Outcome Dependency, Accuracy-Driven Attention, and Individuating Processes." *Journal of Personality and Social Psychology* 53: 431–44.

Neustadt, R. E., and E. May. 1986. *Thinking in Time*. New York: Free Press.

Neyman, J. 1979. *Probability Models: Medicine and Biology*. Berkeley, Calif.: University of California, Statistical Laboratory.

Ng, S. H. 1980. *The Social Psychology of Power*. San Francisco: Academic Press.

Ng, S. H. 1984. "Equity and Social Categorization Effects in Intergroup Allocation of Rewards." *British Journal of Social Psychology* 23: 163–72.

Nisbett, R. E., and L. Ross. 1980. *Human Inference: Strategies and Shortcomings of Social Judgment*. Englewood Cliffs, N.J.: Prentice-Hall.

O'Reilly, C. A., J. Chatman, and D. F. Caldwell. 1991. "People and Organizational Culture." *Academy of Management Journal* 34: 487–516.

Oldham, G. R., and D. J. Brass. 1979. "Employee Reactions to an Open-Plan Office: A Naturally Occurring Quasi-experiment." *Administrative Science Quarterly* 24: 267–84.

Omoto, A. M., and E. Borgida. 1988. "Guess Who Might Be Coming to Dinner? Personal Involvement and Racial Stereotyping." *Journal of Experimental Social Psychology* 24: 571–93.

Orts, E. W. 1995. "Reflexive Environmental Law." *Northwestern University Law Review* 89 (Summer).

Orwell, G. 1949. *1984*. New York: Harcourt Brace.

Park, B., and C. M. Judd. 1990. "Measures and Models of Perceived Group Variability." *Journal of Personality and Social Psychology* 59: 173–91.

Park, B. M., and M. Rothbart. 1982. "Perception of Out-Group Homogeneity and Levels of Social Categorization: Memory for the Subordinate Attributes of In-Group and Out-Group Members." *Journal of Personality and Social Psychology* 42: 1051–1068.

Pavelchak, M. A. 1989. "Piecemeal and Category-Based Evaluation: An Idiographic Analysis." *Journal of Personality and Social Psychology* 56: 354–63.

Payne, J. W., J. R. Bettman, and E. J. Johnson. 1992. "Behavioral Decision Research: Theory and Applications." *Annual Review of Psychology* 43: 87–131.

Perloff, L. S. 1983. "Perceptions of Vulnerability to Victimization." *Journal of Social Issues* 39: 41–61.

Perloff, L. S., and B. K. Feltzer. 1986. "Self-other Judgments and Perceived Vulnerability to Victimization." *Journal of Personality and Social Psychology* 50: 502–10.

Perrow, C. 1984. *Normal Accidents: Living with High Risk Technologies*. New York: Random House.

Perry, S., and J. Dawson. 1985. *Nightmare*. New York: Macmillan.

Petersilia, J., S. Turner, J. Kahan, and J. Peterson. 1985. *Granting Felons Probation: Public Risks and Alternatives*. Santa Monica, Calif: Rand.

Phillips, D. P., and L. L. Carstensen. 1988. "The Effect of Suicide Stories on Various Demographic Groups, 1968–1985." *Suicide and Life-Threatening Behavior* 18: 100–14.

Plater, Z., R. Abrams, and W. Goldfarb. 1992. *Environmental Law and Policy: Nature, Law, and Society*. St. Paul, Minn.: West.

Platt, J. 1973. "Social Traps." *American Psychologist* 28: 641–51.

Platt, J. R. 1964. "Strong Inference." *Science* 146: 347–53.

Quattrone, G. A., and E. E. Jones. 1980. "The Perception of Variability Within In-groups and Out-groups: Implications for the Law of Small Numbers." *Journal of Personality and Social Psychology* 38: 141–52.

Railton, P. 1986. "Moral Realism." *Philosophical Review* 95: 163–80.

Rand, A. 1971. *The Fountainhead*. New York: New American Library.

Rawls, J. 1971. *A Theory of Justice*. Cambridge, Mass.: Harvard University Press.

Rawls, J. 1993. *Political Liberalism*. New York: Columbia University Press.

Reason, J. 1990. *Human Error*. New York: Cambridge University Press.

Regan, D. T. 1971. "Effects of a Favor and Liking on Compliance." *Journal of Experimental Social Psychology* 7: 627–39.

Reitze, A. 1989. "Environmental Policy: It Is Time for a New Beginning." *Columbia Journal of Environmental Law* 14(1): 111–56.

Rescher, N. 1975. *Unselfishness*. Pittsburgh: Pittsburgh University Press.

Reynolds, L. 1993. "Debate Is Brewing over Employees' Right to Privacy." *HR Focus* 70(2): 1–4.

Riley, T., and S. T. Fiske. 1991. "Interdependence and the Social Context of Impression Formation." *Cahiers de psychogie cognitive* 11: 173–92.

Ritov, I., and J. Baron. 1990. "Reluctance to Vaccinate: Omission Bias and Ambiguity." *Journal of Behavioral Decision Making* 3: 263–77.

Ritov, I., and J. Baron. 1992. "Status-quo and Omission Bias." *Journal of Risk and Uncertainty* 5: 49–61.

Rohrmann, B. 1994. "Risk Perceptions of Different Societal Groups." *Australian Journal of Psychology* 46: 15–163.

Rolston, H. 1994. *Conserving Natural Value*. New York: Columbia University Press.

Rorty, R. 1993. "Putnam and the Relativist Menace." *Journal of Philosophy* XC: 1–36.

Rosch, E. 1973. "On the Internal Structure of Perceptual and Semantic Categories." In *Cognitive Development and the Acquisition of Language*, ed. T. E. Moore. New York: Academic Press.

Rosch, E. 1978. "Principles of Categorization." In *Cognition and Categorization*, ed. E. Rosch and B. B. Lloyd. Hillsdale, N.J.: Erlbaum.

Roseman, E. 1981. *Managing Employee Turnover*. New York: AMACOM.

Rosenbaum, B. L. 1973. "Attitude Toward Invasion of Privacy in the Personnel Selection Process and Job Applicant Demographic and Personality Correlates." *Journal of Applied Psychology* 58: 333–38.

Ross, L., and R. Nisbett. 1991. *The Person and the Situation*. New York: McGraw-Hill.

Roth, A., and K. Murnighan. 1982. "The Role of Information in Bargaining: An Experimental Study." *Econometrica* 50: 1123–42.

Rothbart, M., and M. Taylor. 1992. "Category Labels and Social Reality: Do We View Social Categories as Natural Kinds?" In *Language, Interaction and Social Cognition*, ed. G. R. Semin and K. Fiedler. London: Sage.

Rothbart, M., and O. John. 1993. "Intergroup Relations and Stereotype Change: A Social-Cognitive Analysis and Some Longitudinal Findings." In *Prejudice, Politics, and Race in America*, ed. P. M. Sniderman, P. E. Tetlock, & E. G. Carmines. Stanford: Stanford University Press.

Rothbart, M., and O. John. 1985. "Social Categorization and Behavioral Episodes: A Cognitive Analysis of the Effects of Intergroup Contact." *Journal of Social Issues* 41: 81–104.

Rothbart, M., and S. Lewis. 1988. "Inferring Category Attributes from Exemplar Attributes: Geometric Shapes and Social Categories." *Journal of Personality and Social Psychology* 55: 861–72.

Rothbart, M., and S. Lewis. 1994. "Cognitive Processes and Intergroup Relations: A Historical Perspective." In *Social Cognition: Impact on Social Psychology*. P. Devine, D. Hamilton, and T. Ostrom, ed. New York: Academic Press.

Rothbart, M., N. Sriram, and C. Davis-Stitt. 1996. "Social Categories and the Fate of Atypical Group Members." *Journal of Personality and Social Psychology*.

Rothbart, M., S. Fulero, C. Jensen, J. Howard, and P. Birrell. 1978. "From Individual to Group Impressions: Availability Heuristics in Stereotype Formation." *Journal of Experimental Social Psychology* 14: 237–55.

Rothschild, N. M. 1978. "Rothschild: An Antidote to Panic." *Nature* 276: 555.

Rousseau, D. M. 1995. *Psychological Contracts in Organizations*. Thousand Oaks, Calif.: Sage.

Royal Society, The. 1992. *Risk: Analysis, Perception, and Management*. London: Author.

Ruderman, A. J. 1986. "Dietary Restraint: A Theoretical and Empirical Review." *Psychological Bulletin* 99(2): 247–62.

Ruderman, H., M. Levine, and J. McMahon. 1986. "Energy-Efficiency Choice in the Purchase of Residential Appliances." In *Energy Efficiency: Perspectives on Individual Behavior*, ed. W. Kempton and M. Neiman. Washington, D.C.: American Council for an Energy Efficient Economy.

Ruscher, J. B., and S. T. Fiske. 1990. "Interpersonal Competition Can Cause Individuating Processes." *Journal of Personality and Social Psychology* 58: 832–43.

Ruscher, J. B., S. T. Fiske, H. Miki, and S. Van Manen. 1991. "Individuating Processes in Competition: Interpersonal versus Intergroup." *Personality and Social Psychology Bulletin* 17: 595–605.

Sabini, J., and M. Silver. 1982. *Moralities of Everyday Life*. Oxford: Oxford University Press.

Sackheim, H. A. 1983. "Self-deception, Self-esteem, and Depression: The Adaptive Value of Lying to Oneself." In *Empirical Studies of Psychoanalytic Theories*, Vol. 1, ed. J. Masling. Hillsdale, N.J.: Lawrence Erlbaum.

Sagar, H. A., and J. W. Schofield. 1980. "Racial and Behavioral Cues in Black and White Children's Perceptions of Ambiguously Aggressive Acts." *Journal of Personality and Social Psychology* 39: 590–98.

Salovey, P. 1992. "Mood-Induced Self-focused Attention." *Journal of Personality and Social Psychology* 62: 699–707.

Samuelson, C. D., and S. T. Allison. 1994. "Cognitive Factors Affecting the Use of Social Decision Heuristics in Resource-Sharing Tasks." *Organizational Behavior and Human Decision Processes* 58: 1–27.

Samuelson, W., and R. Zeckhauser. 1988. "Status Quo Bias in Decision Making." *Journal of Risk and Uncertainty* 1: 7–59.

Schadron, G., and V. Y. Yzerbyt. 1991. "Social Judgeability: Another Perspective in the Study of Social Inference." *Cahiers De Psychologie Cognitive* 11: 229–58.

Schein, V. E. 1977. "Individual Privacy and Personnel Psychology: The Need for a Broader Perspective." *Journal of Social Issues* 33: 154–67.

Schelling, T. C. 1960. *Strategy and Conflict.* Cambridge: Harvard University Press.

Schelling, T. C. 1978. *Micromotives and Macrobehavior.* New York: Norton.

Schlenker, B. R., M. F. Weigold, and J. R. Hallan. 1990. "Self-serving Attributions in Social Context: Effects of Self-esteem and Social Pressure." *Journal of Personality and Social Psychology* 58: 855–63.

Schlesinger, A. M. 1992. *The Disuniting of America: Reflections on a Multicultural Society.* New York: Norton.

Schnaiburg, A. 1980. *The Environment: From Surplus to Scarcity.* New York: Oxford University Press.

Scott, W. G., and D. K. Hart. 1979. *Organizational America.* Boston: Houghton Mifflin.

Seligman, M. E. P. 1975. *Helplessness.* San Francisco: Freeman.

Selznick, P. 1969. *Law, Society, and Industrial Justice.* New York: Russell Sage Foundation.

Sen, A. 1983. "Positional Objectivity." *Philosophy and Public Affairs* 20: 119–38.

Senge, P. 1990. *The Fifth Discipline.* New York: Doubleday.

Sheridan, T. B. 1980. "Human Error in Nuclear Power Plants." *Technology Review* 82(4): 23–33.

Sherif, M., and C. W. Sherif. 1953. *Groups in Harmony and Tension.* New York: Harper.

Shlyakhter, A. I., D. M. Kammen, C. L. Broido, and R. Wilson. 1994. "Quantifying the Credibility of Energy Projections from Trends in Past Data: The US Energy Sector." *Energy Policy* 22: 119–31.

Shweder, R. A., and E. S. Bourne. 1984. "Does the Concept of the Person Vary Cross-Culturally?" In *Culture Theory: Essays on Mind, Self, and Emotions,* ed. R. A. Shweder and R. A. LeVine. Cambridge: Cambridge University Press.

Simmons, D. D. 1968. "Invasion of Privacy and Judged Benefit of Personality Test Inquiry." *Journal of General Psychology* 79: 177–81.

Simon, H. A. 1989. *The Sciences of the Artificial,* 2nd ed. Cambridge, Mass.: MIT Press.

Singer, P. 1982. *The Expanding Circle: Ethics and Sociobiology.* New York: Farrar, Straus & Giroux.

Sitkin, S. B., and R. J. Bies. 1993. "The Legalistic Organization: Definitions, Dimensions, and Dilemmas." *Organization Science* 4: 345–51.

Skowronski, J. J., and D. E. Carlston. 1989. "Negativity and Extremity Biases in Impression Formation: A Review of Explanations." *Psychological Bulletin* 105: 131–42.

Slovic, P. 1987. "Perceptions of Risk." *Science* 236: 280–85.

Slovic, P., B. Fischhoff, and S. Lichtenstein. 1979. "Rating the Risks." *Environment* 21(3): 14–20, 36–39.

Slovic, P., B. Fischhoff, and S. Lichtenstein. 1980. "Facts and Fears: Understanding Perceived Risk." In *Societal Risk Assessment: How Safe is Safe Enough?* ed. R. Schwing and W. A. Albers, Jr. New York: Plenum Press.

Slovic, P., B. Fischhoff, and S. Lichtenstein. 1985. "Characterizing Perceived Risk." In *Perilous Progress: Technology as Hazard,* ed. R. W. Kates, C. Hohenemser, and J. Kasperson. Boulder, Colo.: Westview.

Slovic, P., S. Lichtenstein, and B. Fischhoff. 1984. "Modeling the Societal Impact of Fatal Accidents." *Management Science* 30: 464–74.

Slovic, S., and T. Dixon, eds. 1992. *Being in the World*. New York: Macmillan.

Smith, A. [1759]1976. *A Theory of Moral Sentiments*, ed. A. L. Macfie and D. D. Raphael. Oxford: Oxford University Press.

Smith, A. [1776]1976. *Wealth of Nations*. Oxford: Oxford University Press.

Smith, H., and T. R. Tyler. In press. "Justice and Power: Can Justice Motivations and Superordinate Categorizations Encourage the Advantaged to Support Policies Which Redistribute Economic Resources and Encourage the Disadvantaged to Willingly Obey the Law?" *European Journal of Social Psychology*.

Smith, H. J. 1994. *Managing Privacy: Information Technology and Corporate America*. Chapel Hill, N.C.: University of North Carolina Press.

Smith, V. K. 1989. "Can We Measure the Economic Value of Environmental Amenities?" Presidential address delivered at the fifty-ninth annual meetings of the Southern Economic Association, Orlando, Fla.

Snyder, M. 1984. "When Belief Creates Reality." In *Advances in Experimental Social Psychology*, Vol. 18, ed. L. Berkowitz. Orlando, Fla.: Academic Press.

Snyder, M. 1992. "Motivational Foundations of Behavioral Confirmation." In *Advances in Experimental Social Psychology*, Vol. 25, ed. M. P. Zanna. San Diego, Calif.: Academic Press.

Solomon, R. C. 1992. *Ethics and Excellence*. New York: Oxford University Press.

Sommer, R. 1969. *Personal Space: The Behavioral Basis for Design*. Englewood Cliffs, N.J.: Prentice-Hall.

Special Issue on Social Contract Theory in Business Ethics. 1995. *Business Ethics Quarterly* 5.

Spranca, M., E. Minsk, and J. Baron. 1991. "Omission and Commission in Judgment and Choice." *Journal of Experimental Social Psychology* 27: 76–105.

Stallen, P. J. 1980. "Risk of Science or Science of Risk?" In *Society, Technology, and Risk Assessment*, ed. J. Conrad. London: Academic Press.

Stark, A. 1993. "What's the Matter with Business Ethics?" *Harvard Business Review* May–June, 38–48.

Starr, C. 1969. "Societal Benefit Versus Technological Risk." *Science* 165: 1232–38.

Staub, E. 1989. *The Roots of Evil: The Origins of Genocide and Other Group Violence*. New York: Cambridge University Press.

Staw, B., and J. Ross. 1987. "Behavior in Escalation Situations: Antecedents, Prototypes, and Solutions." In *Research in Organizational Behavior*, Vol. 9, ed. L. Cummings and B. Staw. Greenwich, Conn.: JAI Press.

Staw, B. M. 1980. "The Consequences of Turnover." *Journal of Occupational Behavior* 1: 253–73.

Staw, B. M. 1990. "Rationality and Justification in Organizational Life." In *Information and Cognition in Organizations*, ed. L. L. Cummings and B. M. Staw. Greenwich, Conn.: JAI Press.

Staw, B. M., and J. Ross. 1989. "Understanding Behavior in Escalation Situations." *Science* 246: 216–20.

Steckmest, F. W. 1982. *Corporate Performance: The Key to Public Trust*. New York: McGraw-Hill.

Stevens, L. E., and S. T. Fiske. 1995. *Forming Motivated Impressions of a Powerholder: Accuracy Under Task Dependency and Misperception Under Evaluation*, Unpublished Manuscript. University of Massachusetts at Amherst.

Stone, C. D. 1972. "Should Trees Have Standing?" *Southern California Law Review* 45: 450–501.

Stone, D. L., and C. Bowden. 1989. "Effects of Job Applicant Drug Testing Practices on Reactions to Drug Testing." In *Academy of Management Best Paper Proceedings*, ed. F. Hoy. Atlanta: Academy of Management.

Stone, D. L., and D. Kotch. 1989. "Individuals' Attitudes Toward Organizational Drug Testing Policies and Practices." *Journal of Applied Psychology* 74: 518–21.

Stone, D. L., J. E. O'Brien, and W. Bommer. 1989. "Individuals' Reactions to Job Applicant Drug Testing Practices." Paper presented at the annual conference of the American Psychological Society, Washington, D. C. (June)

Stone, E. F., and D. L. Stone. 1990. "Privacy in Organizations: Theoretical Issues, Research Findings, and Protection Mechanisms." In *Research in Personnel and Human Resources Management*, Vol. 8, ed. K. M. Rowland and G. R. Ferris. Greenwich, Conn.: JAI Press.

Storms, E. 1994. "Warming Up to Cold Fusion." *Technology Review* 97: 19–29.

Strickland, L. H. 1958. "Surveillance and Trust." *Journal of Personality* 26: 200–15.

Stubbs, J. P., and J. D. Bozarth. 1994. "The Dodo Bird Revisited: A Qualitative Study of Psychotherapy Efficacy Research." *Applied and Preventive Psychology* 3: 109–20.

Studley, J. 1989. "Financial Sacrifice Outside the Private Sector." *National Law Journal*, March 27, 1989, 16.

Suls, J., and C. K. Wan. 1987. "In Search of the False-Uniqueness Phenomenon: Fear and Estimates of Social Consensus." *Journal of Personality and Social Psychology* 52: 211–17.

Sundstrom, E. 1986. *Work Places: The Psychology of the Physical Environment in Offices and Factories*. Cambridge: Cambridge University Press.

Sundstrom, E., R. E. Burt, and D. Kamp. 1980. "Privacy at Work: Architectural Correlates of Job Satisfaction and Job Performance." *Academy of Management Journal* 23: 101–17.

Swasy, A. 1993. *Soap Opera: The Inside Story of Procter & Gamble*. New York: Times Books.

Tajfel, H. 1969. "La categorization sociale." In *Introduction á la psychologie sociale*, Vol. 1, ed. S. Moscovici. Paris: Larousse.

Tajfel, H. 1970. "Experiments in Intergroup Discrimination." *Scientific American* 223(2): 96–102.

Tajfel, H., M. Billig, R. Bundy, and C. Flament. 1971. "Social Categorization and Intergroup Behaviour." *European Journal of Social Psychology* 1: 149–78.

Tallmer, M. 1987. "Chemical Dumping as a Corporate Way of Life." In *Corporate Violence*, ed. S. L. Hills. Totowa, N.J.: Rowman & Littlefield.

Tannen, D. 1990. *You Just Don't Understand: Women and Men in Conversation*. New York: Morrow.

Taylor, D. M., S. Wright, F. Moghaddam, and R. Lalonde. 1990. "The Personal/Group Discrimination Discrepancy: Perceiving My Group but Not Myself to Be a Target for Discrimination." *Personality and Social Psychology Bulletin* 16: 254–62.

Taylor, S. E., and J. D. Brown. 1988. "Illusion and Well-being: A Social Psychological Perspective on Mental Health." *Psychological Bulletin* 103: 193–210.

Taylor, S. E., J. V. Wood, and R. R. Lichtman. 1983. "It Could Be Worse: Selective Evaluation as a Response to Victimization." *Journal of Social Issues* 39: 19–40.

Tetlock, P. E. 1985. "Accountability: The Neglected Social Context of Judgment and Choices." *Research in Organizational Behavior* 7: 297–332.

Tetlock, P. E. 1991. "An Alternative Metaphor in the Study of Judgment and Choice: People as Politicians." *Theory and Psychology* 1: 451–75.

Tetlock, P. E. 1992. "The Impact of Accountability on Judgment and Choice: Toward a Social Contingency Model." In *Advances in Experimental Social Psychology*, Vol. 25, ed. M. P. Zanna. San Diego, Calif.: Academic Press.

Tetlock, P. E., L. Skitka, and R. Boettger. 1989. "Social and Cognitive Strategies for Coping with Accountability: Conformity, Complexity, and Bolstering." *Journal of Personality and Social Psychology* 57: 632–40.

Thagard, P. 1989. "Explanatory Coherence." *Behavioral and Brain Sciences* 12: 435–502.

Thaler, R. H. 1991. *Quasi-rational Economics*. New York: Russell Sage Foundation.

Thibaut, J., and L. Walker. 1975. *Procedural Justice*. Hillsdale, N.J.: Erlbaum.

Thibaut, J. W., and H. H. Kelley. 1959. *The Social Psychology of Groups*. New York: Wiley.

Thompson, L., and G. Loewenstein. 1992. "Egocentric Interpretations of Fairness and Interpersonal Conflict." *Organizational Behavior and Human Decision Processes* 51: 176–97.

Thompson, M. 1980. "Aesthetics of Risk: Culture or Context." In *Culture or Context*, ed. R. C. Schwing and W. A. Albers, Jr. New York: Plenum Press.

Tolchinsky, P. D., M. McCuddy, J. Adams, D. C. Ganster, R. Woodman, and H. L. Fromkin. 1981. "Employee Perceptions of Invasion of Privacy: A Field Simulation Experiment." *Journal of Applied Psychology* 66: 308–13.

Tomarken, A. J., and D. S. Kirschenbaum. 1984. "Effects of Plans for Future Meals on Counterregulatory Eating: Where Have All the Unrestrained Eaters Gone?" *Journal of Abnormal Psychology* 93: 458–72.

Triandis, H. C., C. McCusker, and C. H. Hui. 1990. "Multimethod Probes of Individualism and Collectivism." *Journal of Personality and Social Psychology* 59: 1006–20.

Turner, C. F., and E. Martin, eds. 1984. *Surveying Subjective Phenomena*. New York: Russell Sage Foundation.

Turner, J. C., P. J. Oakes, S. A. Haslam, and C. McGarty. 1994. "Self and Collective: Cognition and Social Context." *Personality and Social Psychology Bulletin* 20: 454–63.

Tversky, A. 1969. "Intransitivity of Preferences." *Psychological Review* 76: 31–48.

Tversky, A., and D. Kahneman. 1973. "Availability: A Heuristic for Judging Frequency and Probability." *Cognitive Psychology* 5: 207–32.

Tversky, A., and D. Kahneman. 1974. "Judgment Under Uncertainty: Heuristics and Biases." *Science* 185: 1124–35.

Tversky, A., and D. Kahneman. 1981. "The Framing of Decisions and the Psychology of Choice." *Science* 211: 453–58.

Tversky, A., and D. Kahneman. 1991. "Loss Aversion in Riskless Choice: A Reference-Dependent Model." *Quarterly Journal of Economics* 106 (4): 1039–61.

Tversky, A., P. Slovic, and D. Kahneman. 1990. "The Causes of Preference Reversal." *American Economic Review* 80: 204–17.

Tversky, A., S. Sattath, and P. Slovic. 1988. "Contingent Weighting in Judgment and Choice." *Psychological Review* 95: 371–84.

Tweney, R. D., M. E. Doherty, W. J. Worner, D. B. Pliske, C. R. Mynatt, K. A. Gross, and D. L. Arkkelin. 1980. "Strategies of Rule Discovery in an Inference Task." *Quarterly Journal of Experimental Psychology* 32: 109–23.

Tyler, T. R. 1988. "What Is Procedural Justice?" *Law and Society Review* 22: 301–55.

Tyler, T. R. 1990. *Why People Obey the Law*. New Haven: Yale University Press.

Tyler, T. R. 1993. "Legitimizing Unpopular Public Policies: Does Procedure Matter?" *Zeitschrift fur Rechts-sociologie* 14: 47–54.

Tyler, T. R. 1994a. "Governing Amid Diversity: The Effect of Fair Decision-Making Procedures on the Legitimacy of Government." *Law and Society Review* 28: 809–31.

Tyler, T. R. 1994b. "The Psychology of Authority." Unpublished manuscript, University of California, Berkeley.

Tyler, T. R., and E. A. Lind. 1992. "A Relational Model of Authority in Groups." In *Advances in Experimental Social Psychology*, Vol. 25, ed. M. Zanna. New York: Academic Press.

Tyler, T. R., and G. Mitchell. 1994. "Legitimacy and the Empowerment of Discretionary Legal Authority: The United States Supreme Court and Abortion Rights." *Duke Law Journal* 43: 703–815.

Tyler, T., and R. Hastie. 1991. "The Social Consequences of Cognitive Illusions." In *Handbook of Negotiation Research*, Vol. 3, *Research on Negotiation in Organizations*, ed. M. H. Bazerman, R. J. Lewicki, and B. Sheppard. Greenwich, Conn.: JAI Press.

Tyler, T. R., and H. J. Smith. In press. "Social Justice and Social Movements." In *Handbook of Social Psychology*, 4th ed., ed. D. Gilbert, S. Fiske, and G. Lindzey. New York: McGraw-Hill.

Tyler, T. R., and P. Degoey. In press. "Collective Restraint in a Social Dilemma Situation." *Journal of Personality and Social Psychology*.

Tyler, T. R., and R. Dawes. 1993. "Fairness in Groups: Comparing the Self-Interest and Social Identity Perspectives." In *Psychological Perspectives on Justice*, ed. B. A. Mellers and J. Baron. Cambridge: Cambridge University Press.

Tyler, T. R., and R. J. Bies. 1990. "Beyond Formal Procedures: The Interpersonal Context of Procedural Justice." In *Applied Social Psychology and Organizational Settings*, ed. J. S. Carroll. Hillsdale, N.J.: Lawrence Erlbaum.

Tyler, T. R., E. A. Lind, and Y. Huo. 1994. "Culture, Ethnicity, and Authority: Social Categorization and Social Orientation Effects on the Psychology of Legitimacy." Unpublished manuscript, University of California, Berkeley.

UK Health and Safety Executive. 1993. *The Costs of Accidents at Work*. (HS)G Series.

Uleman, J. S., and J. A. Bargh, eds. 1989. *Unintended Thought*. New York: Guilford Press.

Vallacher, R. R., and D. M. Wegner. 1987. "What Do People Think They're Doing? Action Identification and Human Behavior." *Psychological Review* 94: 3–15.

van Schie, E. C. M., and J. van der Pligt. 1990. "Influence Diagrams and Fault Trees: The Role of Salience and Anchoring." In *Contemporary Issues in Decision Making*, ed. K. Borcherding, O. I. Larichev, and D. M. Messick. Amsterdam: North-Holland.

Vandivier, K. 1987. "Why Should My Conscience Bother Me?" In *Corporate Violence*, ed. S. L. Hills. Totowa, N.J.: Rowman & Littlefield.

Varca, P. E., and M. James-Valutis. 1993. "The Relationship of Ability and Satisfaction to Job Performance." *Applied Psychology: An International Review* 42: 265–75.

Velasquez, M. G. 1992. *Business Ethics*. Englewood Cliffs, N.J.: Prentice Hall.

Vidmar, N., and D. H. Flaherty. 1985. "Concern for Personal Privacy in an Electronic Age." *Journal of Communication* 35: 91–103.

Wade-Benzoni, K. A., A. E. Tenbrunsel, and M. H. Bazerman. 1995. "Egocentric Interpretations of Fairness in Asymmetric, Environmental Social Dilemmas: Explaining

Harvesting Behavior and the Role of Communication." Working paper, Northwestern University.

Wade-Benzoni, K. A., and M. H. Bazerman. 1996. *Positive Illusions, Self-serving Biases, and Environmental Sensitivity: Disconfirmability and Framing of Self-evaluations.* Working paper, Northwestern University.

Wagenaar, W. A., and J. T. Reason. 1990. "Types and Tokens in Road Accident Causation." *Ergonomics* 33: 10–11, 1365–75.

Wagenaar, W. A., J. Groeneweg, P. T. W. Hudson, and J. T. Reason. 1994. "Promoting Safety in the Oil Industry." *Ergonomics* 37: 1999–2013.

Wagenaar, W. A., P. T. W. Hudson, and J. T. Reason. 1990. "Cognitive Failures and Accidents." *Applied Cognitive Psychology* 4: 273–94.

Walster, P., G. W. Walster, and E. Berscheid. 1978. *Equity: Theory and Research.* Boston: Allyn & Bacon.

Walzer, M. 1994. *Thick and Thin.* Notre Dame: Notre Dame University Press.

Wandersman, A. H., and W. K. Hallman. 1993. "Are People Acting Irrationally?" *American Psychologist* 48: 681–86.

Warner, F., and D. H. Slater. 1981. *The Assessment and Perception of Risk.* London: The Royal Society.

Warren, S. D., and L. D. Brandeis. 1890. "The Right to Privacy." *Harvard Law Review* 4: 289–320.

Wason, P. C. 1960. "On the Failure to Eliminate Hypotheses in a Conceptual Task." *Quarterly Journal of Experimental Psychology* 12: 129–40.

Watson, D. 1982. "The Actor and the Observer: How Are Their Perceptions of Causality Divergent?" *Psychological Bulletin* 92: 682–700.

Weaver, G. R., and L. K. Trevino. 1994. "Normative and Empirical Business Ethics." *Business Ethics Quarterly* 4: 129–44.

Weber, J. G. 1994. "The Nature of Ethnocentric Attribution Bias: In-group Protection or Enhancement?" *Journal of Experimental Social Psychology* 30: 482–504.

Weber, M., F. Eisenführ, and D. von Winterfeldt. 1988. "The Effects of Splitting Attributes on Weights in Multiattribute Utility Measurement." *Management Science* 34: 431–45.

Weick, K. E. 1993. "Sensemaking in Organizations: Small Structures with Large Consequences." In *Social Psychology in Organizations: Advances in Theory and Research,* ed. J. K. Murnighan. Englewood Cliffs, N.J.: Prentice-Hall.

Weiner, B. 1971. *Perceiving the Causes of Successes and Failures.* Morristown, N.J.: General Learning Press.

Weiner, B. 1980. *Human Motivation.* New York: Holt, Rinehart & Winston.

Weiner, B. 1985. "Spontaneous Causal Thinking." *Psychological Bulletin* 97: 74–84.

Weiner, B. 1995. *Judgments of Responsibility: A Foundation for a Theory of Social Conduct.* New York: Guilford Press.

Weiner, B., J. Amirkhan, V. S. Folkes, and J. A. Verette. 1987. "An Attributional Analysis of Excuse Giving: Studies of a Naive Theory of Emotion." *Journal of Personality and Social Psychology* 52: 316–24.

Weinstein, N. D. 1980. "Unrealistic Optimism About Future Life Events." *Journal of Personality and Social Psychology* 39: 806–20.

Weinstein, N. D. 1984. "Why It Won't Happen to Me." *Health Psychology* 3: 431–57.

Weinstein, N. D. 1989. "Optimistic Biases About Personal Risks." *Science* 246: 1232–33.

Weisz, J. R. 1991. "Culture and the Development of Child Psychopathology: Lessons from Thailand." In *Rochester Symposium on Developmental Psychopathology*, Vol. 1, ed. D. Cicchetti. New York: Cambridge University Press.

Weitz, B. A., S. B. Castleberry, and J. F. Tanner. 1992. *Selling: Building Relationships*. Homewood, Ill.: Irwin.

Werhane, P. H. 1989. *Adam Smith and His Legacy for Modern Capitalism*. Oxford: Oxford University Press.

Werhane, P. H. 1994. "The Normative/Descriptive Distinction in Methodologies of Business Ethics." *Business Ethics Quarterly* 4: 175–80.

Werhane, P. H. 1996. "Moral Imagination and the Search for Moral Decision-Making in Management." In *New Avenues for Business Ethics*, ed. R. E. Freeman. Oxford: Oxford University Press.

West, S. G. 1975. "Increasing the Attractiveness of College Cafeteria Food: A Reactance Theory Perspective." *Journal of Applied Psychology* 60: 656–58.

Westin, A. F. 1967. *Privacy and Freedom*. New York: Atheneum.

Westphal, J. D., and E. J. Zajac. 1995. "Who Shall Govern? CEO/Board Power, Demographic Similarity, and New Director Selection." *Administrative Science Quarterly* 40: 60–83.

Wildavsky, A. 1992. *Searching for Safety*. New Brunswick, N.J.: Transaction Books.

Wilson, J. Q. 1993. *The Moral Sense*. New York: Free Press.

Wood, J. V., and K. L. Taylor. 1991. "Serving Self-relevant Goals through Social Comparison." In *Social Comparison: Contemporary Theory and Research*, ed. J. Suls and T. A. Wills. Hillsdale, N. J.: Laurence Erlbaum.

Woodman, R. W., D. C. Ganster, J. Adams, M. C. McCuddy, P. D. Tolchinsky, and H. Fromkin. 1982. "A Survey of Employee Perceptions of Information Privacy in Organizations." *Academy of Management Journal* 25: 647–63.

Woodside, A. G., and J. W. Davenport. 1974. "Effects of Salesman Similarity and Expertise on Consumer Purchasing Behavior." *Journal of Marketing Research* 11: 198–202.

Worchel, S., J. Lee, and A. Adewole. 1975. "Effects of Supply and Demand on Ratings of Object Value." *Journal of Personality and Social Psychology* 11: 198–202.

Wynne, B. 1980. "Technology, Risk and Participation." In *Society, Technology, and Risk Assessment*, ed. J. Conrad. London: Academic Press.

Wynne, B. 1994. "Public Understanding of Science." In *Handbook of Science and Technology Studies*, ed. S. Jasanoff, G. E. Markle, J. C. Petersen, and T. Pinch. Thousand Oaks, Calif.: Sage.

Young, B., R. Mountjoy, and M. Roos. 1981. *Employee Theft*. Sacramento, Calif.: Assembly of the State of California Publications Office.

Yzerbyt, V. Y., G. Schadron, J.-Ph. Leyens, and S. Rocher. 1994. "Social Judgeability: The Impact of Meta-informational Cues on the Use of Stereotyping." *Journal of Personality and Social Psychology* 66: 48–55.

Yzerbyt, V. Y., J.-Ph. Leyens, and F. Bellour. 1993. "Social Judgeability and Motivation: The Ingroup Overexclusion Effect." In *Studies of the Self and Social Cognition*, ed. M. F. Pichevin, M. C. Hurtig, and M. Piolat. Singapore: World Scientific Publishing.

Zalud, B. 1989. "The Conflicts of Privacy." *Security* 26(10): 38–41.

Zawadski, B. 1948. "Limitations of the Scapegoat Theory of Prejudice." *Journal of Abnormal and Social Psychology* 43: 127–41.

Zebrowitz, L. 1990. *Social perception*. Pacific Grove, Calif.: Brooks Cole.

Zelasny, M. D. 1990. "Rater Confidence and Social Influence in Performance Appraisals." *Journal of Applied Psychology* 75: 274–89.

Zentner, R. D. 1979. "Hazards in the Chemical Industry." *Chemical and Engineering News* 57(45): 25–27, 30–34.

Zey, M. 1992. *Decision Making: Alternatives to Rational Choice Models*. Beverly Hills, Calif: Sage.

Index

Boldface numbers refer to figures and tables.